TWO NATIONS, MANY CULTURES
ETHNIC GROUPS IN CANADA

Two Nations, Many Cultures

Ethnic Groups in Canada

EDITED BY

Jean Leonard Elliott
Department of Sociology and Anthropology
Dalhousie University

Prentice-Hall of Canada, Ltd., Scarborough, Ontario

Canadian Cataloguing in Publication Data

Two nations, many cultures

Bibliography: p.

ISBN 0-13-935205-8

1. Canada – Population – Ethnic groups – Addresses,
essays, lectures.* 2. Canada – Foreign population –
Addresses, essays, lectures. I. Elliott, Jean
Leonard, 1941-

FC104.T86   301.45'1'0971   C78-001486-3
F1035.A1T86

© 1979 by Prentice-Hall of Canada, Ltd.
Scarborough, Ontario

Prentice-Hall, Inc., Englewood Cliffs, New Jersey
Prentice-Hall International, Inc., London
Prentice-Hall of Australia, Pty., Ltd., Sydney
Prentice-Hall of India, Pvt., Ltd., New Delhi
Prentice-Hall of Japan, Inc., Tokyo
Prentice-Hall of Southeast Asia (PTE.) Ltd., Singapore

Design by John Zehethofer

Printed and bound in Canada by Webcom Limited

ISBN 0-13-935205-8

1 2 3 4 5 W 82 81 80 79

Contents

Part Three The Other Ethnic Groups: The Non-English in English Canada

Acknowledgements

A number of persons assisted with the preparation of this work, and I wish to express my gratitude here. The typing of the manuscript was undertaken efficiently by Joan Kelly, Pam Lutz, and Mary Morash. In addition I am indebted to Marta Tomins and Veronica Orocio of Prentice-Hall for their editorial assistance and expedition of the book's publication.

Preface

The debate on ethnicity in Canada has become intertwined with the concept of *nation*. The term *nation* is being used quite ambiguously by Canadians; to a large extent this lack of clarity can be traced to the two standard dictionary definitions of the word. On the one hand, a nation is defined as an aggregate of persons of the same ethnic family, speaking the same language or cognate languages; on the other hand, a nation is defined as a body of people in a particular territory who are sufficiently conscious of their unity to seek or to possess a government peculiarly their own.

Given the lack of uniformity in the everyday usage of a key concept like nation, there is little wonder that there is disagreement concerning the existence and status of nations within Canada. This book of readings on Canadian ethnic groups focuses on the theme of "the nations within". Attempting to come to grips with the reality of the nations within, it is hoped, is not in the nature of a sterile, academic exercise. The recognition of the existence of nations within Canada and a resolution of their status are matters of great urgency and moral concern.

A consideration of the ethnic group *qua* nation is not encapsulated by Canada's historic French/English dualism. In fact, both the French and English spheres of Canadian life are undergoing redefinition to the point that to speak of French Canada or English Canada today does not indicate a precise referent. Both entities—French Canada and English Canada—have assumed mythical proportions in Canadian life. In reality, francophones and anglophones in Canada are split by regional factionalisms and a heterogeneous ethnicity. A francophone from Manitoba may have little in common with a francophone from Quebec City, Toronto, or Moncton; the case of an algophone from these regions may be similar. Regions in Canada are *real* factors contributing to the identity of people. When region and ethnicity combine, as is the case with the Scots in Nova Scotia or the French in Quebec, we have perhaps a more dramatic effect on the level of an individual's ethnic identity than is found when an ethnic group is spread thinly across regions or when a single region contains a potpourri of ethnic groups.

In addition to the traditional French/English cleavage in Canada and the matter of regional loyalties, there is a third division within Canadian society that pits Native Peoples against non-Natives. In both a moral and a legal sense, the Native Peoples have strong arguments supporting their struggle for the recognition of their nations in the Northwest Territories. Although the Native Peoples may be relatively few and fragmented by language, culture, and region, they are attempting to unite in their struggles to decolonize their lands.

The organization of this book reflects the three basic divisions within Canada that may serve as catalysts for change—Native Peoples, French Canada, and the non-British segment of English-speaking Canada. In their own way, each is seeking self-definition and an ultimate accommodation to the federal system—even if this means an attempt at "opting out". For this reason, the mainstream of Canadian society, the dominant British charter group, has not been included in this collection. While the British charter group at some point in time may have to react to the forces of change put into motion by the non-British segments of the Canadian population, the former's role may tend to be one of reaction rather than action.

Within each division, articles were selected to illustrate the range of strategies ethnic groups use in the process of working out their identities and accommodations to the larger society. Some of the newer Third World groups to establish a presence in Canada, such as the East Indians and the West Indians, are included. Unfortunately, it was not possible to include all established groups or groups of recent origin; sampling within region and within Canada's ethnic mosaic was necessary. Given the enormous diversity of cultures within Canada, it is hoped that some representativeness was achieved. Groups such as the Icelanders who have been somewhat neglected to date with respect to their inclusion in ethnic collections were sought, while larger groups such as the Dutch or the German were omitted as the latter groups have appeared more frequently in readily available, published material. Similarly, the ethnoreligious minorities such as the Amish and Hutterites were omitted. The voluntary segregation of the communal sects has effectively removed them from the general arena of debate concerning the status of ethnic groups in Canada.

As much as possible, an attempt was made to have the people who belong to an ethnic group or nation speak for themselves. Thus there are, for example, Native People articulating the identity and "land claim" issues of concern to Native People; a Polish Canadian examining multiculturalism among the Poles; and a Franco-Ontarian writing on the subject of ethnic boundaries among Franco-Ontarians. Also in keeping with the attempt to have authors addressing topics internal to groups they have empathy with, female contributors have discussed the experiences of female immigrants of Czech and Slovak and West Indian origins.

In these studies of ethnic groups various theoretical perspectives have been employed to reflect the choice of the contributor as well as the particular problem or issue under focus. The procrustean bed of forcing all data to a single perspective was avoided. There has been minimal reliance on a single imported or professional perspective. The intent was to deal with the Canadian reality rather than to apply a pre-existing theory to Canadian society or test particular versions of standard ethnic behavior models. Ethnic groups have different histories in Canada. Consequently, with respect to some of the more recent and smaller ethnic groups like the Spanish and the Arabs, our analyses are at the simple level of description. With other ethnic groups more numerous and long-standing, such as the Chinese and Ukrainians, our analyses are more complex and our theories more broadly based and logically compelling. Through this variety of perspectives it is hoped that a better understanding of the aspirations of Canadians as well as a range of potential options concerning ethnicity and nationhood will emerge.

Although the concept of an ethnic group *qua* nation may be a stumbling block for some, the intensity or political forcefulness of an ethnic group's aspirations does not necessarily diminish to conform to the wishes of "outsiders". For Canadians who wish to view Canada as a *modern society*, ethnic membership may be passé or antithetical to what it means to be modern. In a modern society, one's membership in the larger society is based on citizenship—equally extended to all, rather than upon such ascribed characteristics as age, sex, race, or ethnic group membership. These latter characteristics are thought to describe the social organization of traditional or primitive societies. Inasmuch as people will act in terms of the labels or categories that are meaningful to them, the study of ethnic groups in Canada is fundamentally relevant to Canada's future—regardless of one's particular view of the importance of the "ethnic factor" in the life of modern societies. Ethnicity seems to persist in modern societies long after sociologists have heralded its demise.

TWO NATIONS, MANY CULTURES
ETHNIC GROUPS IN CANADA

J. L. ELLIOTT

Introduction
Canada: Two Nations, Many Cultures?

This collection of readings was compiled in the months following the Parti Québécois victory in Quebec in late 1976. The Parti Québécois government is committed to bring before the Quebec electorate a referendum on sovereignty association with Canada. In English Canada the aftermath of the Parti Québécois election has been characterized by much soul-searching, some indignation and some support, with anglophones tending to view the separatist stance as an issue of "national unity". In Quebec, the debate over national unity is focused more in terms of the viability of *les deux nations* concept that underlies the Canadian confederation.

Although all Canadians would agree that the *concept* of "two nations" in Canada refers to the two founding peoples or charter groups (the French and the English), consensus ends here. Interpretations differ concerning the implications of the historic French/English dualism for present-day Canada. Opinions differ on how anglophones and francophones can be recognized with respect to constitutional guarantees in such areas as minority language rights without slighting the contributions of the other ethnic groups in Canada.

Perhaps the fundamental question that persists is: Are there two nations in Canada? The lack of agreement in response to this question is indicative of the national unity crisis in our midst. The answer to this question—aside from depending on one's definition of nation—reflects one's knowledge of Canadian history as well as one's thoughts on self-determination and perhaps one's own ethnic background. There are essentially three positions that are voiced:

(1) Canada is one nation in the sense of being a nation-state, a political unit, that has representation in such international bodies as the United Nations. Although attitudes toward institutional bilingualism may vary, it is acknowledged that Canada is officially bilingual on the federal level. The Official Languages Act received the support of all major parties. Within this view of Canada, Quebec is a province like all others.

(2) The federalist view as articulated by such spokesmen as the current Prime Minister, P. E. Trudeau, is compatible to some extent with the

above view, but it also acknowledges the two-nation principle. It considers the French nation as not coterminous with Quebec but extending throughout Canada wherever communities of French Canadians are found. This view of Canada as two nations stresses the partnership element in the confederation of French and English that rests on mutual cooperation for the good of the whole. Institutional bilingualism is fully supported inasmuch as it guarantees that Canadians can receive certain federal services in the language in which they are taxed as they travel and live throughout Canada.

(3) A third position, which has become identified with such groups as the Parti Québécois, considers Quebec as the French nation in Canada. Within this view, a nation is defined as a territory inhabited by those of the same ancestral or ethnic background who share a common language and culture and regard themselves as a people. Quebec is not a province like the others; it is the homeland of the French Canadians, a distinct nation within Canada.

Quebec

Bilingualism on the federal level is the classic example of "too little, too late" for some Quebec nationalists. In an attempt to assure the survival, and, indeed, the flourishing of the French Canadian culture in North America, a strategy of retrenchment was thought to be called for by those Quebec nationalists who are disillusioned with the 1867 vision of a two-nation Canada, given the 1978 reality. The combined effects of the tendency of francophones outside Quebec to assimilate to the anglophone community and the prevailing climate in English Canada that is not conducive to the maintainance of the French culture have meant that French Quebeckers have tended to "write-off" French Canada outside Quebec. When French Canada became redefined as Quebec, "sovereignty association" with Canada was advanced as a logical next step forward by the nationalists within the Parti Québécois.

To such groups as the Parti Québécois, who view the Canadian confederation as a partnership that has failed, Quebec occupies the status of a colony within Canada. These Quebec nationalists would be inclined to entitle this volume: *Canada and her Internal Colony* or *English Canada and the French Colony within*. The model of Quebec as a colony refers to the perceptions by the Québécois that they are controlled unduly by Ottawa; that they are not "masters in their own house"; that they lack autonomy in cultural and economic affairs, and, as importantly, that the Province of Quebec has been bled systematically by anglophone economic elites.

Could Canada's "internal colony" assume an equal-nation status if various constitutional reforms were undertaken? This is no longer an interesting question for the Parti Québécois as it was answered in the negative on the formation of the political organization committed to Quebec independence. However, for some segments of Quebec society and for the Quebec nationalists outside the Parti Québécois this question is primary. It should be remembered that the Parti Québécois government of Rene Lévesque was voted into office on a "good government" platform with the matter of independence to be decided at a future date by referendum. It would be a mistake to assume that all Parti Québécois voters, even those who accept the validity of the "colony within" model, would opt for independence as the best way of righting the imbalance that exists in the relations between French and English Canada. It is possible for some Quebec nationalists to find room for Quebec within the federalist framework.

English Canada has not been oblivious to the unequal union between the two nations that developed steadily after the signing of the partnership in Charlottetown in 1867. The commitment of English Canada to this partnership and its desire to strengthen the two-nation foundation sparked such measures as the ameliorative Royal Commission on Bilingualism and Biculturalism during the government of Lester Pearson. Following a recommendation from the Commission, the Official Languages Act was proclaimed. Subsequent legislation in the 1970s was directed at instituting bilingualism in the federal civil service. By 1978, bilingualism priorities were shifting to the so-called "youth option" whereby it was thought desirable that more school children in Canada should have the opportunity to learn their two official languages.

English Canada

So far I have addressed the problem of circumscribing the French nation in Canada in a way agreeable to all Canadians. To delimit the parameters of the English Canadian nation is also not without its share of problems. In 1838, when Lord Durham surveyed the dissension between the French and the English in the Canadas, he summed up what he saw in Lower Canada as "two nations warring in the bosom of a single state." As a solution, he recommended the assimilation of the French by the English. The Confederation that followed some thirty years later was not a strategy on the part of the English to assimilate the French. Leaders like Cartier from Lower Canada were principal participants in the forging of the Confederation agreement. In fact, Lower Canada was in many respects more convinced concerning the benefits to be accrued from Confederation than was Nova Scotia who feared domination from Upper Canada. English Canada at the time of Confederation was rife with many of the same regional disparities that plague it today. It would be grossly inaccurate to assume that English Canada spoke with a strong, single voice and foisted Confederation upon a weaker Lower Canada (Quebec).

To the regional differences in English Canada that existed at the time of Confederation are added the regional differences that stem from the populating of the West with immigrants who were largely non-British and non-French. European immigration canceled the Anglo-French alliance in the West that was hoped for by Lower Canada. With the settlement of the West, Canada went from an essentially bicultural land to one that was decidedly multicultural. So-called English Canadians today are more accurately referred to as anglophones as their linguistic usage may be the most prominent cultural characteristic they share.

The problem of correct terminology for the Canadian people was noted by Hugh MacLennan in the course of his writing *Two Solitudes*. "No single word exists, within Canada itself, to designate with satisfaction...a native of the country. When those of the French language use the word *Canadien*, they nearly always refer to themselves. They know their English-speaking compatriots as *Les Anglais*. English-speaking citizens act on the same principle. They call themselves Canadians; those of the French language French-Canadians." Since the writing of this novel set during World War I, the terminology dilemma has intensified. Our solitudes, reinforced by regional differences and history, have multiplied.

The lack of communication between regions is sometimes discussed in the context of the elusive Canadian identity. Anglophones seem to lack a core identity that unites them and sets them apart from the British and the Americans. Just as Quebec has been subjected to the status of a colony *vis à vis* the anglophone economic community, so also has English Canada experienced the economic and cultural dependency characteristic of a colony in its relations to the "mother country" and its powerful neighbor to the south.

English Canada not only lacks a cultural coherence of its own, but it is also divided on such issues as the protection and granting of minority language rights at the provincial level. New Brunswick is the only province that officially recognizes French and English at the provincial level. Quebec is quick to point out that the anglophone minority in Quebec has fared better than the francophone minority in the rest of Canada on such matters as the education of children in the official language of their choice.

Finally, anglophones are divided in their view concerning self-determination for Quebec and the constitutionality of a possible, peaceful "separation" of Quebec from Canada. If the referendum on sovereignty association were to be positive, the other provinces might tend to disagree on the legitimacy of the steps that would follow. From the vantage point of self-interest, Atlantic Canada potentially would have more to lose from Quebec separation than the West, for example. The question of the hypothetical use of illegitimate means to bring about Quebec sovereignty would find anglophones also divided with respect to what might constitute an appropriate response. Ever since the War Measures Act was invoked in 1970 to control the alleged potential of widespread terrorism in Quebec, civil libertarians in all provinces have been split on whether a suspension of basic liberties can ever be justified as a defense of liberty. Under what conditions does resort to the sword by one combatant justify its use by the other?

Native Peoples

It has been convenient for Canadians to overlook the fact that their country was built on land on which the Native People had prior claim. Although Europeans have used the words "Indian" and "Eskimo" to refer to the original occupants of North America, the original people call themselves, for example, Inuit, Dene, Micmac, Malecite, Montagnais, Algonquin, Mohawk, Ojibway, Cree, Sioux, Chipeway, Huron, Tlingit, Salish, Haida, Nishga and Kwakiutl. The so-called Indians and Eskimos in North America are members of the Fourth World—aboriginal people who live within nation-states.

The plight of the Fourth World is being gradually articulated by Native People who are organizing to bring about cultural and political self-determination and a recognition of their territorial integrity. Although their efforts have tended to fall under the general rubric of "land claims", their goal is much broader than the establishment of simple real estate rights.

The Fourth World in Canada is not interested in a cash settlement for their land claims; they reject "the beads and trinkets approach". Natives are primarily interested in controlling the "development" of their land, and their own future as a distinct people. They wish to assure development that is ecologically sound and compatible with their traditional way of life. The Mackenzie Valley pipeline investigation conducted by Chief Justice Berger was the first instance in Canadian history that Native People were meaningfully consulted and their voice heard with respect to the use of their land. The Berger report recommended that no development should take place before the land claims of the Native People are settled. It also seriously questioned the wisdom of pipeline construction in the Mackenzie Valley.

For historical reasons, more Native People have tended to learn English rather than French. Anglophone native groups in Quebec have run head-on into Quebec language legislation. The natives fear that their organizational efforts will be fragmented if, in addition to their own languages, they must learn both French and English. Yet some natives seem to draw strength from the Québécois struggle and see hope that its settlement will mean a similar resolution for their own. John Amagoalik, director of Inuit land claims in the Northwest Territories, drew this parallel:

> When the Prime Minister says to the Québécois that it is possible for them to be self-determining within Confederation; when he gives them assurances of the survival of their language and culture; when he promises a new Canadian federalism, we take him at his word. We, too, believe these things are possible, and we will stand as testimony to this truth as we move toward the conclusion of our negotiations.
>
> *Globe and Mail,* January 28, 1978

Many Canadians, Native People included, are questioning the current federal arrangement. Can the British North America Act contain the aspirations of the various Canadian "nations" and peoples or are revisions called for? Canada, an experiment in the confederation of "nations", will continue to evolve until agreement is reached on how many "nations" are contained within its borders.

PART ONE

Native Peoples

Introduction

The Native Peoples in Canada today are attempting to reverse the historical process that has left them, in effect, a colony of the larger society. Through decolonization, the Native Peoples hope to regain control over their own lives, institutions, and the development of their own land, and to resolve such basic questions as who is and who is not a member of their community or nation. The legal leverage the Native Peoples are employing in their struggle toward decolonization rests on the establishment of their aboriginal rights and title to the land that they and their ancestors have occupied since prehistoric times. With a settlement of land claims that is acceptable to the Native Peoples, they will stand to reclaim not only their land, but also their pride. Thus, the intent of this section is to describe (1) the goals of the decolonization process from the point of view of the Native Peoples, (2) the poverty of the Native Peoples that stems from their colonial status—in particular, the reserve system, and (3) the discriminatory aspects of the Indian Act and related bureaucratic arrangements that affect the life chances of native men and women.

George Manuel and Michael Posluns have termed as the "Fourth World" all indigenous people who have experienced European intrusion. The Native Peoples in Canada are united with other Fourth World members in a common struggle to regain control of their own land and destiny. The authors argue for the necessity of establishing aboriginal rights so that the future direction of the use of native land can once more be in native hands.

The Dene call attention to their Fourth World status in the Statement of Rights issued at Fort Simpson in the Northwest Territories in 1975. The Dene are the 11 000 people of native ancestry who live in the Mackenzie District, including the Dogribs, Loucheux, Slaveys, and Chipewyans who speak the Athapascan or Dene dialects. The word *Dene*, which is common to all the languages of the Mackenzie, means "all the people". Although the Dene Declaration has not been recognized by the larger society, it has served to unite many of the Native Peoples and has signalled the start of the long, slow process of decolonization.

The Inuit refer to their land as *Nunavut*. Their position on aboriginal rights is outlined by the native organization, *Inuit Tapirisat*. Unlike the treaty Indians, the Inuit have not signed any treaties with the Canadian government. For the Inuit, therefore, it is not a matter of their ever having "sold" their claim: their aboriginal rights have never been extinguished. Their goal is to have their aboriginal rights recognized within the political context of the larger society.

History, for the most part, is written from the vantage point of the *colonizer*, not the *colonized*. Consequently, the colonized do not see their own lives reflected in the history books of the dominant society—at least not with any dignity. An enlightening sketch of Canadian history from the native point of view is provided by Howard Adams. As a Métis (a person of mixed native and European ancestry), Adams is aware that not until Métis history is acknowledged by the larger society will the Métis be able to know and take pride in the Métis past.

The Indian reserves were established as the white society's response to the "troublesome" presence of the Native Peoples in their midst. From the outset, the reserves have been unable to support life; Indians on reserves live a life of grinding poverty, with disease and mortality rates higher than those of the larger society. Seeking a better life, many Indians have migrated from the reserve to the city. The few that are successful by white standards, we call "assimilated"; the many that fail are simply called "Indians".

The movement from the reserve to the city is one aspect of the more general rural-to-urban migration. While there is a considerable return migration from the city to the reserve, the Native Peoples in recent decades have been experiencing an overall urbanization at a rapidly accelerating pace. W. L. Stanbury studies the impact of the urban way of life on Indians living in British Columbia cities. For Indians to "make it" in a city, is it necessary for them to deny their Indian background? Since the data are interpreted by non-Indians, one should be aware that if the same data were seen through the eyes of the Native Peoples, alternate interpretations might result. In many respects, however, the uninterpreted data are sufficient to illuminate the status of the urban Indians surveyed.

Many Indians temporarily leave the reserve to take their chances in the city. These attempts at upward social mobility have potentially different consequences for native men and women. Women face discrimination in seeking employment, especially if they dare to step outside the racial and sex-typed occupational norms. The Indian Act confers unequal status on native men and women. Native women, for example, who marry non-Indians lose their status under the Act and are no longer entitled to such privileges as reserve housing, whereas Indian men who marry non-Indian women remain entitled to it. This sexism in the Indian Act is attributed to the white society and not to the Indian culture.

Harold Cardinal, an Indian leader, argues, however, that a repeal of the Indian Act is not the solution because the Act is a two-edged sword. On one hand, it serves as a legal framework in which the Indians may negotiate with the federal government on such issues as land claims. On the other hand, the arbitrary definitions of who is an Indian in terms of the Indian Act serve to divide the Native Peoples politically and culturally. Cardinal's article on native women points out the various shortcomings of the Indian Act and the steps Native Peoples are taking to have it amended.

SELECTED REFERENCES

Abler, Thomas S., et al., eds. *A Canadian Indian Bibliography, 1960-1970.* Toronto: University of Toronto Press, 1974.

Berger, Thomas R. *Northern Frontier, Northern Homeland: The Report of the Mackenzie Valley Pipeline Inquiry.* Ottawa, 1977.

Brody, Hugh. *The People's Land: Eskimos and Whites in the Eastern Arctic.* Markham, Ont.: Penguin Books, 1975.

Campbell, Maria. *Halfbreed.* Toronto: McClelland and Stewart, 1973.

Chamberlin, J. E. *The Harrowing of Eden: White Attitudes toward North American Natives.* Toronto: Fitzhenry and Whiteside, 1975.

Cowan, Susan, ed. *We Don't Live in Snow Houses Now: Reflections from Arctic Bay.* Ottawa: Canadian Arctic Producers, 1976.

Dosman, Edgar J. *Indians: The Urban Dilemma.* Toronto: McClelland and Stewart, 1972.

Frideres, J. S. *Canada's Indians: Contemporary Conflicts.* Scarborough, Ont.: Prentice-Hall of Canada, 1974.

Graburn, Nelson, H. H. *Eskimos without Igloos.* Boston: Little, Brown, 1969.

Hutchison, George, and D. Wallace. *Grassy Narrows.* Toronto: Van Nostrand, 1977.

Nagler, Mark. *Natives without a Home.* Don Mills, Ont.: Longman Canada, Ltd., 1975.

Pelletier, Wilfred, and T. Poole. *No Foreign Land: The Biography of a North American Indian.* Toronto: McClelland and Stewart, 1973.

Pimlott, Douglas H., et al., eds. *Arctic Alternatives.* Ottawa: Canadian Arctic Resources Committee, 1973.

Richardson, Boyce. *Strangers Devour the Land.* Toronto: Macmillan, 1975.

Robertson, Heather. *Reservations are for Indians.* Toronto: James Lewis and Samuel, 1970.

Smith, Derek G. *Canadian Indians and the Law:: Selected Documents, 1663-1972.* Toronto: McClelland and Stewart, 1975.

Watkins, Mel, ed. *Dene Nation: the Colony within.* Toronto: University of Toronto, 1977.

GEORGE MANUEL
MICHAEL POSLUNS

The Fourth World in Canada*

The Fourth World has always been here in North America. Since the beginning of European domination its branches, one by one, have been denied the light of day. Its fruit has been withered and stunted. Yet the tree has not died. Our victory begins with the knowledge that we have survived.

The celebration of the Fourth World, its real test of strength, and its capacity to endure, lies more with our grandchildren than with our ancestors. It is they who must cultivate the tree as a whole and honor the unique qualities of each root and branch.

Our grandfathers faced and endured the physical violence of wars, famine, and disease. They survived. We endured the social violence of legal disabilities and administrative oppression. We survived. Now there is the possibility that our grandchildren may yet face the danger of material success. They shall survive. Our history and our faith in the future are united. We are neither the beginning nor the end.

Constitutions are a collection of customs and practices that are recorded in whatever way seems suitable at the time that the practice was found good to the people who lived under it. Yet, however loosely recorded, however many sources must be consulted to put together all the pieces, that constitution does stand as a valid symbol of the hopes and aspirations, customs and beliefs, traditions and taboos of the people who live under it at the present moment. It is more than a symbol; it is the very substance of the nation and its culture.

Why then should it be so hard to understand the root and branch of the Indian nations? Our claim to a special place in the past and future history of North America? Our belief that if the Canadian mosaic arises sensibly out of the history and culture of Canada, the case for Indian nationhood arises at least as clearly out of the history and culture that the Indian nations of North America have shared?

The way to end the custodian-child relationship for Indian people is not to abolish our status as Indians, but to allow us to take our place at

* Reprinted from George Manuel and Michael Posluns, *The Fourth World: An Indian Reality*, Don Mills, Ontario: Collier-Macmillan Canada, 1974, by permission of authors and publisher.

the table with all the rest of the adults. Indian status has too often been described as "special" by those who want to create an argument to get rid of it. Indian status is neither more nor less special than those special provisions that have been made for different provinces, at Confederation and since, in order to make it possible for them to work within the partnership of Canada. These provisions recognized the unique needs of different peoples and groups and have been preserved because the differences have been found real. Yet everyone insists that they do not confer special status because they only create conditions for the different groups to become equal partners.

Why should there be a different kind of equality for us as Indian people than for the other groups of Canadians who share both a common history and a common territory that distinguish them from other Canadians? It is true that not all Indian people share a common territory in the way that a province occupies a single territory. Yet we can only imagine that our relationship with this land and with one another is far deeper and more complex than the relationship between the people of any province and their land, their institutions, or one another.

The Indian peoples cannot be brushed off with the multicultural broom to join the diverse ethnic groups that compose the Third Element of Canada, that is, those who are neither French nor English. When the Englishman speaks of "the Mother Country", the French-Canadian can still reply "Maitre Chez Nous"; the Jew can build his freedom in North America with the faith that if it fails there is yet another Promised Land; and the Eastern European who becomes an ardent Canadian nationalist still believes himself to be in exile from his native land. It seems as if every element in the Canadian mosaic is carved from a split personality. This itself is enough to distinguish the Indian peoples from the multicultural society.

When we say, "The Earth is Our Mother," we are saying that Canada is our Promised Land. Where other people look "homeward" for the medicines to heal themselves, this is our home. If the exiled condition in which Eastern Europeans believe themselves can only be ended with a change in the relationship between their Mother Country and the neighboring Great Powers, our exile can be ended only with a change in our relationship with Canada. We know that many of those people who have come to our shores to find freedom will not go home when their country is liberated. On that day their freedom will be the freedom to choose. This is the freedom of the Fourth World. We ask no more for ourselves that the many immigrant groups ask for themselves. We do expect the same freedom and autonomy in our Mother Country as they demand in theirs, and ours. This is equality.

We are neither an ethnic group nor a province of Canada. Although there are elements in both models that are useful, neither one will really work very well for us. The imposition of models on those who did not have a hand in the design has been the problem throughout our history. Clearly, the right to design our own model is the first step toward the Fourth World. Home rule begins with the opportunity to build that model with all the ingredients that the tides of history have washed up on our shores.

What is useful in the provincial model is that it teaches us that constitutional provisions and agreements have commonly been used to guarantee local autonomy and preserve the customs, traditions, and values of those people who have been able to make their political presence felt. The basic concept of making special provisions for special needs, far from being a strange anomaly as some contemporary political leaders have led us to believe, has been an accepted way of making room at the table for those whom the present partners were prepared to welcome.

The ethnic model teaches us that a Confederation founded on the belief in "two founding groups" can broaden its perspective when it appears to be politically expedient to do so. That is a source of enormous hope and confidence. If Confederation can endure past the racial myths that were the midwives at its birth, there can be no finer proof that institutions survive through the will of men as much as through their purely economic virtues.

If there is no single model on which to build either a route or a vehicle into the Fourth World there is both a common philosophy and a common fuel. The philosophy has been born from the desire to resolve two dilemmas that have been imposed through the conditions of unilateral dependence. We know that no Canadian government will ever deal fairly with the Indian peoples until we can negotiate from a position of strength. We also know that the kind of integration based on mutual respect and acceptance of each other's values as valid for the other will never happen until Indian people achieve the same standard of living as that enjoyed by city-dwelling, middle-class, white Canadians. The political and social dilemmas meet every time the Canadian taxpayers are told of the vast sums spent by their Department of Indian Affairs. Led to believe that this money is somehow directed for our benefit, the taxpayer resents the expenditure and wonders how people can be so foolish that they fail to benefit when millions of dollars are spent on their behalf.

The energy to move away from this situation comes from the realization that the way to remain Indian is to dispel the myths that have given rise to these false dilemmas in the first place. Most Indian people not only want to remain Indian but do not believe that there is any conflict between wanting to live decently and even comfortably, and wanting to maintain and develop our own way of life as Indian people. Remaining

Indian does not mean wearing a breech-cloth or a buckskin jacket, any more than remaining English means wearing pantaloons, a sword, and a funny hat. Yet on ceremonial occasions all people dress in the manner of their forefathers to remind themselves where they came from and who they are.

Remaining Indian means that Indian people gain control of the economic and social development of our own communities, within a framework of legal and constitutional guarantees for our land and our institutions. Without those guarantees, our people and our institutions remain in a defensive position, and our only weapon is passive resistance. With the constitutional and material support to carry on that development, there would be no dilemma. The racial myths that were created to justify the seizure of our land base will only be fully dispelled when we have received the legal recognition of our effective title to the lands that remain to us, and sufficient grants to compensate for what is lost that we can afford to develop what does remain. Only then will we be able to demonstrate that there is no conflict between wanting to live comfortably and wanting to develop within our own traditional framework.

The desire for legal recognition of our aboriginal and treaty rights has taken on a religious perspective. But, as in most natural or traditional religions, the spiritual has not been separated from the material world. Recognition of our aboriginal rights can, and must be, the mainspring of our future economic and social independence. It is as much in the long-term interest of the non-Indian peoples of North America as in our own interest that we be allowed our birthright, rather than that governments and churches perpetuate the Christian conspiracy that renders us the objects of charity while others enjoy the wealth of our land.

Immigrants to North America have long been considered on the basis of their skills and their usefulness to the economic development of the country. Unfortunately for the Gross National Product, we did not apply at the Immigration Office. The skills that those immigrants brought with them were at least the portable portion of their birthright. We, the first people of the land, must recover our birthright so that we can choose whether to become a part of the North American economy or to develop within our own value system.

The Dene Declaration*

We the Dene of the N.W.T. insist on the right to be regarded by ourselves and the world as a nation.

Our struggle is for the recognition of the Dene Nation by the Government and people of Canada and the peoples and governments of the world.

As once Europe was the exclusive homeland of the European peoples, Africa the exclusive homeland of the African peoples, the New World, North and South America, was the exclusive homeland of the Aboriginal peoples of the New World, the Amerindian and the Inuit.

The New World, like other parts of the world, has suffered the experience of colonialism and imperialism. Other peoples have occupied the land—often with force—and foreign governments have imposed themselves on our people. Ancient civilizations and ways of life have been destroyed.

Colonialism and imperialism is now dead or dying. Recent years have witnessed the birth of new nations or rebirth of old nations out of the ashes of colonialism.

As Europe is the place where you will find European countries with European governments for European peoples, now also you will find in Africa and Asia the existence of African and Asian countries with African and Asian governments for the African and Asian peoples.

The African and Asian peoples—the peoples of the Third World—have fought for and won the right to self-determination, the right to recognition as distinct peoples and the recognition of themselves as nations.

But in the New World the Native Peoples have not fared so well. Even in countries in South America where the Native Peoples are the vast majority of the population there is not one country which has an Amerindian government for the Amerindian peoples.

Nowhere in the New World have the Native Peoples won the right to self-determination and the right to recognition by the world as a distinct people and as Nations.

While the Native People of Canada are a minority in their homeland, the Native People of the N.W.T., the Dene and the Inuit, are a majority of the population of the N.W.T.

---

* Reprinted by permission of the Indian Brotherhood of the Northwest Territories.

The Dene find themselves as part of a country. That country is Canada. But the Government of Canada is not the government of the Dene. These governments were not the choice of the Dene, they were imposed upon the Dene.

What we the Dene are struggling for is the recognition of the Dene Nation by the governments and peoples of the world.

And while there are realities we are forced to submit to, such as the existence of a country called Canada, we insist on the right to self-determination as a distinct people and the recognition of the Dene Nation.

We the Dene are part of the Fourth World. And as the peoples and nations of the world have come to recognize the existence and rights of those peoples who make up the Third World the day must come and will come when the nations of the Fourth World will come to be recognized and respected. The challenge to the Dene and the world is to find the way for the recognition of the Dene Nation.

Our plea to the world is to help us in our struggle to find a place in the world community where we can exercise our right to self-determination as a distinct people and as a nation.

What we seek then is independence and self-determination within the country of Canada. This is what we mean when we call for a just land settlement for the Dene Nation.

Nunavut—"Our Land"*

Introduction

Inuit Tapirisat of Canada, or Eskimo Brotherhood, was founded in 1971 when an organizing committee of Inuit decided it was time for the Native People of the Arctic to speak with a united voice on a host of issues concerning development of the North, education of their children and preservation of their culture.

Initially, headquarters were established in Edmonton, but in 1972 the offices were moved to Ottawa when it became obvious the ITC needed better access to the federal government and closer communication with government officials.

A lot has happened since then. The Committee for Original People's Entitlement (COPE) representing the Inuit of the Western Arctic, became an affiliate of ITC. Other affiliated organizations are the Northern Quebec Inuit Association, the Labrador Inuit Association, the Baffin Region Inuit Association, Kitikmeot Inuit Association (representing the Central Arctic from offices in Cambridge Bay), and the Keewatin Inuit Association with headquarters in Rankin inlet.

The affiliated organizations look after day-to-day problems and concerns in their communities and regions, but their presidents also sit as members of the ITC board of directors. The national organization concentrates on national issues but helps out with community or regional problems when requested to do so. For example, ITC head office frequently goes to bat for Arctic communities when the government is asked to restrict development or exploration work in areas where local residents believe the environment and wildlife are threatened.

In short, Inuit Tapirisat is dedicated to preserving the culture, identity, and way of life of the Inuit and to helping them find their role in a changing society. To that end, an Inuit Cultural Institute has been established at Eskimo Point, and a language commission is exploring the possibility of adopting a standard system of writing in the Inuktitut language. A legal aid office has been opened at Frobisher Bay. A major communications research project is under way.

A non-profit housing corporation has been established, and a $48 000 contract has been signed with Frontier College of Toronto to draw up a

---

* Reprinted with permission from the *Inuit Tapirisat of Canada*.

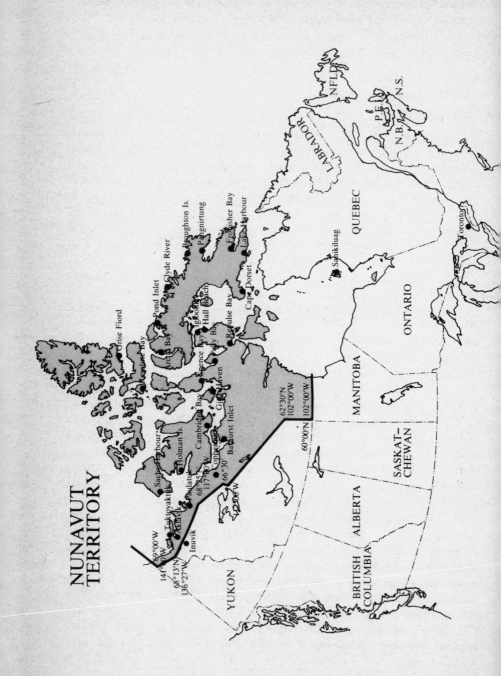

management training program designed to fit the special needs of Inuit. An Inuit Development Corporation is being established as the business arm of ITC to enable the people of the Arctic to administer the resources and assets which will come under their control when a land claims agreement is reached with the government of Canada.

Land Claims

In the short history of Inuit Tapirisat, by far its most significant project is the Inuit land claims proposal for the Northwest Territories. It is probably the most comprehensive proposal of its kind ever presented in North America, the product of three years of intensive research and field work covering the legal aspects, renewable and non-renewable resources, and the documentation of actual land use and occupancy over the centuries.

The land use and occupancy study, directed by Dr. Milton Freeman of McMaster University, shows that from prehistoric times the Inuit have used and occupied virtually all of the 750 000 square miles of land generally north of the treeline, and an estimated 800 000 square miles of northern ocean. This research, along with an exhaustive study of renewable resources directed by Dr. Gordon Nelson of the University of Waterloo, and a survey of non-renewable resources by geological consultant Pedro Van Meurs of Ottawa, went into the preparation of a proposed agreement in principle drawn up by ITC's legal consultant, Prof. Peter Cumming of York University.

But lest there be any misunderstanding, ITC's land claims proposal is not another example of white man in the south deciding what is best for Inuit in the North. At successive annual meetings of Inuit Tapirisat, delegates from all regions of the Arctic gave their organization's board of directors a strong mandate to proceed with the land claims project. And while the consultants were preparing their studies, ITC field workers were actively seeking the views of the people in the communities, talking to them about the issues and collecting their suggestions.

All of this hard work and effort culminated in a historic meeting of Inuit held at Pond Inlet, Northwest Territories, from October 28 to November 2, 1975. More than 100 voting delegates from 32 Arctic communities attended. Resolutions passed by their community councils empowered them to vote on behalf of their people. For six days and some long nights, the delegates plodded through the lengthy land claims document clause by clause, questioning some of the points, voting to make amendments to some of the important sections, and finally passing a resolution authorizing ITC to begin negotiations with the federal government. What the delegates did in effect was declare that the Inuit are willing to share the land which they have never surrendered by treaty or otherwise.

Because the Inuit are neither greedy nor unreasonable, they are not asking for outright ownership of their entire 750 000 square miles of traditional lands; in fact, ownership of land as southern Canadians understand it is a concept that had always been foreign to the Inuit. The land had always been there for the people to use and occupy. However, the people realize now that if their native environment is to be preserved for future generations, they must have a piece of paper establishing ownership under Canadian law of enough land to ensure their survival. So they are asking for ownership of 250 000 square miles of land, which will be selected in such a way that each Arctic community has at least 2 500 square miles. The remaining 500 000 square miles north of the treeline would be surrendered, but with certain conditions attached. Among those conditions, the Inuit would retain exclusive hunting, fishing and trapping rights. And the Inuit want a share of the revenue from development of natural resources. A royalty of 3% has been suggested.

The Inuit want to be self-sufficient. One really unique feature of their land settlement proposal is that it will not cost the taxpayers of Canada anything. They are not asking for a cash settlement, because the Inuit land is not for sale. In fact, they are offering to pay back, with interest, the money provided by the federal government (more than $2 million) to finance their land settlement research.

The revenue from resources would go toward financing a comprehensive social and economic development program, and operations of the new Inuit Development Corporation. The whole philosophy behind ITC's proposal is to permit the Inuit to gain some control of their social, cultural and economic destiny. To that end, they are also suggesting a first step toward self-government by the creation of a new territory to be known as Nunavut, which means "Our Land". Nunavut would comprise all 750 000 square miles of the traditional Inuit lands, and its system of government would be similar to that of the existing Northwest Territories, with an appointed commissioner and an elected council. Since the majority of electors would be Inuit, Native People would assume a degree of control over industrial development and such things as environmental protection and wildlife conservation.

And then eventually, perhaps there will be a Province of Nunavut. The Inuit are not separatists. They are Canadians. But they don't want to be colonial subjects. They want to be partners in Confederation. When one considers the unbelievably barren nature of the Arctic terrain and the effects of a climate that is harsh and cruel by southern standards, 250 000 square miles is really not very much.

Look at it this way. In the fertile agricultural areas of Ontario, according to Statistics Canada, the average farm earning 51% or more of its revenue from livestock covers an area of 209.1 acres. In Alberta, where the grazing land is not quite as lush and the climate somewhat more severe, the average livestock operation requires 1 025.5 acres. In the Arctic, it takes up to tens of square miles of land to support one caribou. That is why it is so unreasonable to think in terms of 5 square miles per family, as has been suggested for native land settlements in other parts of the North.

In an exhaustive study of Arctic renewable resources carried out for Inuit Tapirisat, Dr. Gordon Nelson of the University of Waterloo says that "Inuit hunters range over hundreds or thousands of square miles, so land settlement must be thought of on an entirely different scale than elsewhere in Canada."

There are lessons to be learned from history when it comes to negotiating a land agreement with the Inuit. In the 19th century, when the arid plains of western Canada were being settled, homesteaders were allowed 160 to 320 acres for farming. This size was based on the experience of raising crops on the moist lands of eastern Canada, but was totally unrealistic for the dry land of the west. It took decades of trial and error, countless farm failures and untold human misery before farms of 1 000 acres or more—large enough to support a family—could be established by those lucky enough to emerge as winners in the long struggle against other settlers and the environment.

Dr. Nelson concludes in his report that the same principle applies in the Far North. "Much land must be placed in control of the Inuit and conservation agencies of government if wildlife and environment are to be protected and traditional hunting and fishing as well as modern commercial renewable resource-based enterprises are to have a second opportunity to grow in the Arctic."

Why an Inuit Land Settlement?

There are good, solid reasons why the people of Canada through their elected government should reach a land sharing agreement with the Inuit of the Northwest Territories. Old-fashioned fair play is one of them. It can be argued that Canada owes a large debt to the Inuit, after so many years of intruding into their land, uninvited, imposing changes in their way of life, exploiting the natural resources of the Arctic without consulting the original inhabitants.

The government of Canada has adopted an enlightened and generous policy of assistance and support for the emerging countries of the Third World. In fairness, can Canadians be any less generous with the first citizens of their own country? But if apathy and indifference should rule out fairness as an argument, how about enlightened self-interest?

The politicians churn out hundreds of thousands of inspired words about maintaining sovereignty over that vast and magnificent land that stretches north beyond the treeline, through the Arctic Islands, almost to the North Pole. But to have sovereignty, one must have occupancy. The Inuit are the occupants. They are the only occupants who want to, or indeed are able to live in the extreme environment of Canada north of the treeline. They are happy to live there, and struggling desperately to preserve what is left of their unique way of life. In fact, until the whiteman came and imported the southern comforts of home, the Inuit were the only ones who knew how to survive in the North.

Recently, southern Canada has been showing a great interest in the Arctic. But this has not been reflected in any eagerness among large numbers of southern Canadians to actually live in the Arctic. They are interested in the North for what they can take out of it.

Canadians are on the threshold of one of the most significant decisions since Confederation. They can help the Inuit achieve self-sufficiency—socially, culturally, and economically. The alternative is continued colonial rule at ever-increasing cost to the Canadian taxpayer, coupled with destruction of the Inuit culture and the consignment of a proud and independent people to a marginal existence on poor wages and government handouts. For the Inuit, it is still not too late to avoid the mistakes which have blighted the history of white society's relationships with Native People.

HOWARD ADAMS

Canada from the Native Point of View*

I grew up in the community of St. Louis, Saskatchewan, which, like Batoche, was founded by French halfbreeds who had fled from Red River in 1870 to escape the persecution by Ottawa's troops and the Ontario Orangemen. It is a town of approximately 300 people, situated on the banks of the South Saskatchewan River. Strung out along the south side of the river for nearly a mile is the main part of the town, centering on the Catholic cathedral and convent.

In World War II, the town was easily identified as halfbreed, Catholic, and French. Halfbreed log shacks were scattered throughout the town; the huge cathedral with its towering steeple, magnificent rectory, and gowned nuns told of the Catholic influence. Many of the townspeople spoke a French patois mixed with Cree and English. Although the majority of the population were Métis—French and Cree—not a single business was owned or operated by us. We remained the casual and unskilled laborers, the depressed and powerless people. The hotel, garage, store, lumberyard, and café were all run by white Frenchmen. A few Anglo-Saxons ran other small businesses and had importance and power in the community quite out of proportion to their small numbers. Dotted along the back roads were more halfbreed shacks, log and mud houses used as permanent dwellings throughout the year, built to accommodate large families and withstand the severe sub-zero Saskatchewan winters. They were typical houses of poor Prairie people. On the north side of the river lived the English Protestant halfbreeds whose ancestors had migrated from Manitoba in the early 1870s via Prince Albert. The French and English halfbreeds on the two sides of the river got along well together.

Typical of most halfbreeds, our family lived in a state of deprivation and at times had to depend on welfare. In spring and fall we worked for white farmers and in summer we tended our gardens and small farms, picked berries, seneca root and rocks, cut brush, and grubbed trees**. In

---

* Reprinted from Howard Adams, *Prison of Grass: Canada From the Native Point of View*. Toronto: New Press, 1975, by permission of the author and publisher.

** cleared farm land of tree stumps.

winter we cut and hauled cordwood and sold it to the white merchants in St. Louis for $1.50 per cord. On Sundays we faithfully went to church to thank God for our "small blessings". We were always reminded to be eternally grateful to the Lord for giving us so much in life.

Halfbreed Resistance to Imperialism

Colonial struggles were taking place throughout western Canada in the 1860s. At the base of the trouble was the conflict between two different economic systems—the old economic system represented by the Hudson's Bay Company and the new industrial system. The new ruling class of British financiers and Canadian industrialists had consolidated its position in eastern Canada and was now extending its empire westward across the Prairies. They wanted not only the land and the resources of the Northwest, but also a capitalist order that would consolidate and further their economic enterprises, so it was natural that they encountered opposition from the old order of the Hudson's Bay Company. The clash of these two economic systems fuelled the hostilities of 1869-70 in the Northwest, which resulted in Rupert's Land being brought under the constitutional authority of the government in Ottawa, the seat of the industrial empire.

Although Native People were involved in this struggle and represented a major force against advancing imperialism, it was basically a civil war between two economic orders. The new capitalist order had to overthrow the political institutions of the old order before it could develop its new society. Up to 1869 the government and judicial system of the Northwest Territories was under the jurisdiction of the Hudson's Bay Company. The government bought the Rupert's Land charter in 1869 in the hope that it could simply transfer power from one set of rulers to another without consulting the people of the land or the Canadian factors of the Bay, the lower rank of rulers in the company. The most important change proposed was the surrender of the Hudson's Bay Company's constitutional authority over Rupert's Land, which would bring the entire Northwest under the jurisdiction of Ottawa. Since the top ruling class of the Bay had become members of the new industrialist class (certain wealthy shareholders of the Hudson's Bay Company, among them Donald A. Smith, had transferred some of their capital to the impending transcontinental railways), Ottawa expected a peaceful subjugation of the Bay empire and a willing surrender of the Northwest Territories. But Ottawa underestimated the strength of the factors within the Hudson's Bay Company. Because they had no share in the $300 000 paid by the government to the Bay and because their wealth and power was derived from the day-to-day fur-trading operations of the company, the factors opposed the transfer of Rupert's Land.

Many Canadian scholars and journalists consider the resulting civil war as a rebellion by the Métis of Red River. Portraying it as a rebellion, however, distorts the objective conditions and consequences of this struggle, justifies imperialist conquest, and at the same time falsifies the heritage of Native People. The struggle of 1869 was *not* a rebellion because it was not an uprising against a constitutional government in existence at the time.

To complete its expansion plan, Ottawa needed the best Northwest lands, not only for the CPR but also as an agricultural area for immigrants. Since a market was needed for manufactured goods, European settlers were needed to perform the function of consumers. Once the buffalo were gone, the Native People were reduced to complete dependency on whites, and the treaties served to justify the seizure of Indian lands. It was government policy to locate reserves on rocky, sandy, and hilly land. Because halfbreeds were not considered aboriginal people, they were not placed on reserves but were confined on farm colonies and rural ghettos. Some halfbreeds were left with no alternative but to become squatters on road allowances.*

Very few halfbreeds took up homesteads, because the intention behind such land settlement plans was to exclude most of the indigenous people who had aboriginal claims. In the first place, the halfbreeds did not have the required down payment, small as it was. But, more important, the halfbreeds had lived in the Northwest Territories long before the government surveyed the land and implemented its homestead policies. Halfbreeds had moved into the Saskatchewan area shortly after the Red River struggle in 1870. They selected sites along the river which they divided into river lots. They built homes and developed their farms. As far as they were concerned, this land belonged to them. Nevertheless, the requirements to qualify for a homestead were restrictive, in the sense that certain bureaucratic and legal matters were involved. Also, homestead regulations demanded that a set number of acres had to be cleared, broken, and cultivated within three years. This regulation alone made it almost prohibitive for halfbreeds to own homesteads, because they lacked the machinery and tools to fulfil such development requirements. Halfbreeds were allowed to buy their river lots after April 1885.

To call the hostilities of 1885 "Riel Rebellion" is not only misleading but incorrect because it implies that Louis Riel alone was responsible for the hostilities. The truth is that he entered only the later stages of a long struggle involving many groups in the Northwest. The war of 1885 was the culmination of a complex struggle that had arisen over the previous two decades between the people of the Northwest and the industrial rulers of Ottawa. Western protests were made by local merchants, farm-

---

* The narrow strips of land between the road itself and the private property on either side.

ers, settlers, workers, Indians, and Métis, and their demands essentially centered around the need for a responsible government to make economic and land reforms. The hostilities of 1885 proved to be an important turning point in the social and political development of Canada. The new rulers established capitalism in the Northwest, and the way was clear for modern agriculture and industrialism to expand through the private enterprise system.

Being a pacifist, Riel believed that justice could be achieved through peaceful methods. When he surrendered he thought he would receive justice through the courts. In the most profound way Riel opposed violence and bloodshed: during both the civil war of 1870 and the resistance of 1885 Riel never carried a gun, nor did he advocate violence. This was Riel's chief weakness as a leader. He was amazingly naive about the willingness of the members of the ruling class to use force to achieve their ends.

While the trial of Riel held the public's attention, Macdonald's cabinet quietly turned its attention to the recovering economy. A little more than two months after Batoche, a bill was introduced in Parliament granting the CPR syndicate an additional $45 million essential to the completion of the railway. As a result of this grant, CPR creditors were paid, workers were returned to work and paid their back wages, supplies were bought for cash and the construction of the railway got under way once again. Financiers from Britain who had previously stopped putting money into the CPR began investing again. On November 7, 1885, nine days before Riel was murdered, the railway line from the West met up with the line from the East and the CPR was at last completed. A new wave of immigrants moved into the Prairies to furnish the land companies with buyers for their land.

The Native Plight in White-Supremacy Canada

To the Indians and the Métis the basic cause of poverty is not the psychological or personal weaknesses of individuals but the economic conditions of the capitalist system. In northern native communities nearly 80% of the adults are either unemployed or live in families whose annual income is under $4 000. Any native who opposes the authorities responsible for this oppression is dealt with directly by such means as withdrawal of welfare, harassment by police, or denial of local services. In 1973 a Catholic priest in a northern community threatened the Métis people with a refusal to administer sacraments and confession if they opposed the policies of the local power structure in the community.

Although the poverty of Métis and Indians is ultimately linked to colonial suppression, it is specifically the result of immediate issues such as the availability of jobs. In practically all areas of employment natives are given menial and low-paying jobs which whites do not want, such as picking stones, harvesting beets, and fighting forest fires. Picking stones and beets are done on contracts, which natives must find for themselves. The rate of pay for fire-fighting is very low, and the workers often fight fires 16 hours a day. Although both white and native men can be conscripted into this job, native men almost exclusively are pressed into fire-fighting, often in dangerous tasks.

The majority of jobs given to Native People are casual and seasonal, hence they are unable to build any security around such jobs. These employment practices force natives into a day-to-day occupational existence. They are unable to plan for a future, or for their children, or think in terms of social mobility within the present employment structure. Even in Métis Farm Colonies*, natives cannot aspire to positions any higher than casual laborers on the farm because all the supervisory positions are held by whites.

A very small percentage of Métis and Indians are in positions where they are meeting the public (as sales clerks, bank tellers, or bus drivers). This reveals a great deal about Canada's racist society and is a major reason for unemployment among natives. Of course, whites will excuse themselves by saying, "Natives are not qualified for these jobs." However, the other side of the coin is that Native People know fully well that there is no use in training for such jobs since they will not get them. They are hesitant to take training that will lead to further discrimination, frustration, and disappointment. They are realistic in their outlook; the fact is that Métis and Indians do not get public positions. As a result, the income of natives is severely restricted, both by the type of work and by the rate of pay. The casual "dead-end" jobs we do obtain have serious psychological effects: they are soul-destroying experiences and force us into hopelessness, frustration, and hostility. Many Indians and Métis families live on social welfare. Since the welfare department does not record payments according to racial origin, it is difficult to obtain accurate figures. However, it is well known that most families on welfare, whether native or white, take it because there is no alternative.

The problem of racism is always present in the schools, particularly with regard to the use of native languages. Many Métis and Indians have been forbidden to speak their native language by their teachers or by official policy. Twenty percent of those interviewed in the 1972 survey claimed they had been punished for using their native language at

---

* Large farms in Saskatchewan Métis communities owned and operated by the provincial government. The work force, except supervisory and administration staff, is exlusively Métis. Employees and their families live in the housing units on the colony.

school. Others had been forbidden to speak their native language because teachers claimed these students were mocking them. This sort of teacher paranoia only serves to increase the cultural differences that exist between native students and teachers. But even though they admit that most white teachers do not associate with natives, the latter often rationalize this discrimination by claiming that "we are of a different culture" and "the teachers are not interested in us".

The vast majority of Indians and Métis do not know who controls the schools in their community, or who decides on the curriculum. Apparently, they are not concerned enough about education to learn about the system of control. Probably they feel it matters little since they would still be powerless to exercise any control once they did know. However, when they do begin to exercise control over their own educational system, changes in white-native relationships in the schools will only take place gradually because of the white-ideal. The rate of change will depend on the rate of decolonization, i.e., on how fast natives can rid themselves of the consciousness of the oppressed. It is therefore unlikely that Native People would approve if schooling immediately changed to a completely native operation. Because of the white-ideal, native parents hold certain expectations of success in the white world for their children. Although these are only superficial and surface expectations, nevertheless they do exist and have to be respected. Native teachers would be generally regarded as incapable of preparing native children for white society. Influenced by the white-ideal, native parents feel that white teachers are better able to direct their children to success in mainstream society, even though the majority drop out before reaching high school. Most native parents would probably oppose full native content in the curriculum at the present time. But, as decolonization progresses, both native parents and students will develop greater determination and pride in their heritage and nation and more confidence in their own ability and increased skills in community control. This will allow Indians and Métis to move towards a greater degree of native administration and instruction in the schools.

Towards Liberation

Indians and Métis will need to fight for independence and self-determination like other Third World peoples. We have to recognize that our rights are what we take, that it requires power to take rights and preserve these rights after they have been taken. Freedom will never be freely given. As soon as our struggle begins to gain momentum, ruling authorities will declare that natives are racist and violent. However, it is impossible for minorities to practise racism effectively because they do not exercise any influence on the society that determines the ideology and attitudes of that nation. Under radical nationalism the masses are the leaders and not the Uncle Tomahawks, or the self-appointed representatives, or the elites. Liberation demands are based on obtaining autonomy in native communities and throwing off the domination of government bureaucrats.

Under the colonial society that has imprisoned Native People, practically all creativity and intellectual development have been smothered. Radical nationalism provides opportunities for exploring and expanding creatively because the excitement and potential of an awakening nation generates rich, flourishing ideas. Red nationalism revives those native cultural traditions that give stability and security to the nation and discards those that oppress the people. The native nation, in a state of archaic suspension for the last hundred years, will break out of its colonial molds. Nationalism will usher in a new humanism and harmony that will set native culture in motion once again and open the doors to new cultural developments. This revival of culture will not be refined or sophisticated but it will be vigorous. Formalism and ritualism will be abandoned in favor of new forms of expression that will depict struggle, freedom, vitality, and hope.

Since red nationalism is essential to Indian/Métis liberation, it must be a spearhead force for the native movement, and must provide the machinery for educating the masses politically. Since cultural awakening is only one stage of liberation, steps must be taken to ensure that the national consciousness will develop its political aspects as well. There is danger in nationalism if this transition is not made at the right time, because colonized people can quickly become involved in cultural nationalism, which is a move backward to further oppression. They must also be on guard against bourgeois nationalism as well as cultural nationalism. Bourgeois nationalism, however, is easily recognized: it is simply a code of patriotism imposed by a ruling class through authoritarian officials and channels, such as schools—it is a purely ritualistic and empty exercise, performed only because one is obligated to participate in displays of patriotism.

Cultural nationalism is a reactionary nationalism that forms part of the ideology of imperialism. It is adopted by or imposed on Third World people in their colonized state and it involves the revival of indigenous native traditions and tribalism. Today, in our awakening, many Indians of Canada are returning to native religion and tribal rituals. The danger in this is that it might begin to sever any links with a progressive liberation ideology. The idea that a return to traditional Indian customs and worship will free us from the shackles of colonial domination is deceptive—a return to this kind of traditional worship is a reactionary move and leads to greater oppression, rather than to liberation. Cultural nationalism is more than behaving and believing as traditional Indians; it is a return to extreme separatism in the hope that colonial oppression will automatically go away. The emphasis is on worship and the performance of ritual behavior, not on politics and liberation. Because cultural nationalism insists on excluding political issues, Indians and Métis accept their colonized political conditions without challenging them. It perpetuates the racist idea of "Indians in their place", and does not allow them to develop a radical consciousness or a reorganized culture that would be in harmony with liberation.

This analysis takes into account the fact that it is not only the native society that is colonized, but Canada and all of its citizens. White Canadians and Indian/Métis are in similar states of colonization. Canada has always been a colony, first of France, then of Britain, and now of America. Although Europeans came to Canada as settlers, they in turn were colonized by the mother country. In 1837 Canadians attempted a struggle for independence, but they were defeated by English imperialists; consequently, the social institutions, legal and political structures, and ideological framework remained under the control of the Imperial government in London and later under the colonial bourgeois administration in Ottawa. Canada is now a colony of America, and what applies to Indians and Métis to some extent applies to white Canadians who have their own national liberation struggle against the empire of the United States. Like Indians and Métis, white Canadians must acknowledge their colonized situation and then direct their national liberation movement from that point. At the same time, Canadians in general will need to develop their radical nationalism. Such a nationalism is beginning to emerge, but work must be done to make sure that it does not remain bourgeois nationalism. The major difference between whites and reds in their colonization is that natives have been molded into a pseudo-apartheid system. Their struggle is therefore a double one: the first and most immediate struggle is against the colonialism of the federal and provincial governments; the second is against the imperialism of the United States. The struggle against the government of Canada is the most immediate because its agents occupy our native communities and dominate our daily lives.

Indians and Métis cannot count on any support from the white working class in their struggle against imperialism, at least not at this time. Part of the working class and its union aristocracy have disappeared into the capitalist ranks. Some unions and workers appear to be primarily concerned with getting a greater slice of the economic pie rather than with promoting a revolutionary struggle. Their energies are directed towards internal organization and economic gain (such as higher wages and pensions) within the capitalist system. Because they have been absorbed into the system as an integral part of capitalism, they have reduced their effectiveness in struggling against it. Historically, white workers of the imperial nation generally have much better working conditions, higher wages, and a higher standard of living than the workers of the colonies. The white workers' good conditions are due partly to the crude exploitation of the native workers in the Third World. Generally, white workers are inclined to oppose liberation and independence for native colonies. White workers tend to identify themselves with the colonizing society, and white supremacy is as much a part of the working class as it is of the ruling class. As jobs become increasingly scarce, white workers react more severely against native workers. The poorer the white worker, the more he is threatened by the native worker, and the stronger are his racist feelings. Since white workers are inclined to see developments in the native struggle as a direct threat to them, they often support the reactionary appeal to enforce "law and order". In this way, they serve the forces of counter-revolution. It is understandable that Indians and Métis identify more with the colonized colored people of the Third World than with the white working class of their own nation. Instead of struggling against capitalism, the majority of workers are inclined to accept it as the best of all possible systems; they believe it only needs to be reformed so that they will receive greater privileges and benefits. Those workers who have become integrated into the capitalist system are not at present a potential source of support for revolutionary change. There are exceptions, of course: many workers and unions in Quebec are in the forefront of struggles against the capitalist system. Nevertheless, there comes a time when all oppressed people must join together in a united struggle and form a new revolutionary class. It appears that this new class will comprise women, youth, natives, and workers. At the same time, the ruling class must be prevented from isolating any one group from the remainder, as they did in 1885 and again in 1970 during the Quebec crisis.

In the Quebec crisis of 1970, the government showed itself completely willing to use violence and jail against people who attempt liberation through violent means, and they would crush a native people's liberation struggle with even greater brutality than they did in 1885. A call to arms by the Native People at this stage would be a call to martyrdom. However, as the native movement develops together with the struggles of other oppressed groups in Canada, there may come a time when guerilla violence will be necessary and appropriate, and we must not hesitate to use it.

We are told that the enemy, colonialism, is the historical oppressor. But we must make no mistake that our oppression is in the forms and institutions of colonialism and in its manifestations, such as racial stereotypes, Indian bureaucracies, welfare, and prisons. Only by transforming the objective conditions can we put a final end to colonialism. For example, we must change the authoritarian schools and government departments, the economic elite who control the masses and the government, and the chauvinist relationships that exist between men and women.

The Indian and Métis are now concerned with giving a native dimension to their lives and actions because identity helps in the struggle against colonialism. This struggle for liberation is a long and arduous one, yet it is for this reason that it must be fought without respite and without compromise. We can do this by working at all levels in the liberation struggle. For instance, some members can work at the neighborhood level in simple organizational and education work, while others can work in a broader way, mobilizing for civil-rights actions and extra-parliamentary confrontations. Finally, there must be a group of natives who are willing and able to work at the sophisticated level of guerilla warfare, both urban and rural. The racism and colonialism that capitalism breeds will always hold us captive in misery, violence, and exploitation. It is time that we recognized our own power and faced the fact that our solutions lie within ourselves. Revolution can be made only by those who are in a state of revolution.

W. T. STANBURY University of British Columbia

Urban Indians in British Columbia*

A Rising Off-Reserve Population

Between 1965 and 1972 the percentage of status Indians living off reserve in Canada increased from 25.6% to 36.3%. The proportion of B.C. Indians living off reserve increased from 14.2% in 1962 to 34.6% in 1972. In absolute terms, the size of the on-reserve Indian population in B.C. has remained virtually constant since 1962. For each of the five major cultural/linguistic groups within the province, the proportion living off reserve has increased. The largest increases were found among Coast Salish people (from 9.0% off reserve in 1962 to 30.2% in 1972) and among the Wakashan/Bella Coola Bands (from 11.0% in 1962 to 38.0% in 1972).

Our sample of 1 095 off-reserve residents, amounting to a one-in-six sample of the B.C. off-reserve population aged 15 to 65, collected in the summer of 1971, indicated that one third had spent less than two fifths of their lives on reserve. Forty-four percent of our sample had spent more than three fifths of their lives on reserve. Almost 14% of the members of our sample were born to parents living off reserve. We believe that, virtually independently of government policies, a greater proportion of Indian people in B.C. and in the rest of Canada will be living in urban centers in the future. Our concern is whether or not both the Indian people and the dominant white society are prepared for the urbanization of the native population.

Reasons for Living Off Reserve

In answer to the question, "Why do you live off the reserve?" employment provided the single most important reason. This response was given by 35% of the men and 19.7% of the women. Forty-two percent of men aged 25 to 49, and 45.8% of those currently employed, lived off the reserve because there were no jobs on reserve or because the distance to their job was too great to permit them to live on a reserve. Economic necessity was

---

* Reprinted from W. T. Stanbury, *Success and Failure: Indians in Urban Society*. Vancouver: University of British Columbia, 1975, by permission of the author and publisher.

therefore the single most important reason, making our results similar to those of other studies of Indians in urban centers.

Another reason given for living off the reserve was "a general preference for life off reserve". One quarter of the men and one fifth of the women lived off reserve for this reason. Lack of housing on the reserve was another reason given by 13.9% of the women and 9.7% of the men in the sample, most of whom were older people.

Forty-four percent of our sample planned to return to the reserve to live and almost the same proportion did not plan to do so. The remainder was undecided. Some 29.3% planned to return if there was a house available on the reserve, 20.2% planned to return when they retired, and 22.6% identified the reserve as their home or said that they preferred reserve to urban life. About 14% said they would return if there was a job on reserve or if they became unemployed.

A Young and Rapidly Growing Population

Status Indians account for 1.1% of the nation's population and 2.3% of British Columbia's population. When non-status Indians are included, Native People represent almost 5% of the total population of the province. Between 1944 and 1972 the status Indian population of B.C. almost doubled, increasing at an average annual rate of 2.45% compared with the rate of 2.24% for the total Canadian population. The causes of the growth of the Indian and non-Indian population were quite different. All of the increase in the Indian population was due to natural increase (the number of births minus the number of deaths). A large component of the increase in the total population was accounted for by immigration rather than the rate of natural increase. In the 1960s, the rate of natural increase for B.C. Indians declined from 35 to 27 per 1 000, while that of the entire province fell from 15.8 to 9.3 per 1 000. In 1970, therefore, the rate of natural increase of B.C. Indians was three times that of non-Indians.

The most important result of the sustained high rates of natural increase of the Indian population is that 45% of the Indian people in 1971 were under age 15 and 30% were under 10. The percentages for the province were 28% and 18% respectively. The age distribution of the off-reserve population is only a little different from that on reserve; the proportion under age 15 is less than one percentage point apart. There is, however, a higher proportion of people aged 50 and over living on reserve (11.3%) than off reserve (7.0%). In every age group within the 15–64 range, the proportion of women off reserve is greater than that of men.

The second most important result of sustained high rates of natural increase is the large size of most Indian families. The 1971 Census indicated that rural Indian women (primarily on reserve) aged 15 and over who had married had borne an average of 4.7 children each, compared with 2.7 for rural non-Indian women. Urban Indian women averaged 3.6 children in contrast to 2.3 for non-Indian women. Almost two fifths of the rural Indian women had borne six or more children. Of the rural Indian women aged 55 and over, 31% had borne nine or more children. A comparison of the 1954 data for a sample of reserve residents with those for 1971 suggests that family size has declined (in terms of the number of children born to women ever married), but the decline in infant mortality means that the "effective family size" (children over one year) has remained about the same. For a given level of income (and many Indian families have low incomes), a larger number of children implies a significantly lower per capita income.

Our survey of off-reserve residents, well over four fifths of whom lived in urban centers (over 1 000 population), indicated that an average of 5.4 people lived in an Indian household, compared with 3.1 as the household average for the total B.C. urban population. Over two fifths of the Indian households consisted of six or more people. On average, non-family members accounted for one third of the total Indian household but only one eighth of non-Indian households. Although we could not make precise comparisons, reserve households seem to be about the same size as off-reserve households, but the average size of reserve families is greater.

Coming to the City: Adjusting to Life Off Reserve

Thirty-eight percent of our sample knew both other Indians and some non-Indians in the city when they arrived. Thirty-seven percent knew only other Indians when they first arrived. Fifty-five percent of our respondents received some help during their first month in the city. In slightly over one half of such cases, the help was provided by relatives, in 13% it came from friends, and in 32% from a social worker or clergyman. We note that the Department of Indian Affairs was not mentioned as a source of assistance. Where help was received during the first month, it took the form of assistance in getting housing in 17% of the cases, the form of cash in 7%, and in a similar proportion of cases the new migrant was shown around the city, primarily by friends and relatives. Two fifths of those who received help had virtually all their needs met, primarily, again, from friends or relatives, the traditional source of assistance to new migrants.

To what extent are urban Indians subject to racial discrimination? On the basis of questions relating to stores and cafes, hotels, government offices, landlords, and the police, we did not find that discrimination was pervasive. Fifteen percent of the sample reported negative experiences in stores and cafes, 16% reported negative experiences in hotels, and 14%

had negative experiences with landlords. One fifth and just over one quarter of the sample reported negative experiences in government offices and with the police, respectively. A higher proportion of younger people reported incidents of discrimination than older people. To put our data in perspective, we would like to know the extent of discrimination against other minorities and, specifically, how discrimination constrains the opportunities of urban Indians in British Columbia.

Mobility

Majority of the people in our sample had been living in the town where we interviewed them for six years. One third, however, had been residents for less than one year, and one half had lived there for three years or more. On average, our respondents changed their place of abode once every 18 months. Families of three or more had changed their dwelling place once every 25 months, or about twice as frequently as the Canadian average. The number of months between intracity moves generally declined as the size of the town increased, perhaps reflecting the larger absolute supply of rental accommodation in larger urban centers.

Members of our sample had lived in an average of 6.2 places off reserve (for at least one month) inside or outside of B.C. and an average of 4.4 different cities or towns within the province. With an average age of 32, these data would suggest that B.C. Indians are a mobile population. Mobility was inversely related to the proportion of life spent on reserve, the number of months in the current town of residence, and the number of months since the individual had lived on reserve for one month or more. Residents of all regions experienced lower mobility than Vancouver residents. All other variables, including marital status, income, number of months self-supporting, perceived discrimination, and Indianness Index were statistically insignificant predictors of mobility in terms of the total number of cities or towns where the members of our sample had lived or the number of different cities or towns within B.C. where members of our sample had lived.

Marital Status, Illegitimacy, and Children in Care

The proportion of the B.C. Indian population (aged 15 and over) that is married is substantially lower than that of the total B.C. population. The 1971 Census indicates that 66.2% of the B.C. population are married (or separated), but only 42.65% of the total B.C. Indian population, and 38.3% of the off-reserve population are married. Data collected in 1954 indicated that 60.5% of the Indian population (aged 15 and over) were married or separated.

The decline in the preference for marriage is matched by a corresponding rise in the proportion of Indian births that are classified as "illegitimate". In 1961, some 34.6% of the status Indian births were illegitimate. In 1972 this proportion had risen to 56.5%. Indian Affairs data revealed that in 1971, two fifths of all single Indian women in B.C. had one or more children. Cause and effect are difficult to discern here, but sections of the Indian Act provide that a status Indian woman who marries a non-Indian loses her status. This represents a substantial disincentive to such marriages. If she simply lives with a man, however, their children are defined as status Indians. In our sample, over two thirds of the common-law relationships that we could identify as such consisted of a status Indian woman living with a non-Indian or with a non-status Indian.

Large families, limited resources, and the high rate of illegitimacy have been associated with a doubling of the number of status Indian children coming into the care of the province's Superintendent of Child Welfare. In 1973, proportionate to the number of children 19 and under, four times as many Indian children were in care as non-Indians. Children of Indian racial origin (status and non-status) account for almost 30% of the total number of children in care, but only 5% of the total children in the province.

Using a broader measure of the incidence of child welfare problems, the rate for status Indians was almost eight times that for non-Indians in 1972. Almost two fifths of the status Indian children came into care because of the "inability of parents to provide necessary care," and 18.0% came into care because of "desertion or abandonment."

The number of Indian children placed in adoption has been increasing over the past decade. Of the 472 status B.C. Indian children adopted between 1961-62 and 1970-71, less than one fifth were adopted by status Indian parents. Indian people in the province are most concerned about the low percentage of placements in status Indian homes.

Closing the Education Gap

Perhaps the most outstanding evidence of the progress of the Indian people in the province is the rise in their level of educational attainment over the past three decades. We found a strong inverse correlation (−0.528) between age and education (the highest grade completed). For those aged 55 to 64 in our sample of off-reserve residents the median number of grades completed was 4.1. For those aged 20 to 24, the median was 9.9 grades completed. A survey of B.C. Indians (most of whom were living on reserves) made in 1954 indicated that the median level of education for those aged 46 and over was only 1.3 grades and that for those aged 15 to 25 it was 6.5 grades. Forty-eight percent of our 1971 sample had at least a secondary school education, whereas the 1961 Census showed that only 19.0% of those aged 15 and over had a similar level of education.

The education gap is closing, particularly among younger people, but it is by no means closed when we examine the total adult population. For example, we estimate that 37.5% of off-reserve Indians (1971) have not completed even an elementary school education, compared with 18.6% of all Canadians in 1967. Among those aged 20 to 24, we found that 29.2% of our sample had an elementary education, 67.6% had a secondary school education, and 3.2% had attended university. The comparable percentages for the B.C. population were 10.7, 66.0 and 23.3, respectively. Indian retention rates remain far below those for non-Indians in B.C. Only 12% who were in grade one in 1958-59 entered grade twelve in 1969-70. For the total province the rate was 82.6%

Most importantly, the aspirations parents have for the children's educational attainment are rising, and they are positively related to the parents' own level of education. In response to the question "How much schooling do you want your children to have?" the proportion who replied "university" was 13% for those with eight or fewer grades completed, 20% for those with grades nine to eleven, and 33% for those with high school graduation or beyond.

We found that 35% of the members of our sample had taken one or more special courses or vocational training courses. Sixty percent of these people reported one or more full-time trade courses and three quarters of the courses taken could be described as vocational training. Almost 70% of these vocational courses were of at least six months' duration. Over nine tenths of those who enrolled for a course had completed it. Some 28.5% of the sample responded affirmatively to the question, "Do you have any definite plans or arrangements for any more schooling, training or special courses in the next twelve months?" We found that younger, better-educated Indians were more likely to have taken vocational training and other special courses.

Despite the rise in the level of schooling and the prevalence of vocational training, we found that additional years of schooling and the presence of vocational courses did not significantly increase current earnings when the effects of other variables were held constant. Similarly, higher education did not increase the number of months the individual had been self-supporting. The crucial point here is that virtually all our observations were in the range of zero to thirteen grades completed. It is not surprising that those with grade ten are no more economically successful than those who had completed grades eight or nine. The literature on the economics of human capital indicates that the rate of return on a university education exceeds that of a high school education. To move into the more skilled tradesmen's jobs and into the better white-collar jobs where incomes are higher and more stable, more Indians will have to graduate from high school and obtain a university education.

The State of Indian Health

It is no exaggeration to say that the poor health of the Indian people of B.C. is an enormous tax both on the people who suffer the debility of ill health and also on the non-Indian population that finances per capita public expenditures on Indian health more than double those for the non-Indian population.

It is still relevant to talk about "the right to life" among the Indian population in British Columbia. The median age at death of B.C. Indians is about 44 compared with about 72 for all British Columbians. Even when we account for the fact that the Indian population is substantially younger than the total population, the median age at death of non-Indians is 17 years greater than it is for status Indians. Infant mortality among B.C. Indians in the early 1970s is one third of the rate it was in the late 1930s, but it was still three times the rate for non-Indians in 1971 and 1972, despite the fact that 96% of the later Indian births occurred in hospitals or nursing stations. In 1973 almost two fifths of the infant deaths occurred within 24 hours of birth. Between 1961 and 1970, some 9.1% of all Indian deaths were due to perinatal mortality compared with 2.5% for all British Columbians.

The fictional doctor in Alan Fry's *How a People Die*, remarked "Tell us in fact how a people die and we can tell you how a people live...." Between 1961 and 1970, death by accidents and violence accounted for 28.9% of all Indian deaths in the province—almost three times the proportion for the total population. In 1971, 51.1% of all Indian deaths were accounted for by infant deaths or by accidents and violence. In contrast, only 15.5% of all deaths in B.C. were due to these two causes. On the other hand, we found that the number of deaths per 100 000 population between 1961 and 1970 due to diseases of the heart, cerebrovascular diseases, and malignant neoplasms (such as cancer) were only 34% to 40% of the rates for the total population.

Indians in the Labor Market

In the absence of property income or inherited wealth, level of income depends on the degree of success in the labor market. The level of income from employment, in turn, depends on type of job and stability of employment. These two variables are not, of course, independent of each other. People at the lower end of the occupational structure are frequently beset by periods of unemployment.

We were able to measure the rate of unemployment among B.C. Indians in urban centers only for the summer of 1971. Using the strict interpretation of the Monthly Labour Force definitions, we found the unemployment rate to be 26.9% or more than four times the rate for non-Indians. If we had counted as part of the labor force the "discouraged workers" (or those who were without work and would have been seeking work except that they "believed no suitable work was available in the community") then the unemployment rate would have been 46.5% (54.1% for women, 42.9% for men).

The labor-force participation rate is a crude measure of the degree of attachment to the labor market. If discouraged workers are included, the participation rate among the members of the sample was 69.7%, almost 11 points above that of the total population. If we use the narrower definition and exclude the discouraged workers, the rate for urban Indians was 51.1% or eight percentage points below the total population of B.C. A survey of non-status Indians, also made in the summer of 1971, indicated an unemployment rate of 50% and a participation rate of 64%. While participation rates increased consistently with the level of education of our sample, the level of unemployment was only significantly lower among high school graduates (10.5%, narrow definition) than non-graduates (32.4%, narrow definition).

Occupationally, we have evidence that B.C. Indians living off reserves are reducing their reliance on primary occupations and are enjoying increased representation in white-collar and production/craftsmen occupations. Using pooled data, recording occupational changes over the previous four jobs or by going back at least two or three years, we determined that 10% of the jobs were in managerial/professional/technical occupations (18.7% in the summer of 1971), 7% were in clerical/sales occupations (11.5% in summer of 1971), 19% were in service/recreation jobs, 13% in transportation/communication, 31% in primary occupations, 22% in production/craftsmen jobs, and 9% in labor/unskilled jobs. The comparable figures for Canada in 1971 were 24%, 22%, 12%, 5%, 8%, 24%, and 4% respectively. A measure of the urban Indians' upward occupational mobility is the fact that, in 1961, 42% of all Canadian Indians were in primary occupations, 17% in service/recreation jobs, 16% were in production/craftsmen jobs, and 12% in labor/unskilled occupations. Only 6% were in white-collar jobs.

Level of Income and the Ability to be Self-Supporting

We sought to determine the capacity of Indians living off reserves to be self-supporting, that is not in receipt of financial assistance from friends or from the government in the form of social assistance for the 2½-year period before the interviews in the summer of 1971. We found that 28% of the sample had not been self-supporting for even one month in the 30-month period, but 24% had been self-supporting for the entire period. Just under one half of the members of the sample (48%) had been self-supporting for at least one half of the 2½-year period.

A set of regression equations seeking to identify the "determinants" of the ability of men to be self-supporting found that the following variables had positive coefficients and were statistically significant: age in the 25 to 49 year range compared with men of 15 to 24; high school graduates compared with those with four or fewer grades completed (in only one equation); the presence of a wife in the labor market; union membership; all current occupations, except those in managerial/professional/technical occupations; individual perception of the job situation as good; the Tsimshian/Haida cultural/linguistic group compared with the reference group (Interior Salish).

In terms of their income from employment in 1970, 54% of our sample of off-reserve residents (families and unattached individuals) had incomes of less than $2 000. In contrast, only 26% of all B.C. individuals had incomes of less than $2 000 in 1971. Over one third of those in our sample had no income from employment in 1970. At the other end of the spectrum, only one eighth of the families and unattached individuals had incomes of $8 000 or more in 1970, compared with one third of all B.C. individuals in 1971.

Using the definitions of the Special Senate Committee on Poverty, we estimated that 67.5% of the families and individuals in our sample were below the poverty line in terms of their incomes from employment. When government transfer payments were taken into account, the proportion was still 62.8%, or 2½ times that for the country as a whole. It is apparent that government transfer schemes (family allowances, old-age pensions, and social assistance payments) simply do not fill the poverty gap.

In terms of total income, two fifths of the families of two or more in our sample had incomes under $4 000 in 1970. Only one sixth of all B.C. families were in this income class in 1969. Just over 19% of our sample had total incomes of $8 000 or more in contrast to some 55.8% of all B.C. families of two or more. Yet the data we have assembled indicate that Indian incomes in B.C. have improved sharply over the past decade. For example, in 1961, 51.5% of the reserve families (probably averaging between five and six people) had total incomes under $2 000, and 82.8% had incomes under $4 000. Although Indian incomes have improved (even relative to the rise in the incomes of non-Indians), Indians in B.C. have barely begun to enjoy a taste of the "affluent society".

Cultural Identity

Indians who live in urban centers continue to speak their native language and to teach it to their children. They visit the reserve and attend Indian ceremonies on and off the reserve. They read publications aimed specifically at the native population and tell their children traditional stories and legends.

For almost one third of our sample, English was the only spoken language. Sixty-one percent spoke English and one native language. Interviews conducted in 1954 with a large sample of reserve residents indicated that only 6% of those interviewed spoke only English and 84% spoke English and one Indian language. To make these figures comparable to our own for which all interviews were conducted in English, we excluded the 17% who spoke only an Indian language. In our sample, the proportion speaking only English declined sharply in the older age groups. For example, 45% of those aged 15 to 29 compared with only 7% of those of 50 and over spoke only English and no native language. These data suggest that prominence of the native language is declining over time as a smaller proportion of young people learn their Indian tongue.

Only 14% of the sample used an Indian language at home; 13% used both Indian and English, and 73% said that English was the language usually spoken at home. Again, the percentage of older respondents who reported Indian or English and Indian spoken in the home was much higher than it was for younger respondents.

When asked "What language(s) do your children speak at home?" only 7.4% of those ever married indicated an Indian language and 6.0% stated that both an Indian language and English were used. Yet one half of those ever married said that they or their spouse had made at least some effort to teach the children their native tongue. One third of those ever married had told their children Indian legends and customs "sometimes" or "occasionally", while 16% had done so "often" or "frequently".

As for other measures of cultural identity, we found that 57% attended Indian ceremonies (dancing, potlatches, and so on), and 23% had attended three or more such ceremonies in the previous 12 months. Three quarters of the sample visited the reserve, and some 47% usually made two or more such visits annually.

Thirty-seven percent read one or more publications aimed at Indian people and 16% reported membership in at least one Indian organization (for example, an Indian center). For the most part, the various measures of cultural identity and cultural ties tended to reinforce each other, but the degree of positive interrelationship was much greater within the language-related variables and the non-language measures than between them.

We did not discern any evidence to suggest that Indians living in urban centers must "go white" in order to be economically and socially successful. Certain non-traditional patterns of behavior must be adopted, but these need not result in the loss of cultural identity.

Native Women and the Indian Act*

In 1971 an Indian woman who had lost her status (under provisions in the Indian Act) by marrying a white man, filed an appeal in Ontario courts. The case became generally known as the Corbiere-Laval case. The woman, Mrs. Laval, protested to the courts that she was being discriminated against by reason of sex, and that her rights under the Canadian Bill of Rights thus had been encroached upon by the Indian Act. Shortly thereafter, a Mrs. Bedard launched a somewhat similar court action. Mrs. Bedard had lost her status by marrying a white man, but had returned to the reserve after the marriage broke up. When the community decided to evict her and her children, she launched an action based on the status and rights of the children, again claiming encroachment by the Indian Act upon rights guaranteed by the Bill of Rights.

At the beginning, I don't think that anyone except the federal government was watching these cases with any real interest. Certainly few Indian people paid any attention. By the time the cases reached the Supreme Court level, we became very aware of the implications. If it was found by the Supreme Court of the country that provisions of the Indian Act were invalid because they were inconsistent with provisions of the Bill of Rights, the overall implications were enough to make our hair stand on end!

A dangerous precedent had been set. In a case involving a liquor infraction in the Northwest Territories in the 1960s, an Indian named Drybones was convicted under provisions in the Indian Act. Mr. Drybones successfully challenged that conviction on the basis that it was discriminatory and contravened provisions of the Canadian Bill of Rights. That precedent was in the back of our minds as the cases involving the two Indian women began to attract attention across the country. There appeared to be considerable public support for the women, and various women's groups recognized the cases as a unique opportunity to advance their cause.

In other parts of the country, Indian people were beginning to examine the Canadian Bill of Rights as a basis for challenging certain other provisions in the Indian Act. In British Columbia several people were

---

* Reprinted from Harold Cardinal, *The Rebirth of Canada's Indians*. Edmonton, Alberta, 1977, by permission of the author and publisher.

preparing to challenge a section in the Indian Act which they felt was discriminatory because it denied them the right to hold private property on the reserve. Talk of this nature (let alone action) and the very thought that a decision in favor of the plaintiffs would make the Bill of Rights supreme over the Indian Act, raised all sorts of fears on our part. We were terribly concerned over what effect such a decision would have on reserves as the collective home of Indian people. We did not follow, nor did we want, a system of private ownership, because we felt that this would rip apart our reserve communities in short order.

Another valid concern was that if the women were successful in their suits, our reserves would be opened for settlement by white men, allowing them, through marriage to Indians, to gain ownership of Indian lands. A number of other questions were raised:

(1) Would individual Indians then be free to sell portions of Indian land? This could mean destruction of Indian reserves and the end of Indian landholding.

(2) Would communal band ownership of reserve land cease to exist and be supplanted by individual ownership subject to seizure? Would that entitle non-Indians, related through marriage to Indians, to inherit portions of Indian lands?

(3) Would Indians be subject to some of the provincial laws which do not now apply? Such restrictions would seriously impair, not only the livelihood of many Indians, but also their freedom to pursue their traditional lifestyle.

(4) Would all Indians be deprived of the freedom of choosing between remaining a status Indian or becoming a member of the greater society?

(5) Would Indians be forced off the reserves where their chances of economic development are reasonable, and into urban slums where they would be doomed to perpetual dependence on welfare?

Our alarm, which led to our decision to oppose the two women, was based on our belief that if the Bill of Rights knocked out the legal basis for the Indian Act, it would at the same time knock out all legal basis for the special status of Indians.

In assessing this problem, we had to consider the position we, the Indian organizations, were placing ourselves in. Many government officials appeared confident that the two women would win their cases, and that the Canadian Bill of Rights would be found to be supreme over the Indian Act. When we met with officials of the government, they could scarcely hide their jubilation at the realization that they were being handed a beautiful opportunity to do what they had wanted to do with the Indian Act, but had been unable to get away with in a political forum.

By mid-1972, we were again looking seriously at the need to change the Indian Act. At the National Indian Brotherhood meeting in Edmonton that summer, the Indian Association of Alberta took the position that Indian people had to intervene against Mrs. Laval in the Corbiere-Laval case, the first of the two to reach the Supreme Court. Our position was that it was not the rights of women at stake. If it was decided that the Canadian Bill of Rights was supreme over the Indian Act, that decision would wipe out the Indian Act and remove whatever legal basis we had for our treaties. Thus, the relationship between the Indians and the government would be dramatically affected. What was at stake was the whole relationship between Indians and whites.

The initial response of the National Indian Brotherhood to the Indian Association of Alberta's position was negative. Some of the provincial organizations, particularly in Manitoba and British Columbia, did not want to intervene. They not only felt that Mrs. Laval had a legitimate point of concern, but they feared a political backlash if Indian organizations appeared to be intervening against their own people. When we failed to get unanimous support from the Brotherhood, we decided to take on the case on our own as the Indian Association of Alberta. We were then joined by the Indians of the Quebec Association and by the Federation of Saskatchewan Indians. However, by the time the Supreme Court was ready to hear the Corbiere-Laval case, the Brotherhood was ready to follow our lead, and the intervention then became an action by the national organization representing the provincial ones.

We realized when we decided to intervene that we would, of course, alienate the feminist movement, and that we would also lose some of our traditional public support. It proved one hell of a mess to get into, because no matter what we did, everyone got mad at us, and it was difficult to maintain a sane and rational discussion on the issues involved. We had one other problem that few white people ever appreciated, and that was trying to cool tempers on the reserves where this was a big emotional issue. It seemed that everyone on the reserves had come into personal contact with this problem: it had affected mothers and fathers who had had to make decisions about their daughters; people who had to decide whether or not to leave the reserve to marry someone off the reserve; old people who had had to make decisions about grand-children. This was an issue that had touched everyone personally at one time or another. There was an extremely strong feeling on the reserves that a decision had been made by the women involved, and that they were going to have to live with that decision.

Another element in our midst wanted to turn the cases into a fight between treaty Indians and Métis. The issues were exploited by some Indians who felt we had gone too far in seeking a working relationship with the Métis, and we worked for a hell of a long time just trying to quell that hostility between treaty Indians and the Métis population.

We had a tough time controlling those passions and keeping our people focused on the position that whatever injustices an Indian woman faces under the current provisions of the Indian Act, those injustices can be best rectified when the Indian Act is amended. We freely admitted that such a step was still down the road a way, but insisted that we had to first make sure that we had an Indian Act that was strong enough to stand by itself without being overshadowed by other pieces of federal legislation. That was the focus that we had to maintain, not whether or not women who married off the reserve should lose their status.

We got a lot of crap from everyone, not only the women involved; and we lost, as we had suspected we would, a lot of our traditional white support. Of course, the government was extremely happy to see all this unfold. They were convinced that they were going to get what they wanted. They probably welcomed our intervention because it would give them two birds to kill with one stone—one, they would get rid of the Indian Act, and two, our intervention would get us into so much hot water with our own people that we would be finished as an organization. Fortunately for us, it didn't turn out that way.

One of the direct results was a revived concern over the Indian Act. When the Corbiere-Laval appeal reached the Supreme Court of Canada in February of 1973, the Indian Association of Alberta took as many observers as possible to Ottawa to hear the arguments being presented to the court by both sides. Additionally, as a result of the various studies that we had conducted on our own, combined with the legal research that was done on the case, we intended to present an Alberta brief to the federal government. We asked for two things in our formal presentation. We told the government that we were ready with a task force of resource people, with input from Indian people, and a specific timetable, to draw up a new Indian Act for submission to the government within six months. We realized, of course, that the Supreme Court would not hand down an immediate decision, and we calculated that they would take about six months to prepare it. We wanted to be ready, and we wanted a commitment from the government that if we were ready within six months with a completed new version of the Indian Act, whether the case went for or against us, there would be something in place for Parliament to consider.

We asked for, but did not get at that time, an immediate amendment to the Indian Act which would have put a temporary clause eliminating the threat it faced from the Bill of Rights. Conversely, if that procedure was not possible, we asked that an amendment be put into the Bill of Rights which would state that nothing in that bill would interfere with our treaty rights. What we did get as a result of our presentations was a commitment by Mr. Chrétien to give us resources and people to work with us in coming up with a new Indian Act within the time period we had set.

In February 1973, as a result of the two court actions, we found ourselves in a formal agreement to look at the Indian Act and come up with changes for it within six months. We were pleased with the commitment and confident that we could meet the time frame we had imposed on ourselves. The House Committee on Indian Affairs was skeptical about our ability to meet that deadline, which we established was conditional on receipt of the financial resources pledged by Mr. Chrétien.

We immediately started discussions with the bureaucrats who would have to implement the general agreement that had been arrived at between the Minister and ourselves, and they said, "Give us a budget estimate and we will get started, or at least we will see how we can respond." Because our timetable was so tight, we submitted a budget that same month.

Then we discovered that the Department of Indian Affairs was not prepared to provide the necessary funding. Instead of starting on the project, we found ourselves involved in a budget fight with the Department. After several futile sessions with Indian Affairs, the Brotherhood asked us, the Alberta Association, to pursue the negotiations so that we could get started on the Indian Act research. But after we had submitted our fourth or fifth budget estimate, each time revised and made more specific, we advised the Brotherhood to tell the Department to go to hell with any further requests for budgets. We asked Indian Affairs to state clearly and precisely just how much money they would make available. That way at least we could tell what kind of work we could do with the resources we were to have. We were limited to the numbers and types of resource people we could afford, and it depended on the total amount of money to be made available to us for resource people, for consultations across the country, and even for clerical work. We couldn't make a proper start until we knew what we were going to be able to spend.

During the budget battle, Mr. Chrétien publicly asserted that he had given $1 million to the Indian Association of Alberta to draw up a new Indian Act. He asked what had happened to that money, complaining that he had not received a progress report. The statement made it look as though we had made off with the money from the federal government, giving nothing in return. The statement was probably partly a response to the pressure we had been putting on the Department to come through with the money they had pledged. We promptly notified Mr. Chrétien that we intended to sue him for libel unless that statement was withdrawn. Mr. Chrétien hastily withdrew his statement and delivered a written apology to me as President of the Indian Association of Alberta.

It was a year later, in the spring of 1974, before the Brotherhood finally reached an agreement with the Department of Indian Affairs on a budget for the work. Of course the deadline had passed, but the work we subsequently did proved we could have met our goal sooner had the money been made available promptly.

Immediately after the agreement, we put together a team of Indian people from various reserves and various walks of life, along with resource people. After three months of examining the Indian Act section by section, they came up with a draft proposal. We officially presented our findings to the National Indian Brotherhood on August 5, 1974 and asked for a later date to make the presentation to the Department because we wanted to give an opportunity to various organizations to respond to the draft recommendations contained in the proposal. By the end of October 1974, still well within our timetable, we presented the proposals to the new Minister of Indian Affairs, the Honorable Judd Buchanan.

There was no public discussion of the proposals that we submitted. The government reacted very coolly, and it was our understanding that they had begun to work on their own draft of an Indian Act to be submitted to the federal cabinet.

There was no agreement on handling amendments to the Indian Act, only agreement that amendments were needed. Our proposal was a lock, stock, and barrel revision of the entire act. We took the opportunity in our first meeting with the federal cabinet in the fall of 1974, shortly after the demonstration on Parliament Hill, to bring to the cabinet's attention our desire and determination to have the Indian Act amended, and the cabinet agreed to put the matter on the agenda for the next meeting in February 1975. At that second meeting, the cabinet committee said that it preferred a step-by-step revision of various sections rather than an immediate overall revision of the act, and we agreed to go along with this. We won a vitally important commitment that no changes to the Indian Act would be introduced in Parliament by the Department of Indian Affairs, without first having such changes cleared through a joint meeting of the National Indian Brotherhood executive council and the cabinet committee especially set up to meet with the Brotherhood council.

Prior to the Bill of Rights cases that swung our attention back to the political urgency of the Indian Act revisions, many bands and organizations had achieved considerable success with their work on claims settlements. We got agreement nationally that in the revised Indian Act, there should be an opting-out provision along the lines of the federal-provincial agreements of Prime Minister Lester Pearson's day. Where a band or a province had won special legislative guarantees of their rights in a settlement agreement, and feared losing those advantages to provisions of the new Indian Act, they would be allowed to opt out; that is, to be governed by the special legislation attached to their settlements rather than by the new Indian Act.

That was the final compromise that we arrived at internally on the Indian Act. From the onset the Alberta study team felt (and so did the leadership) that what was needed was a study document that dealt not only in broad concepts, but came up with specific recommendations and specific means to implement those recommendations.

On the question of membership, which was really the crux of the problem in the Corbiere-Laval case, the study team made two recommendations. First, that when a non-Indian marries an Indian, the non-Indian spouse would not gain status and the children would not have status. The Indian spouse would not lose status, and that is substantially different from the present provisions. If this clause has been in effect, the Corbiere-Laval case would never have come up. The second recommendation covered the situation which had spawned the Bedard case. In a non-Indian-Indian marriage, the couple would not be allowed to remain on the reserve while married, but the Indian spouse would be permitted to return to the reserve if the non-Indian spouse died, or if they were divorced. This would solve a major problem faced by Indian women in such circumstances.

In the case of inter-tribal marriages, the Indian Act simply provides a so-called patriarchal solution: a woman who marries a man from another reserve transfers to the husband's reserve. The new provisions would provide equality and a free choice: both the man and the woman would retain their tribal memberships, and the children would have the option of choosing which tribe to belong to when they reached the age of twenty. All would be entitled to live on the reserve of their choice. Provision was made that any Indian who marries an American Indian retains his or her Canadian Indian status, and the American spouse may be listed as a member of the Canadian tribe.

PART TWO

The Second Nation: The French in Canada

Introduction

When Prime Minister Trudeau addressed the U.S. Congress in 1977, he observed, "The success of our efforts in the first century following Confederation was promising but by no means complete. . . . We have not . . . created the conditions in which French-speaking Canadians have felt fully equal or could fully develop the richness of the culture they had inherited. And therein is the source of our *central problem today* (emphasis added)." This section examines this "central problem" from a regional and historical perspective, focusing on the ethnic factor in the lives of Canadians of French ancestry.

The Québécois

The historical background to the so-called central problem as it concerns Quebec is presented through the eyes of a Quebecker, Marcel Rioux. Quebec is the homeland of about 80% of the francophones in Canada. Rioux's article highlights the rise of the Quebec State (as opposed to the French Canadian nation), the objectives of the Royal Commission on Bilingualism and Biculturalism, the federalist's definition and response to the Quebec question, and the alternative offered by Quebec.

If one were to speak of Quebec as the central problem today, it would be erroneous to suggest that the roots of the problem are shallow or that the nationalistic sentiments of the Québécois are not as legitimate as those expressed by others. The Québécois aspirations are only problematic for those English-speaking Canadians who do not wish to accommodate them. The anglophone media often portray Quebec as an annoying thorn-in-the-side of an otherwise tranquil Canada. Danielle Lee offers an alternative view for those who consider Quebec nationalism as either recent or illicit. Lee traces the evolution of nationalism in Quebec, linking ideological to structural change. She stresses the fact that nationalism is not new in Quebec; it has assumed different shapes and has found various expressions over the years. She concludes with an evaluation of separatism as a possible next step in the evolutionary process.

Stephen Richer and Pierre Laporte's article questions how *real* the cultural differences are that presumably exist between the anglophones and the francophones. Although the likelihood of either cultural or social class factors completely eclipsing the other in importance as a determinant of behavior is slight, what is the relative importance of culture as opposed to class for outcomes such as status attainment? The research

52

model adequate for an empirical resolution of this question is put forth and existing data are fit to the model.

The wide social class differences that exist today between the francophone and anglophone communities were even more sharply drawn and reflected in the educational system of the province before the Quiet Revolution in the early 1960s. During the Duplessis era prior to the 1960s, higher education for the francophones was limited to the children of a small circle of elites who trained in the classical colleges for careers predominantly in law, medicine, and the Church. In contrast, anglophone education tended to emphasize engineering, technical and scientific training, and commercial skills preparatory to the business world. In 1967, educational reforms were instituted with the establishment of *les collèges d'enseignement général et professionel* (CEGEPS). This new educational system aims to increase the access of the lower social classes to higher education and offers curricula designed to bring francophone education in line with anglophone education. The CEGEPS operate on a bilingual, free-tuition basis and are spread throughout the province. They are similar to junior colleges and serve approximately one third of the Quebec high school graduates.

Ann Denis' study of students in an anglophone CEGEP in Montreal reveals that students from the other ethnic groups are over-represented and some French Quebeckers are enrolled as well. This finding is consistent with other research that shows the tendency of immigrant groups and native-born francophones to assimilate to the English community. The educational aspirations of the CEGEP students in this study are analyzed by social class, ethnicity, and sex. Bearing in mind that generalizations drawn from an empirical study may be limited by the social conditions existing at the time of the study, Denis' study provides a model for the type of research that would have to be done periodically to determine changes in the educational aspirations of the different ethnic groups, social classes and sexes.

Francophones outside Quebec

Francophones outside Quebec participate in a broad range of social and political contexts. Even within the same province, they may have in common only their language and the reality of a larger society that may be alternatively supportive, disinterested, or, perhaps, aggressively hostile. Such variations in the social milieu, coupled with ethnic differences among francophone groups, make francophone organizational efforts somewhat problematic.

Taking the case of francophones in Ontario, Danielle Lee and Jean Lapointe and Thomas Maxwell discuss the presence of a francophone identity in some areas and absence in others, and the societal factors that tend to explain this. Lee and Lapointe analyze the structural changes that have taken place in the ethnic boundaries of the Franco-Ontarians. For the most part, the latter trace their ancestry to the founding French settlers in Canada. Many Franco-Ontarians are related to the Québécois as both groups are descended from very old French Canadian families. Because of the divergent histories of Quebec and Ontario, unique ethnic identities are emerging in each province. Lee and Lapointe relate the changes in ethnic boundaries to the new modes of Franco-Ontarian ethnicity they encompass.

The vibrant ethnicity emerging among many Franco-Ontarians, however, stands in juxtaposition to the "invisible" French unearthed by Maxwell within the same province—the francophones of Toronto. We learn from Maxwell's research that just as the presence of certain structural conditions may predict ethnicity, so also may their absence predict assimilation. The francophones in Toronto are geographically and structurally heterogeneous in their origins; they do not reside in the same neighborhood; they occupy all social strata and classes of the community; they are diversified in their religious behavior; and by their presence in Toronto, it is assumed that they are trying to succeed within English Canadian society. Thus, it is not surprising that the Toronto francophones are "invisible". The structure of social rewards in Toronto does not encourage francophones to orient their lives along an ethnic dimension.

While maintaining an ethnic identity may be a problem in a metropolis like Toronto, ethnicity is not necessarily preserved in rural areas. In the Atlantic provinces, for example, the Acadians, descendants of the early 17th century French settlers who were expelled in the mid-18th century by the British, and who subsequently returned after the Peace of Paris, are struggling to keep their culture intact. Recent attempts at modernizing fish processing have had an impact on the Acadian life style. Nanciellen Sealy investigated the effects of modernization on the traditional status of men and women in a small New Brunswick community. It was assumed that ethnicity mediates the modernization process. Acadian culture and traditional sex roles stand to be eroded by economic development with women perhaps benefiting less than men.

In the West, French ethnicity was weakened by an influx of Central European immigrants. C. Jaenen offers a historical account of the cultural battle for survival that francophones have waged in the West on behalf of the "two nation" concept of Confederation. French Canada's survival in the West—if only in a token way—has been achieved seemingly against all odds. French was only briefly recognized as an official language on the provincial level in Manitoba, and throughout the West, French language instruction in the schools assumed the status of a foreign language. The linguistic factor was cross-cut by religious sentiments. While English Protestants tended to oppose French Catholics, non-French speaking Catholics tended to support the French Catholics on some political issues on the assumption that Catholics of all languages should band together. The net effect of this support may have been a weakening of the francophone position. Nevertheless, remnants of French ethnicity persist in the West as well as in such communities as St. Boniface, Manitoba.

SELECTED REFERENCES

Beattie, Christopher. *Minority Men in a Majority Setting: Middle-Level Franco-phones in the Canadian Public Service.* Toronto: McClelland and Stewart, 1975.

Cameron, D. *Nationalism, Self-Determination, and the Quebec Question.* Toronto: Macmillan, 1974.

Clark, Andrew Hill. *Acadia.* Madison: University of Wisconsin Press, 1968.

Clement, Wallace. *The Canadian Corporate Elite: an Analysis of Economic Power.* Toronto: McClelland and Stewart, 1975.

Cook, Ramsay. *Canada and the French-Canadian Question.* Toronto: Macmillan, 1968.

———. *French-Canadian Nationalism.* Toronto: Macmillan, 1969.

Dion, Léon. *Nationalismes et politique au Québec.* Montreal: Hurtubise H.M.H., 1975.

Dorge, Lionel. *Introduction à l'étude des Franco-Manitobains.* Saint Boniface: La Societe Historique de Saint Boniface, 1973.

Falardeau, J. C., ed. *Essais sur le Québec contemporain.* Quebec: Les Presses de l'Universite Laval, 1953.

Henripin, Jacques. *Immigration and Language Imbalance.* Ottawa: Information Canada, 1974.

Henripin, Jacques, and E. Lapierre-Adamyck. *La fin de la revanche des berceaux.* Montréal: Presses de l'Université de Montréal, 1974.

Jackson, John D. *Community and Conflict: A Study of French-English Relations in Ontario.* Toronto: Holt, Rinehart and Winston, 1975.

Joy, Richard. *Languages in Conflict.* Toronto: McClelland and Stewart, 1972.

Milner, Henry. *Politics in the New Quebec.* Toronto: McClelland and Stewart, 1978.

Milner, S. H., and Henry Milner. *The Decolonization of Quebec.* Toronto: McClelland and Stewart, 1973.

Morris, Raymond N., and C. Michael Lanphier. *Three Scales of Inequality: Perspectives on French-English Relations.* Don Mills, Ont.: Longman, 1977.

Piotte, J. M., ed. *Quebec occupé.* Montréal: Editions Parti-Pris, 1971.

Posgate, Dale, and K. McRoberts. *Quebec: Social Change and Political Crisis.* Toronto: McClelland and Stewart, 1976.

Thomson, Dale C., ed. *Quebec Society and Politics: Views from the Inside.* Toronto: McClelland and Stewart, 1973.

Trudeau, Pierre E. *Federalism and the French Canadians.* Toronto: Macmillan, 1968.

Wade, Mason. *The French Canadians, Vol. 1, 1760-1911; Vol. 2, 1911-1967.* Toronto: Macmillan, 1968.

Québécois

MARCEL RIOUX   University of Montreal

Quebec in Question*

In his year-end speech in 1968, General de Gaulle expressed the hope that the French people of Canada would obtain a free hand in the management of their national life. The journalists at once remarked that the General had been more insistent on this point than the previous year. When asked to comment on this statement, Prime Minister Trudeau was said to have agreed with the General. How was this possible? "The General was speaking of French Canada," Trudeau is said to have replied, "not of Quebec." The essence of the Quebec problem lies, in fact, in this distinction.

To speak of French Canada (or of the French people of Canada) is to speak of Canadians who speak French and who live in all parts of Canada. The problem is therefore one of bilingualism or, at the most, of biculturalism, and the solution is to be reached through the agency of the central government, the Canadian State. Federalists are happy to grant the name "French Canada" to the totality of French-speaking people scattered throughout the Canadian territory. Ottawa could, at the outside, even tolerate that this population be called the French-Canadian nation, because so defined, the word "nation" refers only to characteristics of language and culture; moreover, Ottawa remains the government of these two "nations" because the population referred to is distributed over the entire territory of Canada. The French-speaking people thus remain the traditional minority of about 28% defending their minority rights while experiencing a progressive anglicization. All is safe and sound. No attack has been made on the political and economic power structure, nor on the important sectors of government and administration which continue to be controlled by the central government in Ottawa, the capital of the two

---

* Reprinted from Marcel Rioux, *Quebec in Question*, Toronto: James Lewis and Samuel, 1971, with permission of author and publisher.

"nations". Here is the most perfect status quo, the very thesis of Mr. Trudeau. For the federalists, Quebec is one province out of ten; it can make no claims to represent the French-Canadian nation because there are still French-speaking people living in the other nine provinces.

In the 1960s a great change occurred, revolutionizing the situation. Quebeckers began to make a distinction between Quebec and French Canada. On the one hand, there is a population of French-speaking people distributed throughout Canada. This population has, in varying degrees, a common heritage of language, religion, tradition and custom. This cultural element represents about 28% of Canada's total population. Federal government statistics show that outside of Quebec this population is becoming anglicized at various rates of speed; in British Columbia 60% of this group have been assimilated. For Canada as a whole, it will be a lost cause sooner or later; the steamroller of English-speaking North American culture will soon leave nothing but a few remnants of this language and culture.

On the other hand, there is a vast land three times larger than France where the French-speaking people are a great majority, namely Quebec. Since 1867, this territory has had a government and an administration with limited constitutional powers, but still perhaps capable of exercising enough leverage to safeguard most of what we call French-Canadian culture. On the evidence, to do this requires a reevaluation of the Quebec State, the only collective instrument that the French Canadians possess. In Quebec the French-speaking people own only a small share of the economy, the industry, and commerce. All they have is a mini-state, a territory, a culture and the desire to live together and to develop themselves. Under the pressure of public opinion, Quebec provincial governments have timidly endeavored, since 1960, to affirm the existence of the Quebec State and to control, as far as possible, those economic and political decisions which affect the life of their people. They have adopted measures to strengthen the role of the State in economic life. They soon realized, however, that the most important powers required by a modern industrial state were held by the national government of the other nine provinces, in all of which the English-speaking people were in the majority. Quebec public opinion showed a surprising degree of unanimity that favored more power for the Quebec Sate, and a significant part of the population now demanded full political powers. It is here that the Quebec question arises. We are no longer dealing with French-Canada, with bilingualism and biculturalism, but with the powers of the State of Quebec and with the collective life of the people of Quebec. The issue is not merely that of nationalism, racism or prejudice towards anyone; it is also a question of life or death for a nation of six million people. The fate of Canada's French-speaking people will be decided in Quebec itself. French Canada's culture is finished—in Newfoundland, in

British Columbia, and even in Ottawa. A century of Confederation has proved that.

Trudeau's rise to power in Ottawa was the federalists' most spectacular reply to the separatists, but the central government had been actively working against separatism many years before the appearance of Trudeau. In July 1963, well aware of the seething discontent in Quebec, the Canadian government, in the best British tradition, appointed a Royal Commission "to enquire into and report on the present state of bilingualism and biculturalism in Canada and to recommend measures that would be taken to ensure the development of Confederation according to the principle of equality between the two founding nations, taking into account the contribution of other ethnic groups to the cultural enrichment of Canada, as well as measures to be taken to safeguard this contribution."

In 1965, in their first public document, the commissioners opined that "Canada, without being fully conscious of the fact, is passing through the greatest crisis in its history." Curiously enough, Quebec is no exception to the rule; as in every colonial situation, the dominant power is always behind the times, and unaware of how conscious its subjects are of the society that is made for them. For a century, French-speaking people have fought for an acceptance of bilingualism by the federal government. If Ottawa had been aware of this problem before, events might have taken a different course. The federal government was prepared to accept bilingualism only at a time when Quebeckers, declaring themselves a majority in their own country, were taking on attitudes and political stances which went far beyond bilingualism. As in every other colony, it's a case of too little or too late. The problem that interests Quebeckers at the moment is the question of monolingualism in Quebec; the bilingualism that Quebeckers had frequently demanded for Canada as a whole no longer seems a worthwhile goal to many French Canadians.

Let us recognize clearly, here in Quebec, that when the members of any group—nation or class—are subjugated to another group and see that they are considerably weaker than their masters, they ask only for equality. When the dominated group becomes more and more aware of its strength and the balance of power seems to shift in its favor, it demands all the power and all the culture for itself. This is plainly what is happening in Quebec today.

Almost everyone who lives here agrees that there are serious problems in Quebec, but there are many conflicting explanations for this state of affairs and many proposals to remedy it. The supporters of the status quo, i.e., the Canadian Confederation, say that Quebec has not quite caught up with the rest of Canada, that the problem of Quebec is a problem in regional economic disparity, more or less the normal situation in any federated system, as certain regions develop more rapidly than others. The remedy is equally simple: apply the appropriate economic policies to correct this state of affairs. Most federalists see Quebeckers as the authors of their own misfortune: if instead of electing so many reactionary governments and investing so much energy in defense of their collective rights, each one of them had striven to succeed in his particular field, Quebeckers would be in much better economic shape today. If instead of holding fast to outmoded practices and obsolete values they took an active part in the modern life of North America, they would not have to complain about being oppressed. This view implies the thesis (openly stated, moreover) that Canada is one people, one nation, one State composed of several ethnic strains—the English- and French-speaking being the two principal ones—and that the government will take all necessary measures to ensure the continued existence of one nation. This is one of the chief replies made to the Quebec question.

The other reply—given by the great majority of Quebeckers—is that a French-speaking nation exists in Quebec and that it has the right to a great measure of political autonomy; for many Quebeckers, this nation has been dominated continually since 1760. Today, in spite of occasional fits of frustration and impatience, it has become aware of this state of domination and is struggling for political independence. This is the reply which explains why there should be a Quebec question.

DANIELLE JUTEAU LEE   University of Ottawa

The Evolution of Nationalism in Quebec*

The 1976 provincial election in Quebec brought to power the Parti Québécois, which is committed to what has been commonly referred to as separatism, and opened a new chapter in the history of a people pursuing the goal of survival. Although *la survivance* is a constant in this history, the ideology behind this goal has evolved because nationalism is affected by overall changes in the social structure of a collectivity. This article analyzes the impact of three major social processes—industrialization, urbanization, and political modernization—on the evolution of nationalism in Quebec, and focuses on the form, intensity and foundations of nationalism. Social processes have affected nationalism by transforming the social structure of the collectivity, by modifying its relations with other collectivities, by increasing the overall awareness of the population to its boundaries, and by changing the boundaries themselves.

Nationalism

Nationalism will be tentatively defined as the ideology which legitimizes the goal of survival of a nation-community, also called an ethnico-national formation. A nation-community is characterized by a common origin, history, territory, culture, institutional framework, language, identity, and solidarity, as well as collective projects outlining its present and future social organization. None of these traits by itself, however, is either sufficient or necessary for the existence of a nation-community (Dion, 1975: 16). The terms in this definition are elaborated on further by the author (Juteau Lee and Lapointe, 1978).

Shared ethnicity is defined by Vallee (1975: 165-66) as the basic factor of inclusion/exclusion. The system of interaction it generates can be examined by the two factors—cultural and structural—which define ethnic boundaries. The cultural criteria include language, religion, and lifestyle. A collectivity can also be examined in terms of its structure: the various spheres within which cultural patterns are institutionalized, such as the religious, educational, economic, and political. These factors can only be distinguished at the analytical level; at the empirical level, it is useful to determine which set of criteria is emphasized by a given collectivity. Finally, those who are interacting must possess a common feeling of identity, belongingness, solidarity, and loyalty.

---

* Written expressly for *Two Nations, Many Cultures: Ethnic Groups in Canada.*

This definition of ethnicity has several implications. It goes back to the French concept of nation; it does not include state-nations, such as Canada and Switzerland, which are political-legal-territorial formations. Ethnico-national formations (or nation-communities) differ from ethnic groups because they possess a higher degree of enclosure. They are more than an aspect of class, even though their history is inseparable from class structures and modes of production (Ryerson, 1972: 224). While classes embody relations of property and work in the context of a mode of production (Ryerson, 1972: 224), nation-communities embody relations based on a common origin, a shared culture and institutional framework. Nation-communities are not ideological phenomena and nationalism is not simply an ideology manipulated by certain classes; the conflict between nation-communities is different from the conflict between the sexes or social classes because it questions the legitimacy of the political-legal-territorial framework which encompasses their relations.

A definition of ethnico-national formations or nation-communities does not constitute an explanation of their emergence. However, the subject is not discussed here since we are limiting this study to an analysis of the evolution of nationalism. Nation-communities are constantly changing, and their cultural and institutional boundaries fluctuate.

When nation-communities pursue the goal of survival, they are, in effect, aiming at maintaining distinct boundaries. This implies self-sufficiency, or the capacity of a community to function autonomously in implementing its normative culture and collective goals (Parsons, 1968: 461). Nationalism can now be defined as the ideology which legitimizes the goal of self-sufficiency pursued by the members of a nation-community. Although this definition embodies the essence of nationalism, there are many types of nationalisms, because nation-communities offer many peculiarities, as they differ both in space and time.

Nationalism can be classified according to its dimensions and types. Economic nationalism is the ideology which legitimizes the aim of a collectivity to function autonomously in implementing its normative culture and collective goals in the economic sphere. Political nationalism legitimizes the aim of a collectivity to function autonomously in implementing its political culture and goals. Cultural nationalism legitimizes the collectivity's goal of functioning autonomously in implementing its cultural patterns. Each of these nationalisms can be traditional or modern. It is traditional when self-sufficiency is defined as the maintenance of existing institutional patterns by means of relative isolation from other collectivities; the emphasis rests on content. Nationalism is modern when self-sufficiency is equated with control over internal institutions and over external relations with other collectivities; the emphasis is on form. The main emphasis is conditioned by the overall characteristics of the nation-community. A past-oriented and relatively autarkic community will

define self-sufficiency in traditional terms, while a community characterized by self-steering will develop a modern nationalism.

Finally, nationalism, and more specifically political nationalism, must
be differentiated from separatism, an ideology which rejects the existing
political-legal framework that unites collectivities. Secessionism is therefore one means of achieving political self-sufficiency. The approach presented here differs from other analyses of nationalism which treat it as a
one-dimensional ideology and which equate political nationalism with
secessionism or separatism (Smith, 1971: 168).

While a clarification of the conceptual haze surrounding nationalism is
not offered as an explanation of its emergence, a few basic points can be
made. Nationalism emerges when a nation-community perceives that its
goal of boundary-maintenance is threatened by other collectivities. More
specifically, economic nationalism appears when the goal of economic
self-sufficiency is perceived to be threatened by the economies of other
collectivities; political nationalism emerges when a community perceives
that its capacity for decision-making in the political sphere is threatened;
cultural nationalism emerges when its cultural distinctiveness is threatened (acculturation).

The Evolution of Nationalism

A study of the evolution of nationalism in Quebec must account for
changes in the dominant type of nationalism, for the intensification of
nationalism, and for the emergence of separatism as a "real" option. It is
hypothesized that three interrelated factors—industrialization, urbanization, and political modernization—are responsible for the evolution of
nationalism. These factors appeared as a consequence of an expanding
Anglo-American capitalism.[1]

Industrialization is the development of a very high level of technology
fostered by the systematic application of knowledge. It entails the growth
of the secondary and tertiary sectors of the economy at the expense of
the primary, and the growing specialization of economic roles and units
of economic activity. It is characterized by an increase in the degree of
centralization and size of units of production and in the complexity of
markets, by the growing division of labor and ensuing modifications in
the occupational system (Eisenstadt, 1966: 3-7). The extent of industrialization can be measured by indicators such as the size of the labor force
in the three economic sectors, the changes in occupational categories and
in the number and size of firms, in the Gross Provincial Product and in
income per capita.

Urbanization is a process whereby the population in urban centers
increases at the expense of that living in rural farm/non-farm areas. This
population shift from countryside to the cities occurs because of indus-

trialization and internal deficiences brought about by a high birth rate and the shortage of farmland. The urban population of Quebec, as a percentage of total population, increased from 44.5% in 1911 to 66.8% in 1951 and 80.6% in 1971 (Kubat and Thornton, 1974: 12-15).

Industrialization and urbanization eroded the foundation of social organization of the Quebec collectivity, namely the farm-parish-extended family complex. They also destroyed the balance which formerly existed between economic institutions and the other institutions of the community. The political, religious, educational institutions did not function to meet the requirements of an industrial economy, and the former systemic responses were no longer adequate. The existence of strong flexible centers and structural autonomy enabled the emerging elites to displace the old ones and to implement an active response (Deutsch, 1961; Eisenstadt, 1966 & 1968; Germani, 1964) which increased the scope and intensified the power of the central, legal, and administrative agencies of the society (Eisenstadt, 1966: 4).

Political modernization involves the growth of the provincial state and can be assessed in terms of a rise in such indicators as (1) the number and expertise of bureaucrats, (2) the level of government expenditures as a percentage of Gross Provincial Product, and (3) the proportion of provincial expenditures relative to municipal spending. Political modernization also involves the emergence of self-steering, that is, of the capacity of a government to control its own affairs and to direct its own behavior:

> Real self-steering differs both from the past-determined path of a bullet and from the environment-determined path of driftwood. The behavior of a self-steering system cannot be predicted wholly from its environment or from its past. Self-steering consists in combining the effects of the past of a system with those of its present, and the effects of its environment with those of its own inner structure and processes (Deutsch, 1970: 144).

Self-steering means that the existing norms will be defined in terms of ongoing situational exigencies rather than traditional value-orientations.

The specific historical combination of these independent variables in the evolution of nationalism will be briefly examined. An unusually high birth rate combined with the lack of available land and the pattern of land transmission created an internal contradiction within French-Canadian society (Miner, 1963: 237). This resulted in the ensuing migration of an estimated 337 058 French Canadians to the United States between 1870 and 1910 (Paquet, 1964: 328). Industrialization, which began at the beginning of the century, accelerated after the Second World War and exerted new pressures in the direction of urbanization. These changes in the economic sphere of the collectivity rendered ineffective the existing political and cultural institutions. For example, the policies of the Duplessis regime and the programs of the educational system did not meet the requirements of an industrialized society. As their ineffectiveness grew, so did the size of a "disposable group", that is, of people detached from former commitments and free to form new attachments (Deutsch, 1971: 288). The emergence of this group did not insure the immediate implementation of measures dealing with existing strains, and political modernization occurred later, in the form of the Quiet Revolution during the Lesage government in 1960.

These three major social processes affected the evolution of nationalism by modifying the social structure of the nation-community, changing its relations with other collectivities, increasing the overall awareness of the community to its threatened boundaries, and altering the boundaries themselves. First, the modification of the existing social structure of the collectivity rendered ineffective the former means of boundary-maintenance, as preserving existing patterns was no longer possible. As self-steering continued to grow, it modified the community's response to a changing social organization and transformed the means to attain "survival". Increasing environmental impingements destroyed relative isolation as a means of boundary-maintenance. These changes are responsible for the dominant form of nationalism. Second, these factors increased the politically relevant strata of the collectivity and consequently the awareness of, and identification to, societal boundaries. The increasing level of nationalism was evidenced in the shift from "we" the French Canadians to "we" the Québécois. This shift, for the first time in history, made separation or secession a potentially possible strategy.

Traditional Nationalism

The nationalism that emerged around the middle of the 19th century until the Second World War had two distinctive features. First, the bearer of this ideology was the French-Canadian collectivity which shared a common ethnicity, history, and territory. As early as 1760, this collectivity, "les Canadiens", had differentiated itself from the mother country; this process was accentuated by a change in metropolis, the return to France of government officials, and the French Revolution. As a result of the Conquest in 1760 and the American Revolution in 1776, "les Canadiens" and "les Anglais" lived side by side, and became French and English Canadians. The boundaries between both groups were established mainly in terms of their cultural differences—language, religion, and lifestyle. This cultural pluralism gave birth to structural pluralism, as evidenced by the British North America Act. At this stage, the criteria underlying group boundaries were mainly ascriptive. French Canadians constituted a primordial kinship-ethnic and religious group, and their territorial reference was Canada. Any descendant of this group, whether he/she lived in Manitoba, Ontario or Québec belonged to the French-

Canadian collectivity. The feelings of group solidarity, "we-ness" and mutual loyalty had no provincial boundaries. The Riel episode (1885), the Manitoba (1890) and Ontario (1912) school crises, extended the French-Canadian solidarity beyond the province of Québec. The nationalism of conservation was rooted in the French-Canadian collectivity as a whole.

Second, this nationalism was essentially conservative and past-oriented. Although boundary-maintenance remains a constant goal today, the means to achieve it have changed. These means are determined both by external (level of environmental impingements) and internal (type of social structure) factors. If a collectivity possesses a certain amount of closure, it will tend to favor relative isolation as a means to preserve its boundaries. If it values established cultural patterns and rejects change, it will define survival in terms of maintaining existing patterns of culture. Self-sufficiency will then imply the preservation of the institutional patterns which define the existing boundaries of the collectivity as well as its isolation from other collectivities.

Traditional nationalism can be examined with respect to its three dimensions—economic, political, and cultural. *Economic nationalism* is the ideology which legitimizes the desire of a collectivity to function autonomously in implementing its normative culture and collective goals in the economic sphere. It implies the maintenance of existing economic patterns and of the boundaries between the economic institutions of French and English Canada. Savaria (1975: 118-19) has demonstrated how the Conquest revitalized, in Quebec, the differentiation of classes of a pre-capitalist origin. Most French Canadians were located, as farmers, artisans and small manufacturers, within the small-scale merchant mode of production, which was subordinated to the capitalist mode of production. As a result, economic nationalism was first defined in terms of agriculturalism (Brunet, 1958: 113-66) as expressed in the thought of Mgr. Pâquet, V. Barbeau, A. David (Trudeau, 1969: 36). The existence of a self-sufficient economy based on agriculture insured the cultural and economic isolation of French Canadians and thus served as an effective means of maintaining boundaries.

The predominance of this agriculturalist ideology also indicates that boundary-maintenance meant maintenance of existing economic and demographic patterns. The expansion of Anglo-American capitalism (Faucher and Lamontagne, 1953; E. C. Hughes, 1965; W. F. Ryan, 1967) and the demographic growth of French Canada rendered these means of maintaining boundaries ineffective; economic nationalism was gradually defined in terms of internal control over industrial development. While the growing economic dependency made impossible the control over the process of production, policies such as "l'achat chez nous" ("buy

Quebec") provided a way of isolating the network of distribution and created boundaries at that level of the economy. The strength and dominance of the clerical elite facilitated the retention of the agricultural-ist ideology in spite of its ineffectiveness; very few measures were taken to implement economic self-sufficiency.

Political nationalism also emphasized isolation as a means of maintain-ing the boundaries of a collectivity still defined as French Canadian. From Sir George-Etienne Cartier to Henri Bourassa and Wilfrid Laurier, the main position was one of unity in duality. The latter advocated pan-Canadianism, the development of a Canadian "we" resting on citizenship and cultural pluralism. (Cook, 1969: 147). Even Tardivel, an advocate of a strong French-Canadian nationalism and an opponent of Bourassa maintained that " ... our people are the French-Canadian people; we will not say that our homeland is limited to the Province of Québec, but is French-Canada; the nation we wish to see founded at that time appointed by Providence is the French-Canadian nation" (Cook, 1969: 147). Although the Tardivel-Bourassa disagreement can be found throughout this part of Quebec's history, the system of reference is always French-Canada/Canada; one thinks of *Le Bloc Populaire Cana-dien, L'Institut Canadien, Les Jeunes-Canada,* and *Les Jeunesse Libérales-nationales* ... (Milner and Milner, 1973: 112-27). The demands for the greater autonomy of the French-Canadian collectivity of Quebec were always legitimized in terms of the French-Canadian nation. Separatism remained an idea which could not germinate, since its structural basis was absent; as an ideology separatism could only be actualized with the emergence of a Québécois-bounded collectivity. Finally, the main thrust of Quebec provincial governments, as clearly indicated during the Duplessis regime, was a defensive one. "L'anti-étatisme" confined the State to a passive role (Brunet, 1958), namely the protection and defence of provincial rights from federal intervention. The mission of the Quebec State was to guard French-Canadian culture; its role consisted in main-taining strong boundaries between the cultures and polities of Quebec and Canada (Kwavnick, 1973: 63).

In this traditional context, *cultural nationalism* implied the maintenance of existing patterns of culture and the idealization of the past. It expressed itself in the battle against "anglicisation" and "anglicanisation". When the boundaries of a collectivity are defined mainly in terms of cultural factors (language, religion, and lifestyle), boundary-maintenance is equated with the maintenance of distinct cultural characteristics; the loss of any of these distinctive traits was considered as contributing to the disappearance of French Canadianism. This definition of boundary-maintenance in terms of non-change creates an internal impediment to self-sufficiency, since a collectivity which is enslaved by the weight of its past cannot successfully adapt the effects of its past with those of its present.

Modern Nationalism

By destroying the former patterns of social organization and rendering old solutions ineffective, industrialization, urbanization and political modernization altered the means best suited to achieve self-sufficiency and consequently, transformed nationalism itself.

The industrialization of Quebec brought about the disintegration of the small-scale merchant mode of production, especially in the agricultural sector (Savaria, 1975: 121). These changes rendered the policies of a past-oriented government ineffective, especially in economic and educational matters. The Duplessis regime still favored the development of agriculture, the "back to the land" movement and the maintenance of an outmoded educational system, while encouraging increased foreign investments.

At the beginning of the 1950s, the capacity of the Quebec collectivity to be self-sufficient was strongly handicapped by internal and external factors. The impediment created by past-orientations explains why, between 1945 and 1960, the emerging change-oriented elites were anti-nationalist, or at least, non-nationalist. Because survival was equated to non-change, the emerging elites rejected nationalism. The increasing conflict between old and new elites was eventually partly resolved with the election of the Quebec Liberal party in 1960. The Quiet Revolution brought about political modernization, as measures dealing with the new conditions created by industrialization and urbanization were implemented. The emphasis changed from maintaining old patterns to coping with ongoing situational exigencies. (The Liberal slogan during the 1960 election campaign was: "Il faut que ça change" or "change is necessary.")

The Quebec collectivity altered the means to achieve its basic goals; new solutions were required, since the old arrangements could no longer cope with the demands created by a new form of social organization. As boundary maintenance was transformed, so was the dominant type of nationalism. As self-sufficiency became dissociated from the maintenance of existing patterns, it became defined as the capacity to control the internal institutions in the best interests of the collectivity. The electoral slogan of the Liberal party in 1962, "Maîtres chez nous" or "masters in our own home" reflected this change, and the decisions implemented by this party showed that the elites committed to the catching-up ideology were not anti-nationalist.

Industrialization, urbanization and political modernization not only modified the dominant type of nationalism but also destroyed the former state of relative isolation of this community and laid it open to further impingements from outside collectivities. Nationalism could no longer ensure the relative isolation of the economic, political, and cultural boundaries of the collectivity so that it had to develop its capacity to control interchange relations with the significant surrounding collectivities. Nationalism was now defined as the capacity of the collectivity to control its internal institutions and its external relations with other collectivities. This modern nationalism will be examined in terms of its economic, political, and cultural dimensions.

The industrialization of Quebec broke down its former state of relative isolation and increased its dependency vis-à-vis other collectivities. Many authors   (Milner and Milner, 1973;   David and Maheu, 1971;   Savaria, 1975; St-Germain, 1973) have examined this process in terms of the dependency of the French-speaking collectivity in Quebec. The modernizing elite took many steps to increase the role of the state in economic matters, by creating the "Conseil d'orientation économique du Québec", the "Société générale de financement", the "Régie des rentes du Québec", the "Société générale forestière", the "Société québécoise d' exploration minière", and many other agencies. Economic nationalism aimed at increasing Québec's autonomy in the economic sphere and dealt with the consequences of industrialization. These solutions, however, implied a tacit acceptance of the overall capitalist framework of the economy.

The expanding Anglo-American capitalism also increased impingements in the political sphere. As a result of industrialization, urbanization, the Depression, and the Second World War, the federal government created a single taxation system for the country. The Wartime Tax Agreements created a *de facto* situation where the federal government raised almost all the public revenues and spent almost all the public money. Insofar as power is related to expenditure, the provinces exerted little power. At the same time, the growing expenditures in health, welfare, and education fell under provincial jurisdiction. What was distinctive about Québec was the linking of a struggle over federal and provincial taxing powers to a struggle of the French-Canadian people to fulfill itself. The Québec government chose to opt out of joint cost programs and accepted the new direction that resulted. The federal government abandoned programs with a narrow and specific content in favor of broadly defined programs in which the provinces set their own priorities within broadly defined national priorities. Political nationalism detached itself from the former type of isolationism and legitimized new means of controlling relations with the federal government. During this period, constitutional alternatives proliferated. None of the parties who offered solutions favoring an increase in the collectivity's control over its political functions questioned the basic political framework. Those who did had to form new political parties and/or movements.

Industrialization, urbanization, and political modernization also modified cultural nationalism by increasing internal and external pressures for changes. They destroyed the old patterns of social organization since the French-Canadians were no longer predominantly rural, agricultural, and Catholic. They broke down the former cultural isolation of French Canadians. Urbanization often meant moving to Montreal, a city which now comprised a sizable proportion (33.7%) of non-French mother-tongue (Rapport Gendron, 1972, Vol. 1: 13). Industrialization often meant working for English Canadians since 87% of the establishments in Montréal were owned by Anglo-Canadians or Americans (Raynauld, 1967: 185). The studies done for the Gendron Commission confirmed that francophones had often been obliged to use English as a language of communication. When francophone respondents were asked whether they encountered difficulties when using French, 13% answered positively (Etude E 17, 1973: Table 91); for the educated group (13+ years of education), the proportion was 26%. Among the francophones experiencing difficulties, 69% did so in Montreal. The same study showed that the exposure of francophones, especially the well-educated, to English media is quite high (Etude E 17: tables 22, 50, 65).

During the 1960s and the early 1970s, various Quebec governments expressed the new cultural nationalism by increasing grants to artists and to public libraries and by creating a Ministry of Cultural Affairs whose job was to develop new forms of cultural expression. Various measures that were proposed aimed at increasing Québec's control over cultural matters and dealt with the Official Language of Québec, the establishment of an overall policy in the field of language and immigration, a revision in the role of the Ministry of Cultural Affairs, and the continuing negotiations in the area of communications. Cultural nationalism was now defined in terms of cultural sovereignty, which implied an internal and external control over cultural boundaries rather than the maintenance of existing patterns of culture.

As the expansion of Anglo-American capitalism modified the internal structure of the collectivity and the nature of its relations with surrounding collectivities, all the dimensions of nationalism were transformed. The emphasis on the maintenance of existing patterns and relative isolation was replaced by a concern for controlling internal institutions and external relations with surrounding collectivities. The main thrust was to free the system of its past orientation. Although some efforts were made to free it from its environment, all the measures implemented by the political elite fell within the existing framework; there was no fundamental rejection of capitalism, of federalism, or of the acquired rights of the anglophone minority in Quebec.

In addition to transforming nationalism from its traditional to modern expression, industrialization, urbanization and political modernization intensified it. An intensified nationalism results from an increase in (1) the strength of environmental impingements, (2) the number of people subjected to them, and (3) the presence of politically relevant strata in the society. History teaches us that communities do not automatically reject external domination.

Political modernization intensifies nationalism by increasing a collectivity's awareness of, and identification to, institutional boundaries; by transforming the relationship between center and periphery; and by extending the boundaries from the local to the provincial plane. The provincial state gradually penetrates the local layers of community organization. Factors which are positively related to awareness, such as education and the mass media, are widely disseminated, and the inequalities between competing groups are brought into focus.

It is beyond the scope of this analysis to examine these factors in greater detail. However, we want to mention that nationalism among the francophones in Quebec was first noted among the better educated, higher salaried, and urban (Montreal) segment of the population.

Separatism as a "Real Option"

The symbolic transformation of Quebec's boundaries has made the emergence of separatism a "real option". As an ideology that is grounded in social reality, separatism may muster support. At present, however, Quebec is experiencing an identity crisis typical of a transitional stage. The erosion of the traditional criteria defining group boundaries has made it difficult to differentiate insiders from outsiders. The disappearance of the former patterns underlying solidarity and affiliation has not automatically led to the creation of new criteria.

To some extent the province has taken responsibility for providing a new basis of affiliation and has assumed a more active voice in decisions concerning the economic, educational, and health and welfare institutions in Quebec. This move directly and visibly affects those who reside in Quebec. Territoriality has become an important basis for identification since, by definition, a State has jurisdiction over a given territory. The substitution, by the Lesage administration, of "l'Etat du Québec" for the former expression "le gouvernement provincial" is indicative of this process. Since "l'Etat du Québec" governs those who reside in Quebec, the French-Canadian nation-community has disappeared as new group boundaries emerge. This transformation was crystallized in the recognition of a Québécois social identity.

The implications of this shift in the criteria defining the boundaries of the nation-community and in the ensuing patterns of affiliation and identification cannot be minimized. Marx maintained that "The emergence of ideas which can serve as an effective challenge to the dominant order depends on the formation of class relationships which generate a structural base for the new ideology" (Giddens, 1971: 209). It is our contention that a similar process occurs in the case of other types of relationships including those encompassed within the boundaries of ethnico-national formations. Marx said that while the idea of communism has been expressed a hundred times in history, the real possibility of a communist revolution presupposed the existence of a revolutionary class (1968: 51, 62). It is suggested that while the idea of separatism has been expressed a hundred times in the history of Quebec, the actual separatist movement today presupposes the existence of a Québécois nation-community. This does not mean that separatism will necessarily happen, but it does imply that scenarios will be affected by this transformation. Decisions are being made to maximize the interests of the Québécois collectivity and to insure its self-sufficiency. The cultural duality of Canada, at the federal level, is no longer a concern to "les Québécois" since the French-Canadian collectivity no longer exists. For a while, measures aimed at increasing the self-sufficiency of the Québécois collectivity in the economic, political and structural spheres will be varied and conflicting.

In the political sphere, the possible alternatives to separatism are the status quo, decentralization, special status, or sovereignty-association. The means chosen will be those which will maximize the capacity of "les Québécois" to control internal political decisions. In the economic sphere nationalism can lead to a continuing acceptance of capitalism, its replacement by state-capitalism, or socialism. In the cultural sphere, nationalism may lead to an increase in control over communications and immigration, and the creation of linguistic policies that will clearly define who belongs to the Québécois collectivity—the francophones or all residents of Quebec.

All these scenarios concern the self-sufficiency of Quebec, not Canada and not French Canada. The existence of different social classes and interest groups and the respective degree of power they wield will determine how the tide of events would go. For example, the upper class in Quebec might support capitalism coupled with increased control over immigration. The proletariat might support socialism and be indifferent to cultural policies. Because of the significance of the boundaries of nation-communities, the proletariat of Quebec may refuse alliances with the proletariat outside Quebec or with the other social classes in Quebec. The phenomenon of class *versus* ethnic consciousness is at times difficult to discern as one may be obscured by the other.

Conclusion

This analysis has emphasized that nationalism is an ideology rooted in social reality. Consequently, any attempt to explain its transformations must deal with those factors which modify the nation-community in which it is embedded. The modifying factors are not purely ideological phenomena as they constitute significant systems of interaction. In the case of Quebec, the expansion of Anglo-American capitalism brought about the industrialization, urbanization, and political modernization of a traditional society. These interrelated social processes transformed and intensified nationalism, potentially creating the structural basis for the actualization of separatism.

ENDNOTE

1. A more comprehensive treatment and operationalization of these three independent variables can be found in the author's unpublished doctoral dissertation (Juteau Lee, 1974: ch. IV & V).

SELECTED REFERENCES

Brunet, M. *La présence anglaise et les Canadiens; étude sur l'histoire et la pensée des deux Canadas.* Montréal: Beauchemin, 1958.

Cook, R. *French-Canadian Nationalism: An Anthology.* Toronto: Macmillan of Canada, 1969.

David, H., and L. Maheu. "Problèmes sociaux, contradictions structurelles, et politiques gouvernementales," pp. 87-140, in J. M. Piotte, ed., *Quebec occupé.* Montréal: Editions Parti-Pris, 1971.

Deutsch, K. W. "Social Mobilization and Political Development." *American Political Science Review*, 55 (September 1961), pp. 494-514.

———. *Politics and Government: How People Decide Their Fate.* Boston: Houghton Mifflin Company, 1970.

——— . "Social Mobilization and Development," pp. 388-93, in S.N. Eisenstadt, ed., *Political Sociology.* New-York: Basic Books, Inc., 1971.

Dion, L. *Nationalismes et politique au Québec.* Montréal: Hurtubise HMH, 1975.

Eisenstadt, S. N. *Modernization: Protest and Change.* Englewood Cliffs, New Jersey: Prentice-Hall, Inc., 1966.

———. "Introduction," pp. XI-XXX, in S. N. Eisenstadt, ed., *Comparative Perspectives in Social Change.* Boston: Little, Brown and Company, 1968.

Faucher, A., and M. Lamontagne. "History of Industrial Development," pp. 23-37, in J. C. Falardeau, ed., *Essais sur le Québec contemporain.* Québec: Les Presses de l'Université Laval, 1953.

Germani, G. "Social Change and Intergroup Conflicts," pp. 391-407, in I. L. Horowitz, ed., *The New Sociology.* New York: Oxford University Press, 1964.

Giddens, A. *Capitalism and Modern Social Theory.* Cambridge, Mass.: Cambridge University Press, 1971.

Government of Québec. *Rapport de la Commission d'enquête sur la situation de la langue française et sur les droits linguistiques au Québec* (Rapport Gendron); Livre 1, La langue de travail (1972); Etude E 17, Les mass média, l'attachement à sa langue et les modèles linguistiques au Québec en 1971 (1973).

Hughes, E. C. *French Canada in Transition*, First Phoenix Edition. Toronto: University of Toronto Press, 1965.

Juteau Lee, D., and J. Lapointe. "The Emergence of Franco-Ontarians: New Identity, New Boundaries," in J. L. Elliott, ed., *Two Nations, Many Cultures: Ethnic Groups in Canada*. Scarborough: Prentice-Hall of Canada, 1979).

Juteau Lee, D. "The Impact of Modernization and Environmental Impingements upon Nationalism and Separatism: The Quebec Case." Unpublished PhD. dissertation, University of Toronto, 1974.

Kwavnick, D. *The Tremblay Report*. Toronto: McClelland and Stewart Limited, 1973.

Marx, K., and F. Engels. *The German Ideology*. Moscow: Progress Publishers, 1968.

Milner, S., and H. Milner. *The Decolonization of Quebec*. Toronto: McClelland and Stewart Limited, 1973.

Miner, H. *Saint-Denis: A French-Canadian Parish*. Chicago: Phoenix Books, University of Chicago Press, 1963.

Paquet, G. "L'émigration des Canadiens-Français vers la Nouvelle-Angleterre, 1870-1910: Prises de vue quantitatives." *Recherches Sociographiques* V:3 (1964), pp. 319-70.

Parson, T. "Systems Analysis: Social Systems," pp. 458-73, in *The International Encyclopedia of the Social Sciences*. New York: Macmillan and Free Press, 1968.

Raynauld, A. "La propriété des entreprises au Québec." Unpublished report presented to the Royal Commission on Bilingualism and Biculturalism, 1967.

Ryan, W. F. *The Clergy and Economic Growth in Quebec (1896-1914)*. Québec: Les Presses de l'université Laval, 1966.

Kubat, D., and D. Thornton. *A Statistical Profile of Canadian Society*. Toronto: McGraw-Hill Ryerson Ltd., 1974.

Ryerson, S. "Quebec, Concepts of Class and Nation," pp. 211-29, in G. Teeple, ed., *Capitalism and National Question in Canada*. Toronto: University of Toronto Press, 1972.

Saint-Germain, M. *Une économie à libérer*. Montréal: Les Presses de l'université de Montréal, 1973.

Savaria, J. "Le Québec est-il une société périphérique?" *Sociologie et Sociétés* 7 (Novembre 1975), pp. 115-27).

Smith, A. D. *Theories of Nationalism*. London: The Camelot Press, 1971.

Trudeau, P. E. "Québec on the Eve of the Asbestos Strike," pp. 32-48, in R. Cook, ed., *French-Canadian Nationalism: An Anthology*. Toronto: Macmillan of Canada, 1969.

Vallee, F. "Multi-Ethnic Societies: The Issues of Identity and Inequality," pp. 162-202, in D. Forcese and S. Richer, eds., *Issues in Canadian Society: An Introduction to Sociology*. Scarborough, Ont.: Prentice-Hall of Canada, Ltd., 1975.

STEPHEN RICHER   Carleton University
PIERRE E. LAPORTE   La Régie de la Langue Française

Culture, Cognition, and English-French Competition*

Introduction

French Canadians are greatly under-represented in the professional and technical occupations, as well as in the upper echelons of business and industry.[1] Attempts to explain this extensive social and economic inequality have ranged from an emphasis on regional variables[2], to power relationships[3], and finally, to a consideration of hypothesized cultural differences between French and English Canadians.[4] With respect to cultural differences, however, one aspect of culture that has not been fully understood in the context of unequal status attainment between anglophones and francophones is the factor of cognition or cognitive style (Richer and Laporte, 1971).

Historically, a consideration of cultural differences between French and English Canadians has tended to focus on the influence of such institutions as the church, the school, and the family. The more common factors that have been related previously to the relative status attainment of the two groups are summarized in Figure 1. It had been previously argued by the present authors (Richer and Laporte, 1971) that cognitive style was an important mechanism through which the factors in Figure 1 give expression to the differential life chances of English and French

FIGURE 1 *Major factors previously related to English success*

French:	General religious dominance Absence of Protestant Ethic Church-controlled educational system Ruralism Authoritarian family structure	⟶ Relative failure
English:	Less religious dominance Presence of Protestant Ethic Secular educational system Urbanism Egalitarian family structure	⟶ Relative success

* Written expressly for *Two Nations, Many Cultures: Ethnic Groups in Canada.*

75

Canadians, their relative successes, failures, and status attainments. It is the purpose of this presentation to specify more fully what is meant by cognitive style and to suggest the impact that this aspect of culture may have on the lives of anglophones and francophones.

Cognitive Style

Cognitive style is the pattern of thought that is a manifestation at the personality level of the group's wider value system. Cognitive style acts as an *intervening variable* linking French and English Canadian values, on the one hand, with status attainment, on the other (see Figure 2). The societal condition under which cognitive style translates into the higher status attainment for English Canadians is anglophone dominance in the occupational sphere. In Figure 2, this condition is referred to as "English in Power." Since in an economic sense this has been the case historically, and if we assume that groups in power will impose their mode of defining and solving problems on their subordinates, then French Canadians will be at a distinct disadvantage in the work world in their competition with anglophones. As we suggested in our earlier work, if the standards of performance are " ... efficiency in terms of time and specificity of solution ... [the French Canadian] is not cognitively equipped for this kind of competition ... [he or she] will feel stress, will fail, will be frustrated, and [will] ultimately perceive the English as the cause of ... failure" (Richer and Laporte, 1971: 149).

FIGURE 2 *A cultural model of status attainment in Canada*

Linguistic Origin	(A) General Historical Cultural Factors →	(B) Values →	(C) Cognitive Style →	IF → English in power, then	(D) Status Attainment
French:	Religious dominance Absence of Protestant Ethic Ruralism Authoritarian family structure	Collectivistic orientation Present orientation	Relational Means orientation (non-closure)		Low
English:	Less religious dominance Presence of Protestant Ethic Urbanism Egalitarian family structure	Individualistic orientation Future orientation	Analytic Goal orientation (closure)		High

It is necessary to outline the dimensions of cognitive style that are relevant to our model. To date, there has been some misunderstanding of our attempt to highlight the importance of the cognitive factor. Zureik, for example, in his introduction to Volume 1 of *Socialization and Values in Canadian Society*, describes our work as "more or less a repetition of earlier works by Rosen (1959) and Strodtbeck (1958) regarding the relationship between achievement orientations and ethnicity" (Zureik, 1975: 19). The works referred to, however, are basically value studies. Rosen and Strodtbeck are attempting to describe the general package of values and motivations ostensibly necessary for success in North American society. As well, they present data showing the extent to which this package is manifested by various ethnic groups.

Rosen or Strodtbeck does not attempt, however, to show the implications of these values for cognitive processes, particularly in the areas of *problem definition* and *execution*. In defining problems, people are essentially responding to a set of stimuli. They may see these stimuli in two ideal-typical ways: as forming a gestalt, or interrelated whole, or as separate units capable of being handled independently of the wider set. One might call the former type "relational" thinkers, the latter, "analytical". In *executing* problems one may be concerned mainly with goal achievement or with the means themselves. Again, these are ideal-typical extremes. The two dimensions yield four types of cognitive style, exemplified in Figure 3.

It is our contention that French Canadians are more likely to be found in Cell 1 and English Canadians in Cell 4. The argument is that if one is a member of a group in which collectivist values predominate (i.e., where the individual is expected to subordinate his wishes to those of the group), he will also, in his perception of stimuli, see the whole as dominating the composite parts. That is, *he will perceive the relationship between parts and whole as he sees the relationship between himself and his wider group.* Highly integrated, high-consensus systems will produce rela-

FIGURE 3 *A typology of cognitive styles*

		Mode of Problem Definition	
		Relational	Analytical
		1	2
Modal orientation to problem execution	Means	Non-closure in task performance	
		3	4
	Goal		Closure in task performance

tional people, while less integrated, individualistic systems will produce analytical ones. Further, groups with future-oriented value systems will produce goal-oriented people, and groups with present-oriented value systems will produce means-oriented people. Clearly, relational-means oriented types will take longer to complete tasks, although the solution will probably reflect a less superficial exploration. We term this process a "non-closure" pattern.

It is quite clear from this restatement that Rosen's need-achievement measures and what we have in mind by cognitive style are analytically separate phenomena, though quite possibly related to one another. Our task now is twofold:

(1) To examine the existing empirical evidence linking various parts of the model to one another, and

(2) To examine the major alternative explanation for French-English differences in status attainment.

We shall engage in a discussion of each of these and conclude with a comment on the implications of our thesis for recent developments in Quebec.

Empirical State of the Model

As we have outlined it, a complete test of the model must meet five requirements:

(1) A demonstration of relationships between linguistic origin and values $(A \rightarrow B)$; linguistic origin and cognitive style $(A \rightarrow C)$; and linguistic origin and status attainment $(A \rightarrow D)$.

(2) A demonstration that the major intervening variables between A and B are extent of religious dominance, extent of ruralism, and extent of authoritarian family structure.

(3) A demonstration of relationships between B and C, B and D, and C and D.

(4) A demonstration of the presence of our major condition, i.e., that English Canadians are in a position to directly impose their values and cognitive style on French Canadian workers.

(5) A demonstration of the tenability of the purely logical statistical deductions from the model. For example, if the model is correct we should find a clear-cut hierarchy of correlation sets (i.e., $^r AB$ should be greater than $^r AC$, which in turn should be greater than $^r AD$. Also, $^r BC$ should be greater than $^r BD$). Further, certain partial correlations, given good measurement, should be close to zero (i.e., $^r AC.B$; $^r BD.C$ and $^r AD.BC$) (Blalock, 1970; Duncan, 1966).

When the current state of knowledge is set against the above criteria, it is quite clear that the model is largely untested. Taking the set of relationships enumerated in requirement 1, only the A→D relationship stands up under careful empirical scrutiny. French and English Canadians *do* vary significantly in status attainment. Porter's work showed French Canadians to be under-represented in professional and technical occupations as well as in the upper echelons of business and industry (Porter, 1965). More recently, Clement's *Canadian Corporate Elite* (1975) reinforced Porter's conclusion, as did Sales' large-scale survey of the Quebec industrial elite (Sales, 1976). Working with a sample of 1 211 Quebec industrial firms, Sales shows that the French Canadian presence in both ownership and top-level management is (proportionately) conspicuously weak. Only 27% of the firms in his sample are French Canadian owned, while 37% have a French Canadian in the top management position. Further, the larger the firm the greater the under-representation of French Canadians in both ownership and top management (Sales, 1976).

Here is perhaps the place to point out that besides providing additional proof of low French Canadian status attainment, Sales' data provide some evidence for our major condition [requirement (4) above]. That is, a large percentage of French Canadians in Quebec working in the industrial sector are in firms controlled by anglophones. The set of work and production standards in these organizations is thus likely to reflect anglophone values and cognitive orientation.

While the A→D relationship has been demonstrated to hold, however, the other two listed under requirement (1) are in a much more tenuous state. Firstly, we have at best scattered support for the thesis that English and French Canadians do indeed hold different values along the lines suggested. Of the two values salient for our argument, the individualism-collectivism difference emerges relatively clearly. As early as 1959 Rosen showed French Canadians to be among the latest ethnic groups to require independence training for their children, with Anglo-Protestants among the earliest. Further, Taylor, in a much debated article, suggests that greater preoccupation with the family was partially responsible for lower French Canadian success as entrepreneurs (Taylor, 1964). Finally, in a recent study based on the Kluckhohn value scheme, young French Canadian Manitobans scored higher on collaterality and showed greater "perceived group consensus" than their English-speaking counterparts. The authors conclude, . . . "these data . . . provide support for the hypothesis that French Canadians are more group-oriented while English Canadians are more individualistically-oriented" (Shapiro and Perlman, 1976: 53).

The same study, however, finds their French Canadian sample to be significantly more future-oriented than the English Canadian group. On the other hand, data from the *Career Decisions* project show that French Canadians in Quebec place much more importance on luck and destiny in achieving success in life than Quebec anglophones (Breton and McDonald, 1967: 156-57). Such an orientation is consistent with a present focus, since it excludes the idea of rational planning of one's life goals. The inconsistency might possibly be due to the difference between the samples; in any event the most prudent stance at this point must be to await further work.

Regarding the connection between linguistic origin and cognitive style, our review of the literature failed to turn up studies explicitly addressing this relationship. Even the Shapiro and Perlman study alluded to above, which ostensibly aimed at testing our model, did not attempt to get at this key intervening variable. The focus was rather on the issue of value difference, certainly an important component of the model, but in our view a secondary one.

The failure to confront the issue of cognitive style might be related to the perceived difficulty of making the concept operational. There are at least three tacks one might take regarding this problem. Firstly, there is a fairly large body of literature in psychology organized around this topic. Although the field is somewhat clouded (Boocock, 1972), there are, as we have suggested, two major modes of reacting to stimuli which tend to reappear in the various studies. The first is typically termed the relational mode and refers to the classification of stimuli in terms of their functional interdependence. One thus attempts to fit the stimuli together into a logical system: everything must be connected to everything else. This relational mode implies non-closure – there is no action on a task until it is placed within a larger context and all its implications understood. Those manifesting an analytic mode, on the other hand, respond to stimuli and to parts of stimuli as discrete units. There is no attention to their interconnectedness, to their common gestalt; they are handled independently. This implies a pattern of closure—quicker solutions to tasks. Perceptual tests for measuring these phenomena are readily available in the literature. These are largely of an abstracting and classificatory variety and appear to produce high reliability and validity (Witkin, 1962; Broverman, 1960; Kagan, et al., 1960, 1963; Kagan, et al., 1964; Beller, 1967; McCain, 1968).

This type of measure, however, is less desirable, we would argue, than one which emerges from an actual problem-solving situation. The cognitive differences we hypothesize are best captured, we think, through either a simulation of everyday work-setting problem solving or, most preferably, through observations in the work setting itself. In our first paper (Richer and Laporte, 1971), we argued for Sales' type small group experiments which would yield data for French and English groups on time to solution, instrumental versus socio-emotional behavior, satisfaction with the problem-solving process, as well as modes of conceptualizing the problem itself. A similar follow-up study of linguistically mixed groups interacting under English supervision (as in the modal Quebec firm) would also be desirable. It has come to our attention that some studies of this nature are now under way at the University of Ottawa, although no results are yet available.

Perhaps the most productive approach would be to observe French and English Canadians actually carrying through job-related problems in the work setting. How do English and French workers begin attacking a problem? How are problems conceptualized by the two groups? Are these conceptualizations modified when occasions arise at work for English-French contact? If so, how? Regarding the actual execution of the problem, how, if at all, does this process differ between the two groups? What is the relative reliance on external information as inputs to the problem's solution? (For example, how much consultation takes place with fellow workers in each case? How much information is gleaned from secondary sources such as records, books, journals?) What is the nature of the solution in both groups (*vis à vis* speed and completeness of explication of alternative possible solutions)? Assumedly such research would produce highly valid measures of cognitive style which would at the same time be isomorphic with salient everyday processes.

Turning now to requirement (2) above, the object would be to refine the A→B relationship by showing that it reduces considerably with religious dominance, ruralism and family structure controlled. In much of the discussion of the so-called "cultural" argument the concept French is viewed automatically as a proxy for historic ruralism, Catholic dominance and authoritarian family structures. While these variables and linguistic origin are undeniably correlated (Shapiro and Perlman, 1976; Garigue, 1968; Lambert, et al., 1971), this is quite different from showing that they are the prime mechanisms through which linguistic origin affects values. A systematic value comparison of English Catholics, French Catholics, English Protestants and French Protestants (an admittedly scarce group in Quebec) would enable us to make some statements about the religious link. Religiosity measures would also aid in clarifying the argument. For example, our model implies that practicing French Catholics would be more likely to display certain values than non-practicing ones. In an analogous fashion, one could compare rural and urban French and English Canadians. Again the original linguistic origin-value relationship should reduce considerably with the rural-urban variable partialed out. The same strategy would apply to the family structure variable. To our knowledge no systematic examination of the interplay among these variables has yet been done, yet this is vital to the model's credibility.

The same conclusion applies to the third requirement—the demonstration of relationships between values and cognitive style, values and status attainment, and cognitive style and status attainment. Do people with a certain value and cognitive style emphasis really tend to "make it" in Canadian society? Further, what is the state of the relationship between values and cognitive style itself? Are they best viewed as separate though related phenomena, as we have viewed them, or are they so intertwined that they are more usefully treated as sub-dimensions of a more general factor? A factor analytic study of these variables would appear to be called for.

Given the above state of knowledge it is clear that we are a long way from being able to incorporate the four variables into a path model of the kind implied by requirement (5). Such a step, however, would be the ultimate goal in attempting to verify our argument.

An Alternative Explanation

The position might be taken that the thorough test of the model advocated above is not sufficient in itself to justify adoption. One might argue that the model is by and large consistent with an approach which would emphasize the *structural* barriers to French Canadian mobility. Such an explanation would likely be embedded in a Marxist and/or conflict perspective and might take the following form:

(1) The low position of French Canadians is a result of the historical domination of a capitalist class.

(2) In order to maintain their position of power, English Canadians actively discriminate against French Canadians in the economic sector.

(3) The so-called cultural model represents simply a rational response of French Canadians to their objective condition of power-impotence in the economic sphere. That is, the value and cognitive style differences by linguistic origin only reflect social class differences and not an ethnic difference at all.

This argument implies, then, that controlling for social class origin will virtually eliminate any independent effects of language on values, cognitive style and status attainment. The introduction of social class into our model is thus a vital step if one is to produce a complete picture of the dynamics involved.

Conclusion

The satisfactory investigation of the two competing explanations for French-English differences in status attainment is, we believe, of utmost importance. The ostensible impetus behind the separatist movement is the protection of French Canadian culture. While it would be presumptuous to argue that the value and cognitive style aspects we have singled out are the major ingredients in this cultural composite, we nevertheless believe them to be of more than incidental importance. If it could be shown that our model is basically sound, the Parti Québécois position becomes difficult to oppose. "Making it" would be shown to be synonymous with adopting an English Canadian set of values and cognitive style, a sacrifice which many French Canadians may not be prepared to accept. In short, upward mobility would necessarily mean assimilation. Support for this "tradeoff" thesis comes from some data presented by Vallee and Shulman (1969) on the correlates of language loss among non-Quebec francophones. Generally, they show an inverse correlation between in-group strength (as measured by such indicators as institutional completeness, group resources and representation in political and administrative structures) and individual status attainment (as measured by income and education). That is, the stronger the French *community*, the lower was found to be the occupational and educational success of its members. Further, and most important for our argument, this pattern of high in-group strength and low status attainment is associated with high language *retention*. Conversely, Vallee and Shulman found low in-group strength and high individual status attainment to be correlated with high language *loss*, i.e., linguistic assimilation. As we have suggested, then, the price for francophone upward mobility as it concerns the group may be akin to linguistic or cultural genocide. A separate Quebec society with institutions reflecting the French Canadian view would be the logical alternative to the present Canadian society that favors assimilation.

If, however, the value, cognitive style and ultimately status attainment differences are shown to be largely social class based, the arguments for separation and the pending language policies become greatly weakened. French Canadian culture would be revealed as essentially equivalent to lower class culture, and hence indistinguishable from that of lower class anglophones. A systematic government effort to open up occupational opportunities to French Canadians would be a logical policy consequence: a program which would eventually produce linguistic balance in the economic sector without the fear of cultural prostitution. Separation is clearly not a necessary condition for this to occur. Even if one tried to make this argument, the nationalist/cultural appeal would no longer be effective.

Clearly the above represents the two extreme outcomes of putting the model to the test. Since the world is invariably more complex than sociological paradigms, the truth will be somewhere in between. However, some information on the nature and extent of cultural differences between English and French Canadians would be preferable to the current state of relative ignorance. Such data would offset somewhat the polemical rhetoric which constitutes so much of the current debate on independence.

ENDNOTES

1. For two of the many relevant works, see Everett C. Hughes, *French Canada in Transition* (Chicago: University of Chicago Press, 1963); and John Porter *The Vertical Mosaic* (Toronto: University of Toronto Press, 1965).
2. See, for example, Albert Faucher and Maurice Lamontagne, "History of Industrial Development," in *French Canadian Society*, Vol. I, Marcel Rioux and Yves Martin, eds. (Toronto: McClelland and Stewart, 1964), pp. 257-70.
3. See Michel Brunet, "L'inevitable inferiorité économique des Canadiens Francais," in *La Presence Anglaise et Les Canadiens* (Montreal: Beauchemin, 1964), pp. 221-32. For another "power type" explanation, see Richard J. Ossenberg, "The Conquest Revisited: Another Look at Canadian Dualism," *Canadian Review of Sociology and Anthropology* (1967), pp. 201-18. Finally, see the structural approach of Raymond Breton and Howard Roseborough, "Ethnic Differences in Status," in *Canadian Society*, 3rd. ed., Bernard Blishen, *et al.*, eds. (Toronto: MacMillan, 1968), pp. 683-701.
4. Among the relevant works here are John Porter, *op. cit.*, and N. W. Taylor, "The French Canadian Industrial Entrepreneur and His Social Environment," in *French Canadian Society*, *op. cit.*, pp. 271-95.

SELECTED REFERENCES

Beller, E. K. "Methods of language training and cognitive styles in lower-class children." Paper read at the annual meeting of the American Educational Research Association, New York, February 1967.

Blalock, H. M., ed. *Causal Models in the Social Sciences*. Chicago: Aldine, 1970.

Boocock, S. S. *An Introduction to the Sociology of Learning*. Boston: Houghton Mifflin, 1972.

Breton, Raymond, and John McDonald. *Career Decisions of Canadian Youth*. Department of Manpower and Immigration, 1967.

Broverman, D. M. "Cognitive Styles and Intra-Individual Variation in Abilities." *Journal of Personality*, 28 (1960), pp. 240-56.

Clement, W. *The Canadian Corporate Elite*. Ottawa: Carleton University Press, 1975.

Duncan, O. D. "Path Analysis: Sociological Examples." *American Journal of Sociology*, 72 (1966).

Garigue, P. "The French Canadian Family," in B. Blishen, et al., eds., *Canadian Society: Sociological Perspectives*. Toronto: Macmillan, 1968.

Kagan, J., et al. "The psychological significance of styles of conceptualization," in J. F. Wright and J. Kagan, eds., *Basic Cognitive Processes in Children*. Monographs of the Society for Research in Child Development, 28 (1963), pp. 73-112.

———. "Conceptual style and the use of affect labels." *Merrill-Palmer Quarterly*, 6 (1960), pp. 261-78.

———. "Information processing in the child: significance of analytic and reflective attitudes." *Psychological Monographs*, 78 (1, whole No. 578), 1964.

Lambert, W., et al. "Child Training Values of English Canadian and French Canadian Parents." *Canadian Journal of Behavioural Science*, 3 (1971).

McCain, F. "The relation between cognitive style and associative performance in verbal and pictorial concept formation tasks." Unpublished study, Indiana University, 1968.

Porter, J. *The Vertical Mosaic*. Toronto: University of Toronto Press, 1965.

Richer, S., and Pierre Laporte. "Culture, Cognition and English-French Competition," in J. L. Elliott, ed., *Immigrant Groups*. Scarborough, Ont.: Prentice-Hall of Canada, 1971; reprinted in D. Koulack and D. Perlman, eds., *Readings in Social Psychology: Focus on Canada*. New York: Wiley, 1973.

Rosen, B.C. "Race, Ethnicity and the Achievement Syndrome." *American Sociological Review*, 24 (1959).

Sales, Arnaud. "Les Industriels au Quebec et leurs roles dans le Development Economique." Interim report presented to Industry and Commerce of Quebec, Montreal, 1976.

Shapiro, L., and D. Perlman. "Value Differences Between English and French Canadian High School Students," *Canadian Ethnic Studies*, VIII: 2 (1976).

Strodtbeck, Fred C. "Family Interaction Values and Achievements," in *Talent and Society*. D. C. McClelland, et al., eds. Princeton: D. Van Nostrand, 1958.

Taylor, N. W., "The French Canadian Industrial Entrepreneur and his Social Environment," in M. Rioux and Y. Martin, eds., *French Canadian Society*, Vol. 1. Toronto: McClelland & Stewart, 1964.

Vallee, Frank G., and Norman Shulman. "The Viability of French Groupings outside Quebec," in Mason Wade, ed., *Regionalism in the Canadian Community, 1867-1967*. Toronto: University of Toronto Press, 1969.

Witkin, H. A., et al. *Psychological differentiation*. New York: Wiley, 1962.

Zureik, E. "Introduction," in E. Zureik and R. M. Pike, eds., *Socialization and Values in Canadian Society*, Vol. I. McClelland and Stewart, 1975.

ANN B. DENIS   University of Ottawa

Educational Aspirations of Montreal Post-Secondary Students: Ethnic, Sex and Social Class Differences*

Introduction

Much of the analysis of educational aspirations and attainment of students has been in terms of social class differences. Studies have shown that students of higher class backgrounds are likely to have higher educational aspirations and to remain in the educational system longer than those of lower class backgrounds (Breton, 1972; Porter et al., 1973). Theoretical explanations of this phenomenon include Baudelot and Establet's (1971) Marxist interpretation of the school as an agent reproducing the class divisions of the social structure through differential educational offerings and the inculcation of the bourgeois ideology in all who stay in the educational system beyond the minimum school-leaving age.

Bourdieu's (1966) critical functionalist analysis of the educational structure posits that there is only a semblance of equality in the school since students with differing "cultural capital" are educated in a system which is based on the assumption of equal cultural background: those whose background is most similar to that of the school are necessarily at an advantage and remain so throughout their schooling. Only the most talented and hard working of those who do not share this background succeed in school. Most, having internalized the objectively ascribed chances of academic success, adapt their aspirations to the probabilities of success associated with their level of cultural capital. Consequently, they attribute failure to attain the highest possible levels of education to their own lack of ability rather than to any possible inequity in the educational system. Cultural capital itself includes verbal facility, general cultural experience, and information about the educational system.

These theoretical analyses and the empirical data on Canada (Wolfgang, 1975; Carlton et al., 1977) suggest that the Canadian school is a vehicle of the dominant culture, usually typified as the culture of the middle class of the charter groups, the English and, in Quebec, also the French. There is evidence (Breton, 1972) that more rigorous selection has

* Written expressly for *Two Nations, Many Cultures: Ethnic Groups in Canada*. Canada Council Research Grants #S73-0462, #S75-0243, and #S76-1194 which supported this research are gratefully acknowledged.

occurred among secondary school students who are not part of this culture than among those who are. A logical consequence of the Baudelot and Establet analysis is that those who undertake post-secondary studies, having successfully undergone a further stage of selection, have fully internalized the norms and skills of the dominant culture, or at least have learned to function effectively in its terms. However, Bourdieu's model would lead us to predict that selection would nevertheless continue to occur at different rates among students at this level.

Literature on Canadian ethnic stratification (Porter, 1965; Kalbach, 1970; Blishen, 1970) indicates a continuing ranking of ethnic origin categories on the basis of occupation and education. The British charter group is over-represented in categories of higher occupational status and educational attainment, while most other ethnic categories are under-represented at these upper levels. Extrapolating from this literature on Canadian ethnic stratification, particularly with regard to education, and from that on educational aspiration and achievement, we might expect systematic differences in educational aspirations among those of British, French and other ethnic origins, with the last category being far from homogeneous. It is not evident, however, whether the observed relationships are the result of social class differences between ethnic groups, of varying linguistic experience depending on immigration history, of cultural differences associated with the particular ethnic groups or of differences associated with immigration status. On this last point Anisef's study (1975) of Ontario grade 12 students revealed that for males, being Canadian-born of Canadian-born parents was associated with lower aspirations than being an immigrant and/or the child of immigrant parents. For females no such relationship existed. In view of possible class and ethnic variations in sex role socialization as well as interprovincial differences in ethnic distributions and educational structure, it is desirable to control for these variables in any analysis of educational aspirations.

The Socio-Linguistic Contexts

In this examination of the educational aspirations of students in anglophone Montreal's Colleges of General and Professional Education, (CEGEPS), attention is focused on contrasts between members of the charter groups and those of other ethnic backgrounds. Both British and French are treated as charter groups in view of the structural dualism that has existed in Quebec, notably with regard to the economy and to education.[1] The students of French origin in this study are atypical in that they have opted to attend an English institution despite the existence of CEGEPS where French is the language of instruction. Table 1 summarizes the ethnic origin and linguistic composition for the age categories that include most post-secondary students.

There are roughly equal proportions of young Montrealers of British and non-charter group origins. If non-charter group origin is not a disadvantage in terms of access to post-secondary studies, we could expect to find a substantial proportion of the students of non-charter group origin. If, on the other hand, extrapolations about the effect of cultural capital, notably verbal skills, can be made from social class to ethnic analyses, then less substantial non-charter group representation could be expected.

In addition to contrasts in ethno-linguistic composition across Canada, there are differences in post-secondary educational structures. In Quebec all post-secondary students enter CEGEPS after completing their secondary studies. Although a large portion of their program is specific to the pre-university or technology option that they have chosen, some courses are common to both and transfer from one stream to the other is theoretically possible.[2] The CEGEP is tuition-free and in Montreal there are both English and French-language institutions. Francophone CEGEPS tend to have an ethnically and linguistically homogeneous student body, while anglophone CEGEPS are much more heterogeneous in both respects (Escande, 1973; Lipkin, 1971; Denis, 1975; A.S.O.P.E., 1976).

TABLE 1 *Ethno-linguistic composition of the Montreal population, 1971, and sample, 1973*

	Montreal Population* aged 18-24	Montreal CEGEPS Student Sample Men	Women
	%	%	%
Ethnic origin:			
British	15.6	33.1	39.6
French	66.6	15.6	15.0
Other	17.8	51.3	45.4
Mother tongue:			
English	22.3	62.6	66.8
French	68.5	5.8	6.3
Other	9.2	31.6	26.9
Usual language:			
English	24.8	67.8	73.4
French	68.4	8.5	4.8
Other	6.8	23.7	21.8

*Calculated from Census of Canada, 1971 Cat. 92-736 Vol. 1 Part 4, Bulletin 1.4-8. Table 24 and Cat. 92-731, Vol. 1 Part 4, Bulletin 1.4-3, Table 6.

Educational Alternatives

The educational alternatives open to the CEGEP students are: not to complete a diploma or degree, to complete a non-university diploma, or to complete a university degree. Students who planned to complete pre-university CEGEP without completing university as well were classified as not planning to complete a degree, since pre-university CEGEP is primarily a preparation for university. Technology programs provide training that is more directly related to specific jobs, but university degrees are pre-requisite for most high status occupations. Consequently, we will argue that in absolute terms hoping to complete a university degree represents a higher level of educational aspiration than hoping to complete a technology diploma, while not wanting to complete either represents the lowest level of aspirations. In fact, virtually all respondents intended to complete either a technology diploma or a university degree, so comparisons are simply expressed in terms of the percentage hoping to complete university. Since considerable selection has already occurred for all these students, we might expect to find less variations in terms of such independent variables as sex, social class, and ethnic background than if the students were at an earlier stage in their academic career. However, both Boudon (1973) and Bourdieu (1966) argue that similar processes operate at each point in the selection process, so that we might expect evidence of some class and ethnic variations even here.

Independent Variables

Ethnic Origin

This is a somewhat ambiguous, sociologically suspect concept within the Canadian context. It classifies a person in terms of the country of origin of the first ancestor on the *male* side to have come to Canada, and so allows for no differentiation in terms of intermarriage[3], number of generations in Canada, subjective identification or behavioral differentiation. It is useful, however, in providing a basis for comparison with other data sets which use it, including the Canadian census. Moreover, as we have noted, there do seem to be relatively systematic patterns of variation among ethnic origin categories. Recognizing the limitations of this operational definition of the concept of ethnicity, we will attempt to ascertain the basis of the variations in educational aspirations between the charter and other origin groups.

Linguistic Skills

This is considered as one of the most important variables in relation to academic success, and comparisons are made here on the basis of ethnic origin and of a scale of language use.[4] The student's mother tongue and the language spoken with the parents are the indicators used, with English and French as possible charter languages in Montreal. Use of English is given a higher value than use of French in Montreal because we are considering students in institutions where English is the language of instruction. Knowledge of English would therefore be a greater asset in that context than knowledge of French.[5]

Social Class

This variable has been so consistently associated with differential educational aspirations and achievement that a study which did not find this relationship would be somewhat suspect (Breton, 1972). Despite the considerable selection that has occurred by the post-secondary level, particularly among lower class students, the literature (Breton, 1972; Porter et al., 1973; Carlton et al., 1977; Escande, 1973) leads us to predict that there will be a positive relationship between social class and the proportion of students in post-secondary institutions and between social class and the proportion hoping to complete university (rather than technology) programs. Technology programs are said to be more attractive for working class students because they tend to be shorter and have more precise career outlets. However, it is possible that the relationship between program of study and social class will be relatively weak because the initial years of study in both programs are tuition-free, so that forgone income is the only economic disincentive. Moreover, if economic rather than cultural factors account for low participation rates by the working class, we can expect, overall, to find a higher proportion of lower class students at post-secondary institutions in Quebec than, for instance, in Ontario. Two measures of socioeconomic status are used in the analysis: father's occupation, coded by the Blishen scale[6] (Blishen and McRoberts, 1976) and level of instruction of the most educated parent, coded on a four-point scale, from less than completed high school to completed university.

Intervening Variables

Cultural Values

It has been argued (Rosen, 1959; Kahl, 1965; Marjoribanks, 1972) that educational differences among class and ethnic origin groups are due to the degree to which the cultural values of the group result in certain attitudes such as favoring achievement and planning for the future. Such attitudes have been associated with high educational aspirations, particularly in American studies (Breton, 1972). From our interpretation of "hoping to complete university" as representing a higher level of aspiration, we predict that favoring achievement and planning for the future will be associated with a greater likelihood to want to complete university.[7]

Female Sex Role Development

For the female students, two additional intervening variables were introduced. One was the extent to which the women favored combining a paid job and child rearing[8], while the other was whether or not the student's mother worked. Since combining a career and child rearing can involve considerable costs for the women (Denis, forthcoming), one might expect that wanting to do so would be associated with a high level of aspiration. The second variable is an indicator of the existence of a role model for such a combination. In view of the different attitudes to mothers' working held by different ethnic groups, not to mention the differing motivations for working by social class, the relationships here are complex.

Data Analysis

Data were collected in 1973 from a random sample of students in their first year of study in Montreal anglophone CEGEPS and in Toronto universities and community colleges. A total of 1 327 usable questionnaires was obtained (Denis, 1976). Analysis here relates to the Montreal sample of 737 students only. Table 1 shows that 33% of the males and 40% of the females were of British origin and a further 15% of each sex was of French origin. The non-charter origin groups were over-represented among the post-secondary students, but only 17% of the sample said English was neither their mother tongue nor the language used at home. Thus, charter group membership *per se* was not necessarily an advantage, although in these anglophone institutions use of English seemed to have been an advantage. Most of the students of French ethnic origin came from linguistically mixed backgrounds.

The British were under-represented in the lower class and over-represented in the upper class. The Italians showed the reverse, and there was no clear-cut pattern for other ethnic groups. Of the upper class students relatively few did not use English both as their mother tongue and with their parents, but a high proportion of lower class students used English in neither context. Students using French alone or in combination with another language tended to be middle class in origin. Students with at least one parent who had attended university reported use of English only, while those with neither parent completing high school reported use of another language, perhaps in combination with English. There were no systematic patterns of educational background for students who reported French as one of their languages. What emerges, then, is that at post-secondary institutions the widely reported positive relationship between attendance and social class is more characteristic of the British charter group and of those reporting use of English only than of other ethnic categories and of those reporting other patterns of language use.

Educational Aspirations

The total percentage hoping to complete university was 60% of the young men and 51% of the young women. Tables 2 and 3 summarize the educational aspirations of the students by sex, social class, and ethnicity.

From the literature it was predicted that there would be a positive relationship between father's occupation and hoping to complete university, and between parental education and hoping to complete university. The relationship with father's occupation is positive for both sexes. The relationship with parental education is positive when this variable is dichotomized in terms of having at least one parent who attended university.

Of the seven ethnic categories, the British men ranked third highest and French men fifth in terms of the percentage hoping to complete university. For all ethnic categories except northern European, women ranked lower than men. With respect to language, students who used French only or French and English were least likely to want to complete university, while women speaking English and another language and men speaking French and another language were most likely to hope to. This finding can be explained by the more restricted enrolment in technology than in pre-university programs; it is possible that the presence of a number of the French language students is the result of less competition for places in technology programs in the anglophone than in the francophone CEGEPs.[9]

On the whole it seems that the predicted relationships are more characteristic of those of charter group origin than of other ethnic origin categories, and of those using English alone than of those using other linguistic combinations. The positive relationship with father's occupation is more characteristic of men than of women, while the relationship with parental education is stronger for women.

Intervening Variables

The intervening variables were introduced in conjunction with each of the independent variables, ethnic origin, language use, father's occupation and parental education. Whether or not a girl's mother worked was eliminated from the analysis when it became evident that it introduced no significant variations in the percentage of women planning to attend

TABLE 2 Percent aspiring to university completion by ethnic origin and sex, controlling for father's occupation and parental education

| | ETHNIC ORIGIN | | | | | | | | | | | | | | |
| | British (N=253) | | French (N=105) | | Northern European (N=52) | | Southern European (N=117) | | Jewish (N=69) | | Eastern European (N=42) | | Other (N=51) | | Total (N=689) | |
SEX	M	F	M	F	M	F	M	F	M	F	M	F	M	F	M	F
% aspiring to complete university	59.8[1]	50.3	58.3	45.6	46.2	65.4	59.4	41.5	71.4	56.1	52.6	52.2	76.2	63.3	60.1	51.2
(Total N)	(102)[2]	(151)	(48)	(57)	(26)	(26)	(64)	(53)	(28)	(41)	(19)	(23)	(21)	(30)	(308)	(381)
% aspiring to complete university when father's occupation is:																
Low	52.9	40.5	42.9	33.3	16.7	57.1	58.1	42.4	40.0	28.6	70.0	50.0	85.7	36.4	55.8	40.9
(N)	(17)	(42)	(7)	(15)	(6)	(7)	(43)	(33)	(5)	(7)	(10)	(12)	(7)	(11)	(95)	(127)
Medium	59.5	44.7	48.0	45.5	55.6	75.0	70.6	41.2	75.0	70.6	28.6	25.0	62.5	88.9	58.3	53.0
(N)	(37)	(38)	(25)	(22)	(9)	(8)	(17)	(17)	(12)	(17)	(7)	(4)	(8)	(9)	(115)	(115)
High	65.2	58.6	81.3	55.0	60.0	60.0	0.0	33.3	81.8	52.9	50.0	71.4	83.3	66.7	68.8	58.1
(N)	(46)	(70)	(16)	(20)	(10)	(10)	(2)	(3)	(11)	(17)	(2)	(7)	(6)	(9)	(93)	(136)
(Total N)	(100)	(150)	(48)	(57)	(25)	(25)	(62)	(53)	(28)	(41)	(19)	(23)	(21)	(29)	(303)	(378)
% aspiring to complete university when parental education is:																
Neither completed university	58.5	44.0	57.9	39.6	50.0	66.7	59.6	40.0	77.3	54.8	53.3	44.4	73.3	47.1	60.4	45.6
(N)	(82)	(109)	(38)	(48)	(16)	(21)	(57)	(50)	(22)	(31)	(15)	(18)	(15)	(17)	(245)	(294)
At least one completed university	68.4	67.6	57.1	83.3	80.0	66.7	50.0	100.0	60.0	55.6	0.0	75.0	80.0	88.9	65.9	71.2
(N)	(19)	(34)	(7)	(6)	(5)	(3)	(2)	(1)	(5)	(9)	(1)	(4)	(5)	(9)	(44)	(66)
(Total N)	(101)	(143)	(45)	(54)	(21)	(24)	(59)	(51)	(27)	(40)	(16)	(22)	(20)	(26)	(289)	(360)

1. 59.8% of the 102 British males aspired to university completion. The remainder (100% − 59.8% = 40.2% of the 102) aspired to complete a non-university program.

2. Similarly 52.9% of the 17 British males with fathers in low-status occupations aspired to complete university, while 47.1% of them aspired to complete a non-university program. The remaining figures in Table 2 should be read in the same way.

TABLE 3 *Student's mother tongue and language used with parents by ethnic origin and sex, controlling for occupation and parental education*

	Neither one English or French (N=122)		Combination including English and/or French (N=149)		Both English (N=424)		Total (N=695)	
SEX	M	F	M	F	M	F	M	F
% aspiring to complete university	60.0[1]	43.5	54.3	51.9	61.2	53.7	59.4	51.7
(Total N)	(60)	(62)	(70)	(79)	(178)	(246)	(308)	(387)
% aspiring to complete university when father's occupation is:								
Low	59.5[2]	38.9	50.0	43.8	55.9	42.4	56.4	41.7
(N)	(42)	(36)	(18)	(32)	(34)	(59)	(94)	(127)
Medium	60.0	36.8	54.1	60.0	58.2	54.2	57.0	52.6
(N)	(10)	(19)	(37)	(25)	(67)	(72)	(114)	(116)
High	80.0	83.3	60.0	52.4	68.0	58.8	67.4	58.9
(N)	(5)	(6)	(15)	(21)	(75)	(114)	(95)	(141)
(Total=N)	(57)	(61)	(70)	(78)	(176)	(245)	(303)	(384)
% aspiring to complete university when parental education is:								
Neither completed university	60.0	38.9	58.3	46.7	61.2	48.4	60.2	46.3
(N)	(50)	(54)	(60)	(60)	(134)	(182)	(244)	(296)
At least one completed university	66.7	83.3	28.6	70.0	69.4	69.8	63.0	71.0
(N)	(3)	(6)	(7)	(10)	(36)	(53)	(46)	(69)
(Total = N)	(53)	(60)	(67)	(70)	(170)	(235)	(290)	(365)

1. 60.0% of the 60 males who used neither English nor French aspired to university completion. The remainder (100% − 60.0% = 40%) of the 60 aspired to complete a non-university program. Similarly 59.5% of the 42 males who used neither English nor French and whose fathers were in low status occupations aspired to complete university. 40.5% of them aspired to complete a non-university program. The remaining figures in Table 3 should be read in the same way.

2. When the control variables of father's occupation and parental education are introduced, N's do not always add up to the total N for the ethnic category as a whole since some cases are lost due to missing data on the control variables.

university. The scale of favoring the combining of a career and child rearing was retained for women since in most contexts it had a positive relationship with planning to complete university.

The intervening variable related to achievement orientation did not affect the aspirations of the charter groups, and its effect on other ethnic categories was mixed. However, there was a tendency for a higher proportion of students who had a university-trained parent and who argued that connections were important in order to get ahead, to aspire to complete university. Women whose fathers were in high status occupations and who thought connections were important were also more likely to aspire to complete university. Agreeing that connections are important is usually interpreted as an indication of low achievement motivation. One might argue, however, that for certain subgroups of students seeking specific types of occupation this might represent high achievement motivation coupled with a fairly realistic perception of the job market. There are situations where sponsorship can be important in getting a job. One example would be the type of higher status occupation where diffuse qualities based on common background (Porter, 1965; Brazeau, 1958) may be the determining factor in selection among candidates who all meet the formal technical qualifications of the job. Another instance would be the type of job which is not advertised, where potential candidates are approached directly. Those who are not part of the upper middle class at least and women in all classes are at a particular disadvantage in such cases because they are less likely to have access to the relevant interaction networks.

Future orientation did not influence the educational aspirations of British males. However, French students who agreed it was important to plan for the future were more likely to hope to complete university, with the reverse being true for British women. The middle class students who agreed were more likely to aspire to finish university.

To determine more precisely the extent of variation explained by the independent factors and intervening variables, regression analyses were performed. In no case did the extent of variance explained in the proportion selecting a university program exceed 2% for males, and none of the variables were statistically significant. For women, parental education or father's occupation, in conjunction with the woman's attitude about combining an outside job and child rearing, were statistically significant variables in the regression and explained 7% and 4% of the variance, respectively.

Conclusion

It is evident that educational aspirations differ depending on sex, and that even when social class is controlled there are variations in the relationship for different ethnic and language use categories. The positive correlation between social class and university aspiration is more typical of charter group members than of others, and of those using only English. The importance of parental education supports Bourdieu's notion of the relevance of cultural capital, particularly when one contrasts university educated parents and others. There are limitations to its applicability to ethnic differences: otherwise those differing from the dominant school culture in terms of ethnic background would have been under-represented in post-secondary studies and would have articulated lower aspirations than the charter group members. That economic considerations also seem to affect post-secondary attendance is shown by the lower average socioeconomic status of Montreal students in contrast to their Toronto counterparts.

That some of the variables do not result in more clear-cut differentiation in terms of educational aspiration may be a result of chance variation due to the small numbers in certain categories of the sample. It may also indicate that those opting for either post-secondary alternative have already internalized similar configurations of values as Baudelot and Establet's model posits. The complex nature of the relationship merits further attention, with more detailed reference to the structural dualism that characterizes Montreal's economy and school system.

ENDNOTES

1. The data reported here were collected in 1973, prior to the Bourassa government's Bill 22 and the election of the Parti Québécois.
2. The difficulty of transfer depends on the required subjects in the particular programs. It is probably more difficult to change from social science to natural science within the pre-university stream than it is to change from social science (pre-university) to social science (technology).
3. This is a more serious failing for some ethnic categories than for others (Royal Commission on Bilingualism and Biculturalism, 1969, Tables A-40 to A-77).
4. Another analysis of the same data set found differing patterns of aspirations in terms of a scale incorporating both language and birthplace variables (Denis, 1976).
5. In constructing the scale, answers to the questions on mother tongue and language used with parents were recoded as English, French and other, and possible answers were: 0- both other; 1- French and other; 2- both French; 3- English and other; 4- English and French; 6- both English.
6. When father's occupation is collapsed to three categories, these are: low (scores of less than 40 on the Blishen scale); medium (scores of 40-59); and high (scores of 60 and more).
7. On the attitudinal questions, students were asked to indicate their agreement or disagreement with statements on a four-point scale. The statement for future orientation was: it is very important to make plans in life and not be

satisfied with what comes along. Agreement with the statement "a person needs good connections to get ahead in the occupational world" was interpreted as indicating low achievement motivation.
8. The respondent was asked whether as a married woman she would prefer to work full-time, part-time, or have no job outside the home at three stages in her life: with no children, pre-school children and school-aged children. Responses were scored to reflect the type of effort implied in each combination, from 0 for no job with no children to 8 for a full-time job with pre-school children. When preferences at these three stages of the life cycle are considered together, there is a possible range of scores from 3 to 20.
9. Questions in the follow-up questionnaire which respondents are completing a year after finishing their studies will give us some further insight on this.

SELECTED REFERENCES

Anisef, Paul. "Congruence of Ethnicity for Educational Plans Among Grade 12 Students," pp. 122-36, in A. Wolfgang, *Education of Immigrant Children.* Toronto: O.I.S.E., 1975.

A.S.O.P.E. *Analyse descriptive des données de la première cueillette: les étudiants,* Vol. I. Montréal et Québec: Université de Montréal et Université Laval, 1976.

Baudelot, Christian, et Roger Establet. *L'école capitaliste en France.* Paris: F. Maspero, 1971.

Blishen, Bernard. "Social Class and Opportunity in Canada." *Canadian Review of Sociology and Anthropology* 7:2 (1970), pp. 110-27.

Blishen, Bernard, and Hugh A. McRoberts. "A Revised Socio-economic Index for Occupations in Canada." *The Canadian Review of Sociology and Anthropology* 13:1 (1976), pp. 71-79.

Boudon, Raymond. *L'inégalité des chances: la mobilité sociale dans les sociétés industrielles.* Paris: Armand Colin, 1973.

Bourdieu, Pierre. "L'école conservatrice: les inégalités devant l'école et devant la culture." *Revue française de Sociologie* VII (1966), pp. 325-47.

Brazeau, E. Jacques. "Language Differences and Occupational Experience." *The Canadian Journal of Economics and Political Science,* XXIV:4 (1958), pp. 532-40.

Breton, Raymond. *Social and Academic Factors in the Career Decisions of Canadian Youth.* Ottawa: Manpower and Immigration, 1972.

Carlton, Richard, Louise Colley, and Neil MacKinnon, eds. *Education, Change, and Society.* Toronto: Gage Educational Publishing, 1977.

Denis, Ann. "Some Social Characteristics of CEGEP Graduates." *The Canadian Journal of Higher Education* V:2 (1975), pp. 39-56.

_____ . "The Relation between Ethnicity and Educational Aspirations of Post-Secondary Students." Paper read at the National Conference on Ethnic Studies and Research, Regina, 1976.

_____ . "Wife and/or Worker. Sex Role Concepts of Canadian Female Students," in Eugen Lupri, ed. *The Changing Role of Women in Family and Society: A Cross-cultural Comparison.* Leiden: Brill (forthcoming).

Escande, C. *Les classes sociales au Cegep.* Montreal: Parti Pris, 1973.

Kahl, J. "Some Measurements of Achievement Orientation." *American Journal of Sociology* 70 (1965), pp. 669-81.

Kalbach, W. "The Impact of Immigration on Canada's Population." *1961 Census Monograph.* Ottawa: Dominion Bureau of Statistics, 1970.

Lipkin, J. Selection and Allocation of Students in Two Montreal Cegeps. (mimeo), 1971.

Marjoribanks, K. "Achievement Orientation of Canadian Ethnic Groups." *Alberta Journal of Educational Research* XVIII:3 (1972), pp. 162-73.

Porter, John. *The Vertical Mosaic.* Toronto: University of Toronto Press, 1965.

Porter, Marion, John Porter, and Bernard Blishen. *Does Money Matter?* Toronto: Institute for Behavioural Research, York University, 1973.

Rosen, B. "Race, Ethnicity and the Achievement Syndrome." *American Sociological Review* 24 (1959), pp. 47-60.

Royal Commission on Bilingualism and Biculturalism. *The Cultural Contribution of the Other Ethnic Groups*, Vol. 4. Ottawa: Queen's Printer, 1969.

Wolfgang, A. *Education of Immigrant Children.* Toronto: O.I.S.E., 1975.

Francophones outside Quebec

DANIELLE JUTEAU LEE   University of Ottawa
JEAN LAPOINTE   University of Ottawa

The Emergence of Franco-Ontarians: New Identity, New Boundaries*

In recent years, both anglophones and francophones have increasingly used the term "Franco-Ontarian" rather than "French Canadian" in referring to the French community living in Ontario. This new appellation reflects the changes presently affecting the collective identity of this community. In exploring this new identity phenomenon, a case will be made that the identity of an ethnic community is conditioned by its boundaries and that fluctuations in the boundaries of such a community bring about changes in its collective identity.

This analysis, which focuses on the French community in Ontario, will examine the criteria that define the boundaries of an ethnic group, identify the factors responsible for their fluctuation, and determine the impact of such fluctuations on changes in collective identity. Some attention will be given to the type of people most susceptible to acquiring this new identity.

Ethnic Boundaries

Existing definitions of the concept "ethnic group" are numerous, contradictory, and often confusing. In discussing this problem, F. Vallee (1975: 162-202) has suggested an approach that will be retained in this analysis. The distinction he makes between ethnicity and ethnic group is crucial:

> ...ethnicity refers to descent from ancestors who shared a common culture or subculture manifested in distinctive ways of speaking and/or acting. This common culture may have been carried by many different kinds of grouping, such as religious, political, geographical, but in all cases the kinship networks are crucial bearers of the culture (Vallee, 1975: 165-66).

---

* Written expressly for *Two Nations, Many Cultures: Ethnic Groups in Canada.*

Thus we say that an ethnic group is made up of people who share ethnicity (as previously defined), who share some sense of peoplehood or consciousness of kind, who interact with one another in meaningful ways beyond the elementary family, and who are regarded by others as being in the one ethnic category (Vallee, 1975: 167).

Ethnicity thus constitutes the main factor of inclusion/exclusion. When it leads to the emergence of an ethnic group, this group can be examined in terms of its existing system of interaction. A distinct system of interaction implies the presence of cultural and structural factors which define boundaries sharply enough to differentiate the group from surrounding collectivities.

Cultural factors are the cognitive, expressive and evaluative dimensions of ethnicity and include, among others, religion, language and lifestyle. They refer mainly to the content of the system. Structural factors pertain to those institutions which embody culture.

Ethnic communities with parallel and compartmentalized sets of institutions are characterized by structural pluralism (van den Berghe, 1967: 34). In other words, the level of structural pluralism can be determined from the number and type of parallel institutions—educational, religious, economic, and political. By examining the institutional completeness and the organizational capacity of an ethnic community (Breton, 1964: 1974), it is possible to determine its level of enclosure. The meaningful interaction referred to by Vallee can be studied in terms of the structural criteria outlined here.

Communities based on ethnicity, therefore, can be classified on a continuum ranging from ethnic groups that possess a few voluntary associations to nation-states where there is a complete congruence between cultural and structural factors. Although these factors are empirically interwoven, they are analytically distinguishable and mutually irreducible. It follows that the goal of survival, which can be defined as the maintenance of distinct boundaries (Juteau Lee, 1974), can be understood in terms of the maintenance of cultural and/or of structural boundaries. Finally an ethnic group has a subjective dimension which consists of a common identity, a feeling of solidarity, loyalty, belongingness and "we-ness". Because this collective identity is conditioned by the boundaries of the system, there exists an identity which is predominantly cultural and an identity which is predominantly structural.

The transition from a French-Canadian to a Franco-Ontarian identity must be examined in terms of changes in group boundaries that fluctuate over time (Barth, 1969) and in many ways. Horowitz differentiates between the processes of ethnic fusion (where boundaries between one group and another are erased) and ethnic fission (where boundaries are narrowed by the creation of additional groups). In the first case, which is a process of assimilation, fusion may take the form of amalgamation, where "two or more groups may unite to form a new group, larger and different from any of the component parts" (Horowitz, 1975: 115); or it may take the form of incorporation, where "one group may lose its identity be merging into another group which retains its identity" (Horowitz, 1975: 115). In the second case, which is a process of differentiation, fission may take the form of proliferation, where "a new group comes into existence without its 'parent group' losing its identity" (Horowitz, 1975:115); or that of division, when a group separates into its component parts. The process examined here corresponds to differentiation-division. The French-Canadian nation is separating into component parts, namely Québécois, Franco-Ontarians, Franco-Manitobans, Acadians, and so on. When one talks of French Canadians, the context is Canada; the criteria emphasized are *cultural*, such as language, religion, and lifestyle, and they separate the French from the English. When one talks about the Québécois, Franco-Ontarians, Franco-Manitobans, the context is a linguistic one, and the *structural* criteria which underlie group boundaries are emphasized. They outline different institutional spheres and refer to a different territorial basis.

The identity of an ethnic community is inseparable from its boundaries, and changes in this identity can only be understood in terms of changes in its boundaries. Two main sets of factors are responsible for the fluctuations in the boundaries of the French-Canadian collectivity in Ontario: (1) the emergence of a Québécois nation-community (the external factor) that has modified the relations between the French of both provinces; (2) the industrialization and urbanization of the French collectivity in Ontario (the internal factors) that have modified its former means of maintaining boundaries. Because Franco-Ontarians pursue the goal of boundary-maintenance, they will tend to choose means better suited to achieve this goal and will emphasize mainly the criteria which delineate the sharpest boundaries.

Changing Boundaries of the Collectivity

The Collectivity

By 1971, the population of French origin (ethnicity) in Ontario had reached 737 360 (Census of Canada, 1971, Bulletin 1. 3-2), and constituted 9.6% of the total population in that province. It is unevenly distributed within the province; the most important cluster can be found in the Ottawa-Carleton area where there are 117 465 people of French origin (Census of Canada, 1971, Bulletin 1. 3-2, Table 4). There are also many smaller centers in the North and in the East which are predominantly

TABLE 1 *Distribution of those of French ethnicity and French mother tongue, by selected regions in Ontario, 1971*

Region	Total population	French Ethnicity		French Mother Tongue	
		No.	%	No.	%
North[1]	838 690	219 935	26.2	173 310	20.7
East[2]	922 545	218 285	23.7	172 575	18.7
South[3]	5 941 870	299 140	5.0	136 160	2.3
Ontario	7 703 105	737 360	9.6	482 045	6.3

Source: Adapted from 1971 Census of Canada, Bulletin 1.3-2, Table 4 and Bulletin 1.3-4, Table 20.
1. Census Divisions: Algoma, Cochrane, Kenora, Manitoulin, Muskoka, Nipissing, Parry Sound, Rainy River, Sudbury, Thunder Bay, Timiskaming.
2. Census Divisions: Dundas, Frontenac, Glengary, Grenville, Lanark, Leeds, Ottawa-Carleton, Prescott, Renfrew, Russell, Stormont.
3. All the other Census Divisions.

French. The lowest concentrations of French are found in the South; in spite of their relatively large numbers, the proportion of French is lower since they are scattered in heavily populated areas. This pattern has previously been described by Joy (1972) who referred to it as the bilingual belt.

Although certain settlements were established at the beginning of the 18th century in Essex County, most communities were set up during the last century by immigrants from Quebec. Because of population pressures on the land, many Québécois settled in Ontario, along the railroad tracks that were being built, in pulp and paper areas such as Hawkesbury and Sturgeon Falls, and eventually in mine towns such as Timmins. By 1971, 22.3% of the population of French mother tongue residing in Ontario was born in Quebec (FFHQ, 1977: 30).

The goal of survival (boundary-maintenance) was also a predominant one for the French in Ontario. The emphasis was on maintaining linguistic and cultural patterns, and the church played a major role in attaining this goal. The school system was also crucial to the survival of the collectivity, and most of the battles fought by the French community centered around the establishment of French instruction in the province. Regulation 17 in 1913 barred the francophones from receiving a primary education in their own language. Although this regulation was modified in 1927, it was not until 1968 (Jackson, 1975: 31) that the Ontario Legislature officially recognized the existing primary schools and allowed for the establishment of French Language Secondary Schools. Language represents one of the major criterion delineating boundaries, and the capacity of the group to resist linguistic assimilation indicates its vitality. This capacity, as indicated in Table 2, varies in different areas. Obviously, both the absolute and relative numbers of francophones influence the collectivity's capacity to establish the structural basis (meaningful interactions which extend beyond the elementary family) which is

TABLE 2 *Distribution of those of French ethnicity, French mother tongue, and French spoken at home, by selected regions in Ontario, 1971*

Selected Regions	French Ethnicity		French Mother Tongue		French Spoken at Home	
	No.	%	No.	%	No.	%
Great North[1]	85 780	11.6	69 415	14.4	58 195	16.5
Middle North[2]	134 155	18.2	103 895	21.6	82 605	23.4
East[3]	218 285	29.6	172 575	35.8	147 290	41.8
Southwest[4]	97 480	13.2	40 745	8.4	18 175	5.2
South[5]	201 660	27.4	95 415	19.8	46 200	13.1
Ontario	737 360	100	482 045	100	352 465	100

Source: Adapted from 1971 Census of Canada, Bulletin 1.3-2, Table 4, Bulletin 1.3-4, Table 20, and Bulletin 1.3-5, Table 28.
1. Census Division: Cochrane, Kenora, Rainy River, Thunder Bay, Timiskaming.
2. Census Divisions: Algoma, Manitoulin, Muskoka, Nipissing, Parry Sound, Sudbury.
3. Census Divisions: Dundas, Frontenac, Glengary, Grenville, Lanark, Leeds, Ottawa-Carleton, Prescott, Renfrew, Russell, Stormont.
4. Census Division: Bruce, Elgin, Essex, Huron, Kent, Lambton, Middlesex, Oxford, Perth.
5. All the other Census Divisions.

essential for boundary-maintenance. Of course, the capacity of a group to maintain boundaries is also determined by the overall political, legal, and constitutional framework within which it operates.

Boundary Changes

A transformation in the group boundary criteria has brought about a fluctuation in group boundaries and a change of emphasis from cultural to structural factors. The emergence of a Québécois collectivity and the changes in the social organization of the French collectivity in Ontario constitute the two main factors responsible for this transformation. This boundary change process has been reinforced by the dynamic relationship between the French and English in Canada.

Industrialization, urbanization, and political modernization are mainly responsible for the emergence of a Québécois collectivity (Juteau Lee, 1974; 1978: 10). French Canadians were French in ancestry, spoke French, adhered to Catholicism and lived mostly on farms. Cultural factors were emphasized in the definition of group boundaries and were the main basis of identification until the advent of industrialization. Industrialization diminished the importance of religion (decrease in religious practice and in the size of the clergy, secularization of norms and values), accelerated urbanization, and modified the occupational structure. These trends led to the erosion of the main components of the French-Canadian social structure as well as of the former basis of "we-feeling", group-sentiment, and belongingness (Juteau Lee, 1974: 170-74). The gradual disappearance of the boundaries underlying identification is responsible for the collective identity crisis examined by many authors (Bellah, 1970; Eisenstadt, 1966; Rioux, 1969; Smelser, 1968). Although ethnicity remains, the criteria which serve as the basis of this community weaken and are replaced by new ones.

Political modernization is a criterion which will serve as a new basis for defining group boundaries and solidarity. This process corresponds to the growing scope and intensification of the power of the central, legal, and administrative agencies of the society (Eisenstadt, 1966: 4). First, the more active role of the state in provincial matters increases the importance of territoriality, since by definition, a state has jurisdiction over certain boundaries. Since political modernization also involves the penetration of the provincial level of government into local and regional sectors, it modifies institutional boundaries and sensitizes the overall population to such changes. Second, political modernization increases the emphasis on self-steering because it brings about the institutionalization of change. As a result, survival (i.e., boundary-maintenance) is no longer defined in terms of maintaining existing patterns, as the emphasis shifts to the capacity of controlling internal functioning in terms of existing goals and resources (Juteau Lee, 1974: 130). As industrialization and urbanization eroded the criteria underlying group boundaries, political modernization supplied new ones by increasing the salience of the territorial basis of *l'Etat du Québec* and of the collectivity it governed. Consequently, the basis and boundaries of the collectivity were transformed.

The emergence of the Québécois nation-community constitutes the external factor responsible for the changes in the boundaries of the French-Canadian nation. Previously, all the French in Canada belonged to the French-Canadian nation. The changing of the francophone collectivity in Quebec meant that the Québécois excluded from their "we" the francophones in other parts of Canada. This process of differentiation-division, which is painful both for the excluded groups and those who remain, was formally recognized at the 1969 meetings of "les Etats généraux du Canada français". In his analysis, Arès (1969: 100) identified the strong conflicts between the francophones of Québec and those of the other provinces. The initial tension subsided only when the existence of two parallel collectivities and systems of solidarity was accepted.

TABLE 3 *Distribution of rural-urban population, for French mother tongue and Ontario as a whole, 1971*

Ontario	% Urban	% Rural		Total
		Non-farm	Farm	
French mother tongue	76.6%	18.9%	4.5%	100
Total population	82.4%	12.9%	4.7%	100

Source: Adapted from FFHQ, 1977: 28.

Nevertheless, the French in Ontario could have kept their French-Canadian identity. To account for the emergence of a new identity, one must examine internal factors such as industrialization and urbanization. The percentage of people with a French mother tongue who live in an urban area as compared with the population as a whole is presented in Table 3. As a result of the rural-to-urban transition, the occupational structure has been modified; francophones are now represented at all occupational levels.

TABLE 4 *Percentage of labor force (15 years and over) in occupational categories, French mother tongue and Ontario as a whole, 1971*

Occupations	French mother tongue Ontarians	Total Ontario
Managerial, administrative and related occupations	3.2	4.7
Professional and semi-professional	7.4	9.0
Religion	0.3	0.2
Medicine and Health	2.6	3.7
Clerical and related occupations	14.7	17.6
Sales and Services	19.5	20.2
Primary sector	7.4	5.2
Processing occupations	32.9	29.5
Not elsewhere classified	2.2	2.3
Not stated	9.9	7.7
All occupations	199 385	3 354 360

Source: FFHQ, 1977: 41.

The resulting breakdown of isolation as a mechanism for maintaining relative closure and group boundaries has required that strong action be taken to develop greater autonomy in education, health services, and the courts. To achieve a certain level of structural pluralism, the French in Ontario had to exert pressures at the level of *their* provincial government; this course of action has strengthened *their* territorial basis of identification. Thus, the means employed for boundary-maintenance shifted from the defense of traditional patterns to the development of structural pluralism. Consequently, the territorial criterion has been emphasized and has become operative in the definition of group boundaries.

Finally, the ensuing reinforcement of this transition must also be examined in terms of the overall political-legal framework within which French-English relations have evolved in Canada. Although the birth of the Canadian federation can only be understood with reference to the economic context at that time (Naylor, 1972; Clement, 1975), the type of federal system which emerged was adopted in order to solve the political stalemate between Canada East and Canada West in the mid-19th century. The division of the country into provinces each with its own government implied that the British North America Act did not recognize politically the existence of two nations. The areas of jurisdiction were distributed between the federal and provincial levels of government, with the latter controlling mainly the cultural sphere. Since most French Canadians resided in Quebec, the granting of autonomy on a territorial basis constituted a solution at the time; French Canadians in Quebec were relatively safe, since their provincial government had some control over cultural matters and could defend their rights against federal and anglophone encroachments. But historical developments modified the basis of this agreement. Many French Canadians moved to other provinces only to face the abolition of existing privileges. The expansion of provincial jurisdiction into areas such as education, health and welfare led to increased conflicts between federal and provincial governments. The growing scope of provincial government jurisdiction also heightened the provincial basis of identification.

At present, the choices open to the Franco-Ontarian collectivity are limited. For many reasons, it is too late to accept, at the political level, the existence of two nations. Because of changing group boundaries, the French-Canadian nation no longer exists; if it did, it would be unacceptable to the other provinces. Special status for Quebec is also impossible since the other provinces also constitute, in their own way, "des provinces pas comme les autres" or "unique provinces". Separatism is not the solution for the francophone minorities outside Quebec.

Although the existing constitution can be modified and the provincial autonomy augmented, Franco-Ontarians must rely primarily on their provincial government and secondarily on the federal. The latter cannot interfere directly in provincial decisions concerning the francophone or anglophone minorities. The Official Languages Act passed in 1968 recognizes the existence of two linguistic groups and grants French and English an equal status on the federal level. New Brunswick is the only province that is officially bilingual.

The 1976 election of the Parti Québécois has improved, on a short-term basis, the bargaining position of the Franco-Ontarians. Because the political elite of Ontario opposes separation, it has decided to strengthen the position of its French minority. The recent experiment with bilingual courts and the 1977 decision to build a French language secondary school in Essex despite the opposition of the local school board (a first in Ontario) are signs of this changing mood. The Franco-Ontarians themselves are aware that their battle must now be fought in their province, with little help from their Québécois cousins. In a recent publication (FFHQ: 1977), they outlined such a course of action and indicated their respect for, and acceptance of, the victory of the Parti Québécois in 1976.

The Franco-Ontarian Identity

The modification of the criteria defining group boundaries has led to a process of differentiation-division and to the emergence of the Franco-Ontarian identity which can be gauged by a variety of indicators. Spokespersons of the collectivity often make statements which explicitly define or implicitly reflect the collective identity of their community; the various expressions of these people, be they leaders of organizations or poets, constitute useful indicators.

Associations and Organizations

The name chosen by an association or its statement of goals usually reflects the collectivity's definition of itself. At the beginning of this century, the collective identity was definitely French-Canadian. The most important association, founded in 1910, was called *L'Association canadienne-française d'éducation en Ontario* (ACFEO); this name reflects the identity of its founders. In 1914, the *Fédération des femmes canadiennes-françaises* adopted a similar name. Between 1910 and 1960 many associations sprang up throughout the province with regional and local representatives in almost every French-speaking area. These associations operate under the patronage of the ACFEO to which they are affiliated and share its definition of a French-Canadian collectivity. In 1960, there were nine such associations in Ontario (ACFEO, 1960: 169-70).

Many associations adopted the terms "French" and "Catholic" in their names. The term "French-Canadian" was also used by groups like the *Association des hommes d'affaires canadiens-français de Welland*, founded in 1955(ACFO, 1976: 199). During that period, only the *Union des cultivateurs franco-ontariens* (1929) and *l'Association de la jeunesse franco-ontarienne* (1949) used the term "Franco-Ontarian".

At the beginning of the 1960s, the designation "Franco-Ontarian" was used by new associations or old ones involved in a name change. The *Fédération des clubs sociaux franco-ontariens* was founded in 1959. The *Association de l'enseignement français de l'Ontario* (1939) became, in 1963, *l'Association des enseignants franco-ontariens*. In 1969, the *Union catholique des fermières* (1937) changed its name to the *Union culturelle des franco-ontariennes*. The *Association des surintendants franco-ontariens* (school boards) was founded in 1968. Other local organizations also adopted the term "Franco-Ontarian" to identify themselves; for example, the *Club franco-ontarien de l'université d'Ottawa*, founded in 1975, the *Centre franco-ontarien de folklore* of the University of Sudbury, established in 1964, and *Les Campeurs franco-ontariens* of Hamilton, founded in 1967 (ACFO, 1976: 6-50, 279, 473, 267). The term "Franco-Ontarian" also found greater use at the governmental level to designate official organizations. The Ontario Art Council opened a Franco-Ontarian section in 1970. In 1975, the Ministry of Culture and Recreation, in conjunction with the Ministry of Colleges and Universities, created an *Advisory Council for Franco-Ontarian Affairs*. Other recent organizations, such as the *Mouvement c'est l'temps* (1975), *Théâtre-Action* (1971), the *Editions Prise de Parole* (1973) among others, adopt this new collective identity explicitly in their statement of objectives (ACFO, 1976: 156, 372; Cano: 1973).

All these examples, drawn at the level of the organizations and associations of the collectivity, reflect the change that is occurring at the identity level. Of course, the French-Canadian identity has not disappeared. L'ACFEO, now *l'Association canadienne-française de l'Ontario* (ACFO), did not change the term of reference in its name; and as late as 1975, a new organization created in Welland was called *Le Club canadien-français de Welland* (ACFO, 1976: 201).

Analysis of Speeches

An examination of the speeches and writings of the leaders of the community also shows that the term "French Canadian" was replaced by the term "Franco-Ontarian" at the beginning of the 1960s. This tendency is confirmed in a study done by R. G. Guindon (1971). His content analysis of communications presented at the founding meeting (1910) of the ACFEO and at its 50th anniversary meeting (1960) supports our view (Guindon, 1971: 38, 64). If we analyze the four-page circular distributed to thousands of people living in French parishes during the organization of the 1910 meetings, we see that there were two references to "Franco-Americans" (who have already set up an association) but no reference to "Franco-Ontarians". The emphasis lies on the terms French Canadian or French Canadian of Ontario which were repeated six times and which were associated with expressions such as "notre gloire nationale" ("our national glory"), "nos intérêts nationaux" ("our national interests"), "L'avenir de notre nationalité" ("the future of our nationality"), "si nous voulons être un peuple" ("if we want to be a nation") (ACFEO, 1960: 86-90). On the other hand, the subtitle of the report of the celebration of the 50th anniversary of the ACFEO read: "Cinquante années de vie franco-ontarienne' (ACFEO, 1960). In the foreword, the author referred both to "Franco-Ontarians" and "French Canadians". In a one-page speech, one honorary president mentioned the term "Franco-Ontarian" four times and did not refer once to "French Canadians" (ACFEO, 1960: 164-65). Appendix B, which summarized the accomplishments of the association, referred in less than two pages to "Franco-Ontarians" seven times and only once to French Canadians (ACFEO: 168-70).

Artistic Expression

This dimension is important as we believe that artists express the soul and life of a collectivity. In recent years, the Franco-Ontarian collectivity has produced its own poets and musicians who write and sing about the Franco-Ontarian reality. The works of François Lemieux, Robert Paquette, André and Robert Paiement (Coopérative des Artistes du Nouvel-Ontario), Robert Dickson, Claude Belcourt not only refer to this emerging identity but also keenly describe its precariousness, as well as the anxiety and stimulation it produces.

Designations Utilized by Group Members

Another indicator of group identity can be found by examining the terms used in everyday conversation by the members of the group when referring to their collectivity. We will now discuss the use of the terms "Franco-Ontarian" and "French Canadian" made by the subjects of our sample of French-speaking communities of Ontario.

The Bearers of the New Identity

Horowitz (1975: 118-19) has pointed out that an identity can be either contextual (dependent on the specific environment) or autonomous. When the criteria underlying a collective identity are well defined and solidly entrenched, it becomes "functionally autonomous of the stumuli that produced it and may become so internalized as to be invoked in contexts quite different from the one in which it was formed" (Horowitz, 1975: 119). This is the case with the French-Canadian identity. When the objective criteria underlying group boundaries undergo transformations, the fit between boundaries and identification becomes blurred. It is precisely during such a transition that the analyst can identify the contextual variables which give birth to different types and levels of identification. In this case, the main cultural criterion (French language) delineating group boundaries remains; the changes affect the structural level (territorial) of identification (Canadian to Ontarian). There is also a change in emphasis from the cultural to the structural factors. The relative importance of each context can be ascertained by identifying how various social actors define their community, how often they refer to this collectivity, and in what types of situation they do so. These contexts can be defined in terms of the location of group members in social networks and institutional spheres, their level of participation in the affairs of the collectivity, and their commitment to boundary-maintenance.

Between 1974 and 1976, we studied five multi-ethnic communities in Ontario.[1] It became clear through our participant observation and unstructured interviews that both identities coexisted but were not articulated by the same groups. Those involved in social change called themselves Franco-Ontarians; those who defined their ethnic group membership mainly in terms of cultural symbols preferred the term French Canadian.

Active in the political and educational spheres, Franco-Ontarians participate in the life of the community and are sensitized to boundary-change as well as to the legal-territorial framework within which their demands can be articulated and acted upon, namely the Ontario government. Those who call themselves Franco-Ontarians are aware that their battles must be fought at the provincial level, that urbanization and modernization have altered the life of their community, and that new means must be developed in order to achieve the old goal of boundary-maintenance. In this context, it is interesting to note that this group uses the term "Franco-Ontarian" to refer to actual conditions and "French Canadian" when talking about the past or about their predecessors. It is not surprising that the younger generation generally exhibits a Franco-Ontarian identity and the older, a French-Canadian one.

In the media, those who have reached a higher educational level, and those who possess a higher degree of political awareness, as well as students enrolled in French Language Secondary Schools, also define themselves as Franco-Ontarians. The same can be said for the artists. As a group, they possess a very high level of sensitivity, and their awareness of changing group boundaries is expressed in their work. Finally, the new identity is also shared by those who are in contact with Québécois (apart from family ties). They are aware of recent changes in that province, and more important for our purposes, of their exclusion from the new group which has emerged.

A French-Canadian identity is dominant mainly among the group which expresses the evaluative dimension of culture, such as those involved in the religious sphere. They are more sensitive to traditional definitions, and they value the maintenance of existing patterns. They seem to consider themselves as descendants of the original group (which must be kept intact) from which the Québécois have unfortunately detached themselves. Those who have kept strong ties with their Québec side of the family (which constitutes a basis of solidarity) also emphasize the cultural rather than the structural criterion of belongingness. They still feel that all francophones in Canada form a collectivity which should be united by a common bond of solidarity. On the other hand, those who call themselves Franco-Ontarians disagree and are much more ambivalent towards their Québec counterparts.

The new definition of "we-feeling", group belongingness, and solidarity is crucial since it influences the means chosen for boundary-maintenance and affects the strategies utilized for achieving this goal. Franco-Ontarians emphasize structural rather than cultural pluralism; they seek to broaden the institutional completeness of their collectivity and to increase their control over its internal functioning. In terms of their analysis, survival requires the development of a strong collectivity capable of creating new cultural expressions rather than maintaining old patterns which no longer correspond to its changing social organization. The emergence of new collectivities (Québécois, Franco-Ontarian) has also modified political strategies; battles are now fought within the provincial sphere. The destiny of Franco-Ontarians is detached from that of the francophones in Québec.

The factors which are responsible for the emergence of a new collective identity do not insure its diffusion. The population at large has not yet embraced the new Franco-Ontarian definition. Since the term "Franco-Ontarian" has an ethnic connotation, it can be accepted rather easily by all those who share this common ethnicity, as soon as the relevance of its boundaries is felt by the members. But Ontario also has francophone groups of different ethnic origin. In Toronto, for example, there are, apart from the Franco-Ontarians, other francophones such as Acadian, European French, African French, and Franco-Americans (Maxwell, 1977: 152). Whether these groups will ever define themselves as Franco-Ontarians depends on the strength of this ethnic group in mobilizing resources and its willingness to enlarge its boundaries as a means to attain its collective goals. To date, there is little indication that the ethnic boundaries of the Franco-Ontarian community are being expanded to include francophones with origins from outside Ontario.

Conclusion

The examination of the factors responsible for changes in group boundaries and collective identification has shed some light on the emergence of a Franco-Ontarian identity. It has demonstrated that ethnic groups do vary over time and consequently, that communal relations are not writ in stone. Because these changes affect the distribution of resources between the groups and their relative statuses, the importance of examining the criteria which underlie group boundaries has been stressed. Since ethnic groups are more than an epiphenomenon, it is crucial to understand the basis of their formation and transformation. Furthermore, too many analyses of assimilation (incapacity to maintain group boundaries) deal only with indicators such as language spoken in the home, language spoken at work, and media consumption. While these variables allow us to understand the linguistic patterns of individuals, they tell us very little about the viability of an ethnic community. Further studies must emphasize the collective dimension (the structural basis of a collectivity), the factors that support its boundaries, and its capacity to maintain them. They must also examine the relationship between different types of boundaries and the overall distribution of resources within them.

ENDNOTE

1. Further details concerning the methodology of this study may be obtained by contacting the authors.

SELECTED REFERENCES

Arès, Richard. "L'oeuvre des Etats généraux," *Relations* 337 (April 1969), pp. 99-100.

Association Canadienne-francaise d'Education d'Ontario (ACFEO). "Congrès d'Education des Canadiens-Français d'Ontario—1910: Rapport officiel des séances tenues à Ottawa." Ottawa, du 18 au 20 janvier 1910.

————. "Rapport general des fêtes du Cinquantenaire et du quinzieme Congrès general d'Association canadienne-française d'Education d'Ontario." Ottawa, Cinquante années de vie franco-ontarienne, les 20, 21 et 22 avril 1960.

Association canadienne-française de l'Ontario (ACFO). "Bottin des Organismes franco-ontariens," Ottawa, 1976.

Barth, F., ed. *Ethnic Groups and Boundaries*. Boston: Little, Brown, and Company, 1969.

Bellah, R. *Beyond Belief: Essays on Religion in a Post-Traditional World*. New York: Harper and Row, 1970.

Breton, R. "Institutional Completeness of Ethnic Communities and Personal Relations of Immigrants," *American Journal of Sociology* 70 (1964), pp. 193-205.

————. "Types of Ethnic Diversity in Canadian Society." Paper presented at the VIII World Congress, ISA, Toronto, 1974.

Cano. *Des artistes du Nouvel-Ontario*. Sudbury: Les Editions Prises de Parole, 1973.

Census of Canada, Bulletins, 1.3-2, 1.3-4, and 1.3-5, 1971.

Clement, Wallace. *The Canadian Corporate Elite: An Analysis of Economic Power*. Toronto: McClelland and Stewart Limited, 1975.

Eisenstadt, S. N. *Modernization: Protest and Change*. Englewood Cliffs, N.J.: Prentice-Hall, Inc., 1966.

Federation des francophones hors Quebec (FFHQ). *Les Heritiers de Lord Durham*. Ottawa, 1977.

Guindon, R. G. "Essai d'analyse interne d'un discours idéologique." Unpublished Master's Thesis, Université d'Ottawa, 1971.

Horowitz, D. L. "Ethnic Identity," pp. 111-40, in N. Glazer and D. P. Moynihan, eds. *Ethnicity: Theory and Experience*. Cambridge: Harvard University Press, 1975.

Jackson, John D. *Community and Conflict: A Study of French-English Relations in Ontario*. Toronto: Holt, Rinehart and Winston of Canada Limited, 1975.

Joy, Richard. *Languages in Conflict*. Toronto: McClelland and Stewart, 1972.

Juteau Lee, D. "The Impact of Modernization and Environmental Impingements upon Nationalism and Separatism: The Quebec Case." Unpublished Doctoral Dissertation, University of Toronto, 1974.

Maxwell, Thomas R. *The Invisible French. The French in Metropolitan Toronto*. Waterloo: Wilfrid Laurier University Press, 1977.

Naylor, R. T. "The Rise and Fall of the Third Commercial Empire of the St. Lawrence," pp. 1-42, in Gary Teeple, ed. *Capitalism and the National Question in Canada*. Toronto: University of Toronto Press, 1972.

Rioux, M. *La Question du Québec*, Paris: Seghers, 1969.

Smelser, N.J. *Essays in Sociological Explanation*. Englewood-Cliffs, N.J.: Prentice-Hall, Inc., 1968.

Vallée, F. "Multi-Ethnic Societies: The Issues of Identity and Inequality," pp. 162-202, in D. Forcese and S. Richer, eds. *Issues in Canadian Society: An Introduction to Sociology*. Scarborough: Prentice-Hall of Canada, Ltd., 1975.

van den Berghe, P. *Race and Racism*. New York: John Wiley and Sons, Inc., 1967.

THOMAS R. MAXWELL   Wilfrid Laurier University

The Invisible French: The French in Metropolitan Toronto*

Invisible is the one word which describes Canadians of French ancestry living in Toronto in the mid-1970s. The social and historical factors which account for this "invisibility" are the focus of this research.

Patterns of Residential Settlement

Metropolitan Toronto experienced the greatest influx of francophones in its history between the census years of 1961 and 1971. The French population increased by 49.7% from 61 421 to 91 975, while the increase in the total metropolitan population for the same period was not far behind, 43.9% from 1 826 481 to 2 628 130. Consequently, the francophone percentage of the total population increased only marginally, from 3.36% in 1961 to 3.49% in 1971.[1]

In spite of the growth of the francophone population, it is significant to note that there has been no appreciable change in the residential settlement patterns of the newcomers to Toronto. In both core and fringe areas francophones have dispersed residentially across the entire metropolitan area as in previous decades with minimal changes in the densities of particular census tracts. For instance, within the Metropolitan Corporation, only 107 out of 347 tracts show densities of the French in excess of 4% and only eight of these have densities higher than 10%. The highest is a small census tract of only 610 persons, of whom 100 are francophone, for a density of 16.3%. In the fringe area, residential dispersion has been even greater as the highest densities of the French have been 5.2% in Georgetown, 5% in Port Credit, 4.8% in Pickering Township, 4.2% in Ajax and 4.1% in Mississauga.[2]

---

* Reprinted from Thomas R. Maxwell, *The Invisible French: The French in Metropolitan Toronto*, Wilfrid Laurier University Press, Waterloo, Ontario, 1977, with the permission of author and publisher.

French as Mother Tongue

The proportion of the French population acknowledging French as mother tongue has risen from 42.3% in 1961 to 49.5% in 1971, showing that many of the French newcomers came from areas where French was the predominant language in the home. In the 1971 census, the replies to the question, "What language is spoken most often at home?" showed that French mother tongue usage in the home increased 50% over the 1961 level, surpassed only by Italian usage that almost doubled. Table 1 shows the growth rates between 1961 and 1971 of the six largest minority ethnic populations in Metropolitan Toronto listed in order of mother tongue as spoken most often in the home.

TABLE 1 *Growth rates of the six largest ethnic minority populations in Metropolitan Toronto rank ordered by mother tongue usage in the home*

Ethnic group	Population 1961	1971	Increase No.	%	Use of mother-tongue in the home %
Italian	140 378	271 755	131 377	93	70
Polish	58 578	51 185	− 7 393	− 13	38
Ukrainian	46 650	60 755	14 105	30	37
German	80 300	116 640	36 340	45	26
French	61 421	91 175	30 544	50	22
Netherlands	33 434	44 430	10 996	33	09

Source: Census 1961 and 1971.

From the table it is readily apparent that only the Italians have maintained the use of mother tongue in the home most of the time to a high degree. An examination of the settlement patterns reveals significant differences. It must first be acknowledged that the Italians have almost doubled their population in Metropolitan Toronto during the census decade. This tide of newcomers, coming mainly from a single homeland where English is a foreign language, would have promoted the use of Italian in the home to a greater degree than is prevalent among the French to whom English is one of the official languages and was spoken by many of them prior to migrating to Toronto.

The highest concentrations of the French are scattered among 107 census tracts across the city while the Italians are concentrated almost solidly in northwest Toronto. The contrast is heightened when the highest densities of the five major areas of concentration in each ethnic group are compared. For the French, only eight census tracts had densities of over 10% and the highest of these was 16.3% with the average density

12.54%. In contrast, the Italians in their areas of concentration had 63 census tracts with a density of over 10%, with the highest density 76% and the average density 39.6%.

Implications of the Spatial Pattern

No single motive provided a focus for French settlement in Toronto. Rather, the predominance of economic motives has tended to disperse the French throughout the metropolitan area in conformity with the widely-spread character of Toronto's industrial development. This geographic dispersion has two implications for social participation within the French population. First is the virtual isolation of French families from one another even in areas of concentration while in contrast there is social interaction with the surrounding English-speaking population both in the neighborhood and on the job. Second, the absence of any significant concentrations of the French population has left its members without a central focus for ethnic participation and consequent identification within the boundaries of their own culture.

The lack of higher concentrations of the French population not only tends to militate against more extensive use of the French language in the home but also weakens French participation in the civic and provincial matters because of lack of voting power to elect political representation. Thus the pattern of residence has deprived the French of influence in the power structures of the community and the province. Italians have been much more active politically because of concentrated voting power in the city wards. The Italians do not have Italian-language schools, or a radio or television station, although they do sponsor programs, have more ethnic parishes, and are concentrated in the construction and business segment of the work world. But retention of their language and culture is evidently dependent on participation within ethnic boundaries strongly reinforced by their patterns of residential settlement and institutional organization.

Over 12% of the francophone population of Ontario are resident in Metropolitan Toronto. But how many of these have been sending their children to French-language schools within the area? As of January 1977 the enrollment of the five separate elementary schools was 1 304 plus the two public elementary schools of 341, for a total of 1 644. Add the 600 at Ecole Secondaire Etienne Brûlé and the grand total is 2 244.

In general terms, the present French-language school system in Toronto has been serving 31% of the francophone children in whose homes French is spoken most of the time; 15% of the children of francophone families who claim French as mother tongue; and 7.5% of all francophone children of school age within the Metropolitan Corporation. Several factors are relevant to this situation. Toronto possesses only

3% of the French-language schools of the province while hosting over 12% of the provincial population. Secondly, francophone officials in the Department of Education and principals of both elementary and secondary schools complain that it has been difficult to convince francophone parents that an education in French language in a predominantly English-speaking community will not handicap the future careers of the children. Many francophone parents, especially in working-class families, believe that economic security is dependent on knowledge of the English and not the French language and the loss of French culture does not disturb them. Thirdly, it has been much easier to send children to local English schools rather than have them travel long distances by bus to French-language schools. In the fringe area outside of the Metropolitan Corporation the difficulties are compounded for the existing or planned French-language schools because of the lower densities of the French population.

The Quest for Cultural Unity

In traditional French-Canadian society the Roman Catholic parish served as an umbrella organization since it sought to coordinate within its boundaries a variety of parish associations which would meet not only the religious but also the social, recreational, and even the economic needs of the parishioners, all within a French cultural environment. In Toronto, the original parish of the Sacre Coeur, established in 1887, fulfilled this integrative role for only two to three decades as the French population grew rapidly and scattered widely among English parishes. From then on, the downtown working class parish concentrated almost wholly on its religious and welfare roles with little attention to its ethnic role in spite of the efforts of some of the parishioners to change this focus. Most of the growing number of middle-class francophones affiliated with middle-class anglophone parishes. Consequently they had no alternative for the maintenance of the French language and culture but to rely on the organization of ethnic associations which had little or no relationship to the Sacre Coeur parish apart from the few who attended there.

In 1966, eighty years after the founding of the French parish, and in response to a concentration of middle-class francophones in the Don Mills area of northeast Toronto where their children had access to the French-language elementary school, Ste. Madeleine, a second parish, St. Louis de France, was established on Don Mills Road. Essentially a middle-class parish of some three hundred families, its most active associations were among women and children. So it appears to serve a religious rather than an ethnic role, although the latter had found expression in the provision of leadership for francophone associations and the expansion of the French-language school system.

Francophone Associations

With the onus for cultural continuity resting mainly on francophone associations, there were discussions among francophone leaders for several years in the early 1960s concerning the establishment of a cultural center which would provide a focus for francophone social and cultural interaction by coordinating the activities of the existing independent associations. It was hoped that such a center would mobilize kinship, friendship, and religious obligations within the French population in support of an informal authority agency which would bridge the cultural differences resulting from the variety of backgrounds represented among the francophone migrants to Metropolitan Toronto. Long-cherished hopes and plans came to fruition on October 24, 1966, when *La Maison Française de Toronto* became a reality as a Centennial project.

In spite of the ideal of a unified focus of French cultural life in Toronto, it soon became evident that tensions were inherent in the very structure of MFT from the beginning. Four variations in cultural background and outlook were represented in the member associations: the European French who composed most of the 5.6% of francophones in Toronto born outside of Canada; the French Canadians, an overwhelming majority of the francophone population but divided by regional loyalties, linguistic variations and social class; the *Federation des Femmes*, the only working-class association within MFT; and the French-speaking Jews with their variations in religion and lifestyle.

Anglophones have a tendency to group all persons of French ancestry under the single category of "the French". But widely disparate regional and cultural differences in background and experience have so diversified the self-conceptions of francophones in Toronto that they do not see themselves merely as French, but as Québécois, Acadians, Franco-Ontarians, European French, Franco-Americans, and so on. The French language alone is not able to bridge these differences, and may, in the case of linguistic variations, intensify them. In an umbrella organization such as MFT this broad spectrum of regional identifications created barriers to social interaction which frustrated efforts to attain cultural solidarity.

The European French-speaking immigrant population in Toronto has used a different approach to the French language problem in an English milieu. To the French-Canadian they appear to have neglected means for maintaining the French language because they disparage the type of French spoken by French-Canadians and instead of sending their children to the Catholic bilingual schools prefer to send them to the English-speaking schools where, the French-Canadians claim, they are lost to the French-speaking community within a single generation. The French immigrants seem to have reconciled themselves to a transition to an English-language milieu as far as occupational life is concerned, but they have made vastly more use of voluntary associations, cultural and recreational programs, drama, music and the cinema in promoting French language and culture. In this sense the immigrant French have adopted a typical North American agency, the voluntary association, and adapted it to the goals and interests of their own culture.

The expansion of institutional structures such as the French-language schools, voluntary associations and a new parish has been a positive development in the direction of greater institutional completeness. But the contribution of such expansion needs to be qualified in two ways. It serves the small elite among the francophone middle class while contributing little to the rest of the French population. And secondly, when the expansion is viewed in the perspective of the present size of the French population of approximately 100 000, it is hardly commensurate with the rate of growth of that population. The vast majority of francophones still have no alternative but to participate in the institutional structures of the dominant society, a continuation of structural assimilation.

An "Invisibility" Theory

The situation in Toronto is not unique, nor does it present an anomaly among ethnic minorities in modern, pluralistic societies. Abner Cohen, in his *Two-Dimensional Man*, devotes an entire chapter to a discussion of "Invisible Minorities: Some Case Studies."[3] He recognizes that culture is not an independent system; consequently, ethnicity can be understood only when it is analyzed within the particular community context in which it exists, an emphasis on local circumstances. But in spite of such variability, Cohen maintains that there is a consistent structural pattern which is characteristic of "invisible ethnic minorities".[4]

The primary and basic element in the pattern is that members of the migrant minority are residentially dispersed among a heterogeneous urban population with consequent dilution of their cultural distinctiveness and erosion of their ethnic identity. Cohen claims that an ethnic identification is particularly difficult to maintain where the ethnic minority is formally recognized by the state, as in a federation such as Canada, where official status is ensured and guarded by legislation.[5] Members of such minorities may not even consider themselves part of an ethnic group when they have charter group status on the national scene.

In Toronto, the variety of cultural backgrounds within the francophone population has also introduced different conceptions of what cultural boundaries are. A Franco-Ontarian migrant to Toronto who grew up in a community either partially or almost wholly anglophone in character would have a more fluid conception of ethnic boundaries than a migrant from Quebec whose past years were spent in a francophone community with only nominal contact with anglophones. Since 57.6% of the francophones in Toronto were born in Ontario and only 36.6% in other provinces, including Quebec, and 5.6% outside Canada, the variations in the interpretations of cultural boundaries would make unlikely any degree of consensus among francophones. This divergence in the standards governing francophone behavior has tended to isolate language as the only common bond within the French population. And when its cohesive force weakens, as is evident in the low percentage of French spoken in the homes, a final defense against assimilation has been shattered. The residential isolation of francophones remains the critical dimension in boundary maintenance.

A second characteristic of "invisible ethnic minorities" is the weakness of ethnic associations in promoting the cultural survival or continuity of the minority because they are aimed, "not at the development of an exclusive ethnic polity, but, on the contrary, at promoting the successful adaptation of its members to modern urban condition." Cohen sees two reasons why migrants join such associations: temporarily "to get help to adjust to the new social milieu",[6] or because such associations represent "an informal interest grouping".[7] Ethnic groups in the contemporary world are less concerned with the perpetuation of traditional cultures than with the mobilizing of interests which will give them greater access to employment, education, and influence in the power structures at the local and national levels, a political role. The traditional symbols are there, giving the impression of conservatism, but are utilized in a different way,[8] to tie members of the group together in the pursuit of power, privilege and prestige within the host society.[9]

A third characteristic of an "invisible ethnic minority", according to Cohen, is the occupational diversification of the minority labor force to the extent that economic differentiation introduces class cleavages which cut across ethnic boundaries, weakening the distinctiveness of the ethnic culture.[10] The displacement of cultural values by the economic values prevalent in the host society has been a major stimulus for assimilation to the dominant host community. Continued residential dispersion, the slow development of institutional structures, the restriction of cultural activities to an elite among the middle class, and the continuing loss of French as mother tongue, all point indirectly to the preoccupation of francophones in Toronto with economic security rather than ethnic identity.

Conclusion

The major impact of the heterogeneity of the French population and the openness of the host English-speaking society has been to remove both internal and external pressures which would tend to confine social inter-action within ethnic boundaries. Participation outside of ethnic bounda-ries has taken the form of alternative identifications which have progres-sively oriented the members of the French minority towards acceptance of the dominant English-speaking culture. In this context, three alterna-tive identifications have loomed as particularly significant in relation to ethnic identity, namely religious, community, and class identifications.

A *religious* identification has replaced the traditional partnership of the French culture and the Roman Catholic Church. The affiliation of the majority of the French population with English parishes and schools has affected ethnic identity in two ways. The French migrants have discov-ered that religious duties may be performed and vows fulfilled satisfacto-rily in the English as well as the French language. The consequent divorce of religious worship and education from the French language and culture has severed the bond between French ethnic identity and the Catholic Church. This break in the traditional bond has made the role of the French parish and bilingual school as a focus for ethnic identity difficult if not impossible to fulfill.

A *community* identification has emerged as a result of the dispersed pattern of French settlement, reinforced by involvement in the Toronto work world. Some indications of the alternative communal identification are the loss of French as mother tongue; mixed marriages, especially with those of British stock; the predominance of memberships in English associations and of friendships with English Canadians; and the almost universal use of the English mass media.

A *class* identification, strongest among the middle class, has replaced an ethnic identification for two reasons. Socioeconomic differentiation has stratified the French population, and in so diversifying further an already culturally heterogeneous minority, has accentuated the differ-ences now dividing the French population. Conversely, within class strata the similarities of shared experience with the English-speaking population in employment, parish, education, residence, association and style of life have generated rapport and consensus across ethnic boundaries, creating a sense of class unity within a context of ethnic disunity.

These emergent religious, communal, and class identifications, seen as alternatives to an ethnic identification, reflect the impact of institutional participation as a basic condition for the formation and maintenance of group identity. A strong sense of ethnic identity is likely to be fostered only where primary social interaction among the French can be concentrated within ethnic boundaries. In Toronto, however, conditions of employment, residence and acceptance within the host community, together with the diversified character of the French migrant population, have promoted participation outside rather than within ethnic boundaries, with the resultant weakening of ethnic identity for a nominally French population.

ENDNOTES

1. Unless otherwise indicated, the statistics in this study are from the *Census of Canada*, Bulletins CT-15 and CT-21B, 1961 and 1971.
2. In 1961, francophones residing within the boundaries of the urban core area (which became the Metropolitan Corporation) numbered 54 806, while those in the fringe numbered 7 617, just 12.4% of the total. By 1971 the francophone population within the Corporation had increased 31.1% to 71 885, but the fringe had expanded 163.7% to 20 090, or 20.8% of the total.
3. Abner Cohen, *Two-Dimensional Man* (Berkeley: University of California Press, 1974), Ch. 6, pp. 91-98.
4. *Ibid.*, pp. 96, 91f.
5. *Ibid.*, pp. 92, 97.
6. *Ibid.*, p. 93.
7. *Ibid.*, p. 97.
8. *Ibid.*, p. 96.
9. N. Glazer and D. P. Moynihan, eds., *Ethnicity: Theory and Experience* (Cambridge, Mass.: Harvard University Press, 1975), p. 19. See also in this volume, Daniel Bell, "Ethnicity and Social Change," p. 169.
10. Cohen, *Two-Dimensional Man*, p. 94.

NANCIELLEN SEALY   Mount Allison University

Acadian Women: Economic Development, Ethnicity, and the Status of Women*

Contrary to popular opinion, women in modern industrialized societies do not necessarily have a higher status than those in egalitarian and/or pre-industrialized societies (Tomeh, 1975: 44-48),[1] and modernization in some Third World areas has been described as creating "modern [sexual] inequality, the devaluation of female labor, and economic dependence" (Bossen, 1975: 595). If this is so, the relation between development and the status of women in Canadian regions such as northeastern New Brunswick, where federal-provincial development programs have been extensive, may be problematic.

Status may be described in at least two ways—in terms of prestige and in terms of power; although, of course, the two are not mutually exclusive. "High status may be inferred from deferential treatment, or may consist of an actual position of power over basic resources and important decisions" (Brown, 1970: 152). Assessment of socioeconomic change in Saint-Simon[2], an Acadian village in northeastern New Brunswick, indicates that the power and prestige of local women have been eroded, and that development has contributed to this erosion. It is a truism that the effects of development may be unforeseen and even unfortunate, but that women may be especially vulnerable deserves explanation. What is the basis of women's vulnerability in developing areas, particularly in Saint-Simon and northeastern New Brunswick?

Women and Development

Recent contributions to the anthropology of women relate the status of women to a variety of socioeconomic factors. Sacks, in her reexamination of Engels' account of women's status, suggests the usefulness of distinguishing between women's status as social adults and as wives, each position being affected by different criteria. Sacks suggests that "basi-

* A revised version of a paper presented at the Conference on Women, Mount Saint Vincent University, Halifax, Nova Scotia, November, 1976. Sincere appreciation is expressed to Patrick L. Baker who made numerous valuable suggestions regarding this paper.

cally, women are social adults where they work collectively as part of a productive group larger than or separate from their domestic establishment," and their status as wives seems to depend on whether or not (family) estates are owned privately by males (1974: 218-19). Rosaldo similarly stresses implications for women's status arising from the restriction of females' activities to the domestic domain, as opposed to the public (economic and political) domain in which men are active (1974). These points are highly relevant in assessing contexts where sex roles related to work are undergoing modifications and are central to this discussion of the status of women in modernizing societies.

According to Bossen, modernization often brings "under-development" for women (1975: 595). This is particularly apparent in societies, like those in West Africa, where women traditionally held considerable economic power as traders. In this role, women controlled capital and displayed expertise in performing work which was recognized as valuable within the society. Today, women are progressively excluded from this occupation (Bossen, 1975: 593-94). Development strategies used in these situations have often been structured on Western models which stress specialization and hierarchical organization in which men have the most important roles.

Less striking, but perhaps more common, are the effects of modernization in societies where both men and women had traditionally contributed equally to the production of goods for the subsistence and maintenance of the household, or where women largely supported the household through their agricultural activities. In certain cases new means of production have been made available to males, although the productive activities themselves were those customarily allotted to women. Where the redefining of the activity as male rather than female has been accepted, men have gone on to gain control of a larger portion of production and thereby gradually lessened women's importance in such areas (Boserup, 1970: 53-64). Bossen is thus led to conclude that often in developing nations "modernization results in a smaller share for women in the total economy due to restrictions against their entry into many modern occupations and a devaluation of traditional subsistence activities." (1975: 595).[3]

These observations on development and the status of women in the Third World are relevant when we examine development strategies in nations like Canada where particular groups and regions are the focus of planned socioeconomic change. The importance of native groups' definitions of sex roles, and their reciprocal relationship to development strategies, is apparent. Less obvious questions involve development strategies and their relation to role systems of residents in economically depressed areas like the Maritime Provinces. In the Maritimes most persons are descendents of immigrant and charter groups and probably share many of the same assumptions regarding the sexual division of labor as do development agents. Nonetheless, questions remain, for this assessment of socioeconomic change in northeastern New Brunswick suggests that the industrialization of the traditional division of labor contributes to an erosion in women's status.

Village, Region and Development

The northeasternmost part of New Brunswick dips down and forms two islands, Lameque and Miscou. Lameque Island is about a mile from the mainland, to which it is connected by a bridge; the village of Saint-Simon is located on Lameque's eastern coast. Just north of Lameque is the smaller and less populated Miscou Island. These two islands and the narrow peninsular mainland south and west of Lameque make up Shippegan (civil) Parish.

Saint-Simon is similar to many northeastern New Brunswick villages in terms of the ethnic, demographic,[4] and economic features of its residents. Many area residents are descendents of Acadians who, on returning from the *grande dérangement* of the mid-1750s, settled along New Brunswick's northern and eastern coasts and riverways, the least accessible and agriculturally productive areas of the province, where anglophone settlers were few. Today New Brunswickers of French origin make up 37% of the province's population, but in Gloucester County (wherein Saint-Simon is located) francophones comprise 83% of the population. Like most other residents of Shippegan Parish, the 387 villagers of Saint-Simon are francophone, Roman Catholic, and descendents of Acadians.

Fishing and fish processing employ about 60% of the rural labor force in Shippegan Parish, and villagers of Saint-Simon rely very heavily on the fishery. Women represent about 90% of the workers in parish fish processing plants (or *usines*) which is practically the only source of employment available to local women.[5] In this area, fishing and fish processing are limited to the warmer months, and there is thus high unemployment from December through April, when residents must depend on unemployment insurance payments and social assistance. Area incomes are low; in 1961 the average family income in Shippegan Parish was about 37% of the average for Canada as a whole ($1 807:$4 906).[6]

Compounding the poverty of northeastern New Brunswick are serious problems in health and education. In order to tackle some of these issues, the federal and provincial governments, in the mid-1960s, approved the expenditure of $100 million for area development (Poetschke, 1971). School and highway construction have been relatively recent developments and longer range goals include the rationalization of the inshore fishery and the relocation of rural dwellers into approved urban centers. In general the strategies seem to have been aimed at economic growth, "a change in the volume of goods and services produced, [and] of purchasing power" (Belshaw, 1974: 521) of area residents.

These strategies were also implicitly aimed at increasing the complexity of social organization, that is, increasing the specialization and interdependence of roles and institutions. Thus, a rationalization of the inshore fishery entails decreasing the number of fishermen to prevent overfishing and to raise individual incomes of the remaining fishermen. But as an outcome of this strategy, men become dependent on other kinds of labor, especially that in local *usines*.[7] The human costs of such development are that men as wage laborers may experience alienation, either in terms of actual loss of control of economic livelihood, or in the felt loss of control and associated dissatisfaction in work.

Villagers dislike *usine* labor; it is described as boring and tiresome. Men say that they prefer fishing as they are their own bosses—free to come and go as they wish. With "development", this possibility of working for oneself and with those of one's household has diminished. In the Shippegan area, both men and women engage in wage labor at *usines*. So it is not men alone who experience the "benefits" of development.

Changing Economic Participation of Saint-Simon Women

Development programs in northeastern New Brunswick have accelerated processes of change similar to those occurring elsewhere in the world where traditional communities have been progressively modernized and industrialized. Traditionally villagers in Saint-Simon engaged in a combination of inshore fishing and farming. Farming was largely for subsistence purposes and fishing for the production of marketable goods. Fishermen exchanged their catches for supplies and equipment at company stores. Through the early decades of this century, cash realized from fishing seems to have been negligible for most households.

Prior to 1940, fish catches were salted and dried before sale, and much of this processing labor was performed by women.[8] Women daily spread and turned the fish drying on the stages, and, on the return of the boats each day, aided in cleaning and preparing the fish for preserving. Women were also responsible for a wide range of activities in the farm and home—caring for stock and garden, processing and preserving foodstuffs, making clothes and other household items. In short, women were active partners in the production of goods for consumption and sale. At the same time, of course, they often bore and cared for eight, ten or more children.

Around 1940 several fresh fish processing *usines* were founded in the area. Groundfish no longer had to be salted and dried prior to sale, but could be turned over directly to a *usine* representative. Coupled with the creation of the fresh fish processing industry was the increasing mechanization of the inshore fishery and the reemergence of an offshore fishing industry, both of which were stimulated by government funding. The fishing industry received a needed boost from the government at mid-century, and its effects were felt in the form of higher returns for fish sales and increased opportunity for men to purchase expensive boats and equipment, again made available via the provisions of the Fishermen's Loan Board and similar government agencies. Government monies were also provided for building and enlarging *usines*, thus further expanding the fishery and local job opportunities. These developments contributed to the decline and eventual demise of farming interests.[9]

The implications for women's roles have been several. The household no longer cooperates in pluralistic economic activities; some men have several occupations, but in few households do men and women jointly engage in economic enterprises. Women at home have become increasingly specialized; their work is largely restricted to the care of house and children. Some women still maintain vegetable gardens and preserve large quantities of foodstuffs; however, this is less characteristic of younger village women. Compared to their mothers and grandmothers, these younger women are "unemployed"; they produce few goods for household consumption or sale.

Village women denied the traditional role of co-producer may become dependent on their husbands or seek wage labor, usually in *usines*. Such employment is taken during periods when responsibilities for children are lightest—before the woman marries and has children or after her children are of school age. Most women yearly earn only a few thousand dollars through wages and unemployment insurance payments; however, this makes considerable difference in households where the man's income is also low.[10]

Development and the Erosion of Women's Status

Local women's increasing participation in the labor force might suggest that change and development have benefited them. Nearly three and a half times as many women in Gloucester County reported income in 1971 as in 1961 (11 225:3 314), and this compares favorably with the increase of slightly more than two times as many men receiving income in 1971 as in 1961 (20 665:9 580). The lifestyle in Saint-Simon has improved; most households have televisions, many others have major appliances such as refrigerators, deep freezers, stoves and even dishwashers. A few village fishermen have prospered in the offshore fishery, and one such villager has recently purchased a quarter-million dollar fishing vessel. In what ways may women's position be described as eroded?

Ethnicity and Women's Status

The traditional status of Acadian women is closely related to elements of class, age, and a complex of cultural traits which may be equated with ethnicity. As socioeconomic change and development affect these elements, so do they affect the status of local women.

Basic components of Acadian ethnicity are the French language, Roman Catholicism, and a sense of common regional and historical origins. The significance of these components varies according to historical and sociocultural context. Religious influence within schools constituted a conflict issue between Acadians and their non-Catholic neighbors in the 19th century. In this century language has supplanted religion as a contentious issue, but differences in demography, settlement pattern, and historical inter-ethnic group relations influence actual language-based conflict in provincial regions (Sealy, 1977; 1978). All Saint-Simon residents are Acadian, and so the intravillage structuring of interaction is not based on ethnic identity. However, ethnicity does color local life and women's status. This becomes apparent by comparing household and community roles of Saint-Simon women with those of women in Cat Harbour, an Anglo-Canadian outport in Newfoundland.[11]

The roles women play in Saint-Simon and the ecclessiastical parish are those in which household or domestic specializations involving children, education, and religion are conducted at a community level. In general, if a Saint-Simon woman fills the appropriate role within household and community—as responsible wife and mother, as member interested in the running of parish and school—she is accorded a measure of respect that seems absent for women in Newfoundland outports like Cat Harbour (Faris, 1966). In Cat Harbour, life is decidedly "male dominated" with women having little authority within household and community; they are little compensated for their hard work, and instead are the first to be suspected of being "witches" or "jinkers". Female characteristics have negative connotations there, and things that are negatively perceived, such as potentially leaky boats, are symbolically identified as being female (Faris, 1966: 95-99).

Although life in Cat Harbour and Saint-Simon is similar in ways related to the residents' techno-economic adaptations, other sociocultural factors differ and contribute to a more elevated position for women in Saint-Simon, as reflected in deferential treatment of women, the symbolic and public honor accorded to women as mothers and wives, and the representation by women on parish committees. Contributing to this higher status in Saint-Simon are religious affiliation and marriage and residence patterns, factors which are based in, or related to, the ethnic origins of villagers.

The Cat Harbour residents are anglophone and Protestant, either United Church of Canada or Jehovah's Witnesses, and neither seems to supply underlying positive evaluation of women in Cat Harbour (Faris, 1966: 164-73). In comparison, in the parish Catholic church, Saint-Simon residents are regularly exposed to sermons and celebrations honoring the Mother of God, motherhood, and women's role in local domestic life.

Marriage and residence patterns also affect the status of women in the two fishing villages. In Cat Harbour residence tends to be virilocal; about 65% of the wives are outsiders (Faris, 1966: 95) and fall in the category of "strangers" whom native residents of Cat Harbour generally suspect and mistrust. In Saint-Simon, on the other hand, choice of marriage partners is made largely from within the ecclessiastical parish and/or village. Although outsiders are negatively perceived in both Saint-Simon and Cat Harbour, most women in Saint-Simon are not outsiders and, hence, are not negatively perceived for that reason.

Although Saint-Simon women have a higher status than do women in Cat Harbour, they do not have the highest positions in the community and household. Nuns serve various functions in the church and local schools, but in these cases it is the priest who has the primary respect and authority. Though women are elected to serve on various administrative bodies in the parish, a man is traditionally chosen to be the president or the chairman of that body. Thus, deferential treatment is not equivalent to the possession of power, and women's roles remain subordinate to those of men.

In Saint-Simon and in Acadian communities in Nova Scotia (Hughes, et al., 1960: 126-28; 148-49) women are highly valued for their domestic or familial role, which is complementary to, and not necessarily less prestigious than, that of men. As discussed above, the evaluation of women as important household workers has a strong historical basis in fact—women traditionally made a large contribution to subsistence and market economies. However, both domestic-familial and economic bases of prestige have been undermined with socioeconomic change. Today local women are increasingly involved in wage labor, and the effect of this on their highly esteemed traditional role is not clear. It seems that as women increasingly participate in wage labor, such work comes to be expected of them, at least at certain stages of their life cycle, and within the village the ideal role of women may be in the process of redefinition. Working women are alternately praised or criticized, and they themselves are ambivalent about their employment.

Related to this increase in the proportion of working women is a reduction in the average size of families in the village. Fewer children are due to a variety of reasons, including the reliance today on wage labor as opposed to subsistence activities (in which children were productive and useful members) and the local church's diminished role in encouraging large families. Village women married prior to 1940 had approximately twice as many children as their daughters (an average of 10 live births per woman as compared to a projected 5 or 6 live births per woman married between 1960 and 1970). Although rearing four to six children is a considerable task, it is obviously less than that of older women who are highly praised for their work, sacrifice, and devotion to their large families. As domestic roles alter in response to societal change and development, the ideal role will either alter, or the younger women may have to choose on the one hand to elaborate their actual housewife-mother role so that they are as busy and as valued as earlier village women, or on the other hand to receive less prestige than their predecessors.

Age and Women's Status

Age is related to the control of power, and in Saint-Simon middle-aged and young adults run community affairs. Older persons maintain households as long as their health allows, but their last years are often spent in children's households or in the nearby senior citizens' home. In the former case, social changes have modified their role in these households from the traditional norm. For example, reduced family size has curtailed the importance of grandparents as babysitters and thereby reduced their overall influence in the home. Thus, the elders return to the relatively powerless position of their youth and childhood.

Saint-Simon women of different generations vary in their educational and work experiences. Development includes increasing specialization of labor and demands skills and training which older women usually do not possess. Thus, development creates restrictions on older women seeking work and limits their access to positions of decision-making and control over resources.

Social Class and Women's Status

"The most important feature of class is the asymmetrical distribution of power" (Harris, 1975: 396). This asymmetry is reflected in ideology, relationships, and material goods, and one indicator of the latter is income. Northeastern New Brunswick has experienced economic growth; more people are working and for higher wages, and more goods are

TABLE 1 *Average income by sex*

	1961		1971	
	M	F	M	F
Rural non-farm				
Gloucester County	$1 584	$ 908	$3 509	$1 769
New Brunswick	2 807	1 569	5 042	2 282
Canada	3 679	1 995	6 538	2 883

Source: Census of Canada 1961, 1971.

being purchased than ten years ago. However, area incomes still lag behind those of Canadians elsewhere, and women lag behind men, with the size of the income gap between men and women increasing. The data for the 1961-71 period is shown in Table 1.

When 1961 and 1971 incomes in rural, non-farm Gloucester County are compared, it is evident from Table 1 that the average income of men in 1971 is 2.2 times greater than their 1961 income, and the income of women in 1971 is 1.9 times greater than their income in 1961. However, when this increase for both sexes in the county is placed in perspective with the average income in the province and county, it is found that in 1961 the average incomes of men and women in rural, non-farm Gloucester county represented 56 and 58% of those of men and women in New Brunswick, and 43 and 46% of those of men and women in Canada. In 1971 comparable incomes were 70 and 78% of those of men and women in the province, and 54 and 61% of those of men and women in Canada. (See Table 1.) In New Brunswick as a whole, women in 1961 earned slightly more than half (56%) of that of men, and in 1971 the gap had increased such that women earned less than half (45%) of that of men.

Between 1961 and 1971 the consumer price index increased by one third.[12] Villagers' "style of consumption" has altered (Runciman, 1969: 48), but the prosperity of households reflects combined incomes, which are individually low, and government transfer payments. Although some villagers enjoy material possessions like those of many Canadians elsewhere, they do so at a much greater cost.

In spite of development programs, the relative position of area residents has not altered, and the position of women has actually deteriorated; average incomes of women in rural (non-farm) Gloucester County has declined in the ten-year period from 58 to 50% of the income of men. Furthermore, in 1971 in Gloucester County, over seven times as many men as women earned $7 000 or more; in rural Gloucester County nearly eight times as many men as women earned $7 000 or more. More women are working today than in 1961, but their earnings continue to compare unfavorably with those of men.

Development programs have been aimed at stimulating growth in traditionally defined male activities, namely fishing. Today both capital and expertise are controlled by men, but this was not always the case. Traditionally, there was minimal capital to be controlled by men and women, and men were not the exclusive holders of skills and knowledge in economic enterprises. If class differences are defined in terms of differential access to power, basic resources, and decision-making (Harris, 1975: 396-97), then development programs have undermined the class position of women.[13] Thus, a hidden cost of development in the region appears to be a widening differential in the socioeconomic position of the sexes.

Implications

The socioeconomic changes in Saint-Simon and the region represent a microcosm of the changes occurring elsewhere in North America as rural communities have been progressively incorporated into a larger, industrial and market-oriented society. A similar pattern occurs in the Third World where western social and economic models of progress have been continuously imposed. Contrary to what might be expected, such change has often been associated with the erosion in the status of women in both domestic and public contexts.

In northeastern New Brunswick women have an increased opportunity to obtain wage labor in *usines*. However, women's participation in the labor force does not reflect an improved status in comparison to that previously held by them or that held by today's men; it indicates the contrary. Development programs in this region are aimed at improving and expanding regional industry, particularly the fishery in which males hold the most powerful and prestigious positions. Employment in the *usines* is little valued by men or women.

Socioeconomic change and development also affect the basis and maintenance of ethnicity in previously distinct groups, and this may partially occur through women. Acadian women have been considered the repository of traditional values and the conveyors of values to children (Hughes, et al., 1960: 128). Women were a source of stability and continuity in the ethnic group and specifically in Saint Simon. Although men left Saint-Simon to work elsewhere in the province or in the offshore fishery, women had little experience beyond the village. As one measure of that isolation, no older village women are bilingual in French and English, while several men of that generation are.

Although Saint-Simon was never isolated from the outside world, the village women experienced a degree of isolation and probably represented a conservative force locally. However, as a result of development, some women, like men, now work beyond the village and island. Women have become the conveyors of extra-village influences, some of which weaken cultural features traditionally distinguishing Acadians from others. This does not imply that Acadians will lose their ethnic identity, but only that their ethnicity may be redefined according to existing sociocultural conditions (Barth, 1969). However, if features associated with ethnicity provide the rationale for the sexual division of labor and for the allocation of power and prestige to women and men, change in these features may alter or even undermine the traditional status of women. In the absence of real opportunities for advancement in the developing society, women may be denied both traditional and modern bases for obtaining high status.

Development programs may have an extra cost for certain individuals and groups, and in northeastern New Brunswick those extra costs have been borne especially by the women. Furthermore, it appears that development strategies may help maintain, rather than eradicate, social inequalities and the exploitation of disadvantaged groups, as indicated within this one Canadian region.

ENDNOTES

1. For an example of a pre-industrial society in which women held positions of considerable power and influence, see Brown's (1970) discussion of women among the Iroquois.
2. Fieldwork took place for seven months in 1971 and 1972. "Saint-Simon" is a pseudonym.
3. See also, Human Resources Development Division 1975; Tinker, et al., 1976; Wellesley Editorial Committee, 1977.
4. Northeastern New Brunswick is predominantly rural and is characterized by high out-migration of working age adults, high birth rates, and concomitantly, a population in which a great number are economically non-productive young people; 60% of the population in northeastern New Brunswick (defined as Gloucester County, Restigouche County, and Alnick Parish of Northumberland County) is less than 25 years of age (Even, 1970: 76-109 passim). In Saint-Simon 62% of the population is less than 25, and 5% is 65 years of age or more; hence, only a third of the villagers are active adults, a proportion similar to that of active adults for the area as a whole.
5. See Community Improvement Corporation Planning Department 1968.
6. In 1971 the average family income in Shippegan Parish had risen to 51% of the average for Canada as a whole ($4 913; $9 600).
7. Some fishermen resist specialization; they fish twelve weeks, and then work in *usines* for another two to three months, depending on job opportunities.
8. Inshore fishermen in recent decades have fished lobster, groundfish, and herring; today lobster fishing provides their main source of income.
9. Much of northeastern New Brunswick does not constitute good farmland, and at mid-century the area as a whole began a decline in farming activity. Villagers in Saint-Simon considered that the decline and absence of local

farming today was due to its being no longer financially advantageous.

10. Most households receive various types of transfer payments from the government, such as child and youth allowance, unemployment insurance payments, and pensions.

11. It is preferable to compare Saint-Simon women with women of an anglophone Protestant fishing community in New Brunswick; however, appropriate studies of such communities are not available. Newfoundland outports like Cat Harbour differ from Saint-Simon in ways other than their residents' ethnicity. As a result of historical, demographic, and geographical factors, the Newfoundland outports have remained more isolated and have maintained a more traditional, near peasant way of life than have New Brunswick's Acadian fishing villages. Faris' study of Cat Harbour is a "classic" in the anthropological literature on Atlantic Canada and provides a rich description against which comparisons can be drawn.

12. *Canada Yearbook 1973*, p. 842.

13. Sex stratification entails at least two dimensions. Housewives derive a status from that of their husbands, and employed women derive a status from their employment. It is this latter dimension to which my comments are related. For a discussion of women as minority group, caste, and class, see Eichler, 1973.

SELECTED REFERENCES

Barth, Fredrik, ed. *Ethnic Groups and Boundaries*. Boston: Little, Brown and Company, 1969, pp. 9-38.

Belshaw, Cyril S. "The Contribution of Anthropology to Development." *Current Anthropology* 15:4 (1974), pp. 520-26.

Boserup, Ester. *Woman's Role in Economic Development*. London: Allen and Unwin, 1970.

Bossen, Laurel. "Women in Modernizing Societies." *American Ethnologist* 2:4 (1975), pp. 587-601.

Brown, Judith K. "Economic Organization and the Position of Women Among the Iroquois," *Ethno-history* 17 (1970), pp. 151-67.

Canada Year Book 1973. Ottawa: Statistics Canada, 1973.

Census of Canada 1961, 1971. Ottawa: Statistics Canada, 1961 and 1971.

Northeast New Brunswick, Outline Community Plans: Shippegan. Fredericton, N.B.: Community Improvement Corp. Planning Department, 1968.

Eichler, Margrit. "Women as Personal Dependents," in Marylee Stephenson, ed., *Women in Canada*. Toronto: New Press, 1973, pp. 38-55.

Even, Alain. "Le Territoire Pilote du Nouveau-Brunswick ou les blocages culturels au développement économique." Thèse pour le doctorat en économie du développement, Rennes, 1970.

Faris, James C. "Cat Harbour: a Newfoundland Fishing Settlement." *Newfoundland Social and Economic Studies No. 3*. St. John's, Newfoundland: Institute of Social and Economic Research, Memorial University of Newfoundland, 1966.

Harris, Marvin. *Culture, People, Nature*. New York: Thomas Y. Crowell Inc., 1975.

Hughes, Charles C., et al. *People of Cove and Woodlot*. New York: Basic Books, Inc., 1960.

Poetschke, L. E. "Regional Planning for Depressed Rural Areas—The Canadian Experience," in John Harp and John R. Hofley, eds., *Poverty in Canada*. Scarborough, Ont.: Prentice-Hall of Canada, Ltd., 1971.

Rosaldo, Michelle Z. "Women, Culture and Society: A Theoretical Overview," in Michelle Zimbalist Rosaldo and Louise Lamphere, eds., *Women, Culture, and Society*. Palo Alto, California: Stanford University Press, 1974.

Runciman, W. G. "The Three Dimensions of Social Inequality," in Andre Beteille, ed., *Social Inequality*. England: Penguin Education, 1969, pp. 45-63.

Sacks, Karen. "Engels Revisited: Women, the Organization of Production, and Private Property," in Michelle Zimbalist Rosaldo and Louise Lamphere, eds., *Women, Culture, and Society*. Palo Alto, California: Stanford University Press, 1974, pp. 207-22.

Sealy, Nanciellen. "Diverses perspectives dans l'étude de la survivance du groupe ethnique acadien." *Les cahiers* 8:2 (1977), pp. 53-64.

_____. "Language Conflict and Schools in New Brunswick," in Martin L. Kovac, ed., *Ethnic Canadians: Culture and Education*. Regina, Sask.: Canadian Plains Research Centre, University of Regina, 1978.

Tinker, Irene, et al., eds. *Women and World Development*. New York: Praeger Publishers, 1976.

Tomeh, Aida K. *The Family and Sex Roles*. Toronto: Holt, Rinehart and Winston of Canada, Ltd., 1975.

Women and National Development in African Countries: Some Profound Contradictions. Human Resources Development Division of the African Training and Research Centre for Women, United Nations Economic Commission for Africa, *The African Review* XVIII:3 (1975), pp. 47-70.

Women and National Development, The Complexities of Change. Wellesley Editorial Committee, *Signs* 3:1 (1977).

CORNELIUS J. JAENEN   University of Ottawa

French Roots in the Prairies*

Three Phases in French Canadian History Prior to the Present Era

Bilingual and Bicultural Communities (Circa 1768-1890)

"Thirty years ago, we who speak French were called by everyone purely and simply 'Canadien.' Others were known as English, Scotch or Irish. Lately the fashion has grown up of calling others Canadians and distinguishing us as French."

Father Lewis Drummond, 1886[1]

In the first phase of Prairie ethnic history, Manitoba and the section of the Northwest Territories, which eventually became Alberta and Saskatchewan, were bilingual and bicultural communities. Their francophone and anglophone communities were balanced (with a slight French preponderance) in demographic, institutional, and constitutional terms. This is an aspect of our history which is often ignored. It may explain as much about the present as it tells us about the past.

Multiculturalism (Circa 1890-1917)

In phase 2, the Prairies received a large influx of Eastern Canadian migrants (mostly from Western Ontario) and continental European immigrants. This radically altered the demographic base, gave rise to demands for institutional changes and even constitutional changes, and resulted in a flirtation in the school system with cultural pluralism and multilingualism. From 1897 to 1916, Manitoba had a public school system which permitted instruction in English and any other language on the bilingual pattern. This system also gave rise to a number of non-English teacher

---

* A revised version of two papers, "The Manitoba School Question: an Ethnic Interpretation," *Proceedings of the National Conference on Ethnic Studies and Research*, Regina, October, 1976; and "Prairie Schooling and Bilingualism," *Proceedings of the 12th Annual Convention of the Canadian Association for the Social Studies*, Regina, October, 1976. Reprinted with permission of author and publishers.

training schools, to ethnic teachers' associations, school trustees' organizations, and others. In Saskatchewan this phase was marked by two distinct, but not altogether unrelated, school issues: the emotional separate school debates starting in 1905 and the bitter bilingual instruction debates which took on national proportions in 1917.

Anglo-Celtic Dominance (Circa 1917-1962)

The Anglo-Celtic dominant society asserted itself in phase 3 through such institutions as the centralized provincial school systems, civic indoctrination, and cultural reorientation so as to assimilate immigrant groups and homogenize the community according to its Anglo-conformist ideology. This is related historically to the anti-alien feeling of the First World War, the war hysteria and the postwar reactionary politics. It was a difficult time for the minorities in Canada—ethnic, cultural, religious, occupational. It was the period in Prairie educational history when the task of the rural country school, staffed by zealous, young Anglo-Saxon teachers, was to assimilate what was thought to be "the hordes of foreigners' children", while "keeping the French-Canadians in their place", with the effect that the position of the Anglo-Celtic dominant sector was consolidated.

Phase 1: French/English Dualism

Each phase is marked perhaps more by its passing than by any single event in its short duration. Principal Robert Falconer of the University of Toronto saw the first phase, a transplantation of Eastern Canadian society, as a perpetuation in the West of the dualism which had characterized Central Canada and produced Confederation. He wrote:

> Older Canada sent out her sons to possess new lands, and these first settlers belonging to the stronger races from which the older portions of Canada were colonized established the type of new life. Older political, social and religious ideals are so essentially inherent in the character, that, like hardy seeds wafted by ocean current to distant shores, they reproduce in the new environment fruit similar in quality to that which was found in their former home.[2]

Unfortunately, the old prejudices, dissensions and factionalism of the East were transferred along with the better qualities to the new seedbed of Western Canada where they took good root and flourished.

The Manitoba School Question marked the end of the first phase. It can be regarded, apart from the religious argument of the feasibility of confessional streaming within a public system, as marking the end of practical dualism (biculturalism) in the West. It had not been possible to maintain the dominant dualism through either migration or immigration. The francophone community was the first to lose its position, until by 1891 it was a small minority. There were unsuccessful efforts to attract Quebec settlers, to repatriate Franco-Americans and to induce francophone Europeans to help maintain parity with the Anglo-Celtic community and so keep alive the bilingual and bicultural community which the federal Conservatives had enshrined in the Manitoba Act of 1870 and which the federal Liberals had enshrined in the North-West Territories Act of 1875.

The Catholic schools were not taught exclusively in French because there was a recognition on the part of the clergy that immigration, and especially migration from Eastern Canada, was altering the demographic balance, which had existed in Manitoba at the time of Union, in favor of Anglo-Celtic peoples and Protestants.[3] As early as 1877, *Le Métis* sounded the alarm, calling on all francophones to unite "to resist tyranny and to defend liberty of conscience and the rights of the minority on the school question, as well as on all other questions".[4] There was no hostility to English settlement *per se*, only fear that the bicultural character of the West would be undermined. In that same year (1877), Father Lacombe, in correspondence with Bishop Taché concerning the colonization of the West by francophones, deplored the difficulty in obtaining bilingual teachers for Catholic schools. He went to Europe to recruit because Quebec was a very unfruitful source of bilingual teachers. In 1883, thanks in good measure to Lacombe's efforts, a French (Breton) order of teaching sisters which operated schools in England sent five bilingual teachers to Brandon, five to Prince Albert and four to the Métis settlement of St. Laurent. In rural homogeneously French settlements such as Ste. Anne or St. Pierre, Taché could continue to send unilingual teachers.[5]

As criticism of the dual confessional school system grew, in large measure because the system no longer comfortably fitted the sociocultural contours, there developed an ethnic tension. Superintendent T. A. Bernier of the Catholic public schools in Manitoba warned in his annual report for 1886 that immigration was threatening dualism and therefore francophones would have to mount an "eternal vigilance".[6] Electioneering politicians sometimes called for the abolition of the official use of French. One widely circulated pamphlet of 1887 called for the exclusion of French "from our legislature, from our courts, from our statutes, and from our public schools".[7] The francophone community, at least its clerical leaders, seemed to place faith in the alleged visit of Messrs. Alloway and Greenway to the Archiepiscopal palace in St. Boniface in 1888 to deliver a Liberal pledge to Rev. Father Joachim Allard, Vicar General, that the official status of French and the dual school system were not in danger.[8]

There would develop the hypothesis that the federal and provincial Liberals—Mowat, Laurier, Greenway—deliberately provoked the Manitoba School Question in 1890 in order to break the basis of Conservative power, i.e., the alliance between tolerant Ontario Toryism and the conservative Quebec Bleus. According to this conspiracy thesis, which Rev. Father Gonthier expounded in a letter to *abbé* Lindsay, and which was sent to the Vatican Secretary of State on the occasion of Prime Minister Laurier's visit to Rome in August 1897, the Manitoba Liberals undertook to restore or retain the rights of French instruction under a centralized non-sectarian school system.[9]

The arrival of the Mennonites and the Icelanders in the 1870s had given rise to the assumption that these ethnic bloc settlements would eventually have their schools incorporated into the Protestant/English school system. There was little in the austere pietistic religion of the Mennonites or the Lutheranism of the Icelanders to indicate any affinity with the Catholic brand of public schooling. Furthermore, many of the Ontario migrants to Manitoba, adherents for the most part of the Methodist or Presbyterian churches, spearheaded fundamental changes in the Manitoba constitution: the abolition of the Legislative Council; changes in the system of representation, substitution of the municipal for the parish system of local government; and abrogation of the status of French in the provincial courts, legislature and official records. These changes altered the bicultural basis of Manitoba and moved it away from the Quebec model to the Ontario model.

The Icelandic immigration which began in 1875 was marked by a strong attachment to public schooling and a steadfast determination to learn English and to become assimilated. This was all the more remarkable because they had founded their ethnic reserve, New Iceland, on the west shore of Lake Winnipeg in the territory of Keewatin just north of the Manitoba provincial boundary.[10] Swedes and Russian Jews also trickled into the province, but they did not acquire reserves of land and they, like the Icelanders, did not attempt to establish their own school system. In other words, in 1890 there were immigrant groups which did not challenge the model of Anglo-conformity or the institution of common non-sectarian public schools.

It is significant that when Manitoba passed an act creating a centralized Department of Education, to replace the dual confessional Board of Education, and an act to abolish Catholic public schools, much of the rhetoric revolved around the concept of "national" schools. It was not only the French, but also Mennonites, Icelanders, Germans, Poles, Swedes and Jews who had to be channelled into the assimilating experiences of the public school, somewhat on the model of the American public school. Archbishops Taché and Langevin responded to the abolition of the dual confessional system by opening "free schools" (*écoles libres*) in opposition to "national schools" in areas of heterogeneous settlement and by encouraging taxpayers, trustees and teachers to retain the essential religious and ethnic qualities in areas of homogeneous settlement. The school legislation was still silent on the matter of language(s) of instruction so that French could be employed with equal justification in the public school system and in the private or parochial schools.

Although francophone colonizing agents, especially the colonizing clergy, redoubled their efforts to find suitable teachers as well as settlers, Langevin's resistance movement against the legislation of 1890 ran into problems. Firstly, the Manitoba government brought down further legislation in 1894 requiring that any school not operating according to the Act would not be called a Public School and therefore would not qualify for the legislative grant. Municipalities could no longer grant money to, or levy and collect taxes for the support of, schools operating as francophone *écoles libres* or Mennonite church schools. Secondly, the European immigrants did not always see eye to eye with their French-Canadian coreligionists on matters of public schooling; they often required what Dom Benoit of Notre-Dame de Lourdes called "re-educating".[11] Thirdly, many teaching orders in Quebec and continental Europe which were approached with a view to staffing schools in Manitoba and the Northwest Territories showed little interest in the Canadian West. The immediate result was that a number of schools in francophone districts—e.g., St. Claude, St. Alphonse, St. Eustache—decided to come under the public school umbrella. Finally, although most Mennonite elders had as strong objections to the school legislation as had Archbishop Langevin, they failed to form a common front with the francophone Catholics against the "godless schools".

Soon after becoming Prime Minister in 1896, Laurier expressed his pessimism about restoring the francophone dominant role in the West:

> ... for my part I have never had ... a great confidence that we could ever have many immigrants from France. The French people do not emigrate, but remain at home. If it were possible to have from France an immigration, not from towns and cities, but from the rural portions of the country, we would certainly have a most valuable class of settlers. I think, however, that a good deal more is to be had from the British Isles themselves.[12]

As continental Europeans began to respond to the Sifton immigration policy, some Canadians expressed the fear that the Anglo-Celtic group might share the fate of its French founding partner in the West. In 1899, W. F. McCreary, the Commissioner of Immigration at Winnipeg (to cite but one example), informed Clifford Sifton that there was a prevalent feeling in the West that the "charter groups" were being neglected in the immigration efforts. McCreary warned the minister:

There is a cry, unfortunately, very prevalent throughout this Province and the West generally, not only among our enemies but among our friends, that the Government are doing more for the Doukhobors and the Galicians than they are for either French or English settlers—and even our papers here do not put this matter in the correct light.[13]

The defeat of the federal Conservative government in 1896 and the assumption of power by the Laurier Liberals made possible the famous Laurier-Greenway Compromise (more accurately it was a Tarte-Sifton agreement) which was announced on November 19, 1896 and which was incorporated into the new school Act of 1897. Clause 10 of the agreement read: "Where ten of the pupils in any school speak the French language (or any language other than English) as their native tongue, the teaching of such pupils shall be conducted in French (or such other language) and English upon the bi-lingual system".[14]

For the first time, Manitoba legislation laid down specific provisions for language(s) of instruction. Although each school district could have only a single bilingual character (e.g., English-German, English-Ruthenian), the province could have an unspecified number of bilingual systems according to the ethnic communities which petitioned the authorities. The legislation invited the development of inspection services, teacher training programs, curricula, centralized examinations and authorized textbooks for each of these bilingual fragments. The Icelanders openly favored the English public schools, but the "French" (Canadiens), "Germans" (mostly Mennonites) and "Ruthenians" (Ukrainians) organized their own teachers' associations and conventions and their own school trustees' associations and conventions.

The Compromise of 1897 could be interpreted as a shift in emphasis from religion to ethnicity. The *Manitoba Free Press* was later to publish the following explanation of this bilingual provision:

In order to avoid exciting anti-French prejudices in Ontario and elsewhere, the concession as to bilingual teaching was not limited to the French, but was made general to all non-English residents in the Province of Manitoba in the expectation that it would be taken advantage of only by the French and by them in a limited degree and by a few and diminishing number of Mennonite communities.[15]

The Catholic hierarchy, at least its ultramontane bishops, had not been a party to this compromise. On the contrary, the negotiations carried on with Manitoba Liberal officials by Israel Tarte and Henri Bourassa did not satisfy Archbishop Langevin, largely because he was excluded from their confidence. Langevin attacked the language clause which placed Franco-Manitobans "on the same basis as the coming hordes of the future that Sifton saw". In a sermon delivered in his cathedral church, he protested:

...we who came as the pioneers into the country, who discovered it, have not more than the last arrivals, we whose rights are guaranteed by the constitution, are placed on the same footing as those who came from Ireland or the depths of Russia, we are not better apportioned than the Chinese and the Japanese.[16]

Henceforth, bilingualism would mean English and any second language and would not be restricted to French-English dualism that historically had preceded the flow of foreign immigration.

But this did not necessarily work to the disadvantage of the francophone communities. Whereas in 1896 there had been only 25 French schools in the public system, by 1900 there were 84 schools under the jurisdiction of Robert Goulet, inspector of French-English schools. Two years later, there were 105 such schools and only six *écoles libres* in Manitoba. In the provincial election of 1899 the Conservatives called for the defeat of the Greenway government and the *règlement défectueux*, i.e., a "defective, imperfect, insufficient" remedy as Leo XIII's encyclical *Affari Vos* called it.[17] But the Liberals argued that a vote for them was a vote for the certainty of preserving their present concessions and the hope of obtaining further ones. The provincial trend was for the Conservatives, but the three predominantly French-Canadian constituencies of St. Boniface, La Vérendrye and Carillon all returned Liberal members.

The French-English bilingual schools continued to experience problems in finding qualified teachers as those who were eager to leave France, because they viewed the secularization of education there as persecution, knew no English, and Quebec teachers seemed increasingly unwilling to learn English or come West. Moreover, the bilingual teachers in the system were not always fully qualified and it became increasingly difficult to obtain provisional authorizations or to dissimulate their true professional status. In 1902, for example, one third of the teachers in the French-English bilingual schools had no diplomas. Moreover, Archbishop Langevin acknowledged in 1908 that he sometimes had to employ threats to convince parents and trustees in francophone districts to maintain French instruction.[18]

In the Northwest Territories the only concession to the immigrant ethnic communities was what remained of the language of instruction clause which the French Canadian charter group had enjoyed. When Manitoba set up what were virtually French, German, Ukrainian and Polish teacher training institutes or normal schools, Saskatchewan followed cautiously with a Training School for Teachers for Foreign-speaking Communities in Regina, and Alberta with an English School for Foreigners at Vegreville. It appears that the farther one went West the greater was the insistence that Canada was British and English-speaking. Manitoba called her school for Ukrainians a Ruthenian Training School, Saskatchewan said hers was for Teachers for Foreign-speaking Communities, while Alberta insisted hers was an English School for Foreigners!

Phase 2: Multiculturalism

In this second phase—a virtual first experiment with multiculturalism—there was misunderstanding as to the goals or purpose of the school legislation and practice. At the inauguration of the new provinces of Alberta and Saskatchewan in 1905, Sir Wilfrid Laurier gave the immigrants his ideal for their integration into the host society:

> Let me say to one and all of our new fellow-countrymen...Let them be Britain's subjects...We do not anticipate, and we do not want, that any individuals should forget the land of their origin, the land of their ancestors... Let them become Canadians, British subjects, and give their heart and soul, their energy, their vows to Canada, to its institutions, to its king, who like his illustrious mother, is a model constitutional Sovereign...[19]

What the provincial bureaucrats expected from the bilingual system was ethnic social disintegration and assimilation, not cultural transmission of group values and ethnic perpetuation. The arrival of the first wave of Ukrainian and Polish immigrants in 1897, ostensibly to engage in farming but forced by circumstances to turn also to the railways, mines and lumber camps, gave the bilingual system a new dimension. Those who settled in rural Manitoba, east of the Red River in marginal farm lands, in the Interlake country, and in the parkland belt west from Clan William along the south of the Riding Mountains and around Dauphin could be expected to make some demand for bilingual schools. The parents, although largely of peasant origins, gave the impression of being sufficiently motivated to realize the benefits of schooling for their children. A typical inspectoral report read: "The large number of Galicians who have lately settled in the vicinity of Stuartburn has increased the school population of this district to a considerable extent. The children are bright, intelligent and most anxious to acquire a knowledge of the English language. They are well-behaved in school and easily managed".[20] As the Ukrainians became aware of the possibility of organizing bilingual schools they naturally favored these. The provincial authorities were faced with the immediate problem of finding qualified teachers to staff such schools, also with the long-range problem of ascertaining the results of an expansion of the bilingual system to encompass an undetermined number of ethnic groups.

However much Archbishop Langevin had deplored the granting of equal school rights to all ethnic minorities, he very soon rallied to the concept and sought to exploit it to Catholic advantage. He obtained from Premier R. Roblin in 1901 a promise for support of Ukrainian, Polish and German schools.[21] In public addresses he strongly defended the teaching of the mother tongues of the immigrant communities, telling Catholic audiences in particular that in preserving the Ukrainian, Polish and German tongues the faith was being preserved.

Schools must be established among them in which the English language will be taught according to the requirements of the law, but since the law concedes bilingual instruction, that is to say instruction of another tongue besides English for those who do not speak the latter, these strangers have the right to have their children taught in their own language, and that is their most ardent wish. But if all admit that English must be taught in Manitoba schools, not all are also of the opinion that one must teach also the mother tongue of the Galicians; a few even have proclaimed very loudly that it would be better to teach only English everywhere! An exhorbitant, unjust and dangerous pretention which endangers the peace of our country.[22]

This was an extension of the traditional French-Canadian ultramontane ideology of the inseparable relationship between language and religion.

Similarly, the Anglo-Celtic Protestants were not unaware of the advantages to be gained through support to the ethnic minorities. The Presbyterians in particular promoted an interest that had developed in 1898 when two young "Galicians" called on the Principal of Manitoba College requesting entrance in order to obtain "an English education". Dr. James Roberston, Superintendent of Home Missions in Western Canada, indicated in a public interview that the Ukrainians "should be put into the great Anglo-Saxon mill and be ground up" because "in the grinding they lose their foreign prejudices and characteristics".[23]

It was only a matter of time before the Archdiocese of St. Boniface and the Home Missions Board of the Presbyterian Church found themselves in open competition for the souls of Slavic immigrants and for the control of their schools, including control of the teacher training institutions and the inspection services which were natural bureaucratic outgrowths of the legislative provisions of 1897. In 1901, Archdeacon Fortin and Dr. Reid, a medical missionary at Sifton, called a closed meeting to discuss the possibility of bringing all Ruthenian-English bilingual schools under the direction of Manitoba College; Archbishop Langevin called a mass meeting of Catholic educators on January 5, 1902 to publicize his opposition to this segment of public schools coming under sectarian Protestant control. About ten days later, a joint meeting of Catholic and Protestant representatives was held at the Winnipeg City Hall to discuss the question of education of immigrant children. No new solutions were proposed, but at least the Fortin-Reid plan had been blocked.

In February 1905, the Roblin Conservative government opened a Ruthenian Training School in Winnipeg for the preparation of Ukrainian and Polish young men who would teach in the bilingual schools. The school was headed by a Yorkshireman who initially viewed the enterprise as "an act of self-preservation on the part of the state", but who later came to view his task as one of great national service in character building, civilizing and Christianizing teacher-candidates. The school was soon relocated in Brandon, near an English Normal School, away from the seat of Catholic strength, and in the Minister of Education's predominantly Anglo-Celtic riding. The few Ukrainian instructors associated with the institute were of known Protestant leanings.

Archbishop Langevin protested vigorously and extracted the promise that a training school for Polish teachers would be organized in Winnipeg. But he was filled with bitterness when a Protestant was proposed as Principal of this second institute. He wrote confidentially to Premier Roblin:

> If things are such, and if you cannot see your way through granting us a Normal School for Galicians with a principal and, perhaps, an assistant, that we can trust, my idea is that we better leave aside the scheme; but the feeling of our Galicians, Poles and Ruthenians in Winnipeg and outside, and the feeling of other Catholics will be bitter against the Government and I will not blame them. Why did Mr. Rogers promise me so positively a Normal School for *our* Galicians if this school falls in the hands of our adversaries as it was the case with the first normal school now in Brandon and when Catholic pupils are under a Presbyterian ruling.[24]

The assumption of the chief officials in the Department of Education was that Manitoba would be an English-speaking and British province. Bilingual schools were a stage in the achievement of this ideal and were not conceived as being a permanent feature of the multilingual and multicultural province.

Archbishop Langevin and his clergy, by seeking to unite all Catholic ethnic minorities in order to obtain a recovery of the school rights enjoyed prior to 1890, failed to counterbalance the Anglo-Celtic dominant group. More important, they failed to obtain parity between francophone and anglophone communities. Indeed, through identification of the Franco-Manitoban cause with that of the immigrant groups, they paved the way for a permanent identification of Franco-Manitobans as just another fragment of the multi-ethnic mosaic.

Phase 3: Anglo-Celtic Dominance

The phase of experimental multiculturalism came to a close during the heated legislative debates on education in the three Prairie Provinces at the time of the First World War. The Mennonites were under particular pressures because of their pacifism, "separation from the world", and their use of the German tongue which was declared to be an "enemy language". In fact, the pressure on them had begun in Manitoba in 1907 with the flag-flying legislation. The Hon. Colin Campbell, in moving second reading of the patriotic legislation, quoted a London speech of

Henry Ward Beecher in which he was alleged to have said:

> It takes them (emigrants to USA) a little time to get used to things, but whenever the children from foreign immigrants, of whom we have eight million born and bred in our land, whenever these children have gone through our common schools they are just as good Americans as if they had not had foreign parents. The common schools are the stomachs of the republic, and when a man goes in there he comes out after all, American.[25]

By 1918, Dr. Harold Foght, the American educator who was asked to evaluate the Saskatchewan public school system, advised that all Mennonite children should be brought forcibly into the public schools and that their private schools should be shut down by the government.

> Once the crust is broken, the Old Coloniers will probably learn as did their brothers in the United States, that it is quite impossible to retain their religion in its old-time purity, even though they accept the tongue of the land in which they and their children live.[26]

It might surprise you to know that more than one Quebec bishop opined that these persecuted Mennonites might make good settlers in the Eastern Townships of *la belle province*.

The inter-war years were marked especially by the Anglo-conformist attempt to gradually integrate the New Canadians, as they were now being called, through the education of their children in schools which were specifically designed for the purpose. The rural one-room school as conceived by educators like J. T. M. Anderson was to become a social, cultural and educational center for the whole community. Anderson explained his concept of the schools to a national education convention in Winnipeg in 1919:

> The paramount factor in racial fusion is undoubtedly the school. It is the national melting pot. We must give it our undivided support. The great battle for better Canadian citizenship is being fought by our school teachers. They are the generals in the home field.[27]

In these schools the pupils would be instructed in good English usage, proper civic attitudes, and in such ancillary matters as personal cleanliness, proper dietary habits, good sportsmanship and patriotic lore. To achieve these objectives it was essential to recruit for each community the "ideal young teacher" imbued with a strong sense of mission, also to exclude the poorly qualified teacher of the community's ethnic background. In numerous districts, especially in Ukrainian and Mennonite communities where the school trustees were quite adept in the democratic administration of their public schools and the hiring of teachers from their own ethnic group, the Departments of Education of the three Prairie provinces arbitrarily suspended local self-government, appointed an Official Trustee and sent in "strong young teachers of a better class". In some areas, notably in northern Alberta, the reaction was the so-called Ruthenian School Revolt.

There was some feeling that not all ethnic groups should have been permitted to come to Canada. Even Stephen Leacock disapproved of immigrants from Slavonic and Mediterranean lands because he believed they were peoples of a so-called lower industrial and moral status. One aspiring poet expressed the Anglo-conformist attitude to non-Nordic peoples:

> They are haggard, huddled, homeless, frightened at—they know not what
> With a few unique exceptions they're a disappointing lot;
> But I take 'em as I get 'em, soldier, sailor, saint and clown
> And I turn 'em out Canadians—all but the yellow and brown.[28]

Phase 4: Multiculturalism

Now we seem to have come full circle. The narrow and bigoted phase 3 has been replaced with a new attempt at multiculturalism, a partial recycling of the earlier phase 2. Without facing head on the dimensions of phase 4 and the current issues surrounding multiculturalism in the West, let us ask the question: why did phase 3 occur? In other words, where did the concept of a compulsory, unilingual British Canada upon which phase 3 was based originate? If these sentiments are still with us today, the chances of a successful phase 4 multiculturalism are nil.

The notion that Canada is a unilingual British country can be traced to a number of historical experiences. First of all, and this is obvious, the Anglo-Celts were among the early European colonizers of what later became Canadian territory. Everyone is aware that, after the Amerindian and Inuit immigrants, the French and the English were the earliest colonizers.

Secondly, the concept is rooted in what I would term the Conquest mentality. There lingers the idea—and I even hear it expressed today by otherwise well-informed people—that the Acadians were conquered in 1713, that the Canadiens were conquered in 1760, and that the Métis and Canadiens in the West were conquered in 1885. The implication seems to be that conquered peoples are second-rate citizens, that they have lost their rights and their identity, that they must forever be servants in their own house. Historically, of course, *the French-Canadians are British subjects by choice and not by conquest.* France did not have to cede Canada in the peace negotiations of 1762—she threatened in fact to re-open the hostilities of the Seven Years' War if Britain did not accept Canada rather than Guadeloupe as the prize of war! And the French-Canadians, by the capitulation and the later peace treaty, were entitled to relocate in

French territory if they wished. They chose not to. They reaffirmed their choice, as a majority, to be British subjects at the time of the American Revolution, the War of 1812, the rebellions of 1837 and at Confederation. Anglo-Celtic reaffirmations of loyalty to the British North American institutions have been no more numerous.

Thirdly, the United Empire Loyalist experience has traumatically marked British North America and it has even influenced subsequent British immigrants. When the Loyalists came to Canada they came as a minority, as displaced persons, to a British colony which was French-speaking, which had Canadien institutions and civil law. Naturally, they wished to be themselves, to order their society along their traditional lines. They were a people still tied to "old country" apron strings. Britain was once again perceived as their homeland. In this they were different from French-Canadians whose European ties were already largely severed and who regarded Canada as their homeland. *The United Empire Loyalists became our first political separatists.* They agitated for separate and special status, and they won! Thereafter, Canada was dualistic, each section of which had its own set of institutions and dominant language. But they also had a concept of minority rights and guarantees in each section. This was carried over into the Confederation charter and later into the Canadian West. And, not surprisingly, it is a concept which many Anglo-Celts have never abandoned. When Premier W. M. Martin was hard-pressed by patriotic societies, Orange lodges, trustees associations, Grain Growers associations, and others in 1918-19 to remove all permissive legislation for the teaching of French along with other languages in Saskatchewan, he answered:

> The question of the French language, however, raises an entirely different question. The people of Canada are made up of two nationalities and each of these nationalities, to my mind must be prepared to be generous to the other. Only in this way will unity of the two races be created and a better understanding exist.[29]

On another occasion he wrote about the "historical position of the French people in Canada". He argued they were native-born Canadians and not immigrants. On another occasion he said:

> It has never been the policy . . . of the British Empire to attempt to force down the throats of any people who came under its charge their own language. The policy has been the opposite.[30]

Thus, while the United Empire Loyalist experience contributed to the development of a concept of a British and English-speaking Canada it also influenced a significant number of the elite to see Canada as a bicultural community.

Fourthly, the mythology of a Canadian northern character is closely tied in with the belief in Nordic or Aryan superiority, with British imperial sentiment, with Social Darwinism combined with a concept of a civilizing mission towards lesser breeds, with Protestant libertarianism and aggressive missionary zeal, and with unabashed Anglo-Saxon racism. These sentiments were publicly proclaimed by such organizations as Canada First, the Imperial Federation League, the Orange Lodge, the patriotic societies and the Ku Klux Klan. At times, benevolent societies, teachers and trustees organizations, farmers organizations, religious corporations and political groups lent their support to and became the vociferous mouthpieces of such views.

Finally, there was a fear that Canada would become Balkanized and lose all national identity and national direction unless an integrated society were created. The United States often served as the model for Canadians in dealing with the integration of immigrants. Not that the melting pot thesis was necessarily adopted, but at least the necessity for common public schools, civic indoctrination and inter-group contact through occupational and professional organizations, through cultural and social associations, through political activities, was adopted.

The assumptions of the immigrants relative to what was required of them could be at variance with the assumptions of the dominant group. Many of the European immigrants assumed that in Canada they would be permitted to retain their language and customs, that there would be no pressures for rapid assimilation similar to what was experienced by immigrants in the United States. Canada did not have an organized program of republican indoctrination, citizenship courses, and the like, which characterized American reception. Some of the newcomers to the Prairies may have been aware of the heterogeneity of the British Isles, of the multilingualism and multiculturalism of the far-flung British Empire, of the historic dualism of Canada, and of the concept of unity under the Crown which was more tolerant of diversity than was consensus-based republicanism. There had never been just one way to be British, nor for that matter to be Canadian, therefore their cultural identity did not seem threatened in adopting a new political allegiance. When this kind of understanding of Canada—a Canada which was multicultural—was challenged, especially during the First World War, some of the New Canadians reacted by demanding their "rights" and privileges.

It may well be asked on what grounds were such assumptions about multiculturalism and diversity, with no pressures for integration or assimilation to be exerted upon them, founded. The view that in Canada there would be no need to renounce "old country" folkways first originated in the immigration propaganda of the various agents who, in competition with American and Argentinian agents, were recruiting settlers. The

Ukrainians certainly were not ignorant of the special concessions and formal guarantees that had been made to the Mennonite and Doukhobor communities as a condition of their establishment on the Prairies. Indeed, the existence of such special concessions for certain ethnic communities readily could be assumed to imply no forced assimilation for any immigrant group.

Furthermore, many immigrants discovered their homestead lots on the Prairies with little in the way of structured, organized social, political and economic life to demand their conformity. There was a sufficient lack of organization and preparedness on the part of the host society to permit the newcomers to interpret the laissez-faire situation as one which encouraged cultural pluralism.

Moreover, the settlement pattern in bloc ethnic rural communities and in city ghettoes may have reinforced the interpretation that Canadian policy was for the retention of ethnic identity. Ethnic reserves encouraged retention of the mother tongue, traditional institutions, patterns of social intercourse, and established folkways. To conclude that the Canadian authorities, in planning the settlement of the Prairies, accepted cultural pluralism as the pattern of society, and that they rejected forced assimilation or integration, was both logical and evident. At least, so it may have seemed to many immigrants.

Finally, if any further proof was required on the part of immigrants for such an assumption of multiculturalism, it seemed to have been clearly indicated in the bilingual school system introduced in Manitoba in 1897, and the special provision for instruction in languages other than English in the rest of the Prairies. Given this tradition, perhaps there is sufficient ground for optimism that the new multiculturalism may be more solidly institutionalized and durable than the old.

Conclusion

The history of Prairie settlement is similar to earlier European patterns in Eastern Canada in the sense that the French preceded the British, but fate ordained that they should form a dual community. This duality distinguishes Canada from the American republic where unity has been predicated, at least since the Revolution, on uniformity and a certain degree of homogeneity. The Canadian West's French roots made the Prairies more receptive to polyglot and multicultural development. However, the multi-ethnic *épanouissement* eventually aided in the reduction of the francophone community's status from a founding and charter member to that of a minority among numerous minorities. Only the Anglo-Celtic community profited, in the long run, from the integration of immigrant groups on the Prairies. Today, only a lack of historical perspective could obscure the fact that multiculturalism has arisen out of dualism in Canada and that bilingualism reinforces our northern and distinctively Canadian identity on a continent which tends to emphasize homogeneity rather than minority rights.

ENDNOTES

1. L. Drummond, "The French Element in the Canadian North-West," *Transactions of the Historical and Scientific Society of Manitoba*, No. 28 (1887), p. 14.
2. Sir Robert A. Falconer, "The Unification of Canada," *University Magazine*, Vol. VII (February 1908), p. 4.
3. The decennial census of 1891 indicated that out of a population of 108 017 in Manitoba, only 7 555 had been born in Quebec, while 46 630 had been born in Ontario. The total number of Roman Catholics was 20 571 or less than one fifth of the total population.
4. *Le Métis*, January 18, 1877.
5. I am much indebted to Professor Robert Painchaud of the University of Winnipeg who generously shared information relating to schools.
6. *P.A.M.*, PR 10/7, Department of Education, Letterbook of Superintendent of Catholic Schools, Report for 1886.
7. P. H. Attwood, *A Jubilee Essay on Imperial Confederation as affecting Manitoba and the Northwest* (Winnipeg, 1887), p. 15. I differ with Lovell Clark and others who maintain that there was little or no dissatisfaction with the school system prior to 1889 and that D'Alton McCarthy's intervention provoked a sudden assault on the system. W. L. Morton puts it into its correct historical context: " ... the feeling was there. The grievance existed. The people's mind had only to be directed to it, and the moment attention was drawn to it, the province of Manitoba rose as one man and said 'We want no dual language— and away with separate schools as well'." W. L. Morton, *Manitoba: A History* (Toronto, 1957), p. 244.
8. Jean Des Prairies, *Une Viste dans les Écoles du Manitoba* (Montreal, 1897), pp. 10-12. I am much indebted to M. Gilbert Comeault of the Provincial Archives of Manitoba for bringing to my attention important documents on this subject.
9. "Mémoire sur la question des Écoles de Manitoba," *Revue d'histoire de l'Amérique française*, Vol. VI, No. 3 (décembre 1952), Gonthier to Lindsay, July 3, 1897, pp. 440-42.
10. F. H. Schofield, *The Story of Manitoba* (Winnipeg, 1913), Vol. 1, pp. 380-82; James A. Jackson, *The Centennial History of Manitoba* (Winnipeg, 1970), pp. 118-19, 151.
11. *A.A.S.B., Fonds Langevin*, Dom Benoit to Msgr. A. Langevin, October 1, 1896.
12. House of Commons, *Debates*, September 24, 1896, pp. 1934-35.
13. Public Archives of Canada (*P.A.C.*), MG 27, Sir Clifford Sifton Papers, II D 15, W. F. McCreary to Sifton, April 13, 1899.

14. *P.A.M.*, RG2, D1, Executive Council, "Memorandum of Settlement of School Question," Ottawa, November 16, 1896.
15. *Manitoba Free Press*, January 13, 1916.
16. *Winnipeg Tribune*, November 23, 1896.
17. *Le Manitoba*, October 25, 1899. The text of the encyclical is given in the *American Catholic Quarterly Review*, Vol. XXIII, No. 2 (April 1897), pp. 189-95.
18. *A.A.S.B.*, Fonds Langevin, Msgr. Langevin to Armand Lavergne, n.d., 1908.
19. Cited in J. Castell Hopkins, "Educational Problems and Conditions in Alberta," *Canadian Annual Review of Public Affairs, 1905* (Toronto, 1906), pp. 224-25.
20. Manitoba, *Report of the Department of Education, 1897* (Winnipeg, 1898), Inspector A. L. Young's report, p. 35.
21. *A.A.S.B.*, Fonds Langevin, Langevin to R. Roblin, January 28, 1901; also, Memorandum to Hon. Roblin, 1901, Letterbook 1900-1901, p. 646.
22. *Les Clôches de Saint-Boniface*, Vol I (January, 1902), p. 8. Langevin had already obtained the promise of Belgian Redemptorists to serve as priests in Ukrainian parishes. The clearest statement from Archbishop Langevin concerning the policy of linking the School Question, European Catholic immigration, and Franco-American repatriation is contained in a letter to a colonizing priest in 1898. Cf. *A.A.S.B.*, Fonds Langevin, Letter Book I, Msgr. Langevin to abbé Jean Gaire, April 5, 1898. Clarification of the question of francophone immigration to the West and the role of the Catholic Church will have to await the publication of the doctoral thesis of Professor Robert Painchaud, University of Winnipeg, to whom I am grateful for the above reference. In a memorandum to the Canadian hierarchy and to two East European cardinals, Langevin maintained that a common front would force a favorable settlement of the School Question. *A.A.S.B.*, Fonds Langevin, Memorandum to the Canadian episcopate and to Cardinals Rampalla and Ledowchowski, September 27, 1901.
23. *Manitoba Free Press*, November 15, 1898.
24. *A.A.S.B.*, Fonds Langevin, Msgr. Langevin to R. Roblin, February 6, 1909, pp. 331-33.
25. *Manitoba Free Press*, January 15, 1907.
26. Harold W. Foght, *A Survey of Education in the Province of Saskatchewan, Canada* (Regina, 1918), p. 150.
27. *Regina Leader*, October 25, 1919.
28. R. J. C. Stead, "The Mixer," quoted in R. C. Brown and Ramsay Cook, *Canada 1896-1921: A Nation Transformed* (Toronto: McClelland and Stewart, 1974), p. 73.
29. *Archives of Saskatchewan (A.S.)*, M4, Hon. W. M. Martin Papers, File 53 (7), Martin to H. R. Walker, Kindersley, January 2, 1919, folio 18444.
30. *Ibid*, Debate of December 19, 1918, p. 18534.

PART THREE

The Other Ethnic Groups:
The Non-English in English Canada

Introduction

Canadians have tended to view immigration with a large measure of ambivalence. The one exception to this general ambivalence, perhaps, is the immigration from one's own particular mother country—the country of one's ancestors. Immigration from countries unrelated to our own Old World roots has met more relative disfavor. The uncertainty of our response to immigration may be highest regarding "the other ethnic groups"[1]—immigrants who are neither British nor French.

Immigration and the Canadian Mosaic

What has been Canada's immigration experience? How has immigration helped in shaping the Canadian identity? J. L. Elliott relates the evolution of immigration policy to the more general social and economic conditions present at the time. The spin-off effects of immigration are not always apparent at the time the policy is formulated.

The diversity of Canada's ethnic mosaic reflects not only the wide range of countries that have sent immigrants to Canada, but also the diversity of immigrants from *within* the same country. Italy, Yugoslavia, Russia, and China, for example, contain numerous ethnic groups. The fact that ethnic groups, especially those that refer to nation-states, are internally differentiated is often overlooked by outsiders who tend to view ethnic groups in a one-dimensional, stereotypic way. J. Nagata points out that the rich diversity found within specific ethnic and national origin groups may militate against the development of a unity of purpose or shared experiences among members. Relations between subgroups within ethnic groups may range from indifference, to conflict, to mutual support. Therefore, it may be more accurate to speak of *identities* rather than *identity* when assessing the impact of immigration on an ethnic community or society as a whole.

Finally, how is the cultural diversity of the Canadian people who comprise the mosaic cemented together? How do our societal institutions function to make us one people? The confusion surrounding the Canadian identity, some would say, is simply the failure of our social institutions to adequately mold the collectivity into a unified whole. D. Millett considers how the church as a social institution functions to integrate members with mother tongues other than French or English. Millett focuses on the mainstream or dominant churches that offer services in the non-official languages. Participation in church services may provide opportunities for shared experiences and understandings, regardless of the fact that the services are conducted in different languages.

In order to fully appreciate the complexity of the Canadian identity with respect to its core values, origins, and changes over time, it would be advantageous to evaluate all the various social institutions in terms of participants, language in use, and the consequence of this participation for the identity of various ethnic groups. The following section considers the experiences of various European immigrant groups and the nature of their ethnicity within Canada.

European Immigration

European immigrants, the traditional source of settlers for North America through the first half of the 20th century, may be referred to as the "old" immigrants as opposed to the "new" immigrants in the current period from non-traditional source countries in the Third World. The old immigrants were selected with reference to such criteria as the ease with which it was believed that they would assimilate into Canadian life. Immigrants recruited under the "preferred nations" guideline tended to come largely from Germany, the Netherlands, and Scandinavia, and especially from the British Isles.

The smallest Scandinavian country, Iceland, has a history of emigration to Canada. The Icelandic immigration to Canada, J. Matthiasson argues, has resulted in an "assimilation paradox". While one might expect the Icelandic Canadians to be prime targets for assimilation, given their relatively small numbers and early history in Canada in which they did not oppose Canadianization, such is not the case. The Icelandic Canadians have developed a "cultural dualism" that enlivens and gives a new direction to their ethnicity. In many respects the Icelandic Canadians are a study of controlled assimilation.

Large-scale immigration from the Mediterranean region stems from the beginning of the postwar era. Although the Italians have been by far the largest group represented, all Mediterranean countries have participated. Grace Anderson examines the internal differentiation within the Spanish-speaking population in Canada. Since they are a linguistic group, various ethnic backgrounds are represented.

Both the Portuguese and Italians share a pattern of migration characterized by an early phase of male contract labor followed by a later phase of chain migration involving the sponsorship of family members. R. Harney traces the development of the Italian community in Toronto; its origins predate the rise of Mussolini in Italy. Since the Italian community has experienced various streams of migration, its internal differentiation is greater than the Portuguese community, the latter being smaller and more recent in origin.

The Slavic peoples evidenced a high degree of internal differentiation in Europe. Upon migration, some of the old world loyalties as well as conflicts carried over; others disappeared or were modified through encounters with the new society. Likewise, a new ethnicity arose in some instances to meet their needs and fit the reality of the new social structure. A Matejko and A. Anderson evaluate the diversity they find within their respective groups—Poles and Ukrainians—with regard to the weakening or the strengthening of the forms of ethnic expression over time.

In addition to the matter of the "many branches", the internal differentiation within the Slavs takes the form of a generational split. Any group with members of different ages might anticipate a "generational gap", and ethnic groups are no exception, especially those which have experienced successive waves of new members. Generational differences among the Poles may be more acute than among the Ukrainians. The successive waves of immigration involving Poles included different social class groupings with the more recent Poles tending to be highly educated as opposed to the earlier group comprised largely of peasants.

The 1968 wave of Slavic immigrants involved approximately 12 000 Czechoslovakian political refugees. J. Horna monitored the progress this group made in adjusting to life in Canada. On the whole, they were professionally and technically educated and had given little, if any, prior consideration to a move to Canada. Horna's data suggest that the rapidity of their adjustment to Canada relates, in large measure, to the sex of the immigrant. Men tended to regain the status they lost, on first entry to Canada, faster than women. The continuation of the "depressed entrance status" of women is interpreted with reference to the status of women in the larger Canadian society.

The Jews belong to a myriad of ethnic groups. The Jewish immigration to Canada spans the "old" and the "new" immigration in terms of the source countries involved. The Jews from North Africa and the Middle East have come in recent times while the earliest Jewish settlers were from Europe. The most active migration to Canada from Europe, of course, occurred at the time of the Hitler holocaust. Although the Jews have settled in all provinces, they tend to be urban dwellers. W. Shaffir offers an account of Jewish immigration with particular attention to the Montreal Jewish community which dates back to the early days of the city. As members of the anglophone community, the Jews constitute a "double minority" in Quebec. Within the Montreal community, the Chassidim "branch" adds to the extensive internal differentiation of the Jews.

Third World Immigration

Racial Prejudice and Discrimination

Great Britain has had a numerically more significant history of non-white immigration than Canada stemming from the immigration of Commonwealth citizens to the mother country. The continuing problems that Great Britain is facing as a multi-racial society are compared by A. Richmond with those that Canada is confronting. If economic factors lead to the perception that whites are pitted against non-whites in competition for such scarce resources as jobs, housing, and higher education, limited racial and ethnic conflict could erupt in Canada in a similar manner to Great Britain. Drawing on the experiences of Great Britain and Canada, Richmond assesses the dimensions of non-white immigration and the possible status of the Blacks in the future.

J. S. Turrittin has given her attention to a special subgroup of Black immigrants: the lower-status Caribbean female. It is her thesis that the migrant culture that prepares women to come to Canada helps to smooth, in part, their adjustment once they arrive. Although the women Turrittin interviewed "don't look for prejudice," this does not mean that none is encountered. The women, many of them employed as maids, have as a group a long history in Canada that predates the new immigration policies. Female domestic laborers have been traditionally recruited from the West Indies under various "special arrangements". This legacy stereotypes Black women in the employment market and retards their mobility from domestic work.

Asian Immigration

Asian immigration in the time of the "old immigration" was governed by a series of double standards. The Chinese immigrant, viewed as a source of cheap labor, was recruited under some economic conditions and discouraged under others. A series of "head taxes" regulated the flow of Chinese immigration into Canada until 1923 when the Chinese were completely barred from entry. Graham Johnson discusses the impact that the early discriminatory regulations, the predominantly male migration, and the prohibition of female immigration have had on the family life of the Chinese until the current policy came into effect.

Early Japanese immigration was governed by a policy different from the one that regulated the Chinese. Japanese immigrants were fewer and tended to settle in fishing communities along the West coast. During World War II when Japan was the enemy, the fishing boats and farmland of Japanese-Canadians were confiscated by the Canadian government. In the postwar era, the Japanese immigrants tended to settle in Ontario. V. Ujimoto attempts to discern the cultural factors associated with the new Japanese immigrants that might affect their adjustment to the Canadian work world.

In spite of the harsh history that the Japanese in North America experienced, the Japanese-Canadian and the Japanese-American have remained remarkably non-bitter, earning the reputation of being a "model minority" for their hard work and achievement. The Japanese "presentation of self" tends to be a pleasing one as judged from the perspective of the larger society.

N. Buchignani deals with the phenomenon of the "presentation of self" as it occurs in the everyday life of the Fijians, an East Indian subgroup in British Columbia. As a result of the "new" immigration, the Fijians have become a sizable East Indian ethnic group that is not clearly visible to the larger society. Because it is difficult to tell them apart from the total East Indian population, the outsider tends not to interact with a Fijian East Indian as a *Fijian*, but as an *East Indian*. The effect of this blocked communication on the Fijians and the coping mechanisms that they employ in order to deflect prejudice and ill treatment are discussed within the framework of symbolic interaction theory.

Arab Immigration

Until recently, Arab immigration to Canada was heavily male in composition. As such, it was similar to the Chinese. Migratory streams that are not composed of complete family units tend to be heavily male. B. Abu-Laban traces the evolution of Arab immigration from the period when Arab countries were on the "non-preferred" list to the present day when they enjoy an equal status with the traditional European source countries.

Although equal to European countries in terms of formal status, immigrants from Arab countries continue to be poorly understood with information about their cultures generally lacking in the larger Canadian society. Abu-Laban's research serves as the groundwork in an effort to bridge the communication gap between the vast majority of non-Arabs in Canada and the relatively few Canadians of Arab background. It should be remembered, though, that the Arabs themselves are varied, containing cultural, national, linguistic, religious and ethnic subgroups.

ENDNOTE

1. This phrase was chosen by The Royal Commission on Bilingualism and Biculturalism to designate the ethnic mix in Canada that is neither Charter group French/English nor Native People in origin. *Report of the Royal Commission on Bilingualism and Biculturalism*, Book IV, "The Contribution of the Other Ethnic Groups" (Ottawa: Queen's Printer, 1970).

SELECTED REFERENCES

Anderson, Grace M. *Networks of Contact: The Portuguese and Toronto.* Waterloo: Wilfrid Laurier, 1974.

Anderson, Grace M., and David Higgs. *A Future to Inherit: The Portuguese Communities of Canada.* Toronto: McClelland and Stewart, 1976.

Awan, Sadiq Noor A. *The People of Pakistani Origin in Canada.* Ottawa: Canada-Pakistan Association of Ottawa-Hull, 1976.

Clairmont, D. H., and Dennis W. Magill. *Africville: The Life and Death of a Canadian Black Community.* Toronto: McClelland and Stewart, 1974.

Cohn, Werner. *The Gypsies.* Don Mills, Ontario: Addison-Wesley, 1973.

Frucht, Richard, ed. *Black Society in the New World.* Toronto: Random House, 1971.

Glasrud, Bruce A. *Race Relations in the British North American Colonies.* Chicago: Nelson-Hall, 1977.

Gregorovich, Andrew, ed. *Canadian Ethnic Groups Bibliography.* Toronto: Department of the Provincial Secretary and Citizenship of Ontario, 1972.

Harney, Robert F., and Harold Troper. *Immigrants: A Portrait of the Urban Experience 1890-1930.* Toronto: Van Nostrand Reinhold, 1975.

Head, Wilson A. *The Black Presence in the Canadian Mosaic.* Toronto: Ontario Human Rights Commission, 1975.

Henry, Frances. *Forgotten Canadians: The Blacks of Nova Scotia.* Don Mills, Ontario: Longman, 1973.

Hughes, D. R., and E. Kallen. *The Anatomy of Racism: Canadian Dimensions.* Montreal: Harvest House, 1974.

Isajiw, Wsevolod W. *Ukrainians in American and Canadian Society.* Cambridge, Massachusetts: Harvard Ukrainian Research Institute, 1976.

Ishwaran, K. *Family, Kinship and Community: A Study of Dutch Canadians.* Toronto: McGraw Hill-Ryerson, 1977.

Kallen, Evelyn L. *Spanning the Generations: A Study in Jewish Identity.* Don Mills, Ont.: Longman, 1977.

Kealey, Gregory S., and Peter Warrian, eds. *Essays in Canadian Working Class History.* Toronto: McClelland and Stewart, 1976.

Klassen, Henry C., ed. *The Canadian West.* Calgary: Comprint, 1977.

Kohl, Seena B. *Working Together: Women and Family in Southwestern Saskatchewan.* Toronto: Holt, Rinehart, and Winston, 1976.

Kovacs, Martin L. *Ethnic Canadians: Culture and Education.* Regina, Sask.: Canadian Plains Research Center, 1977.

Kurelek, William, and A. Arnold. *Jewish Life in Canada.* Edmonton: Hurtig, 1976.

Migus, Paul M., ed. *Sounds Canadian: Languages and Cultures in Multi-Ethnic Society.* Toronto: Peter Martin, 1975.

Palmer, Howard. *Land of the Second Chance: A History of Ethnic Groups in Southern Alberta.* Lethbridge, Alta.: The Lethbridge Herald, 1972.

——. *Immigration and the Rise of Multiculturalism.* Toronto: Copp Clark, 1975.

Immigration and the Canadian Mosaic

J. L. ELLIOTT   Dalhousie University

Canadian Immigration: A Historical Assessment

Introduction

While no one would question the significance of immigration for the development of Canadian society, one may not be as readily aware that immigration has served Canada in ways that extend beyond the original need to populate a vast territory, supply a labor force or add cultural diversity to the life of the whole. The greater reality surrounding immigration is not fully reflected in our nation-building myths and our image of our society as an ethnic mosaic. Over and above the usual costs and benefits that we tend to associate with immigration, the mass movements of people to Canada over the years have had an impact on what many of us might consider to be some of the more pressing issues confronting us today—national unity and minority language rights.

Canada in the late 1970s is beset with conflicts. In addition to the problem of national unity, the conflicts arising from such issues as aboriginal rights and regional disparities do not stem solely from broken promises and good intentions gone astray. The conflicts that plague us today may be traced, in part, to the immigration policies of our past and the economic concerns that shaped them.

Impact of Immigration

If we were to begin an assessment of the impact of immigration with the Confederation era, we would see immediately the consequences of immigration for the Native Peoples. When the Canadian Pacific Railway was completed in 1885, the West was "opened" to immigrants. Before the land could be "opened", the Native Peoples had to be "cleared" from it.

Some would see a tragic irony in the fact that in order to populate the Prairies, the existing settlements of Métis and Cree were first destroyed. The West was populated with immigrants in orderly bloc settlements; the orderliness obscures the fact that before "free land" could be offered generously to the land-hungry peasants from central Europe, it was confiscated from its prior inhabitants.[1]

The ultimate development of the West as an extension of English Canada undermined the balance of power between the French and English segments of the country. Legitimate nationalistic concerns of the French in the West were gradually eroded through legislative changes at the provincial level; French was relegated to the status of a foreign language in the schools and its use denied in the courts.

The losses sustained by the French outside Quebec were a close match to the ground lost within Quebec as a result of immigration. Immigrants to Quebec typically have assimilated to the anglophone community, succumbing to the lure and security of the anglophone-dominated economic sector. Native-born French Quebeckers as well as immigrants have been swayed by economic enticements, often to the detriment of their culture. Being bilingual has been traditionally a prerequisite to economic advancement in Quebec if one's mother tongue were French. Bilingualism on the part of minority cultures is often the first step toward assimilation.

Not only has the Quebec culture been diluted by immigration, but it also has been numerically weakened by mass French Canadian emigration to the United States. In the last decades of the 19th century, concurrent with the settlement of the Prairies, there occurred in Quebec what Richard Joy has termed "the fatal hemorrhage";[2] the U.S. Census of 1900 indicated that one third of all French Canadians in North America resided south of the Canadian border. Many settled in New England textile communities. The Canadian Census of 1901 showed French Canadians as constituting 5% of the population of what are now the three Prairie provinces. One of the major "ifs" of Canadian history is: if the French Canadian migration had been encouraged to go West instead of South, would the "two-nation" aspect of the Canadian identity have proved to be a more broadly-based reality?

It was not until the Great Depression of the 1930s that Quebec emigration to the United States and European immigration to Canada ceased sufficiently for Quebec to begin to recoup demographic losses through excessive fertility. The phenomenally high birth rate in Quebec has been termed "the revenge of the cradle" because of its potentially important political implications. However, *la revanche* was short-lived. In the postwar years the birth rate fell; immigration to North America resumed, and Quebec's efforts to rebuild its numerical strength *vis à vis* English Canada were for naught.

Although Quebec has suffered from immigration, Ontario has benefited. After immigrants were recruited to secure the hinterland in the West, they were sought to meet the labor needs of the burgeoning industrial economy of Ontario. Aided and abetted by immigration, the industrialization of Ontario's "golden horseshoe" proceeded to the relative exclusion of the rest of the country. From the Confederation era to 1911, the largest cluster of immigrants were found on the Prairies which held 41% of the total foreign-born population of Canada. Sixty years later, the Prairies were the domicile of only 16% of the foreign-born with over 50% living in Ontario.[3] Ontario's growth and development would not have been possible without the majority of postwar immigrants settling there.

Industrialization in central Canada, made possible and strengthened by immigration, fostered regional disparities as well as the development of "the vertical mosaic" documented by Porter.[4] The vertical mosaic describes the outcome of certain historical processes like immigration that resulted in the hierarchical ordering of the various ethnic groups in the social structure. Individuals on the top-most rungs of the social ladder tend to be members of the British charter group. The British elites traditionally have monitored the mobility of the other ethnic groups in Canada, including the French charter group, with the exception of some francophone elites in Quebec. Thus, the process of immigration has favored some regions over others and has encouraged the growth of a vertical, social class dimension in Canadian life. Social class in Canada tends to be highly related to ethnicity.

While immigration has had a fundamental impact on ethnic stratification, Freda Hawkins reminds us that Canada is not simply "a 'nation of immigrants.' ... this is not the central fact of Canadian history. The central fact is the existence of the two founding races (sic) and the relations between them."[5] The stresses and strains associated with the immigration process have occurred within the context of uneasy French/English relations. Immigration policies have evolved in this context.

The Evolution of Immigration Policies

The impact of immigration in any historical era is related, in part, to the immigration policy in force at the time. The management of immigration in Canada spans several distinct eras (see Table 1). It is useful to think of the Confederation era through 1895 (the free-entry period), the beginning of selective immigration in 1896 up to World War I (the old immigration), the period between the wars when immigration ebbed, and the post-World War II era to the present (the new immigration).

The charter group designation for the French and British refers to the fact that the first permanent settlements in Canada were either French or

TABLE 1 *Canadian immigration: policy and change (1861 – 1977)*

Historical period	Decade	Population at start of decade (000's)	Immigration as a percentage of average decade population	Migration Immigration	Estimated Emigration	(000's) Net Migration	Immigration policy	Primary destination and type of immigrant
Confederation to 1895	1861-1871	3 090	7.5	183	375	− 192	free entry (exception: first B.C. "head tax" on Chinese. 1885.)	Eastern Canada settled by immigrants from British Isles, N.W. Europe and USA.
	1871-1881	3 689	8.8	353	440	− 087		
	1881-1891	4 325	19.7	903	1 109	− 206		
The Sifton era to W.W. I 1896-1914	1891-1901	4 833	6.4	250	380	− 130	selective immigration. objective: land settlement	Prairies settled by farmers, many from Central Europe
	1901-1911	5 371	28.0	1 550	740	810		
War and economic depression (1914-1945)	1911-1921	7 207	20.2	1 400	1 090	310	restrictive measures.	Urban settlement as well as rural.
	1921-1931	8 788	12.6	1 203	974	229	Chinese Immigration Act. 1923. visas first issued. "sponsorship" begins.	War refugees. Jewish and other displaced persons
	1931-1941	10 377	1.4	150	242	− 092		
Postwar era (1946-1961)	1941-1951	11 507	4.4	548	379	169	liberalization. 1952 Immigration Act. objective: population increase to "absorptive capacity".	Urban areas in Central Canada. Southern European immigration begins many in manufacturing occupations.
	1951-1961	14 009[1]	9.6	1 543	462	1 081		
The Current phase	1961-1971	18 238	7.2	1 429	705	724	"points system". 1967. objective: universalistic criteria.	Urban settlement continues. Third World immigration begins. many professional and technical workers.
	1971-1976	21 568	–	984	–	–		

Sources: W. E. Kalbach and W. W. McVey, *The Demographic Bases of Canadian Society*, Toronto: McGraw-Hill, 1971, Tables 1.4 and 2.2.
W. E. Kalbach, *The Effects of Immigration on Population*, Department of Manpower and Immigration (Ottawa, 1974), Tables 1.1 and 1.2.
1972 *Immigration Statistics*, Dept. of Manpower and Immigration (Ottawa, 1974), Table 1.
1976 *Immigration Statistics*, Dept. of Manpower and Immigration (Ottawa, 1977), Table 2.
Immigration and Population Statistics, Dept. of Manpower and Immigration (Ottawa, 1974), Table 1.4.
1. Includes Newfoundland.

British. The earliest census in New France in 1608 records 28 settlers. By 1765, the population had reached 69 810. Since French emigration virtually halted after the Treaty of Paris, the French Canadian nation tends to be descended from this early nucleus.[6]

The French and the British, however, were not the only settlers in the early period of Canadian history. During the first census following Confederation, the Blacks ranked fifth among the ethnic groups, with only the Germans and Dutch more numerous (Census of Canada, 1870-71, Vol. 1, Table 3). The Blacks came to Canada with their Loyalist masters during the American Revolution and the War of 1812 and settled largely in the Maritimes. It was not until the current era, however, that Blacks emigrated in sizable numbers from the Caribbean (see Table 2). The Maritime provinces never regained their popularity as a destination for immigrants, consistently losing population through out-migration.

Canada's first Immigration Act was passed in 1869 but a period of free entry lasted until 1896, with the appointment of Clifford Sifton, a Manitoba businessman, as Minister of the Interior. The period of free entry ended sooner for the Chinese, however. Since the Chinese had been allowed entry into Canada primarily for work on the CPR, its completion in 1885 meant that they had become surplus laborers. British Columbia responded in 1885 with a "head tax" of $50 on every new Chinese immigrant. This tax was raised several times in the following years until the Chinese Immigration Act in 1923 barred their entry.

Sifton inherited an economic situation which demanded the immediate settlement of the West. His selective immigration policy tended to place prior agricultural experience over national origin concerns. It was a

TABLE 2 *Selected major source countries of postwar immigrants*

Country (Rank order, 1976).	1976	1974	1972	1970	1968	1946-1967
Great Britain	19 257	33 088	16 637	26 497	37 889	827 567
West Indies[1]	15 066	24 441	8 696	12 456	7 563	35 800
USA	14 278	22 454	19 176	24 424	20 422	244 280
China[2]	13 301	15 264	7 209	5 377	8 382	46 765
India	8 562	16 016	6 746	5 670	4 675	24 995
Portugal	6 194	17 268	9 280	7 902	7 738	57 427
Italy	4 008	5 818	4 847	8 533	19 774	409 414
Greece	2 429	5 654	4 008	6 327	7 739	80 216
France	2 415	2 811	1 880	4 410	8 184	82 877
TOTAL	85 510	142 814	78 479	101 596	122 366	1 809 341

1. Includes Caribbean area.
2. Includes Hong Kong and Taiwan.
(Source: *Immigration Statistics*, Dept. of Manpower and Immigration (Ottawa).

selective policy in the sense that non-agriculturalists were not wanted. Sifton's Deputy Minister in 1900 stated, "If a settler is one who has been engaged in agricultural pursuits in the old land ... whether he is rich or poor, Galician, Austrian, Russian, Swede, Belgian or French, we believe it most desirable to encourage him to occupy our land and to break up our soil ... "[7]

In spite of Sifton's vigorous efforts to attract and keep settlers, Canada registered a negative net migration between the decades 1861 to 1901. As inducements to farmers, such as the Doukhobors, Sifton may have made promises which were later impossible to keep. The rural, pacifist communal sect of Doukhobors numbering about 7 000 entered Canada in 1899 on Sifton's invitation. Fleeing Tsarist persecutions in Russia, the religious group hoped it could live life in Canada without interference from the government. By 1905, however, Saskatchewan confiscated more than half their land holdings because their religious convictions prevented the Doukhobors from taking the oath of allegiance to the Crown that was necessary to acquire final title to the land.[8]

The unconfirmed expectations experienced by the Doukhobors may have been repeated by other ethnic groups that came to Canada with the thought of recreating their cultural life as they had known it in the old country. Although Sifton left office in 1905, his successor Frank Oliver continued the expansionist immigration policy up until the start of World War I. The all-time peak was reached in 1913 when over 400 000 people came to Canada. Faced with integrating this diverse mass of immigrants into a coherent social system, voices favoring cultural pluralism did not win out.[9] By World War I, German was considered as an "enemy language", and French was just another foreign tongue among many. If promises of a cultural mosaic were incentives to make the long trek to Canada, "Anglo-conformity" was among the harsh realities the newcomers faced.

During the war years and the Great Depression, immigration came to a standstill with the exception of refugees and displaced persons. More Jews came to Canada in this era than in any other. Despite the influx of refugees, Canada lost more people in the decade 1931-41 than it gained. Promotional efforts had stopped in 1930, and restrictive immigration measures were introduced. Visas were issued for the first time in order to control immigration at its source.

The gradual transition in the economic structure from a rural to an urban base in the early part of the 20th century meant that the labor needs of the postwar era would be different from those known by Sifton. The rural-to-urban migration within Canada commenced to be followed by an international rural-to-urban migration that would see Europeans from rural areas seeking a new life in Canadian cities.[10]

Prime Minister MacKenzie King set the tone of the postwar immigration policy in 1947 when he advocated immigration as an avenue to population growth and economic development to be pursued up to the "absorptive capacity" of the country. Racial and ethnic selectivity continued, with France in 1949 for the first time joining Britain and the USA on the list of "preferred nations".[11] Some liberalization took place, however, regarding Asians who were allowed to sponsor family members. The immigration from southern Europe began with urban settlement as their destination.[12]

In the postwar period, the sponsorship of Italians snowballed. One study showed that every Italian meant 49 relatives.[13] Only the British were responsible for more arrivals in the postwar period than the Italians, and in the period between 1958 and 1961, the Italian immigration surpassed the British. The chain migration of family members suggested that sponsored immigrants who did not have to be self-supporting might create an intolerable economic burden for their sponsors. The need for control of the sponsorship program became obvious to those concerned with economic questions and social problems associated with the growth of ethnic neighborhoods.[14]

The sponsorship "problem" was resolved in 1967 when the immigration policy underwent a major revision. Sponsored immigrants would now be classified as dependent or non-dependent, with separate regulations applying to each. The modification in sponsorship, however, was overshadowed by the introduction of the "points system" which was also part of the new 1967 policy. Discrimination on the basis of race or national origin was eliminated for all classes of immigrants. Immigrants were to be selected on the basis of points that they earned in nine areas such as education, occupation, and language. At this juncture in immigration policy, the characteristics of the future immigrants were set.

The new immigrants from 1967 to the present have tended to come in greater numbers from the professional, technical and managerial occupations, and from the Third World countries that previously were discouraged from applying. The changes occurring after 1967 in the rank ordering of the "source countries" is presented in Table 2. By 1974, the West Indies had climbed to number 2 position behind Great Britain in the number of immigrants coming to Canada. In fact in any two- or three-year period after the points system, the West Indies contributed approximately as many immigrants as during the entire twenty-year postwar period from 1946-67.

The adoption of the universalistic points system, however, did not put an end to attacks aimed at the racist character of Canada's immigration policy. With the emphasis placed on occupational and educational achievement, Canada was accused of discriminating against developing nations who by definition did not have the manpower and potential that immigrants of the more developed societies had. Furthermore, Canada was accused of robbing the talent that did exist and was not easily replaced; for example, medical and scientific personnel. The points system which was basically a manpower recruitment strategy did seem to encourage "the brain drain".

Inasmuch as policy reflects ideologies within a society, the "Anglo-conformity" mentality that reached its zenith in the pre-World War 1 era gradually had been replaced over the years with official notions of cultural pluralism.[15] That is, the reality of the two-nation concept for Canada was reviewed in the mid-1960s along with the case for fostering multiculturalism. The modernization of Quebec and the "quiet revolution" within her borders in the early 1960s caused a resurgence of nationalism. The Pearson government responded by creating the Royal Commission on Bilingualism and Biculturalism which eventually reported under Prime Minister Trudeau.[16] In 1968 the Official Languages Act established French on an equal footing with English on the federal level. Since the shoring up of the two-nation Confederation was not intended to slight the contributions of the "other ethnic groups",[17] a multicultural policy for Canada was announced in 1971.[18] Thus, the backdrop of the points system was the continuing internal questioning within Canada concerning the dimensions of its own bicultural or multicultural identity.

If Third World immigrants are being welcomed to Canada in keeping with the spirit of multiculturalism, the overall numbers of immigrants may be greatly reduced in the future if the high levels of unemployment that have hit the Canadian economy in the mid-1970s continue. The 1977 Immigration Act called for more provincial input concerning labor needs.[19] All in all, it would seem that MacKenzie King's concept of "absorptive capacity" has been retained in Canadian policy as it pertains to economics and rejected as it pertains to notions of ethnic or racial assimilability.

Immigration and the Canadian Identity

A Canadian identity in a collective sense would have to reflect core aspects of life as shared and experienced by Canadians. Inasmuch as some of the core aspects of life may relate to ethnicity and Canada is not ethnically homogeneous, it may be more accurate to speak of Canadian *identities* rather than identity.

Much ambiguity shrouds the issue of identity in Canada. Even the British charter group whose members tend to occupy the elite positions in the Canadian social structure seem to have an identity that, if not riddled with self-doubt, is far from clear-cut. It has been suggested that the fuzzy Canadian identity can be attributed in large measure to Canada's colonial background and heavy immigration from the mother country, on the one hand, and the diffuse cultural boundaries and two-way traffic of considerable scope between Canada and the United States, on the other hand. The influence of American capital and mass media in Canada should not be underestimated. In addition, the United States is high on the list of "source countries" that have contributed significant numbers of immigrants to Canada consistently over the years (see Table 2).

Compared with the United States, for example, Canada has a higher proportion of foreign-born in its total population.[20] When we consider the complexities involved in internalizing a culture so that one is left with a sense of belonging or identity, we may wish to conclude that the transmission of cultural myths and values and the teaching of history and citizenship may present more of a challenge to a country actively engaged in immigration than to one with a homogeneous population or a static ethnic mix.

It is not clear whether immigrants to Canada and the United States are able to distinguish between the two countries in an accurate fashion on a cultural and political level or whether they tend to view North America as a classic, undifferentiated "land of opportunity". In such a context, distinctions between the "two nation" vision of Macdonald and Cartier and the "one nation under God" to the South may seem trivial. It is precisely such distinctions, however, that would have to be widely known if the Canadian identity were to be set apart from the American.

The warmth of the reception received by immigrants to Canada has depended on whether "Anglo-conformity" or cultural pluralism was in vogue. The future of Canada as a multi-ethnic society, however, rests on more than the presence or absence of an "official" ideology of multiculturalism on the part of the government. It is in the order of an experimental question whether the concept of Canada as a multicultural society can fit comfortably into a bilingual framework. If multiculturalism were enthusiastically endorsed, might not the logic of the "two nation" premise become confused? Such fears have been behind the reluctance of the French Canadian nation to actively support multiculturalism.[21]

Sociologists have been split on their reactions to multiculturalism. While they may recognize the inherent value of different cultures, they may have some reservation as to their equal utility in modern society. As Warren Kalbach has noted, "Perpetuation of cultural forms may ... provide an important source for emotional gratification. Yet, successful retention of language and culture on the part of minority ethnic populations may impede social change by preventing their members from acquiring the skills they need to effectively compete in the ongoing industrial and technological revolution."[22]

Social theorists once assumed that as modernization and industrialization progressed, the ethnic dimension in life would assume less salience.[23] The urban culture, it was thought, would move toward homogeneity. In fact the concept of a world culture or "global village" was not that remote, given the pervasive influence of the mass media. As ethnic concerns became minimized, social differences would find expression along social class lines.

If the relative importance of racial and ethnic factors were superseded by a broader social class based consciousness, the potential for social class conflict rather than racial or ethnic conflict would be present. Although predicted to occur in industrial societies, a class conflict scenario on a revolutionary scale has not been enacted in western countries. On the contrary, a "new ethnicity"[24] has asserted itself. In the United States the failure of the melting pot is recognized.[25] On the part of Blacks, demands for integration have been somewhat tempered by the emergence of "Black pride" and the development of a parallel Black "soul culture". In Great Britain the Scotch and Welsh nationalists are active, and in Quebec, of course, nationalism is strong.

In addition to nationalistic mass movements, a concern with one's "roots" continues to interest individuals and families. The study of genealogy has achieved much popularity. Instead of ethnicity's dying with the development of modern social classes, it has staged a recovery. Perhaps for some ethnicity literally does function as roots, providing stability and continuity amidst bewildering encounters with the forces of social change that challenge traditional identities and customs. The future of ethnicity, however it may evolve with respect to substance and modes of expression, seems assured, regardless of whether it may impede or enhance the mobility of its adherents.

ENDNOTES

1. When the Hudson's Bay Co. in 1869 sold Métis land to the new Dominion of Canada, the local autonomy of the Métis was placed in jeopardy. Fearing possible American intervention, Sir John A. Macdonald in 1869-70 assured Louis Riel, the elected leader of the Red River settlement, in the Manitoba Act that religion, language, land title and local government would be honored. In time, however, the Métis stood in the way of the CPR and the grand economic design of Canada. The last so-called Métis rebellion took place in 1885, the year the CPR was completed. See Mason Wade, *The French Canadians* (Toronto: Macmillan of Canada, 1968), Vol. 1, Ch. 8.

   The Canadian business class wished to bolster staple exports by promoting wheat farming and immigration. For the staple approach to the theory of economic growth, see Harold A. Innis, *Essays in Canadian Economic Theory* (Toronto: University of Toronto Press, 1956).

2. Richard Joy, *Languages in Conflict* (Toronto: McClelland and Stewart, 1972), Ch. 11.

3. W. E. Kalbach, *The Effect of Immigration on Population* (Ottawa: Department of Manpower and Immigration, 1974), Table 2.7.

4. John Porter, *The Vertical Mosaic* (Toronto: University of Toronto Press, 1965).

5. Freda Hawkins, *Canada and Immigration: Public Policy and Public Concern* (Montreal: McGill-Queen's University Press, 1972), p. 34.

6. Warren E. Kalbach and Wayne McVey, *The Demographic Bases of Canadian Society* (Toronto: McGraw-Hill, 1971), Table 1.1.

7. House of Commons Journals 1900, 308 as cited in Robert C. Brown and Ramsay Cook, *Canada 1896-1921: A Nation Transformed* (Toronto: McClelland and Stewart, 1974), p. 55.

8. For a general history of the Doukhobors, see George Woodcock and Ivan Avakumovic, *The Doukhobors* (Toronto: McClelland and Stewart, 1977) esp. Ch. 6. The land in question near Prince Albert was "not far from the region of Louis Riel's last rebellion (p. 148)." Elsewhere, the confiscation has been described as a deliberate "expediency by a new federal Minister of the Interior to break up the Doukhobor communal reserve." Koozma J. Tarasoff, "Doukhobors: Their Migration Experience," in *Canadian Ethnic Studies* Vol. 4, no. 1-2 (1972), p. 2. According to Tarasoff, a similar fate had previously struck the Old Order Mennonites in Manitoba.

9. In 1918, an Order-in-Council from the Borden government prohibited "the publication of books, newspapers, magazines or any printed matter in the language of any country or people ... at war with Great Britain." *Canadian Annual Review, 1918*, p. 580. The Order was in effect until January 1, 1920. Bilingual schools were disallowed in Manitoba in 1916; 61 German/English schools and over 100 English/French schools, for example, were permanently closed. For an account of the events in Manitoba and other provinces, see Werner A. Bausenhart, "The Ontario German Language Press and Its Suppression by Order-in-Council in 1918," *Canadian Ethnic Studies*, Vol. 4, no. 1-2 (1972), and W. Entz, "The Suppression of the German Language Press in September, 1918," *Canadian Ethnic Studies* Vol. 8, no. 2 (1976).

10. A focus on European immigration to major cities has tended to overshadow an analysis of rural poverty. The rural migrant in Quebec and Atlantic Canada seeks "livelihood in the urban centers the nearest to his home community. These are urban centers the least caught up in forces of economic growth." S. D. Clark, "The Disadvantaged Rural Society: New Dimensions of Urban Poverty," *Canadian Society in Historical Perspective* (Toronto: McGraw-Hill, Ryerson, 1976), p. 77.

11. P.C. 2743, June 2, 1949. Laval Fortier was appointed as Deputy Minister of the Dept. of Citizenship and Immigration on January 18, 1950. This appointment was an attempt to involve the previously opposed or indifferent francophones in expansionist immigration. For a historical account, see Jacques Brossard, *L'Immigration: les droits et pouvoirs du Canada et du Quebec* (Montreal: Presses de l'Université de Montreal, 1962).

12. It is an oversimplification, however, to view immigrant streams as farmers followed by urban dwellers. H. Troper, *Only Farmers Need Apply* (Toronto:

Giffin Press, 1972). This source focuses on the pursuit of agricultural workers. Between 1906 and 1914, however, occupational intentions of the immigrants were 37% farming and farm labor, 34% general labor, 15% mechanical, 6% clerical and trade, 2% mining, and the remainder unspecified. Donald Avery presents this data in "Continental European Immigrant Workers in Canada 1896-1919: from "Stalwart Peasants' to Radical Proletariat," *Canadian Review of Sociology and Anthropology* Vol. 12:1 (February 1975).

13. Hawkins, *op. cit.*, p. 51.

14. Harney and Troper call our attention to a distinct anti-urban bias which tends to equate immigrants in cities with "social problems". R. F. Harney and H. Troper, "Introduction: Immigrants in Cities," *Canadian Ethnic Studies* 7:1 (1977).

15. Historical data relating immigration history with shifting ideologies is provided by Howard Palmer, *Immigration and the Rise of Multiculturalism* (Toronto: Copp Clark, 1975).

16. *Report of the Royal Commission on Bilingualism and Biculturalism* Vols. 1-4 (1967-1969). Ottawa: Queen's Printer.

17. *Report of the Royal Commission on Bilingualism and Biculturalism*, Book IV: "The Cultural Contribution of the Other Ethnic Groups," (Ottawa, 1969).

18. In response to Book IV of the Royal Commission, Prime Minister Trudeau on October 8, 1971, announced a policy of multiculturalism within a bilingual framework whereby the government would assist various cultures and ethnic groups. A discussion of this policy and Canadian ethnicity in general is provided by Jean Burnet, "Ethnicity: Canadian Experience and Policy," *Sociological Focus* Vol. 9, no. 2 (April, 1976).

19. The new Immigration Act came into effect April 10, 1978. Applicants are awarded 5 points if they go to a location where their job skills are in short supply. Almost one half of the maximum 100 points are given for employment-related factors. The maximum education rating dropped from 20 to 12 points.

20. In the United States, the percentage of foreign born had fallen to 4.9% in 1965. Ernest Rubin, "The Demography of Immigration to the U.S.," *Annals of the American Academy of Political and Social Science*, Vol. 367 (Sept. 1966), p. 15. In Canada, the percentage of foreign born has not fallen under approximately 13% which it attained in 1901. In 1971, it was 15.3%. Kalbach, *op. cit.*, 1974, Table 2.6.

21. Guy Rocher, "Les ambiguités d'un Canada bilingue et multiculturel," *Le Quebec en Mutation* (Montreal: Hutubise, 1973).

22. Warren E. Kalbach, "Demographic Aspects of Canadian Identity," *Sounds Canadian* Paul Migus, (ed.), Toronto: Peter Martin, 1975), pp. 145-46. The same concern has been voiced by others; for example, John Porter, "Ethnic Pluralism in Canada," *Ethnicity, Theory and Experience*, Nathan Glazer and Daniel P. Moynihan, (eds.) (Cambridge: Harvard University Press, 1975).

23. The assimilationist perspective, as well as the conflict perspective, argued that ascriptively oriented relations would lessen in importance as modernization progressed. Universalistic rather than particularistic criteria would determine social mobility. *Cf.* Peter Blau and Otis Duncan, *The American Occupational Structure* (New York: Wiley, 1967); Parsons, *op. cit.*, 1971.

24. The "new ethnicity" is an emergent phenomenon; as opposed to the "old ethnicity", the new is not thought to be transmitted in a static state from one generation to the next. For a theoretical assessment of the new ethnicity, see William Yancey, Eugene Ericksen and Richard Juliani, "Emergent Ethnicity: A Review and Reformulation," *American Sociological Review*, Vol. 41, no. 3 (June, 1976), pp. 391-403.

25. Data disconfirming, in part, assimilationist theory is presented in Nathan Glazer and Daniel P. Moynihan, *Beyond the Melting Pot* (Cambridge: Massachusetts Institute of Technology Press, 1963). On a policy level, the response to the melting pot's "failure" has been the creation of "affirmative action" programs. In turn, their "shortcomings" are reviewed by N. Glazer, *Affirmative Discrimination: Ethnic Identity and Public Policy* (New York: Basic Books, 1976).

JUDITH A. NAGATA   York University

One Vine, Many Branches: Internal Differentiation in Canadian Ethnic Groups*

Familiarity with some of the facts of life of many ethnic populations both in Canada and elsewhere often reveals a startling degree of internal diversity, differentiation and sometimes even conflict, within what are nominally single and unified communities or groups.

The convention of speaking about "ethnic groups" tends to create an illusion of solidarity and community consciousness which in practice rarely exists. Sociologically, the term "group" implies a certain level of awareness and involvement, and possibly even a potential for action and mobilization, that few actual ethnic groups in Canada are able to achieve. There are exceptions, of course, and these will be discussed, and so will the rather special conditions under which such mobilization and groupness occur.

Misapprehensions about ethnic unity often result from the fact that it is the uninformed outsider looking in (whether the outsider be administrator, other citizen or social scientist), who makes definitions and assumptions as to the nature of the population, usually on the basis of insufficient knowledge of the internal organization, characteristics and self-perception of those concerned. Thus, a sheer lack of information, and possibly also of interest, leads the average white Canadian to classify under a single rubric "Pakistani", a whole spectrum of peoples: Indian, Guyanese, Malay, Filipino, Ceylonese, and others, and to accord similar treatment to all. Likewise, a failure to distinguish Canadian-born blacks, such as those from Nova Scotia, from American blacks and West Indians, respectively, allows the single category "black" to be applied equally to all. Sometimes this gives way to the arbitrary assumption that all are "West Indians".

Alternatively, it is frequently in the interest of members or leaders of a particular ethnic population to attempt to present a unified community image to the rest of the world, and efforts are made to paper over the cracks of internal division or discord. Yet under closer scrutiny, their apparent monolithic character and cultural uniformity tend to crumble, showing little evidence of the unity that is usually assumed to be one of

---

* Written expressly for *Two Nations, Many Cultures: Ethnic Groups in Canada.*

the hallmarks of the "ethnic group". For not only do internal variations exist, but ethnic boundaries are not always as definitive or fixed as might be supposed. People can, and do, change their ethnic status, or else switch from an ethnic to a non-ethnic identity, as we shall see, and this too reflects a less than perfect commitment to, or homogeneity of, the membership.

One of the principal reasons why the outside observer often fails to recognize both the differentiation within ethnic populations and their boundaries, and even to classify as one what insiders would regard as several, is lack of knowledge of the significant criteria of ethnicity, particularly those meaningful to actors in specific social situations. Membership in an ethnic group can be derived from one, or a combination of, a number of possible attributes, of which language, religion, place of birth and origin, are the most common. These attributes, however, are not necessarily isomorphic, and may cross-cut one another in different ways, with the result that different groups and boundaries emerge, depending on the attribute by which they are defined (Darroch & Marston, 1969). Thus the French-speaking peoples of Canada would encompass, for example, the Québécois, the Acadians, those born in France, many persons of Belgian and Swiss origin, and an even wider assortment of peoples originating from Haiti, Martinique, certain francophone African countries, and Vietnam. If religion (such as Roman Catholicism) is used as the defining attribute, however, then a new constellation of peoples would emerge including, for example, the Italians and the Irish, not necessarily coinciding with the same linguistic cluster. Finally, place of birth and/or origin, which likewise do not always correspond, would fragment the unity created by language or religion. Even when the outsider is aware of these various possible ways of carving up populations into "ethnic groups", he is not always able to predict which attribute will be invoked by the actors in any given situation. When, for example, does a "French Canadian", in the context of language or political rights, include the entire spectrum of francophones in Canada or merely the Québécois; and, are preoccupations with separatism also expected to mobilize this expanded body of francophones?

Administrators and government officials are also beset with these problems. As a result, they often create and perpetuate categories and labels which either misrepresent whole populations, or even ignore them altogether. The administrative definitions employed in the census, for example, speak of "Asians", and ignore distinctions between the Chinese, the Japanese, the Koreans, the Indians, the Filipinos, and others of Asian origins. Even where official reference is specifically made to the "Chinese" of Canada, there is usually no hint of awareness of the sometimes enormous gulf which separates the Hong Kong Chinese from his Taiwanese, Cantonese, Hakka, Teochiew or Hokkien "compatriots", whether in the realm of birth, origin or dialect. The census, like the average Canadian, fails to distinguish differences among the East Indians, the Pakistanis, and the Ceylonese, and is even more woefully ignorant of the subtle differences in origin, religion (e.g., Hindu, Muslim, Sikh, Parsee), and language, by which members of the communities concerned draw their own boundaries. Even with the more "familiar" European groups, the finer distinctions, which are often those that create the greatest conflict, are missed in official classifications. For example, the Macedonians of Northern Greece, despite the territory and polity of their birth and origin, do not identify as Greeks, from whom they are separated by many cultural practices, including a totally different language. This cleavage is reflected institutionally within all the so-called "Greek" communities of North America, for example in the organization of Church and associational life. Census classifications tend to reflect the principal directions of official interest, necessity and expediency, with the paradoxical result that all the Asians in Canada are perceived as one, while the British population is meticulously broken down into its component English, Scottish and Irish elements.

Divisions within Ethnic Communities

Internal divisions within ethnic groups take many forms, and are activated in different contexts. Some are more apparent to outsiders than others. The most common causes and patterns of intra-ethnic differentiation will now be examined separately.

Origin and Birth

Among the most obvious internal ethnic divisions are those of region and place of origin, and where different, of birth. Frequently, regional distinctions are rephrased as "sub-ethnic". In most ethnic populations, an almost infinite number of progressive subdivisions is possible, depending on the needs of the situation. Thus, "Italian" as a gross term has little of the solidarity-creating impact of the lesser and more precise identity of "Sicilian" or "Calabrian", or of the even more intense appeals of a specific village within one of these regions. Organizationally, such divisions are reflected in recruitment to and membership in voluntary associations and clubs, and these often compete with one another in sports and forms of ceremonial display, in much the same way that whole country-based ethnic populations may express their opposition to each other. Comparable examples would be the Acoreans, Madeirans, Algarvians, Lisboans and Portēnos of Portugal, or of the Peloponnesians, Cretans, Rhodians and Athenians of southern Greece. At the opposite end of the scale, common origin can be "stretched" to include even broader categories of people, such as the Brazilians who claim commonality with the Portuguese on the basis of their Lusitanian origin, when they wish to take advantage of Portuguese community facilities in Toronto.

The case of the Portuguese and Brazilians is typical of those in which place of origin and actual birth may part company, and the particular identity selected will depend on the advantages to be obtained, the solidarity and cooperation anticipated, or the social distance to be expressed. Opportunities for such selection exist in many other groups, such as those Greeks, Turks and Portuguese born of migrant workers in places like West Germany and Sweden. This could be important, for example, where immigration quotas are determined by country of birth or of last residence, particularly where quotas for place of origin are already filled. In matters of language and cultural loyalty, or even friendship patterns, on the other hand, place of origin would determine "ethnic" identity. Similar oscillations were practised, according to Rioux (1974), by the early French Canadians in this country. When emphasizing their distinctiveness from the French of France, they would refer to themselves as "Canadiens", on the basis of their North American birth. In opposition to the English Canadians, they stressed their (French) origin, and then became Québécois.

It may thus be seen that the identity frame of reference may constantly be changing, either from broad to narrow (more to less inclusive), or from one characteristic to another, according to the immediate context. Normally, the largest possible group with interests in a given issue will be invoked for that purpose (cf. Nagata, 1974).

Cultural Divisions

It often goes unrecognized that frequently, almost as much intra-ethnic cultural variation may exist as occurs between members of different ethnic communities, or between these and the host society. Aside from rural/urban and class differences (see below) and the regional variations discussed above, other factors may contribute to cultural diversity.

One of these factors depends on the generation of the immigrants, and the period in which they left their homeland. Those Japanese and Chinese Canadians who arrived in this country prior to World War II came from societies substantially different from those left by the postwar emigrants. In general, first-generation immigrants of the prewar period display more "traditional" behaviors and are characterized as more "conservative" culturally than the immigrants of a later era. Among the Chinese in particular, these differences may be reinforced by political ideology and commitment, with the post-1949 arrivals being more polarized over the current regime on the mainland than those from the "old" society. Japanese Canadians themselves recognize generational distinctions, and commonly refer to number of generations of residence in Canada as culturally significant, viz. Issei, Nisei, Sansei, Yonsei, and so on.

In addition to the above, considerable individual variation in cultural loyalty and commitment to ethnic institutions and style of life is inevitable. While some members faithfully support community organizations and follow traditional rites of passage and family and religious practices, others are less meticulous. The important point here, however, as Barth (1970) has made clear, is that a sense of personal identity and a tacit recognition of social networks and boundaries, not "the cultural stuff" enclosed by these boundaries, ultimately determine ethnic membership and commitment. An Italian may flout his ancestral Catholic faith, and all the ceremonial, community and family practices which it entails, in favor of Pentecostalism, but he remains, nonetheless, an Italian. Individuals may also be culturally inactive, or acculturated to the host society objectively, yet subjectively consider themselves part of an ethnic community (Gordon, 1964), as many secular Jews in Canada today. Those third-generation Greeks, too, who have become successfully integrated to upper middle class Canadian society, speak only English, and with but residual Greek cultural behavior, may nevertheless regard themselves as more "Greek" than Canadian in a number of social contexts, and subsequently even try to pick up "lost" cultural items, such as music and language, to increase congruence with their subjective identity.

Social scientists now generally accept that culture alone is not a sufficient diagnostic of ethnic identity, because it is amenable to change, and even manipulation, by factors other than mere integration into the host society. Depending on the exigencies of the immediate situation, an individual may play up his ethnic identity, for example, in order to cement his ties with certain business associates of a particular ethnic origin, or the politician soliciting votes, only to forget this identity when it is more expedient to be non-ethnic (or other-ethnic, if any tie at all can be made with another group). In each case, there will be an attempt to adjust cultural behaviors in order to maintain a semblance of credibility and congruence with the ethnic status being claimed.

Class

Probably one of the deepest cleavages within ethnic groups in Canada and elsewhere is that created by stratification and the horizontal lines of class division. Sometimes class divisions hark back to position in the society of origin, and immigrant Greeks of upper class background are commonly heard, in Canada, to make deprecating remarks about the uncivilized mass of their poor and rural compatriots now resident in this country. Equally powerful divisions result from upward mobility achieved within Canada, and again, the Greeks resemble several other groups, such as the Italians (cf. Jansen, 1969), who are split horizontally, between middle and upper class (usually second generation) on the one hand, and working class (normally newcomers) on the other. This gulf is reflected in many of the ethnic institutions (for example, the elitist Church and other associations), to the extent that many of the working class fail to recognize or accept those who claim to be "leaders" of the ethnic community (Nagata, 1969; Jansen, 1969).

One of the problems here is that upward social mobility in countries like Canada invariably involves a greater degree of acculturation (objectively, at least) to the host society, and a greater facility in handling the ways of the wider (non-ethnic) world, particularly in the public sphere. This often results in visible cultural, and sometimes social, detachment from the less successful members of the "same" community. The upwardly mobile and successful tend to identify more closely with their class peers of the host society and of other ethnic origins, such that their own ethnic loyalties may sometimes be set aside in favor of class interest. The French Liberal "leaders" in Quebec could be regarded as more closely concerned with their class position than with their loyalty to the French ethnic cause. As Ossenberg has pointed out (1971), such "Québécois" resemble and associate more closely with the English elites than with working class Québécois. On the other hand, there are elites who genuinely lead their ethnic compatriots, such as the current members of the Parti Québécois government, and they could be described as counter-elites. In this respect, of course, there is less of a threat to ethnic unity.

In a modern, complex society, where most educational and occupational goals increasingly converge, ethnic identity tend to yield to class identity, particularly in areas concerned with economic, social and political advancement. It is true, for example, that most Greeks who enter Canadian political life do so as "ethnically neutral" candidates, often anglicizing their names, and in no way attempting to appeal to ethnic issues or interests. Some Italian leaders, on the other hand, often claim to represent an ethnic constituency, but even these men may be selective, sometimes cultivating their ethnic identity as the primary source of status (as in election campaigns), but at other times reverting to a preoccupation with class interests and status (in the company of fellow politicians), when "Italian-ness" may be of secondary importance.

Upward mobility and elite status frequently create disunity in the ethnic community. They are, however, one of the principal avenues by which these same communities articulate with the host society, and by which political goals in particular can be achieved.

Rural/Urban Differences

The unity of ethnic populations is also modified by rural/urban divisions. This dichotomy often reflects lines of class difference. Rather predictably, rural dwellers tend to be lower on the scale of social stratification, while the elites are frequently urban in origin and residence, and these differences may be greater than the similarities by which the ethnic group is normally identified. The same is true, by extension, of cultural behaviors, which may be so modified by residential and class factors, that the "ethnic core culture" may be substantially unrecognizable from segment to segment of the population. Thus, Montrealers differ from rural Québécois in many respects—linguistic, occupational and in overall style of life. Likewise, the Acadian French in New Brunswick recognize the deep division (now with political overtones), between the Moncton-centered and university-dominated old French elite leadership, and the rural, coastal francophones whom new political leaders have recently risen to represent.

Scale, Size and Distribution

In a country the size and complexity of Canada, the very spatial distribution of ethnic populations militates against a monolithic unity of interest and organization, much less the potential for common action or mobilization. Problems of communication, rural/urban difference and social and geographic mobility, effectively limit group unity. Only in the case of the Québécois does territorial discreteness and solidarity create a condition capable of counteracting some of the other lines of cleavage, and provide the logistical basis for any realistic and concerted action. This comes closer to the "group-like" quality which is rarely found in a dispersed community. It is partly for reasons of residential distribution that the substantial, but isolated, French minorities in Manitoba and New Brunswick do not identify so closely with, or participate in, the Québécois movement, thus making the latter a territorial as much as a cultural or linguistic phenomenon.

Ethnic groups, whether immigrant minorities within a single state or transnational communities (e.g., the Jews, the Italians, and the Japanese), rarely mobilize as true groups for purposes of a common cause. However, groupness and pan-ethnic solidarity emerge in exceptional circumstances. The Middle East crisis, for example, stirred a pan-Jewish consciousness, transcending the many sub-differences mentioned. The Friuli earthquake brought Italians together in a common cause to give aid to survivors. The Japanese centennial in Canada created a feeling of unity within the Japanese community.

At the other end of the scale could be cited the Scots of Canada. Scottish Canadians can be considered as little more than a diffuse category (but by no means a group) of individuals who acknowledge an ultimate common origin and a vague sense of identity. Aside from the occasional burst of cultural revitalization in the form of such rather self-conscious activities as the Highland Games, the Canadian Scots have a low social and cultural profile, and no demonstrable claim to be a true community, in the strict sense of the word.

Mobilization of any group tends to reduce, at least temporarily, cleavages and distinctions at "lower" levels. Thus the German, Russian, Polish and Moroccan Jews set aside their respective differences in their collective opposition to the Arabs, but go their separate ways again when the Middle East question is not salient. The broader coalition is easily interrupted by lesser divisions, and a constant process of alternate fission and fusion occurs, with no permanent, unambiguous and immutable "ethnic" boundaries. Normally, as we have seen, ethnic mobilization follows a pattern of segmentary opposition between different components and combinations of a population, and is usually dependent on the issues of the moment. "Ethnic" identities and labels are then shuffled accordingly.

Conclusion

Ethnic identity is an elusive concept to isolate and pin down. It cannot be defined by culture alone, and indeed, its cultural expression and underpinnings may vary from situation to situation. Further, the social boundaries by which the culture is enclosed are often far from clear, and may shift from time to time, and according to interest. Individuals may alternately espouse and play up an ethnic identity with another competing or non-ethnic identity, such as one of class. The intensity of the ethnic commitment and participation often depends on more immediate, practical and instrumental issues, and personal identity will tend to follow these interests.

Even where ethnic loyalties are fairly constant and predictable, these must not be allowed to obscure substantial internal differences, ranging from those of origin and birth ("sub-ethnic" loyalty), to other forms of cultural variation, class and rural/urban distinctions.

Finally, the groupness and community qualities of ethnicity are frequently overplayed, for the level of consciousness and action, like that of cultural uniformity, is rarely as high as that believed by the outsider.

Mobilization usually only occurs in exceptional situations, and is rarely sustained beyond immediate, short-lived interests, after which the internal, segmentary process of subdivision customarily takes over once more.

SELECTED REFERENCES

Barth, Frederik. *Ethnic Groups and Boundaries*. London: Allen & Unwin, 1970.

Darroch, G., and W. Marston. "Ethnic Differentiation: Ecological Aspects of a Multidimensional Concept," *The International Migration Review* 4:1 (1969), pp. 71-95.

Gordon, Milton M. *Assimilation in American Life: The Role of Race, Religion and National Origins*. New York: Oxford University Press, 1964.

Jansen, Clifford. "Leadership in the Toronto Italian Ethnic Group," *The International Migration Review* 4:1 (1969), pp. 25-40.

Nagata, Judith. "Adaptation and Integration of Greek Working Class Immigrants in the City of Toronto: A Situational Approach," *The International Migration Review* 4:1 (1969), pp. 44-68.

———. "What is a Malay? Situational Selection of Ethnic Identity in a Plural Society," *American Ethnologist* 1:2 (1974), pp. 331-50.

Ossenberg, Richard, (ed.). *Canadian Society: Pluralism, Change and Conflict*. Scarborough, Ont.: Prentice-Hall of Canada, 1971.

Rioux, Marcel. *Les Québécois. Le Temps Qui Court*. France: Editions du Seuil, 1974.

DAVID MILLETT   University of Ottawa

Religious Identity: The Non-Official Languages and the Minority Churches*

Introduction

The "race issue" sparked by recent non-white (primarily Asian) immigration to Canada competes in importance with the issue of Native Peoples. The populations involved are of roughly equal size (between 500 000 and one million) according to how the two groups (non-white immigrants and Native Peoples) are defined. The problems of their American counterparts, whether immigrants or Native Peoples, do not attract comparable attention, dwarfed as they are by the race question (the black American population equals the entire population of Canada).

A significant part of the non-white Canadian immigrant population shares with Native Peoples two complications which go beyond purely racial problems—differences with the dominant whites over language, and differences of religion. Where racial, linguistic, and religious differences combine, they may be greeted periodically with apprehension or outright hostility. Underlying such reactions is the concern that in some basic and unchangeable ways "they" are different from "us", and that "their" beliefs and customs are incompatible with something which, for lack of a better term, is often called "the Canadian way of life", or "the Judaeo-Christian tradition".[1]

Religion provides a target on which such reactions tend to be focused. Asian religions, for example, appear as a visible symbol of all the cultural differences, real or imagined, which white Canadians attribute to the foreign-born. The use, by some immigrants, of non-official languages in their religious services permits these fears to be further exaggerated. In fact, however, most "non-white" immigrants (and most Native People) practise the same religion—western Christianity—as the dominant white group.

White immigrants, while not subjected to racial discrimination, arouse similar though less intense sentiments of anxiety because of their use of

* I wish to thank Professor Kenneth Westhues, of the University of Waterloo, for organizing a conference on religion which motivated much of the research underlying this paper. Thanks are also due to the Faculty of Graduate Studies at the University of Ottawa for financial support, and to Miss Judy Cantwell, for energetic work as a research assistant.

languages other than English or French. Like their fellow immigrants of non-European origin, they tend to concentrate use of these languages in their homes and in their places of worship. Insofar as they do so, they must work out certain accommodations with existing English-language and French-language institutions in Canada. Thus it is that three self-conscious groups—Native Peoples, white immigrants, and "non-white" immigrants—share a common problem of linguistic accommodation.

There are at least five ways in which immigrants and Native Peoples may relate to religious institutions developed by the English-French[2] dominant group:

(1) They could abandon all religious activity, if they have not already done so, and join those Canadians who have no religion (secular assimilation).

(2) They could move, as individuals or families, into churches, sects, and cults of the native-born operating in the official languages and disappear as rapidly as racial and linguistic difficulties permit (religious assimilation).

(3) They could join pre-existing parishes or congregations sponsored by the major churches or sects operating in a non-official language. This may involve exerting pressure to create parishes and congregations which add to the languages already available (linguistic diversification).

(4) They could establish temples, mosques, and other institutions for their own religions if these are not already available in Canada (new formal organizations).

(5) If their religion does not require a formal organization, they could practise it in their own homes, in cultural centers, or in whatever form of religious interaction is traditional in their Canadian communities or in their homeland (new informal organizations).

Our purpose here is to examine option 3: it is through linguistic diversification that Native Peoples and immigrants cause religious structures to respond to their needs, and come to share the religious institutions created by the dominant linguistic groups. We wish to discover the non-official languages in which major churches provide services for Native Peoples, for recent white immigrants, and for "non-white" immigrants. A second question, related to the sense of power among these groups, concerns the way various minority churches are clustered in different regions of Canada. We will return to this question after examining the concept of "minority church" more closely.

Minority Churches

Canadian parishes and congregations which provide services in non-official languages have been our primary source of data. We have called these organizations *minority churches*, as they use in common languages which are likely to antagonize members of the English- and French-speaking dominant groups and lead to discrimination. The minority church concept has been applied in Canada to the development of the Orthodox churches.[3] It was originally used to explain the behavior of religious bodies whose members, because of some sort of persecution, might be expected to adopt a defensive attitude, spurn "the world", and become a sect, but who instead continue to act as a church.

Roger Mehl, using the term to explain why French Protestants display church-like rather than sect-like behavior, claimed that the answer lay in their relationships with a variety of reference groups.[4] In his view, French Protestants have a strong awareness of Calvinists, Lutherans, or Baptists in other lands, and this gives them a sense of strength and security far beyond what one might expect, given their small number and the history of their persecution up to the end of the 19th century.

In Canada similar behavior may be found among non-English- or non-French-speaking parishes and congregations sponsored by large churches. Such groups generally avoid either an extreme "retreat from the world" attitude of introversionist sects, or the "aggressive efforts to change the world" approach of conversionist sects. Instead they accommodate rather easily to their society, in the manner of the large churches to which they are affiliated. I have argued that their sense of strength and security comes ultimately from their awareness of the strength of their sponsors. They know that they are associated, however indirectly, with some of the most powerful institutions of the dominant groups in Canadian society.

It must be emphasized that our interest here is confined to *sponsored* bodies. There are certain immigrant groups, such as the Ukrainians, the Greeks, and the Mennonites, which have established large churches, numbering hundreds of parishes or congregations, and which are also strong forces for linguistic and other aspects of ethnic survival. The members of these bodies draw their sense of security not from a sponsoring body but from the very size of their own churches.[5]

What is of particular interest here are not these large bodies, but those groups which are less secure, on the one hand for purely linguistic reasons (the case of white immigrants), and on the other hand for both linguistic and racial reasons (non-white immigrants and Native Peoples). These will be examined in the order of their major waves of settlement in Canada, i.e., Native Peoples, white immigrants, and non-white immigrants.

The Findings

The Churches Selected

As a first step in our research we contacted a number of major churches and asked if they sponsored any non-official language parishes or congregations. To test whether the group in question really operated as a minority church, we asked if they thought that a newcomer, unable to speak either English or French, would "feel at home" in such a congregation or parish. Their response would thus be a clue as to whether the majority church was providing a sense of strength and security to its members.

Initially we thought that the churches most likely to sponsor minority churches would be the largest and oldest ones in Canada. This assumption seemed indicated by an earlier study.[6] Certain exceptions appeared as the study progressed, and new churches were included, but most of them were found to operate only in English.[7] While we make no claim to have an exhaustive count of all the minority churches in Canada, we do have usable information from the following:

Anglican Church
Baptist Churches (3 kinds)
Church of the Latter Day Saints (Mormons)
Lutheran Council in Canada
Presbyterian Church in Canada
Roman Catholic Church
Seventh Day Adventists
United Church of Canada

In 1971 these churches accounted for over 86% of all Canadians. The response from these churches revealed over 700 congregations and parishes operating in more than 60 languages (see Table 1). They also, of course, offer services in English and French.

The Location of Minority Churches

Canadians, whether Native Peoples, "founding groups", or recent arrivals, are scattered in very complicated ways across the country, in great masses, little islands, or in ribbons of population strung along roads and waterways. In the course of settling in the country they have poured into one region for a while, only to suddenly stop and pour into another. Some areas have had long periods of quiet in which to assimilate newcomers linguistically, while others have been constantly shaken up by the impact of new arrivals.

Some areas do not want newcomers; others are not wanted *by* newcomers. And the pattern is not entirely random. If we take the standard regions of Canada, determined both by physical geography and by the way people have reacted to that geography, we can illuminate the cultural composition of these regions by examining what minority churches are concentrated in them. To do so, we will consider Native Peoples, white immigrants, and "non-white" immigrants in turn.

TABLE 1 *The languages of the minority churches*

A. *Languages of Native Peoples*

1. Algonquin	11. Swampy Cree	21. Nishga
2. Beaver-Slavey	12. Plains (Cree)	22. Ojibway
3. Blood	13. Eskimo (Inuit)	23. Oneida
4. Blackfoot	14. Gitkshan	24. Peigan
5. Carrier	15. Haida	25. Saultaux
6. Chipewyan	16. Kwakwala	26. Sioux
7. Cowichan	17. Loucheux	27. Six Nations (n.s.*)
8. Cree (n.s.*)	18. Micmac	28. Stony
9. Coastal Cree	19. Mohawk	29. Tsimpsean
10. Moose Cree	20. Montagnais	30. Tuscarora

B. *White Immigrant Languages*

1. Armenian	10. Greek	19. Portuguese
2. Croatian	11. Hungarian	20. Roumanian
3. Czech	12. Icelandic	21. Russian
4. Danish	13. Italian	22. Slovak
5. Dutch	14. Latin	23. Slovene
6. Estonian	15. Latvian	24. Spanish
7. Finnish	16. Lithuanian	25. Swedish
8. Flemish	17. Maltese	26. Ukrainian
9. German	18. Polish	27. Yugoslav (n.s.*)

C. *"Non-white" Immigrant Languages*

1. Arabic (includes responses of "Lebanese", "Melchite", and "Maronite")	4. Ge'ez (used in Ethiopian Coptic Church)
2. Chinese (includes Cantonese, Mandarin, and Swatow)	5. East Indian (Hindi not always specified)
3. Creole (Haitian French)	6. Japanese
	7. Korean
	8. Vietnamese

*not specified

Native Peoples

Table 2 provides an indication of how Native Peoples have settled into various regions. We see that those who have abandoned their own religion but still worship in their own language are stronger in the Prairies than in the rest of the country. Insofar as native religions are recovering, after being outlawed for a century, there appears to be a strong population with the potential for practising them, should they choose to abandon Christianity.

Some Indian groups are much stronger than others, ranging from the Cree, with 105 minority churches, to the single tiny congregations of Carrier, or Kwakwala. Such small groups may not find sufficient protection from the white man's world in the white man's church, and may eventually "retire from the world" into little introverted sects.[8] The stronger tribes may evolve into large Indian Christian churches, or may use their growing sense of strength to break out of the colonialism of the white churches (however benevolent and secure), and return to their own religion, or develop some synthesis of native religion and Christianity, as has happened in many areas around the world.[9] Many Inuit, for example, have affiliated with the Baha'i World Faith, which permits retention of most of their original beliefs. The Baha'i do not, however, provide services in the Inuit language.

TABLE 2 *Native language parishes and congregations sponsored by major churches, Canada and regions, 1977*

Language	Atlantic	Quebec	Ontario	Region Prairies	B.C.	Arctic	Canada
1. Algonquin		5					5
2. Beaver-Slavey				2			2
3. Blood				1			1
4. Blackfoot				3			3
5. Carrier					1		1
6. Chipewyan				1			1
7. Cowichan					1		1
8. Cree (n.s.)*		2	16	68			86
9. Coastal Cree		3				1	4
10. Moose Cree		2	6				8
11. Swampy Cree			1				1
12. Plains Cree				6			6
13. Inuit	1	10				48	59
14. Gitkshan					3		3
15. Haida					1		1
16. Kwakwala					2		2
17. Loucheux						4	4
18. Micmac	1						1
19. Mohawk		2	1				3
20. Montagnais	2	7		4			13
21. Nishga					3		3
22. Ojibway			28				28
23. Oneida			3				3
24. Peigan				1			1
25. Saultaux			3	4			7
26. Sioux				1			1
27. Six Nations (n.s.*)			3				3
28. Stony				1			1
29. Tsimpsean					5		5
30. Tuscarora			1				1
Total	4	28	65	92	16	53	258

*not specified

TABLE 3 *White immigrant parishes and congregations sponsored by major churches, Canada and regions, 1977*

Language	Atlantic	Quebec	Ontario	Region Prairies	B.C.	Can.
Armenian		2	1			3
Croatian		1	9	4	2	16
Czech		1	4	1		6
Danish			2	2	1	5
Dutch	1		1			2
Estonian		2	13		1	16
Finnish		1	7		1	9
German		3	13	45	8	69
Greek			1			1
Hungarian		3	24	8	3	38
Icelandic				1		1
Italian	1	9	57	3	7	77
Latin			2			2
Latvian		2	11	1	1	15
Lithuanian		2	6	1		9
Maltese			1			1
Polish	1	4	25	9	2	41
Portuguese		2	26	6	3	37
Roumanian		1	3			4
Russian		1	2			3
Slovak		1	14		1	16
Slovene		1	4	1		6
Spanish		1	7	1	1	10
Swedish			1			1
Ukrainian			4	4	1	9
Yugoslav (n.s.*) coded "Croatian"			1			1
Total	2	38	239	87	32	398

*not specified

White Immigrants

Table 3 shows how European whites have formed minority churches over the years. The pattern of recent immigration is suggested by the 77 Italian parishes and the 37 Portuguese. At the other extreme are large but longer-resident groups such as the Dutch, now mainly assimilated with only two surviving Dutch-speaking parishes, both Roman Catholic. This means that virtually all Dutch members of the United, Presbyterian and Baptist churches are now anglicized.[10] Between these extreme cases, however, we find moderately-sized but persistent groups which cling to churches in their own language, such as the Croatians, Estonians, and Slovaks, with 16 churches each, and the Latvians, with 15. Either these

TABLE 4 *"Non-white" immigrant languages is parishes and congregations for major churches, Canada and regions, 1977*

Language	Atlantic	Quebec	Ontario	Region Prairies	B.C.	Arctic	Canada
1. Arabic		1	2				3
2. Chinese		5	12	5	9		31
3. Creole		1					1
4. East Indian				3			3
5. Ge'ez	nil	1				nil	1
6. Japanese		3	8	3	6		20
7. Korean		2	13	4	5		24
8. Vietnamese		1	1				2
Total		14	39	12	20		85

groups are very attached to their churches for religious or other reasons (perhaps political), or there is a heavier flow of immigration than may appear obvious. The regional distribution of European-speaking minority churches approximates closely the national distribution of population.

"Non-white" Immigrants

Let us now examine the languages of "non-white" immigrants, as presented in Table 4. (As indicated in endnote 1, these are not necessarily non-white people in a racial sense, but are those perceived as extremely foreign, and hence subject to the same discrimination as the non-whites).

Table 4 shows in a striking manner that Ontario now surpasses British Columbia as an area with the most number of recent non-white (primarily Asian) immigrants. The number of minority churches that have sprung up (shown in more detail in Table 5) reflects the change in immigration policy since 1964. The increase in the number of Chinese immigrants, for example, has resulted in the establishment of 31 parishes and congregations. Most striking of all is the appearance of 24 Korean churches, starting from zero in 1968.[11]

Table 5 groups these same churches by Asian, African, and Caribbean origins. It shows which major church has sponsored which group and indicates in more detail the growth of each group since 1968, the date of an earlier study. Forty new churches have been added to the 45 parishes and congregations of 1968; this represents close to 100% growth. As previously indicated (endnote 6), the Jehovah's Witness and Pentecostal Assemblies also support a considerable number of Asian and European-language congregations, but details of their regional distribution are not yet available.

TABLE 5 *Sponsors and growth of "non-white" immigrant minority churches*

Language	Sponsoring Denomination*								Total 1977	Total 1968**	Net Inc.
	Adv.	Ang.	Bap.	L.C.C.	Mor.	Pres.	R.C.	U.C.			
Asian:											
Chinese	1	2	3	3	2	5	6	9	31	21	+10
East Indian			3				—		4	0	+4
Japanese	1	6					1	12	23	18	+5
Korean	1	2	3		1	6	4	7	22	0	+22
Vietnamese							2		2	0	+2
Total	3	10	9	3	3	11	13	28	82	39	+43
African:											
Arabic							3		3	2	+1
Ge'ez (Coptic)							1		1	4	−3
Total							4		4	6	−2
Caribbean:											
Creole							1		1	0	+1
Overall Total	3	10	9	3	3	11	18	28	87	45	+42

* Adv. Adventist
Ang. Anglican
Bap. Baptist
L.C.C. Lutheran Council of Canada
** Adventists and Mormons not included

Mor. Mormon
Pres. Presbyterian
R.C. Roman Catholic
U.C. United Church of Canada

TABLE 6 *Minority churches by region, Canada, 1977*

Population	Atlantic	Quebec	Ontario	Region Prairies	B.C.	Arctic	Canada
Native Peoples	4	28	65	92	16	53	258
White immigrants	2	38	239	87	32		398
"Non-white" immigrants		14	39	12	20		85
All minority churches	6	80	343	191	68	53	741

"Non-white" immigrants, then, have come to constitute a significant part of the minority church scene in Canada. The entire picture can now be summarized briefly in regional terms as shown in Table 6.

The Regional Influence of Sponsoring Churches

By persuading churches to offer services in non-official languages, immigrants and Native Peoples make the churches function as perpetuators of ethnic diversity. Each church has more impact in some regions of Canada than in others. Some regions are dominated by particular churches, and others by different churches. Table 7 shows the impact of each sponsoring church on various regions of Canada, as measured by the regions' ability to support minority churches.

Referring to Table 7, it is interesting to compare the relative strength of Roman Catholics with non-Catholics in each region. In the Atlantic region the six minority churches are all Roman Catholic, and in Quebec Catholic parishes outnumber all others by 48 to 32. In Ontario, as in the

TABLE 7 *Minority churches by sponsoring church, Canada and regions*

Sponsor	Atlantic	Quebec	Ontario	Region Prairies	B.C.	Arctic	Canada
Adv.			7	7	3		17
Ang.		15	41	31	10	32	129
Bap.			37		2		39
L.C.C.		7	35	41	12		95
Mor.		1	6		1		8
Pres.		2	14	2	4		22
R.C.	6	48	167	84	22	21	348
U.C.		7	36	26	14		83
Total	6	80	343	191	68	53	741

Adv. Adventist
Ang. Anglican
Bap. Baptist
L.C.C. Lutheran Council of Canada

Mor. Mormon
Pres. Presbyterian
R.C. Roman Catholic
U.C. United Church of Canada

country at large, Catholics and non-Catholics are virtually equal in this activity, with 167 and 176 respectively. In the Prairies non-Catholics as a whole are more influential, with 107 parishes to the Catholics' 84. On the West Coast the reversal is complete, with the 46 non-Catholics far outnumbering the 22 Catholics. In the Arctic, Catholics and Anglicans share the non-official language parishes, with 21 and 32 respectively. In total we have found 348 Catholic and 393 non-Catholic minority churches in Canada.

Minority Churches and Ethnic Persistence

Minority churches operating in non-official languages (normally a very insecure situation), and yet relatively in harmony with Canadian society, constitute a strong force for ethnic persistence. They provide a locus for a wide range of artistic and recreational activities; since they operate in the tongue of the society of origin, they constantly attract newcomers who are not yet at ease with the English or French language. These newcomers reinforce the use of the national language in the community where the minority church is situated, using the church as a major base for their activities.

In Canada, however, linguistic survival is not only a question for people from overseas; it is also a matter of interest for Native Peoples who speak a great variety of languages and dialects. Because churches are one of a few institutions of the larger society which make use of these languages, examination of minority churches reveals much of what we could not otherwise discover about native churches.

Just why large churches sponsor linguistic minority churches, or how they came to do so, is not entirely clear. There have certainly been economic, political and career interests on the part of both the sponsored and the sponsors or such arrangements would never have developed and survived. Pure religious altruism is hardly adequate to explain such a persistent phenomenon. Whatever the dynamics of the process, the net result has contributed to the vitality of linguistic communities from one coast of Canada to the other.

Summary

As Canada evolves linguistically and in other cultural ways, Native Peoples, the English- and French-speaking dominant groups, and newcomers from Europe, Asia and Africa will jostle with one another for influence, and in some cases, for cultural survival. Minority churches are only one indicator, but a rather useful one, of ways in which people are trying to maintain their language and are succeeding. Examination of institutions produced by these survival efforts, on a regional level and even on the community level, may shed light on local conflict, especially if large institutions seek to absorb groups determined to perpetuate their own linguistic identity.

In the case of minority churches, linguistic persistence need not mean cultural continuity. The parent churches sponsoring minority churches are all representative of European culture. Thus the immigrant from Asia, the native person, and the European newcomer who all happen to be Seventh Day Adventists or Roman Catholic, for example, share a religious culture even though they belong to disparate linguistic groups. They tend to become homogenized in a religious "global village".

In Canada, the major denominations which sponsor minority churches may, at the same time, both facilitate the integration of immigrants and natives by involving them in a dominant institution, and hinder their integration by making it non-essential to learn English or French. The stronger the minority churches are, the more they support other minority institutions, and the more the various ethnic communities tend toward institutional completeness. This cannot help but cause Canadian society to evolve in continuously new directions.

ENDNOTES

1. This is particularly true of people from countries which have traditionally been non-Christian. Even when they are biologically Caucasian, as in the case of the Arabs, and until recently the Jews, a person obsessed by a sense of their "foreignness" may actually come to perceive them as being non-white, and subject them to racial discrimination. On this ground *I have included Arabic-speaking immigrants as "non-white", but with the term in quotation marks to indicate that the category is due to a perceptual distortion.* The effects of this distortion are quite real, and it is this, as well as linguistic differences, which makes their churches minority churches.

2. While Jews were seen as incompatible with a "white Christian Canada" as late as the 1950s, and are still subject to some discrimination, especially in provincial education systems, the position is taken here that they now constitute part of the dominant group, on both the English-speaking and the French-speaking sides. Their religious institutions make linguistic accommodations to immigrants (though not to Native Peoples) in the same way as Christian churches do. The study of Jewish minority churches has not yet been completed, and it is only for that reason that they have not been included here.

3. David Millett, "The Orthodox Church: Ukrainian, Greek and Syrian," in *Minority Canadians*, Vol. 2; J. L. Elliott, ed., "Immigrant Groups," Scarborough, Ontario: Prentice-Hall of Canada, 1971, pp. 47-65.

4. *Ibid.*, p. 59.
5. In Millett (1971) I treated the Hellenic Greek Orthodox Church and the Syrian Orthodox Church as minority churches "on the point of losing their minority church status and becoming full-fledged Canadian churches". In the interim both have grown, and I am now taking the position that they have ceased to be minority churches. To these might be added the Mennonite Church, which now sponsors a Chinese congregation, and which has come to operate mainly in English, rather than in German.
6. Reported in Paul Migus, ed., *Sounds Canadian* (Toronto: Peter Martin, 1974). The two major "surprise" groups were the Jehovah's Witnesses and the Pentecostal Assemblies of Canada. From material received they appear to be the two largest sponsors of minority churches, after the Roman Catholic Church, but their information is not yet in a form which permits a regional analysis. The case of Judaism was another surprise, as indicated in endnote 2.
7. The following denominations were found to be unilingual English:
Netherlands Reformed
Society of Friends (Quakers)
Unitarian
Baha'i
Old Catholic
8. For an account of the Kwakwala Anglican parish, see the popular novel by Margaret Craven, *I Heard the Owl Call My Name* (Toronto: Clarke Irwin, 1967).
9. These phenomena have occurred on the Hobbema Reserve in Alberta. In this situation our definition of minority church seems somewhat defective. It assumes that affiliation with the church of the dominant group (in this case the Roman Catholic Church) provides a sense of strength and security. However, some Hobbema Indians consider it as a liability and have returned to their own religion. The reference groups which give them a sense of strength are no longer white Canadians but other Indians and, more generally, Native Peoples around the world. Whether this has occurred from a sense of strength or from a sense of defeat by whites has not yet been carefully examined.
10. The Reformed Church in America (originally Dutch) also reports that all its Canadian congregations now operate in English.
11. This is a revised version of a table appearing in "The Religion of Immigrants," a paper delivered at a conference entitled "Two Nations at Prayer," University of Waterloo, May 1-3, 1977.

European Immigration

JOHN S. MATTHIASSON   University of Manitoba

The Icelandic Canadians: The Paradox of an Assimilated Ethnic Group*

Introduction

The people of Iceland live within the circumpolar region of the world. Unlike the Inuit, Chukchee or Lapp, they are not native to the region. They are displaced Norwegians who migrated there in a.d. 874 in search of political freedom. Centuries later in 1875, their descendants migrated to Canada and established a republic of New Iceland in the interlake region of Manitoba north of Winnipeg. Today, in such communities as Gimli, Riverton and Lundar, people may be found who speak English with an Icelandic accent and some may, in fact, be bilingual. Subsequent Icelandic migration settled in Winnipeg. These people were joined by families of New Icelanders fleeing small pox epidemics which struck the interlake region. In time Winnipeg became the urban ceter of Icelandic culture in Canada.

I hope to identify some of the cultural patterns which Icelandic Canadians in Winnipeg brought with them from Iceland, but over the years adapted to their new environment. These patterns of adaptation are uniquely Icelandic, reflecting the basic structural features of Icelandic culture dating back to the Viking past and the writing of the sagas.

Historical Background

Visitors to Iceland who are used to tree-covered landscapes find this island a barren place of lava, volcanic mountains and sparse vegetation. Others find a rugged beauty in its austerity. The country has never been an easy place to eke out a living; its inhabitants have suffered countless natural disasters and epidemics in their more than one thousand years of

---

* Written expressly for *Two Nations, Many Cultures: Ethnic Groups in Canada.*

history. The bubonic plague between 1402 and 1404 reduced the population by two thirds (Kristjanson, 121). By 1708, the population was 34 000, not enough to populate a city the size of Brandon, Manitoba. After the initial Norwegian settlement in a.d. 874, the Icelanders were subjected to an extended period of colonialism between 1262 and 1918 when Iceland was ruled by Denmark.

Before the colonial era, the Icelandic spirit of nationalism and independence was demonstrated by the founding in a.d. 930 of the *Althing*, the oldest functioning parliament in the western world. In 1944, Iceland formally severed political connections with Denmark when members of the *Althing* voted to restore Iceland to the status of a republic (Ruth, 10).

Halldor Laxness, an Icelandic writer, characterized Icelanders in his Nobel Prize-winning book, *The Independent People*, as aggressively independent. His sardonic portrayal of this urge for independence aptly captured the main psychological and cultural theme of his fellow islanders. With the restoration of the *Althing* to an independent status, the Icelanders had regained a position of self-determination. Nevertheless, conditions were such that in spite of their deep attachment to their small island, a vanguard of 285 Icelanders chose to break their European ties in 1875 and become participants in the social and cultural experiments taking place in Canada. After a brief time in Ontario, they settled in New Iceland.

In moving to Canada, the Icelanders hoped to find a new land which would allow them to preserve traditions which they felt were basic to their home society. At the same time, they were prepared to sacrifice tradition when it conflicted with assimilation to a new social order. This apparent contradiction or paradox has characterized their life in Winnipeg. While resisting the categorization of "ethnics", they have attempted to continue to be "Icelanders". Two related traditions they sought strongly to preserve were literary writing or publishing and education.

Icelandic Traditions

Literary Writing

The history of both written and oral literary traditions among Icelanders goes back in time to the original settlement of Iceland, and has played a significant role in the type of adaptations which Icelandic immigrants made to Canada. Traditional history pays homage to the sagas and family eddas recounting early times in Iceland. Watson Kirkconnell, a prolific translator of Icelandic poetry, once wrote, "The sagas, taken as a whole, constitute the most important contribution to European literature in the twelve centuries between Virgil and Dante" (Kristjanson, 121).

Rich in literary terms, the sagas also provide the scholar with early source material which is rare for any European population.

The New Testament was translated into Icelandic in 1540, only 15 years after William Tyndale's English translation (Kristjanson, 121). On a more mundane level, literary activities were found in the homes of farmers in isolated homesteads, where it was common to have readings each evening by some member of the family while others went about their work of weaving or repairing implements. It is said that in modern Iceland, more books and periodicals are published yearly *per capita* than in any country in the world.

When the first Icelanders settled in Manitoba, their first goal, other than to make a living, was to create a basis for the continuation of the Icelandic literary tradition in the new world. In 1877, the first issue of *Framfari*, one of the first newspapers in Manitoba and the first ethnic paper west of Ontario, appeared. Because of a factional split among supporters, which was in part responsible for the movement of Icelandic Canadians from New Iceland to Winnipeg, it ceased publication in 1880; it was soon replaced by others. *Leifur*, named after Leif Eirikson, son of Erik the Red, had a brief life, dying after three years of publication also as a result of factional division among subscribers.

In Winnipeg, two Icelandic language weeklies were born within two years of one another. *Heimskringla* was first published in 1886, and *Logberg* in 1888. The names of the two reflect the conflicting tendencies of Icelandic Canadians toward both assimilation and ethnic status. *Heimskringla* is roughly translated as "the round world," symbolizing for its first editors the communality of humanity, while *Logberg* means "the Mount of Laws," suggestive of Icelandic devotion to the *Althing*, the parliament at which each year the laws of the Icelanders were read and used to settle disputes among litigants.

The first editorial in *Heimskringla* was addressed to the question of whether or not, and to what extent, Icelandic Canadians should participate in the Canadian political scene. The conclusion reached was positive. The editorial also asked if Icelanders would be able to maintain their cultural identity in Canada with an increasing involvement in the larger fabric of Canadian society. The answer given was equally positive. Icelandic Canadians were urged to create a political front which would allow them to continue to be a unified community with a common cultural heritage, and at the same time to be Canadians to the fullest extent possible. Later editorials encouraged the formation of an Icelandic labor union and the creation of means to assist new immigrants to adjust to Canadian life (Kristjanson, 124).

Heimskringla began, then, with a strong political orientation. Its editorial policy was to support the Conservative party in Canada and the Democratic party in the United States. *Logberg* took the side of the

Liberal party, and the two papers continued through the years to disagree with one another, and each to claim their own supporters in an ideological rift which in time left all Winnipeg Icelandic Canadians on one side or the other.

Over the years, with the rapid assimilation of Icelandic Canadians, it became increasingly difficult to maintain two Icelandic language newspapers. In spite of their opposing ideological and political orientations, *Heimskringla* and *Logberg* were merged in 1959, under the combined name *Logberg-Heimskringla*. Both papers had attemped to retain contacts between Iceland and the new settlements in Canada by regularly publishing news from Iceland and items for their small numbers of subscribers in Iceland of life in the New World. Both the two original newspapers and their amalgamated successor created a forum for the publication of Icelandic poetry and prose, and in a sense were almost more literary journals than traditional newspapers. With the decline of the use of the Icelandic language in Winnipeg, however, the need for a new organ in English was recognized. Even substantial underwriting by wealthy patrons was not enough to maintain the vitality of *Logberg-Heimskringla*, and it continues its life today with heavy subsidization, facing the growing reality of eventual death. The patterns of adaptation of a generation and more of Icelandic immigrants were to a large extent determined by the editorial policies of the paper which tended to urge Canadianization above ethnic retention. At the same time, they sustained and nurtured an internally directed perspective which encouraged inadvertently the very ethnic awareness which, on one level, they seemed to oppose.

Although these were the most prominent and influential publications, more than 30 were published by Icelanders in Manitoba. Regardless of their life span, all attempted to preserve the Icelandic literary traditions in the Canadian setting. The most vital one today is the *Icelandic Canadian*, a quarterly published in English which was founded in 1942 in an effort to retain the interest of younger Icelandic Canadians who had never learned Icelandic. The *Icelandic* has as an audience those Canadians who have achieved some degree of recognition in the arts, academia or business; it has a heavy literary bent and is one of the main outlets for Icelandic Canadian poets and prose writers who want an Icelandic Canadian audience.

Many Icelandic Canadian writers have made a major impact on Canadian and international literature. Names such as Laura Goodman Salverson, William Valgardson, Stephan G. Stephansson, and Guttormur J. Guttormsson are striking examples. They have continued the saga tradition by demonstrating in a literary idiom the adjustments which Icelandic immigrants made to their new life in Canada. The poetry is rarely psychological. Instead, it typically extolls the dramatic features of the landscapes of Iceland or Canada. Short stories and novels, on the other hand, vividly demonstrated in writings such as Valgardson's *Bloodflowers*, dip into the personalities of pioneers and their offsprings with analytic knives which may wound their Icelandic Canadian readers and tarnish the memories within the Icelandic Canadian psyche. They are reminiscent of the Icelandic writings of Halldor Laxness and Gunnar Gunnarsson which Icelanders found to portray their independent nature accurately, and whom they admire as national heroes, while being disturbed by the sometimes brutal accuracy of their identification of the themes of Icelandic society and personality. Both Icelanders and Icelandic Canadians seem more comfortable with images of the rigors of the landscape they selected for themselves on both sides of the Atlantic than the psychological mirror in themselves which is a reflection of those landscapes. Writing in the New World personifies contradictions inherent in the theme of cultural dualism, a theme I shall return to later.

Education

Icelanders have always cherished education as much as their literary tradition. Marriage in Iceland required literacy; a knowledge of the sagas and eddas was expected of all. Even with the recent introduction of state schools, children were generally literate before entering them, being tutored by parents or grandparents on isolated farmsteads.

NEW ICELAND Emphasis on reading and writing skills was transplanted to New Iceland with the first Icelandic immigrants. It was a mere nine days after their arrival in the interlake area, and before homes had been constructed, that the Icelandic immigrants made a request to the Lieutenant-Governor of Manitoba to have a school provided for their children (Ruth, 1964). In 1875 the first school was opened, with thirty students enrolled (Ruth, 1964). Due to a smallpox epidemic, it was shortly closed, but reopened in 1876 with enrollment increased to 63 students. Emphasis was placed on the learning of English as a second language. Sunday schools for Christian education were founded as soon as ministers arrived to lead the new congregations, and students attending them were given instruction in reading as well as the catechism.

During this early period of settlement, New Iceland was essentially an independent political entity. A constitution drawn up in 1878 made New Iceland virtually a republic of its own, with internally controlled legal and political structures and mechanisms and the right to do everything possible to retain Icelandic traditions and the continued use of the Icelandic language (Ruth, 19). Ultimately, however, the republic was responsible, during its twelve-year life, to the overriding control of the Government of Canada, but because of their geographic isolation, settlers were able to function largely independently. In 1881, the boundaries of

Manitoba were extended to the north, and the republic of New Iceland became part of the larger province.

Although efforts were made to retain the use of Icelandic in New Iceland, the first schools in the area also emphasized the acquisition of reading, writing and verbal skills in English. After a visit to the settlements in 1878, the Federal Minister of Agriculture stated in the House of Commons that he had been impressed with the quality of English spoken by both children and adults (Ruth, 21). Although Icelandic was the official language of New Iceland, from 1875 on it was not used as a language of instruction in day schools. Even in this early period, then, the Icelandic settlers, although given an almost unique opportunity to develop boundary maintenance mechanisms to protect their ethnicity, were beginning to move along the path to assimilation, and apparently consciously so.

In 1889 all schools in New Iceland were taken over by the provincial government's Department of Education. By that time there were five school districts, and in the next few years more were added.

The first immigrants had settled along the western shore of Lake Winnipeg, with fishing being the mainstay of their economy, but gradually they moved inland and farther south, replacing fishing in part or completely with farming. Eventually some settled in large towns such as Selkirk. During this period concern had developed over the possible loss of the Icelandic language among members of the younger generation. In 1901, in response to requests by the Icelandic High School committee, the provincial Department of Education approved the teaching of Icelandic in schools where parents wished it, and the University of Manitoba, where by this time several students of Icelandic background were enrolled, accepted Icelandic as a second language for incoming students and granted credit to these students for previous course work in Icelandic instruction.

WINNIPEG   The first Icelandic immigrants to Winnipeg, who arrived in 1875, found themselves in a growing urban environment in which the mechanisms for cultural preservation which existed in New Iceland were not available to them. Their children began almost immediately to attend regular city schools which differed from others in Winnipeg only because of their high ratio of Icelandic to non-Icelandic students, which was an artifact of the Icelandic immigrants' congregation in the western part of the city in what was to some extent an Icelandic enclave, although in no way a ghetto. Members of the Icelandic community were undismayed by this early exposure of their children to an alien educational system, and in fact encouraged the anglicization process by providing additional instruction in English for children and adults alike in homes, churches and other meeting places in the evenings.

Soon after the first settlement by Icelanders in Winnipeg, several cultural and social organizations were formed which, while having social and recreational aims, also had educational overtones. One in particular, the Icelander's Society, was created to assist newly arrived immigrants to adapt to Canadian urban life. For a while, extra-school educational instruction continued to be carried out by educated individuals acting as individuals, but in 1881 the Advancement Society, which had been founded in 1877, began to coordinate the night school activities. That same year they founded a full-time day school, which at the time was the only separate ethnic day school in Winnipeg. However, the purpose of this school was not to perpetuate Icelandic culture and language in Canada, but rather to speed the process of acquisition of skills believed necessary for adaptation to a new social environment in which the Icelanders were socially, politically, legally and in all other ways a part of a larger, non-Icelandic society. The school was closed in 1883, when it was felt that it had served its purpose, with students now able to compete successfully in the regular school system and fewer adults needing instruction in English.

Children of Icelandic immigrants in both New Iceland and Winnipeg were strongly encouraged by their parents to aspire to university. This goal was a central determining factor behind the efforts in both areas for the emphasis on learning of English and of other parts of the standard Manitoba educational curriculum. The first Icelander in Canada to earn a university degree graduated from the University of Manitoba in 1885. Soon there were others. Typically, these university students aspired to careers in teaching, law and medicine. Few of them took programs geared toward business. Academic and professional avenues seemed to have been ways of reemphasizing the Icelandic traditions of learning and literature, but it must also be recalled that mercantilism had not been a strong theme in Icelandic economic life. For centuries, most merchants in Iceland were Danes operating in a colonial system. There were travelling merchants in Iceland, but outside of major urban centers such as Reykjavik, the capital of the country, there was little involvement in a capitalistic way of life. To a large extent, the people of Iceland were farmers and fishermen, and it was from the rural areas that most immigrants to Canada came.

During the latter part of the 19th century, the Icelandic community in Winnipeg experienced a desire for an Icelandic college of their own. Several abortive attempts were tried, but in 1913 public dissension about the college and what it would do were settled with the opening of the Jon Bjarnason Academy. For the first two years the academy was housed in the Lutheran church which was a central meeting place for the community, and in 1915 it was moved to new quarters in a rented part of a building in the heart of the Icelandic area of Winnipeg. Classes to grade 11 were offered. Most students were from Winnipeg, although there was a smattering of rural enrollments as well. By this time, a religious rift within the Winnipeg Icelandic community was becoming crystallized, with Unitarians on one side and Lutherans on the other. The students at the academy, because of its church connections, were for the main part Lutheran. It had a typical curriculum, but also emphasized a "Christian influence" and training in the Icelandic language and literature. In time, the academy became a center for many cultural activities carried on by voluntary associations dedicated to the retention of Icelandic culture in Canada. It closed in 1940, and the library which had been built up was donated to the University of Manitoba. More of a high school than a college as such, the academy was nevertheless a cultural and educational focus for the Icelandic community, providing a vehicle for ethnic inner-directedness which countered the increasing rates of out-marriage and general cultural and social assimilation.

One last Icelandic Canadian educational venture should be mentioned. The University of Manitoba had accepted Icelandic as a second language, and had given credit for previous instruction in Icelandic to incoming students, but the community was not yet represented at the university level through university courses in Icelandic language or history. Icelandic had been taught for several years at Wesley College, an affiliate of the University of Manitoba, and most Icelandic Canadian students pursuing degrees in the arts attended it, but some prominent members of the community thought that a permanent place for Icelandic studies should be established at the university itself. As in almost all community-wide issues, the community was divided about the feasibility of the establishment of an Icelandic chair. Gradually, however, and in the face of numerous obstacles, funds were raised and in 1952, classes were inaugurated in Icelandic language and literature at the University of Manitoba as part of the new program of the Department of Icelandic Literature and Language. The possibility of the Icelandic language being retained at least as an academic subject in Manitoba had been realized, in spite of an increasing loss of knowledge of it by the children and grandchildren of immigrants. Never heavy in enrollments, the department has swelled in recent years with the enhanced sense of ethnicity among the new generation of the 1970s, who seek an ethnic identity which their parents have lost, or possibly, never had.

Dualism: An Icelandic Cultural Theme[1]

Iceland—a land of "fire and Ice"—is a land of contrasts. Volcanoes erupt periodically with their lava encrusted tops and moltenly alive interiors juxtaposed to mute, but slowly moving glaciers. Frigid waters from glacial rivers spill over gigantic waterfalls such as fabled *Gullfoss*, while the cities of the nation are often heated by boiling water from underground, and people in Reykjavik bathe year-round in warm spring-heated outdoor pools. Iceland is a country still experiencing geological evolution and formation.

The theme of contrast in the Icelandic landscape is reflected in the personalities of the people who inhabit it, and the social and cultural forms they have evolved. It is a country of contrast and rarely of compromise. I have touched on this theme in an earlier discussion of the literary and educational traditions of Iceland and their transformations in immigrant adaptations to life in Manitoba. On the *emic* (or personal) level, many Icelanders and Icelandic Canadians dispute its existence. On an *etic* (or cross-cultural) level, it is a reality which must be examined in an anthropological or sociological analysis of either population.

I have decided to call this cultural theme of contrasts "dualism". Its expression in personality and social and cultural forms is more one of "two-sidedness" than of contrast as such. On the social and cultural level, whenever there is one form of an institution, for example, there must also exist another, often identical in form, yet standing in structural opposition to the first. A few examples are all that can be given here, but hopefully they will illustrate some of the pervasiveness of the theme.

Kin Groups

Closed corporate kin groups, identified with larger farmstead units and its geographical location, composed the basic structural features of Icelandic society. These units (at least in recent times) did not easily cooperate with one another, even when joined by marriages. This pattern may go back to the earliest settlement of Iceland by maverick Norwegian chiefs, and the farmsteads may be a modern continuation of these early chiefdoms. Kin groups, farmsteads and, on a broader level (although not as pronounced), regional groupings such as "the people of Northeast Iceland" stood in structural opposition to one another. This pattern is retained today and is evident in Icelandic political behavior and business practices in the larger centers such as Reykjavik which have experienced extreme population growth in recent years as a result of the increasing urbanization of Iceland. That is, the structure of rural Iceland continues in urban Iceland in the late 1970s.

These kinship-based features are one evidence of the dualism, at least on a social level, which was brought to Canada by Icelandic immigrants in the last century. Their communities were structured around them, and many of the examples of factionalism over issues of education and journalism which I identified earlier were products of this. A deeper analysis of the role played by kin (farmstead and regionally-based) in early Icelandic Canadian adaptations is needed.[2]

Church Organization

Another example of the dualism theme involves church organizations. In virtually every Icelandic Canadian community in Manitoba there were two churches: the Unitarian and the Lutheran. Every North American Icelander saw the first light of day in a Unitarian or Lutheran home, and forever remained a member of one or the other. Families were lined up against one another in political as well as religious issues. A Unitarian did not marry a Lutheran, for the one was Godless and the other a True Believer. But they were brought together through an ancient Icelandic love of debate. A debate over the Trinity supplanted in Icelandic Canadian communities other issues which created both factionalism and cohesion in communities in Iceland.

Voluntary Association

Many Icelandic Canadian voluntary associations have been formed in Manitoba communities and Winnipeg in particular. Many duplicated one another's goals and purposes. When a group of Icelandic Canadians in Winnipeg formed a temperance organization in 1887, a second association was soon formed, and the two worked in opposition to each other while striving for the same aims. Several other examples could be given. A people who have for more than a thousand years struggled to create a society which allowed for independence of spirit and of selfhood have, from the time of formation of the society from which Icelandic Canadians came, thus built and perpetuated a society with built-in structural features which have seemed to militate against the achievement of these goals.

Nevertheless, Icelandic Canadians have consistently worked together to preserve their cultural identity. Perhaps this is seen best in an amalgamation in 1977 of the last two surviving Icelandic Canadian social organizations in Winnipeg which have had large but dwindling memberships: the *Fron* chapter of the Icelandic National League and the Icelandic Canadian Club. The former used the Icelandic language exclusively at meetings, while the latter used English. There was a heated and drawn-out debate about the name of the new organization, but it was resolved. It would not have been a true venture of the Icelandic Canadian community in Winnipeg without it.

Ethnic Identity

Finally, dualism helps us understand why Icelandic Canadians, who for more than 100 years have sought to become non-hyphenated Canadians, still exist as an ethnic group in Winnipeg and elsewhere in Canada. The inward thrust created by structural oppositions has worked against the outward pull of assimilation. The debates have concentrated interest inward. They have militated against total assimilation, while allowing a degree of it to occur. The ultimate example of dualism in Icelandic Canadian culture has been the paradox of a simultaneous drive towards assimilation and cultural retention. The internal factionalism, found on many fronts and a product of structural features brought with them from Iceland has fostered this, and at least in the case of this one ethnic group, helps explain why Icelandic Canadians retain ethnic status within the larger Canadian society.

ENDNOTES

1. My use of thematic analysis varies in some respects from that of Morris Opler, who first used the concept of themes in anthropology. Whereas Opler's approach is highly psychological, mine is both psychological and structural. However, I hope that I still do justice to his concept (Opler, 1945).
2. A joint long-range interdisciplinary research project being carried out by the University of Manitoba and the University of Iceland is investigating this topic along with many others. The research was initiated in 1976.

SELECTED REFERENCES

Gjerset, Knut. *History of Iceland.* New York: Macmillan, 1924.

Kirkconnell, Watson. *North American Book of Icelandic Verse.* New York: Little and Ives, 1930.

Kristjanson, Wilhelm. *The Icelandic People in Manitoba: A Manitoba Saga.* Winnipeg: Wallingford Press, 1965.

_____. "Icelandic Canadian Publications in Manitoba," in *The Multilingual Press in Manitoba.* Winnipeg: Canada Press Club, 1974, pp. 121-29.

Lindal, Walter J. *The Icelanders in Canada.* Ottawa and Winnipeg: National Publishers and Viking Printers, 1967.

Opler, Morris. "Themes as Dynamic Forces in Culture," *American Journal of Sociology,* Vol. 51 (1945), pp. 198-206.

Ruth, Roy H. *Educational Echoes: A History of Education of the Icelandic-Canadians in Manitoba.* Winnipeg: Columbia Printers, Ltd., 1964.

Stefansson, Vilhjalmur. *Iceland: The First American Republic.* New York: Doubleday, 1947.

GRACE M. ANDERSON   Wilfrid Laurier University

Spanish- and Portuguese-Speaking Immigrants in Canada*

Spanish-Speaking Immigrants in Canada[1]

Spanish-speaking immigrants have come to Canada from Spain, Mexico, Central and South America, certain islands of the Caribbean and from the Philippine Islands of the Pacific. These countries were at one time parts of the far-flung Spanish empire. In consequence, Spanish-speaking countries, although now independent from Spain, are linked together by elements of a common history, many common traditions, a similar legal background and the Roman Catholic Church which was founded in Hispano-America by Spanish priests. Of course in areas as vast or far-flung as South and Central America, the Caribbean and the Philippines there are bound to be unique regional elements mixed in with the common Spanish cultural heritage.

In Canada the Spanish-speaking form not only a statistical category based on language, but also a group of immigrants who are frequently serviced by the same social agencies (because of the convenience of a

TABLE 1 *Population by ethnic group (Spanish), Canada and Provinces, 1971*

Province	Population
Newfoundland	110
Prince Edward Island	25
Nova Scotia	640
New Brunswick	310
Quebec	10 825
Ontario	10 330
Manitoba	640
Saskatchewan	210
Alberta	1 305
British Columbia	3 070
Yukon	20
Northwest Territories	30
Canada Total	27 515

Source: Manpower and Immigration, *Immigration and Population Statistics: Canadian Immigration and Population Study*, Ottawa, Information Canada, 1974, p. 12.

* Written expressly for *Two Nations, Many Cultures: Ethnic Groups in Canada*.

206

single translator and interpreter who can serve all of them). In the larger metropolitan centers such as Montreal, Toronto and Vancouver, the Spanish-speaking immigrants tend to separate into two major groups, the Spaniards and the Latin Americans. The latter are further divided into national-origin subgroupings and the former into regional communities such as Gallego or Basque. But in smaller centers such as Victoria the immigrants come together as one group for social occasions. The conviviality is based on a common language of communication, albeit with differing regional accents.

Originally, Spanish explorers, followed by *conquistadores* (conquerors) (both soldiers and priests), set foot on North America in the 16th century.[2]

The Spanish were once the claimants to the whole territory of British Columbia.... The first Spaniards to reach British Columbia may have been the crew of the ship *Los Tres Reyes*... who claimed to have reached the Strait of Juan de Fuca in 1603.[3]

The early Spaniards were only a temporary presence on the west coast of Canada, and they eventually withdrew in 1795 leaving the area to the British.[4] "Contacts between Spain and Canada go back several centuries to the voyages of the intrepid Basque fishermen to Atlantic coastal waters."[5]

During the 19th and early 20th centuries an occasional Spaniard arrived in Canada as a seaman or an adventurer. A very small number came as settlers. Frequently they intermarried with Canadians and became assimilated. Spanish names linger on but their descendants today are francophones or anglophones who may scarcely acknowledge their Spanish heritage.

Between 1920 and 1945 the number of Spaniards (Spanish by nationality and citizenship) who arrived to settle in Canada totalled 408, and a further 2 598 came between 1946 and 1956 inclusive, but in 1957, a year of economic expansion, a total of 1 090 arrived.[6] "Under an arrangement between the Spanish and Canadian governments, a group of 150 families emigrated to Canada as farmers in 1957."[7] By the time of the 1971 census there were 27 515 persons resident in Canada who claimed Spanish ethnic background. In the same year the number of people in selected metropolitan areas who used Spanish as their mother tongue totalled 20 525 and the number speaking Spanish in the home in these same cities was 15 670. The majority of these persons were from Spain.

The immigration status of many Latin Americans is beclouded by changes in immigration rulings. As a consequence, some Latin Americans may be here illegally in spite of their efforts to immigrate legitimately.

TABLE 2 *Number of people with Spanish as the mother tongue, for CMAs, 1971*

CMA[1]	Total	Spanish Males	Females	Total Population	Number of Census Tracts
Calgary	515	285	230	403 310	77
Edmonton	275	145	130	495 695	88
Hamilton	385	185	200	498 530	109
Kitchener	320	175	145	226 845	45
Montreal	8 210	4 180	4 030	2 743 170	570
Ottawa	885	405	480	602 480	120
Quebec	320	165	155	480 515	98
Sudbury	160	90	70	155 415	28
Toronto	7 155	3 650	3 505	2 627 980	447
Vancouver	1 470	710	760	1 082 280	179
Victoria	185	75	110	195 805	41
Winnipeg	645	275	370	540 300	106
Total	20 525	10 340	10 185	10 052 325	1 908

[1]Census Metropolitan Area.
Source: Area Aggregate Tape, IBR, York University, 1971. The author is indebted to Prof. Anthony H. Richmond and Dr. Ravi Varma of the Ethnic Research Programme of York University for extraction of the data from the census tapes, in this table and Tables 3, 7 & 8.

Latin Americans form one of the biggest migratory waves to Canada in recent years. In 1963 there were few Latin Americans in Toronto. By 1973, the number had grown considerably. Most of them do not appear in official statistics. The majority entered Canada as visitors before the Nov. 30, 1972 change in immigration ruling and then applied for landed status from within the country. Most of those who have arrived since the November, 1972 cut-off date have remained with tourist visas and work permits. . . . [8]

The estimates of current numbers of Latin Americans are unreliable since no official statistics exist. The ethnic press, however, reports that many Latin Americans, especially in Toronto, are here illegally. All too little is known about the current situation in Montreal. There is one thesis available which studies six Spaniards in that city in regard to shifting ethnic identity.[9] Studies of Latin Americans are notable by their absence.

Initially the first few Spanish immigrants came to Canada from Spain as young adventurers. The large majority which have come since World War II have arrived with the hope of improving their standard of living. There are notable exceptions, however. The Spanish Civil War (1936-39) triggered a wave of emigration. Most of these persons were held up in other countries of Europe by World War II (1939-45). It was not until 1947 that shipping became available to bring immigrants from Europe to Canada. Table 6 shows the number of refugees, stateless, and displaced

TABLE 3 *Number of people with Spanish as the language spoken at home, for CMAs, 1971*

CMA[1]	Total	Spanish Males	Females	Total Population	Number of Census Tracts
Calgary	345	170	175	403 310	77
Edmonton	150	95	55	495 695	88
Hamilton	295	155	140	498 530	109
Kitchener	290	175	115	226 845	45
Montreal	6 470	3 170	3 300	2 743 170	570
Ottawa	730	360	370	602 480	120
Quebec	165	75	90	480 515	98
Sudbury	105	60	45	155 415	28
Toronto	5 690	2 980	2 710	2 627 980	447
Vancouver	915	455	460	1 082 280	179
Victoria	155	80	75	195 805	41
Winnipeg	360	160	200	540 300	106
Total	15 670	7 935	7 735	10 052 325	1 908

[1]Census Metropolitan Area.
Source: Area Aggregate Tape, IBR, York University, 1971.

persons of Spanish background who sought asylum and were admitted to Canada in various periods from 1947 to 1967.

The other Spanish-speaking group with large numbers of refugees in their midst comes from Latin America. In Chile applications started pouring into immigration offices in 1973 immediately following the right-wing coup which toppled the government of the Marxist Salvadore Allende. Other Chileans attempted to enter Canada from neighboring countries, especially Argentina. "Of some 16 320 Chileans who filed applications with Canadian immigration officials since 1973, 5 300 visas were granted."[10]

Political unrest during the 1970s in Latin American countries (like Argentina and Uruguay) and the Philippines prompted many residents to

TABLE 4 *Estimated numbers of Spanish-speaking Latin American immigrants in Metro Toronto, 1977*

Country of Origin	Population
Ecuador	30 000
Uruguay	20 000
Colombia	10 000
Peru	4 000
Chile	1 000
Other*	5 000
	70 000

*Other countries in Central and South America and also Cuba.

TABLE 5 *Estimated numbers of Spanish-speaking Latin American immigrants in Metro Vancouver, 1977***

Country of Origin	Population
Chile	700
Peru	400
Argentina	350
Mexico	300
Philippines	100
Other*	250
	2 100

*Other countries in Central and South America and also Cuba.
**In addition there are an estimated 400 immigrants from Spain in Metro Vancouver. A sizable number of these persons have spent some time in Latin America.

leave the homeland for a new life in Canada. In times of political chaos, it is often the highly educated and the highly skilled people who leave, probably because they have the means to mobilize resources rapidly. Thus, many of those who come to Canada have professional training as doctors, lawyers, professors, teachers and social workers; or they arrive with entrepreneurial skills, like the small group of Spanish-speaking Filipinos in Vancouver.

Usually in each nationality group only a small percentage of the immigrants hold professional jobs or are employed as large-scale entrepreneurs. Among the Spaniards there are a number who have become very successful restaurateurs. They usually feature French cuisine in their establishments as several of them have learned their skills in France before coming to Canada. Other restaurants in the larger centers of Spanish-speaking immigration cater mainly to immigrants who are nos-

TABLE 6 *Refugees, displaced and stateless persons admitted to Canada as immigrants, by ethnic origin (Spanish), 1947-67*

Years	Numbers Admitted
1947-58	481
1959	3
1960	—
1961	—
1962	2
1963	6
1964	50
1965	20
1966	7
1967	1
Total	570

Source: Manpower and Immigration, *Immigration and Population Statistics: Canadian Immigration and Population Study*, Ottawa, Information Canada, 1974, pp. 44-45.

talgic for "home" cooking. These restaurants are usually regionally-oriented. Most of them hire Spanish guitarists or singers and occasionally dancers. (Flamenco dancing is spectacular and very popular in restaurants catering to the tourist trade.)

In sales and services a small group of the Spanish-speaking find employment. Since many of these immigrants also speak Portuguese they may be serving a dual market in the real estate or insurance fields and in automobile or electronic sales and servicing. Some of the well-educated young women, and, to a lesser extent young men, are entering clerical or secretarial jobs which require English-Spanish or French-Spanish bilingualism. A number of the young people, especially in Quebec, are trilingual. In Toronto, Vancouver, and Montreal the head offices of certain companies who conduct major transactions with Spain or Latin America use the language skills of these young people. The majority employed in clerical jobs, however, are used in a unilingual (English or French) capacity.

Many of the immigrants have been skilled tradesmen before emigration. On arrival in Canada they often find that the jobs for which they feel themselves to be fully qualified are not open to them. This is frequently because employment requires apprenticeship and certification in their trade. In this regard Spaniards are usually better situated than Latin Americans because Spain follows general European practices in many trades. Some Spaniards have been trained in France or Germany under apprenticeship and licensing systems. Their diplomas are more easily recognized because of greater employer and union familiarity with these programs.

Large number of Spanish-speaking immigrants are classified in Canada as unskilled or semi-skilled. Many of these persons have found that there are no vacancies in jobs that would utilize the training that they received in the homeland. For example, many Latin-American men are highly skilled artisans in hand-tooled leatherwork, but the market for these goods in Canada is strictly limited. Many of the women are very skilled in embroidery but can only find factory jobs in the textile trade where high output is imperative. The women find jobs as machine operators and their specific skills go unutilized.

As with most of the newly-arrived immigrant groups with limited education, many Latin-American men in urban areas find employment in semi-skilled or unskilled construction jobs or as janitors in business establishments, offices, and schools. Many immigrants, both men and women, work in factories.

University young people who are here on temporary student visas form a distinct group. Frequently they tend to identify more with their fellow students than with other members of their ethnic group. This is especially the case if the student body from the particular country is large and the immigrant population is small. An example in point is the group of Venezuelan students in Vancouver. On the other hand if the students are the second generation of a refugee group such as the Chileans who were teenagers when they came to Canada with their parents a few years ago, then these students are fully part of their own ethnic community.

Major newspapers in the Spanish language are published in Toronto, Montreal and Vancouver. Many urban centers where there is a sizable aggregation of Spanish-speaking immigrants have their own radio and television programs, usually on a weekly basis. In the larger settlements, Spanish parishes are a lively part of the community and often share a building with Portuguese or Italian parishes.[11] Similarly, social work agencies may service several ethnic groups. A Toronto agency, for example, has clients from Latin America, both Spanish- and Portuguese-speaking (the latter from Brazil), as well as Europeans from the Iberian Peninsula, and also West Indians. Because of the recent arrival of large numbers of immigrants from South and Central America, services are often shared with other ethnic groups; for instance, corner food stores specializing in Portuguese or Italian delicacies often also sell specialties to a Spanish-speaking market as a sideline.

Finally, it should be recognized that the Spanish-speaking in Canada are a very heterogeneous category. In the Kitchener-Waterloo area one research study showed them to be associated with Germany through marriage or through work experience in that country.[12] In the course of the current study the author met Yugoslav and Estonian Argentinians, Peruvian Quechua Indians, Jews from Chile, and German Mexicans in addition to Oriental (Chinese or Japanese) Latin Americans. Many from Latin America or the Philippines, however, claim uniquely European Spanish ancestry (although, of course, Spaniards themselves are a combination of several ancestral strains including the Moors, the latter especially in the South). Latin Americans[13] may be a mixture of indigenous Indian, negroid, Asian or white races. The heterogeneity also is expressed in regional foods, dress and accents. But in Canada the pressure to be with those with whom the immigrant can communicate in his mother tongue often overcomes the diversity of origins.[14]

With respect to the level of conflict or consensus within Spanish-speaking communities, it would seem that this is influenced in large measure by social pressures present within the community and by external sources emanating from the larger Canadian society. Multiple cleavages within the Spanish-speaking communities and the consequent criss-crossing of allegiances may provide a complex web of affiliation. The consensus that may be visible sometimes to outsiders consists of a fragile unity. This unity may be imposed by social agencies providing services in Spanish.

Currently, I am doing research on the internal differentiation within various Spanish-speaking communities in Canada.[15] To date, the factors that seem to be the most divisive for a community are politics, religion, and regionalism. Social class, racial and ethnic factors, and urban and rural differences are present, however, and should not be overlooked. When verbal conflicts and antagonisms erupt, the communities split along one or more of the predictable cleavages. People come together again when countervailing forces occur. In sum, it would appear that the contemporary Spanish-speaking communities in Canada tend to exist in a state of flux between varying degrees of conflict and consensus.

Portuguese-Speaking Immigrants in Canada

The Portuguese-speaking immigrants in Canada come mainly from Continental Portugal and its overseas provinces which include the Azores Islands in mid-Atlantic, and to a lesser extent, from Madeira Island off the coast of Northwest Africa. There are a few Portuguese-speaking Asian immigrants from Macao, a Portuguese Overseas Province, adjacent to mainland China, and another small contingent from Goa, a former Portuguese colony which now forms part of India. A very small number of the immigrant population are "black Portuguese" from the Cape Verde Islands which lie off the coast of West Africa. Also, about 2 000 Portuguese-speaking immigrants are from Brazil in South America, which was a Portuguese colony until the late 19th century.[16] The total number

TABLE 7 *Number of people with Portuguese as the mother tongue, for CMAs, 1971*

CMA[1]	Total	Portuguese Males	Total Females	Total Population	Number of Census Tracts
Calgary	595	315	280	403 310	77
Edmonton	1 665	870	795	495 695	88
Hamilton	2 040	1 055	985	498 530	109
Kitchener	4 350	2 180	2 170	226 845	45
Montreal	12 795	6 445	6 350	2 743 170	570
Ottawa	2 270	1 150	1 120	602 480	120
Quebec	300	145	155	480 515	98
Sudbury	120	75	45	155 415	28
Toronto	39 550	20 105	19 445	2 627 980	447
Vancouver	3 835	1 955	1 880	1 082 280	179
Victoria	500	250	250	195 805	41
Winnipeg	3 150	1 605	1 545	540 300	106

[1]Census Metropolitan Area.
Source: Area Aggregate Tape, IBR, York University, 1971.

TABLE 8 *Number of people with Portuguese as the language spoken at home, for CMAs, 1971*

CMA[1]	Portuguese			Total Population	Number of Census Tracts
	Total	Males	Females		
Calgary	305	165	140	403 310	77
Edmonton	1 145	595	550	495 695	88
Hamilton	1 855	925	930	498 530	109
Kitchener	3 745	1 800	1 945	226 845	45
Montreal	10 310	5 150	5 160	2 743 170	570
Ottawa	1 870	965	905	602 480	120
Quebec	230	120	110	480 515	98
Sudbury	225	115	110	155 415	28
Toronto	36 045	18 390	17 655	2 627 980	447
Vancouver	3 105	1 580	1 525	1 082 280	179
Victoria	275	125	150	195 805	41
Winnipeg	2 930	1 415	1 515	540 300	106

[1]Census Metropolitan Area.
Source: Area Aggregate Tape, IBR, York University, 1971

of Portuguese immigrants in Canada was estimated at 250 000 in 1977.[17] The largest number of these are in Metropolitan Toronto, followed by Montreal, Vancouver and Cambridge (mostly in the former city of Galt).

Although there have been occasional settlers from Portugal in Canada from the 17th century yet these form only a minuscule portion of the total immigration.[18] It is estimated that more than 99% have arrived in this country since 1953. It is not surprising then that a recent study found that 90.4% of the Portuguese persons who are fluent in the language use Portuguese almost exclusively in their homes.[19]

Because many of the early settlers were recruited to work in agriculture or on the railways (especially on the northern or more isolated sections) the educational levels required of the early settlers were not very demanding.[20] Also, since close family members who migrated were sponsored and more distant kin were nominated, the streams of immigrants from small towns and peasant villages of the Azores and from the area north of Lisbon in Continental Portugal tended to have a similar educational level as the original settlers.

After the initial contracts[21] of the early settlers were completed, many of the immigrants tended to move towards the Eastern cities. Many entered work in the various construction fields or in janitorial services. Others entered factory employment. Immigrants arriving from the mid-1960s and into the 1970s have, in large measure, commenced work in the metropolitan areas directly on arrival in Canada. It has been noted elsewhere that the attainment of initial jobs of a sample of Portuguese immigrants in Toronto affected the chances for future jobs and hence social and economic mobility of blue-collar workers.[22]

TABLE 9 *Estimated statistics of Portuguese immigrants in Canada**

Region	Province	City or Town	Date	Estimated Portuguese Population
Atlantic Provinces	Newfoundland	St. John's	1973	40
		Labrador City	1974	80
	Nova Scotia	Halifax	1974	300
Quebec	Quebec	Montreal	1974	35 000
		Quebec City	1974	2 000
		Sainte Thérèse	1974	2 000
		Schefferville	1974	1 000
		Trois Rivières	1974	1 000
		Sept Isles	1974	500
		Sherbrooke	1974	500
		Hull	1975	3 000
Ontario	Ontario	Ottawa	1975	2 000
		Kingston	1973	3 000
		Toronto	1977	102 000
		Oshawa	1974	1 000
		Hamilton, Burlington	1974	6 000
		Oakville	1974	3 000
		Brampton	1976	6 000
		Mississauga, Streetsville	1974	2 000
		Cambridge (formerly Galt, Preston, Hespeler)	1977	12 000
		Kitchener	1976	4 000
		Guelph	1975	1 000
		London	1975	10 000
		Strathroy	1974	2 000
		Leamington, Wheatley	1974	350 (& 1 000 seasonal)
Prairie Provinces	Manitoba	Winnipeg	1973	5 000
		Thompson	1973	1 000
	Alberta	Edmonton	1974	6 000
		Calgary	1973	1 500
British Columbia	British Columbia	Greater Vancouver	1973	15 000
		Victoria	1973	1 000
		Kitimat, Terrace	1973	2 000
		Prince Rupert	1973	1 000
		Prince George	1973	2 000
		Okanagan Valley (especially Oliver, Osoyoos, Penticton)	1973	4 500

*I am indebted to David Higgs, History, University of Toronto for providing statistics on Quebec and the Atlantic provinces. For further details of distribution see Grace M. Anderson and David Higgs, *A Future to Inherit: The Portuguese Communities of Canada* (Toronto and Ottawa: McClelland & Stewart in association with the Multiculturalism Program, Dept. of the Secretary of Canada and the Publishing Centre, Supply and Services Canada, 1976).

There are, of course, a more highly educated minority who may offer leadership to the Portuguese communities. Frequently they are employed as real estate or travel agents, they operate driving schools or write for ethnic newspapers. A few own substantial restaurants. A small number are on the faculties of various Canadian universities or are employed in a professional capacity. The second-generation immigrants are now coming to maturity and are entering high school and a few are continuing to post-secondary education in a wide variety of fields.

Where communities of Portuguese immigrants number several thousands, they usually form their own parishes and endeavor to attract priests from the homeland. In some communities the social life centers around the church hall whereas in others there is a marked split between religious and secular life. The latter often revolves around the soccer associations.[23] The larger communities publish their own newspapers. In many areas of substantial settlement both television and radio programs are available in Portuguese on a weekly basis.

In many metropolitan centers the Portuguese settlement can be described as "institutionally-complete,"[24] all or most of the needed services are available in the mother-tongue. This, of course, can lead to an immigrant ghetto (by immigrant choice). The more highly educated usually move to the suburbs, although they may provide some of the services to the community in the inner cities.[25] Many Portuguese immigrants have reported that Canadians often mistake them for Italians or Spaniards so that few Canadians realize that large numbers of Portuguese immigrants are now in their midst.[26]

One interesting facet of Portuguese communities in Canada is the mutual influence of occupation and family structure. For example, the men of Nazaré, a large fishing village on the Atlantic shore of mainland Portugal, for generations have spent many months of each year on the Grand Banks off the coast of Newfoundland. They are attached to the White Fleet which fishes for cod. This necessity for the working men of the village to spend many months away from home has meant that the wives need to be much more independent. Therefore, it is not such a great step for the men to come to Southern Ontario ports of Wheatley and Leamington for the summers of commercial fishing in Lake Erie. Usually they obtain seasonal work permits.[27] Also, in many of the inland towns and villages of Continental Portugal, when work is in short supply, many of the men migrate to France to find employment, often without their families.[28] Some of these men also come to Canada without their families. Their wives and children may not join them in Canada for a period of several years.[29] Perhaps it is not surprising that these men are willing to work in the far north or on isolated construction projects because separation from their families for prolonged periods has become a way of life for them.

It is also possible, of course, that family structure influences the choice of an occupation. The boys, growing up in a family where the father has been absent for many years during the boys' teenage and early adulthood years, may be prone to select occupations which involve long periods of isolation in all-male work crews, but which are relatively highly remunerated. However, families from the cities are not prepared to endure prolonged periods of separation.[30] The girls are socialized into patterns of independence by the mothers of these families. Such is not the case among the working class of families where the family unit has remained intact and the men of the family have been employed in the local area. The interdependence of family structure and occupation in Portuguese communities in Canada is a subject which warrants further research.

ENDNOTES

1. The material in this section is based on the study by Grace M. Anderson, *Spanish-Speaking Immigrants in Selected Canadian Cosmopolitan Cities* (Simon Fraser University, Dept. of Sociology & Anthropology, and the Latin American Studies Program, Fall 1977). The study was supported by a grant from the Office of the Secretary of State through their program of Visiting Professors of Multiculturalism. Thanks are also expressed to the Department of Sociology & Anthropology and to the Ethnic Research Programme of York University who facilitated the gathering and analysis of data in the Metropolitan Toronto segment of this study.
2. Harold J. Alford, *The Proud Peoples: The Heritage and Culture of Spanish-Speaking Peoples in the United States* (New York & Scarborough, Ont.: Mentor, New American Library, 1972), pp. 4-5.
3. John Norris, ed., "The French and Spanish: Historic Founders," in *Strangers Entertained: A History of the Ethnic Groups of British Columbia* (Vancouver: Centennial '71 Committee, 1971), pp. 200, 202-3.
4. Norris, *op. cit.*, p. 204.
5. *The Canadian Family Tree: Centennial Edition 1867-1967* (Ottawa: Canadian Citizenship Branch, Dept. of the Secretary of State and the Centennial Commission, 1967), p. 304.
6. *Annuaires du Canada*, quoted in P. Justo Saco, o.f.m., "Histoire de L'Immigration des Espagnols au Canada et plus particulièrement dans le Québec et ce qui characterise ce problème," M.A. Thesis, L'Ecole de Service Social, Université Laval, Dec. 1958, pp. 17, 18 & 36.
7. Howard Palmer, *Land of the Second Chance: A History of Ethnic Groups in Southern Alberta* (Lethbridge, Alta.: The Lethbridge Herald, 1972), p. 216.
8. Ana Lizón Alberro and Gloria Montero, "The Land of Beginning Again," *Canadian Forum* (Sept. 1975), p. 23.
9. Ronald Louis Fernandez, "Ethnicity as a Symbol System: A Theoretical Discussion exemplified by Case Studies of Spaniards in Montréal," M.A. Thesis in Anthropology, McGill University, July 1972.

10. "Few Chileans Granted Visas Since 1973 Coup," *Kitchener-Waterloo Record*, Dec. 24, 1976.

11. There are a small number of Sephardic Jews in Toronto and Montreal. See Samuel Sidlofsky, "The Jewish Sepharade Association: Structural Integration of North African Jews in Toronto 1957 to 1962," A paper prepared for presentation at the Canadian Sociology & Anthropology Association Annual Meeting, St. John's, Newfoundland, June 1971.

12. Juanne Clarke and Grace M. Anderson, "Double-hyphenated Canadians: Spanish-speaking Immigrants of German Background in the Kitchener-Waterloo Urban Area of Ontario," Paper presented to the Canadian Sociology & Anthropology Association Annual Meeting, Kingston, Ontario, May 31, 1973.

13. The persons referred to in this chapter as Latin Americans are Spanish-speaking persons. Properly speaking Latin Americans also include other linguistic groups such as French-speaking Haitians, English-speaking Guyanians, and Portuguese-speaking Brazilians. However, the term Latin American has been used throughout in this narrow sense since this is the manner in which they refer to themselves, although, of course they use the term *Latino-americanos* which is the Spanish translation.

14. For a study of the diversity of origins among the Spanish-speakers, see Joyce Lorimer, Sara Keith and Grace M. Anderson, "Selected Bibliography on Spanish-Speaking Immigrants in Canada, 1500-1977," *Canadian Identities Program*, Ottawa: Office of the Secretary of State, 1977.

15. Further findings and details concerning the methodology of this study appear in Grace M. Anderson, "Conflict, Cleavages and Consensus: Spanish-Speaking Immigrant Communities in Selected Canadian Metropolitan Areas," (A paper presented to the International Sociological Association, Research Committee on Migration, Uppsala, Sweden, August, 1978).

16. The information outlined in this study was gathered during the decade 1967 to 1977.

17. A commentary on the reasons for large discrepancies between official and unofficial statistics is given in Grace M. Anderson, "A Commentary on Immigration Statistics: Portuguese Migration to Canada," mimeo., Ethnic Research Programme, York Univ., 1976.

18. Grace M. Anderson and David Higgs, *A Future to Inherit: The Portuguese Communities of Canada* (Toronto and Ottawa: McClelland & Stewart in association with the Multiculturalism Program, Department of the Secretary of State of Canada and the Publishing Centre, Supply and Services Canada, 1976), p. 18. See also revision by David Higgs and Grace M. Anderson, "Portuguese" in *The Canadian Family Tree*, 2nd ed. (Ottawa: Department of the Secretary of State of Canada, forthcoming).

19. K. G. O'Bryan, J. G. Reitz and O. M. Kuplowska, *Non-Official Languages: A Study in Canadian Multiculturalism* (Ottawa: Minister of Supply and Services Canada, 1976), p. 65.

20. See Edith Ferguson, *Newcomers in Transition: A Project of the International Institute of Metropolitan Toronto 1962-1964*, and *Newcomers and New Learning: A Project of the International Institute of Metropolitan Toronto, 1964-1966* (Toronto: International Institute of Metropolitan Toronto, 1964 and

1966); and Grace M. Anderson, *Networks of Contact: The Portuguese and Toronto* (Waterloo: Wilfrid Laurier University Press, 1974).

21. Grace M. Anderson, "A Contract for Portuguese Railway Workers Coming to Canada," mimeo., Ethnic Research Programme, York University, 1976.

22. Grace Merle Anderson, "The Channel-Facilitators Model of Migration: A Model Tested Using Portuguese Blue-Collar Immigrants in Metropolitan Toronto," Ph.D. Thesis, University of Toronto, 1971. See also Grace M. Anderson, "Spearhead Anchorages and Initiation of Networks with Special Reference to the Portuguese Case," mimeo., Paper presented at the National Conference on Ethnic Studies and Research, Canadian Plains Research Centre, Univ. of Regina, Oct., 1976, and Grace M. Anderson, "Institutionally-Oriented Networks," mimeo., Paper presented at the American Anthropological Association Annual Meetings (Network Seminar II), Mexico City, Nov. 21, 1974.

23. Grace M. Anderson and David Higgs, 1976, *op. cit.*, see especially parts 3 and 4.

24. Raymond Breton, "Institutional Completeness of Ethnic Communities and the Personal Relations of Immigrants," *American Journal of Sociology*, LXX, No. 2 (Sept. 1964), pp. 193-205.

25. For further details see Anderson and Higgs, *loc. cit.*

26. A substantial bibliography of the Portuguese in Canada is contained in Anderson and Higgs, *loc. cit.*, pp. 190-98. See also Portuguese-Canadian Periodical Publications, First Supplement, compiled by Grace M. Anderson and David Higgs, *Canadian Ethnic Studies*, vol. v, no. 1-2.

27. For an elaboration of this pattern, see Grace M. Anderson and David Higgs, 1976, *op. cit.*, pp. 83-85.

28. Maria Beatriz Rocha Trindade, *Immigrés Portugais* (Lisbon: Instituto Superior de Ciências Sociais e Política Ultramarina, 1973).

29. Edith Ferguson, *Newcomers in Transition, 1962-1964* (Toronto: The International Institute of Metropolitan Toronto, 1964), p. 33 places the time span between arrival of husband and wife at an average of 3.6 years. Later studies (Anderson, 1974, and Anderson & Higgs, 1976), give every indication that the average time span between arrival of husband and wife has, if anything, been extended in recent years.

30. For a discussion of these contracts see Anderson & Higgs, *loc. cit.*, pp. 127 ff.

ROBERT F. HARNEY   University of Toronto

The Italian Community in Toronto*

The Pre-World War I Community (1900-14)

Between 1900 and 1914, more Italians entered Canada than any immigrant group except those from the British Isles. They came from the ports of southern Italy or through Swiss border points. Others arrived at random, as members of wandering labor gangs or as petty entrepreneurs from the Little Italies of the American east coast. In Italy, the myth of the New World included all of America. For the migrants who wandered throughout the continent looking for work and a reassuring south Italian *ambiente*[1] crossing national boundaries meant less than the first tentative steps from their villages. In 1903, 2 000 of an estimated 3 000 who worked for the Canadian Pacific Railroad came from the United States.[2] The very causes of Italian emigration produced a capricious pattern of settlement. Not only *la miseria* but also the chance to make good wages drew the sojourner. Chain migration, word of mouth about work on North American railroads, and the activities of a variety of agents combined to increase the flow. In 1892, one line, the Inman Steamship Company, was reputed to have 3 500 agents in Europe.[3] Emigration and migration had become a commerce in Italy, where middle class "brokers" served or preyed on their countrymen.

The Commerce of Migration

Canada had her share of men engaged in this commerce. They came from the trickle of Italian settlers who preceded the new immigration. The most important were immigrant bankers and steamship agents who became employment brokers providing unskilled workers for the railroads and the mines.[4] During the 1904 Royal Commission investigation of Italian immigrant labor in Montreal, an agent for one company admitted that "We pay 25¢ a head for rounding them (Italian laborers) up."[5] The men who did the rounding up were known as *padroni*. It should be noted that the immigrants were often peasants from southern Italy who did not see a job as their right but as something to be wheedled from the employer. Accustomed to feigning servility in the face of *signori* and petty bureaucrats at home, they fell easily into the *padrone* system.

---

* A previously unpublished manuscript.

The railroads and other labor-intensive industries sought a docile and cheap work force while Italian migrants wanted high-paying seasonal work. Many of them had come to Canada not to settle but to amass enough capital to improve their petty holdings at home, to provide a sister's dowry, or to gather passage money for other relatives. Between North American industry and the pre-industrial labor force of rural Italy, it was natural that the *padroni* go-betweens should emerge. Men like Antonio Cordasco and Alberto Dini of Montreal had offices or agents in Toronto, New York, Boston, at clandestine migrant depots like Chiasso on the Swiss-Italian border, and in the small towns of Italy. They owned or influenced Italian-language papers in eastern North America, and they provided track gangs for the railroads and electric street railroads of Canada and the northeastern United States. Because the railroads and other industries (often culpable because they used the Italian labor gangs as strikebreakers) hired exclusively through the *padroni*, the immigrants were at the mercy of their exploiters. A notice from the boss, Cordasco, to the labor force reflects the extent of his control.

To the army of the pick and shovel
Italian labourers, bosses and underbosses do not show a double face but only one (be true) have a soldiers courage. Apply to the elegant and solid Italian Bank of Antonio Cordasco if you do not want to weep over your misfortunes in the Spring when the shipments of men will begin. Do not believe that with your dollars or dollar you will be able to get work like your comrades who have been faithful. No, we will inspect our books and money orders and our passage ticket book, and those who will not have their names entered in them in their despair tear out their hair and will call Mr. Cordasco lordship, Don Antonio, let me go to work. No never, will be answered to them, go to those through whom you sent money and so on. A forewarned man is forearmed.[6]

Men, collected in American Little Italies or met by scouts where the Naples steamers docked, then shepherded by interpreters or foremen to remote track work sites, never left their own cultural *ambiente*. Communicating in their own dialect, living on moldy Italian style bread and over-priced sardines in oil supplied by the *padrone*, they dreamed most often not of the rich North American earth around them but of an impoverished *paese* far away. Indeed, CPR officials admitted that it was the clannish and migrant mentality that made the Italian gangs a reliable work force.[7] Initially, cities like Toronto played little role in the life of the migrants. They knew its main railroad stations and dock areas since they waited there before being thrust into the hinterland work force. Staying in "inns" and boarding houses owned by *padroni* or by independent older Italian settlers, girt about by ignorance of English, the migrant worker had little sense of the city as opportunity. Still an Italian immigrant *ambiente* began to emerge in Toronto by the 1890s. Centered first around the train station, wharves, and market, and later in St. John's Ward, a neighborhood developed. There were church services in Italian, but in Toronto it was often a Methodist one at the Little Flower mission before it was a Catholic mass.

For many years, the migrants outnumbered the stable town dwellers in the Italian community.[8] Toronto's Union Station had a superintendent of immigration, the powerful Montreal *padrone* Alberto Dini, who maintained one of several Italian employment agencies on York Street.[9] The city had representatives of twenty-one railroads and after the great fire of 1903 there was much urban construction work. Still the Italian community grew slowly. Montreal was closer to the trans-continental routes and the spurs and interurban lines of Northern Ontario. One Italo-Canadian writer, reinforcing the image of "Toronto the Good" claimed that Toronto did not appeal to the young migrants because of the absence of liquor and women. Montreal had both. "It was the center of attraction for the Italians who came from the West. Instead of facing a dull winter in Toronto, they pushed into the gay port city."[10]

The Growth of an Ethnic Neighborhood

While the Italians in Toronto did not constitute a massive foreign invasion—there were only about 1 000 permanent settlers in 1900 and less than 10 000 by the end of World War I—myth and stereotypes about the Italian and some competition with native artisans did create an atmosphere that reinforced the need for an ethnic neighborhood. Before the influx of unskilled labor, Italians practised trades and lived symbiotically within Canadian society such that their presence was little noticed. Several things were happening that threatened this symbiosis. A subtle change in the new Italian arrivals corresponded to the growth in North America of racial hostility toward southern Europeans.[11] Settlers with small artisan skills were apparently giving way to unskilled migrants. The latter thought like sojourners, did not learn English, were often bachelors and were clearly "lower class" workers. Anti-Catholic feeling and the xenophobia of a small homogeneous city existed in Toronto, but there was no dangerous competition for work in a city recovering from a terrible fire and replete with labor-intensive enterprises.[12] Yet, as early as the late 1880s even the Italian artisans had been stamped with a double stigmata: scab laborers and excitable Latins. An exchange between the counsel and a witness to the Royal Commission on the Relation of Capital and Labour will illustrate the problem.

Q. Are there any Italians doing laboring work?
A. They take the work home, and they run what are known as sweating shops. They are making quite a pile of money, and have a few slaves under them in the shape of women.[13]

Goldwin Smith who wrote at roughly the same time could not resist noting the arrival of Italians in Canada and gratuitously confirmed the stereotype. "There are scatterings of other races, the last arrival being the Italian with his grinding organ and, we hope, without his knife."[14] Within this atmosphere of latent hostility, it was natural for the Italians of Toronto to overcome regional antipathies and to gather together in an "ethnic community".

World War I and its Aftermath (1915-35)

The arrival of an increasing number of women and children required more elaborate institutions. The seasonal nature of some work, combined with a pre-industrial sense of the family as a single economic unit and of the need for a number of minor sources of income, gave diversity to the community. Men who worked as common laborers in summer found work removing snow or hauling in winter; some were scavengers, street entertainers, knife-sharpeners, or fruit peddlers in their spare time. Women picked greens, gathered mushrooms or did piece work in the nascent garment industry. They had come from a setting where work was seasonal, cyclical, marginal. While few of the new Italian Canadians dreamed of rolling wheat fields, they did buy and cultivate arable patches of ground in and immediately outside of Toronto. These properties played a role in the later development of Italian wealth and suburbs in Toronto.

St. John's Ward became the center of Toronto Italian life, a street life with a pace and purpose at variance with the dour and "indoors" north European city around it.[15] From the outset, Italians shared the Ward with the other major group of newcomers to Toronto, the east European Jews. The relationship was not unusual. Humbert Nelli showed that even in Chicago's Little Italy, the Italians rarely exceeded 50% of the total.[16] In New York and Chicago, Jew and Italian lived side by side. R. Glanz claims that the basis of the relationship was an essential lack of competition: Jews tending to trade and Italians to laboring and both to the garment industry.[17] The number of street corner stores that passed from Jewish to Italian hands as the latter moved into the Ward suggests, however, that competition did exist, but that there was rapport at other levels. Neither group worried excessively about threats to endogamy; initially the strength of religion and family was too great on both sides. Both groups accepted a high level of street activity as the inevitable noise, "hustling", and crowding that preceded the "take-off" from green-horn to successful immigrant. Jews in numbers had come north into the Ward before the Italians and had, in modern usage, "blockbusted" for the Italians to follow. Still a typical street of the Ward had Jewish, Italian, and older stock on it. The latter were often "mechanics" (artisans) while the Jews and Italians dominated the storefront and residential pattern. Many older Italians can recount serving as "shabbes goy," the lighters of sabbath fires and runners of errands, for the Orthodox Jews of the neighborhood. Toronto's Little Italy had—along with the Italian Methodist Mission on Elm Street and eventually a parish, The Church of Our Lady of Mt. Carmel—Rumanian and Russian synagogues, some smaller congregations, several Protestant missions to the Jews, and an African Methodist Church. In that sense, St. John's Ward was not just Little Italy, it was the foreign quarter of Toronto.[18]

Occupational Diversification

The growing number of Italians produced both diversity of occupation and upward mobility within the community itself. There were ethnic bankers, postal agents, interpreters, grocers, notaries, steamship agents, and boarding housekeepers. The special food needs of the Italians, although not as likely to cause the proliferation of small shops that ritual required of the Jews, did encourage enterprise. For example, successful pasta factories were started on York Street and later on Centre Avenue in the Ward.[19] Typically, too, a certain number of fruit dealers and merchants began to import provisions (Italian style cheese, canned fish, vegetables, and pasta), and importing led to travel agencies. Bakeries, confectionaries and a few meat markets and grocery stores sprouted to serve the community. Over the years, the Ward had few hotels (saloni) because of Toronto's blue laws; nevertheless, small clubs, boarding houses and a restaurant or two allowed for a glass of wine within the *ambiente*. There was an importer of wine-making equipment as well. Along Elm or Gerrard Streets, Italian was the language of the sidewalks.

Upward mobility in Little Italy was not associated initially with either assimilation or outward mobility. As the choice between laboring in the city and small commercial enterprise grew, status and income varied greatly within the Ward and often within the Italian extended family itself. Brothers living together on Elm or Centre Street might leave their flat in the morning, one to be a brewery worker or street laborer, a second to peddle fruit, and a third to run a grocery and give music lessons downstairs. Only strong parents or expanding business could keep the family destiny a shared one. It was most often the children of the merchants who became the doctors, lawyers, and professsionals of the next generation, and, while there did tend to be families that were more successful than others, independent nuclear families emerged.[20]

Only an impression of the relationship of upward mobility, residential patterns and assimilation is possible now. If we divide the occupations of

Toronto Italians in the period into (1) those self-employed who served the *ambiente* for their fellow Italians (the provisioners, grocers, notaries, steamship agents), (2) those who serviced the non-Italian community (the fruit peddlers and later, the storekeepers, musicians, cobblers and shoe-shine men, tailors, and barbers), and (3) laborers in the nascent industrial structure and those in varieties of street, railroads, sewer, and construction work, we can see the social history of the Ward and the outlying Italian neighborhoods more clearly.

First, one must record the courage and enterprise of men who spoke no English yet chose to live outside the Ward among their clientele.[21] Dependent on the *ambiente*, a high percentage of the barbers, tailors, and peddlers daily commuted back to the Ward, but others dared to move out. Fruit men rose before dawn to buy produce directly from the arriving freight trains and pushed carts many miles through alien streets to sell to the non-Italian community.[22] The logic of "time as money" caused them, as their business prospered, to settle and open stores outside the Ward. By 1912 half the fruit dealers in the city were Italian; by 1924, more than half. In the same period, Italians represented only 5% of the barbers and 3% of the grocers in the city, while the City Directories showed that the Greeks and the Syrians provided sharp competition in shoeshine and cobbling work as well as in producing and selling confectionaries. A very high percentage of the fruit vendors operated outside the Italian receiving areas. They opened stores first in response to the non-Italian consumer, but such shops later became the nuclei of new Italian residential areas. Men who started as fruit vendors then moved on to open grocery stores, then steamship agencies, boarding houses, and even subcontracting—always from one corner store—mediated in many ways between their less city-wise compatriots and the hazards of Toronto. New neighborhoods then were partly artifice, partly spontaneous. Following other groups such as the Jews from the worst to the better housing areas of the city, Italian housing patterns then depended on commerce and industry, from the heavier street construction and primary industries to the sale of fresh fruit.[23]

One sort of distribution that may have been as important as the fruit vendors was that set by the street railway development and by the construction of sheds and warehouses in the train yards of greater Toronto. Just as the railroads played a key role in the settlement of various ethnic groups across the continent, so the substations and junctions created little clusters of foreign laborers, and later their dependents, in various outlying parts of the city. Track maintenance in the severe winter further attenuated the settlement pattern. In the city itself electric street railroads served to distribute the once clustered and alien population. Motormen and conductors who worked the long 11½ and 12-hour shifts on the street railroads found it logical to reside at different turns and junctions on the line.

Not only did subcolonization go on in relation to jobs or better housing, the Ward also began to lose its Italian flavor. At the southern margins along Dundas, the Chinese began to encroach. The old Little Flower Mission became a Mission to the Chinese. The Ukrainians, exiled supporters of Hetman Skoropadsky's government, moved into the top floors of the Ward's two- and three-storey houses. Italian stores in the center and north of the neighborhood gave way not before a new ethnic group but in the face of a growing Bohemia along Gerrard-Hayter, a conscious and striking parallel to the Italian *avant garde* confrontation in New York's Greenwich Village.[24]

Although the Ward remained as Little Italy to many outsiders, it lost to the Clinton-Mansfield section as the primary receiving area for newcomers. By 1935 that area had a United, an Evangelical, and two Catholic Churches with largely Italian communicants. A hotel, the Venezia, steamship agents, and Italian grocery stores were also there. A third neighborhood—following the general northwesterly development of the city and near a major CPR junction—grew up around Davenport and Dufferin. It had fewer storefronts but St. Clements (later Saint Mary of the Angels) and a United Church Mission served the newcomers.[25]

Immigration Disrupted

The war years interrupted Italian immigration to Toronto, but heavy immigration resumed until 1924. Then the combination of Fascism in Italy, fear and hostility over the new American immigration quotas, the tightening of Canadian restrictions on the unskilled, and the Depression stemmed the flow to Toronto almost completely.[26] The consequences for Italo-Toronto were twofold. The Ward and its successors in the west end could no longer be sustained by the continuing flood of greenhorns. As a result, certain stores and institutions in the ethnic neighborhood either atrophied or had to alter their nature. For example, immigrant bankers disappeared or moved into real estate and Toronto-centered activities. The amount of money transmissions to Italy and money changing declined. Ownership of boarding houses and inns passed on to other ethnic groups or disappeared as families became more affluent and immigrant *paesano* boarders dwindled in number. Steamship agencies failed or found their alternatives in importing Italian goods or preparing junkets for the affluent *Americani* of Toronto who wanted to show off their respectability to the newly respectable Fascist Italy. When the Volstead Act in the United States brought Prohibition, restaurant and liquor activities increased in the Italo-Canadian community.[27] Because of all this change, Italians in Toronto by the late 1920s had a full social pyramid. Sons of early settlers were entering the professions, many men who had started as peddlers or manual laborers had become prosperous. For many, community meant only "weekend ethnicity", a trip to one of the Little Italy areas for cheese, pasta, and veal. Others, however, continued to cling to an *ambiente* that they found comfortable, and to a preference for cultural dualism over assimilation.

As their occupational status and levels of acculturation had changed, the associational life of Toronto Italians also changed. From small *paese*-based clubs and mutual aid (burial) societies, they had moved to new institutions that were both more Italian and more Canadian than the initial organizations. Where once there had been clubs such as the Trinacria for Sicilians, there were, side by side with the "home-town clubs", clubs open to all Italians such as the Circolo Colombo and the Società Italo-Canadese, an amalgam of three mutual aid societies. Those who, 20 or 30 years earlier in Italy, had counted a man from a village miles away as a *forestiere* (stranger) now, in the new environment, developed fellow feeling for other Italians. *Campanilismo* did not disappear, hostility particularly between northerners and southerners continued. Still the small size of the Toronto community and the fact that, unlike New York or Montreal, it was not an entrepôt for all people and goods passing from a given village to its colonies in America, meant that continued localism was neither as possible nor as desirable. The struggle against such diverse enemies as Protestant temperance societies and Jansenist Irish clergy increased solidarity among the city's Italians.

The New "Nationalism"

World War I heightened the new "nationalism" among overseas Italians. The so-called *treno degli italiani* that gathered Italian volunteers from Vancouver to the East Coast to serve Italy against the Triple Alliance stopped in Toronto where it was met both by more volunteers and Italian bands.[28] Indeed, there were many varieties of identification. One could be Italian, Italo-Canadian, or a Canadian of Italian descent. Although much of this was self-definition, a statement from the Casa Metodista (Italian Methodist Mission) showed some of the receiving society's confusion about identity. "Our aim is to make good citizens out of Italians and we know that by preaching the Gospel and endeavoring to bring the newcomers to a high spiritual life, they will become good citizens."[29] In World War I, service to the Italian ally was an acceptable form of Canadianism. Dual loyalty would be more difficult later on.

Most of the community stayed suspended between full assimilation (in the form of Protestantism and the changing of patronymics on the one hand) and the remembered Italian origins on the other. Visitors back to Italy found their fractured North American dialect and confident manner alien to their own kinsmen who had stayed behind. At the same time, in Toronto, most felt that prosperity and reasonable acculturation did not require giving up Catholicism or fully giving in to Anglo-conformity.

Men, mostly of humble and petty capitalist origins possessing a high level of Umbertine propriety and respect for property, nonetheless had undergone that part of the North American experience baffling to all immigrants. In Italy, they were used to being despised as *contadini* (peasants) by city people, and as *cafone* (rubes) or *bestie* (manual laborers) by their own upper classes. In Canada they had not expected to be looked down on simply as Italians. Even if they were humble peasants, they came of Europe's "mother culture." As success came to the individual Italian, his need for dignity was heightened. It was proper that part of that dignity should relate to ethnicity, to the place of the Italian nation and of Italians in the world.

It is in such a setting that we should understand the response of Toronto's Italians to the rise of Fascism in Italy. Many, particularly unionists, immediately saw Mussolini as a counter-revolutionary thug. Others, however, could not help but see the new Italy through their own immigrant eyes. Ignazio Silone captured the pathos of their view.

"Descendants of eternal Rome," he began, "O thou my people.... Tell me ... Who was it who brought culture and civilization to the whole Mediterranean and to all known Africa?" "We did," voices replied. "But the fruits were gathered by others." "Tell me again, I pray you, who brought culture and civilization to the whole of Europe, even to the misty shores of England, and built towns and cities where savages had grubbed for food with wild hogs and deer?" "We did," voices replied "but the fruits were enjoyed by others." "Tell me again I beg you, who discovered America?" This time everybody rose to his feet and shouted, "We did! we did! but others enjoy it...." "And tell me again, if you please, who are the people who have emigrated to all the countries of the world to dig mines, build bridges, make roads, dry swamps?..." "We did. We did," they shouted. "And thus you have explained the origin of all your ills. But now, after centuries of humiliation and injustice, Providence has sent us the man who will give our country all its rights that others have usurped."[30]

Mussolini, the champion of the middle classes against Bolshevism, seemed to have won respect and approval for Italy in the world. His solution to the problem of the "red flaggers" and later, the Depression, found support from part of the press in Canada and from many businessmen, academics, and veterans. Respectable Italo-Canadians, full of the patriotism of World War I, could, between 1922 and 1935, support Fascism with the full approval of their fellow Canadians. At last for the Anglo-Saxons, who had never understood the importance of Dante or Verdi, there was an Italian and an Italy to obliterate the image of ragged street musicians and *cafoni* track laborers.

In Toronto, *Il Bollettino*, a paper published from Elm Street, was Fascist-controlled. Attempts to mount anti-Fascist organizations such as Matteotti Clubs met only limited success.[31] For a time a socialist newspaper, *L'Unita*, fought against the official line. With the Lateran Pact and Mussolini's increased popularity in church circles, Fascism became equated with respectability in Toronto's Little Italy. Clergy, businessmen/ advertisers in the local Italian press, *Il Bollettino* itself, Italian officials in the city, and, until the invasion of Ethiopia in 1936, much of non-Italian public opinion in Toronto, made life difficult for "unpatriotic" or "leftist" elements in the Italian community. True to the city's general tendency to a colonial mentality the Italians of Toronto remained under the influence of Montreal organizations such as the Italian United Moral Front or New York organizations like the Sons of Italy. *Il Progresso Italo-Americano*, published in New York, led all other Italian language papers in circulation in Toronto. By 1927, the Fascist government had replaced the Commissioner of Emigration with a Director General of Italians Abroad. Italo-Canadians were considered overseas Italian subjects and not emigrants lost to the mother country.[32] This wooing of the overseas Italians was one reason for Fascism's relative popularity. Centering on the *Casa d'Italia* at Dundas and Beverley Streets, Fascists controlled the life of the community with educational, social, and ideological organizations more familiar among displaced persons or political exiles than among immigrants.[33]

Fascism then was an acceptable political belief in the Toronto of the 1920s and 1930s. Although many Italo-Canadians paid no attention to politics, the lack of sophistication of the immigrant aided the Fascist regime's efforts to reach them. Monarchism, Catholicism, the esteem of their Canadian neighbors, and the general desire for propertied respectability colluded to make it so. For example, the triumphal passage of Italo Balbo and his squadron of hydroplanes on the way to the Chicago World's Fair was a major event for Italo-Canadians, as important as the appearance of a great musical maestro like Caruso. At one level, of course, the roar of huge Savoia-Marchetti seaplanes was a harbinger of Fascism's bombast and belligerence, for Italo-Canadians it was a source of pride in the new Italy: industrialized, a Great Power, and yet evoking Columbus, Vespucci, and the Cabots. The point is that if few Italo-Torontonians were Fascists, fewer escaped some contact with the regime or its programs.

The Chaos of the World War II Era (1936-45)

As Fascist foreign policy became aggression, Canadian public opinion, following that of Great Britain, grew hostile to Italy and to the overt political activity in the Toronto and Montreal Italian communities. At a time when Toronto's Italian women were sending their wedding rings to be melted down to pay for Italy's new imperialism, the Canadian press was denouncing Mussolini's aggression in Ethiopia. Between 1936 and 1940 Italians recognized the possibility of conflict between their primary loyalty to Canada and sympathy for the mother country and her politics. When Italy declared war against Great Britain and her allies, Italo-Canadians were confused and apprehensive. One old Italian, interned as a dangerous enemy alien at Petawawa, had to ask a fellow prisoner whether Italy declared war with France or Germany.[34]

Non-Italians who had flirted with the varieties of Fascism overcame their indiscretions by loyalty and sacrifice during the War. It was not so easy for Toronto Italians. On June 13, 1940 the Minister of Justice announced to the Commons the government's policy toward known Fascists and all those of "Italian racial origins who have become naturalized British subjects since September 1, 1929." The Honourable Minister Lapointe explained that "the very minute that news was received that Italy had declared war on Great Britain and France he signed an order for the internment of many hundreds of men whose names were on the list of the RCMP as suspects. I cannot give the House the number; I have been asked by the head of the mounted police not to do this because it might hamper his work."[35]

One can imagine the terror and upset among the city's people of Italian descent. The RCMP raids were directed only against potential fifth columnists but they appeared inclusive and retrospective in their definition of Fascists. The rumor persisted in Toronto that the RCMP confiscated the guest book of the Casa d'Italia (Casa Fascista) and rounded up everyone on it. More frightening was the violence and vigilantism of the Toronto public. It was reported in the House and in the press that at least 16 Italian storefronts in the city were vandalized when war broke out.[36] Instances of harassment and estrangement occurred with painful frequency in the first days of the war. Then too, while Members of Parliament assured the government that various German groups were loyal Canadian citizens, no Toronto voices there were raised on behalf of the Italians. Far from it. The Member from Broadview warned that "During the Spanish trouble, Italian submarines found shelter on the southeast coast of that country, and Italy has modern submarines that can cross the Atlantic Ocean and return without refueling."[37] Continued American neutrality and the ties of kinship and commerce between Toronto and New York Italians also troubled the legislators.

"This writer goes on to say that we must watch out when Italy enters the war, because of the number of foreigners in the United States, and the German-Italian-Russian spy propaganda. He also says that there are more coloured people in that country than there are in Africa and urges that some organization in the Dominions should cope with these questions before it is too late."[38]

The member for York West congratulated the government on the absence of sabotage in his riding which was "an industrial constituency, one in which we have a large number of foreigners".[39] Thus, the disloyalty of the Italian population was assumed.

The impact of internment on Toronto Italians is hard to assess. It cannot be compared with the removal of the Japanese. No one's property was confiscated. More political and random than racial, the cost to the community was nonetheless terrible. Men who one day held government contracts to produce war material, the next day found themselves shipped to Camp Petawawa where they languished or wasted their talent on road gangs. A Montreal Italian, Mario Duliani, wrote a moving account of life at Petawawa in *La Villa Sans Femmes*.[40] Fascists and Italo-Canadian leaders were interned at the camp, but the real hardship fell on their dependents. Families were left with no livelihood during the difficult first months of the War. Although the church and other organizations cared, help came slowly from group charities lest their efforts be interpreted as support for Fascist sympathizers. During the War, numbers of Italian families from outlying areas and from isolated rural or mining communities moved into the College-Grace and the Dufferin-Brandon areas. They came because of apprehension but also, like others, because of the defense production boom. Paradoxically, some sought rapid assimilation, while others sought shelter in concentrated Italian populated areas.

Migration Resumes (Post-World War II to the Present Era)

The instinctive gathering in of Toronto's Italians during the war had important consequences for the new mass migration of the 1950s. During the war more Italian entrepreneurs had moved from subcontracting and the skilled building trades into heavier and larger construction work. This, in turn, provided some network of job opportunities for unskilled countrymen in the postwar era. The obvious loyalty of Italo-Canadians and the fact that Italy itself by 1943 appeared to be more a victim than a member of the Fascist Axis facilitated the healing of wartime wounds.

The Canadian government's search for unskilled labor in the postwar boom and the possibility of sponsorship renewed the flow of immigrants from Italy. Although the Italo-Canadian community was more Neapolitan and Sicilian in its origins than were the newcomers, it is possible to see that many family chains from the Abruzzi, Molise and Calabria, long interrupted by exclusionist legislation in North America and Fascism in

Italy, became operative again. Large numbers of northern Italians, particularly Friulians and Venetians with little or no connection with the Italo-Canadian community, also arrived.

In a single year like 1956 or 1957, the arriving Italian immigrants outnumbered the 20 000 Italo-Canadians of Toronto.[41] A declining ethnic neighborhood in the west end burgeoned into new "Little Italies", and men who a few years earlier found their *italianità* a liability, now found it an avenue to commercial success. Professionals, children of the Ward's families, relearned Italian or struggled with dialect in order to reach the newcomer.

No careful analysis exists of the role of the Italo-Canadians in the postwar Italian community of Toronto. Even accepting the natural advantages of speaking English and being wise in the ways of the land, one gets the sense that their role was disproportionate. At the same time, it is incorrect to envisage an idyll in which Italo-Canadians led and the newcomers followed. The historical and cultural distance between the two groups was immense. To the newcomers, Italo-Canadians were more like Canadians than Italians or they were "umbertine", that is, fossils of the Age of King Umberto (roughly the equivalent of Victorian). Their sense of probity and even of Italy was remote from that of immigrants who had lived through Fascism and the Allied occupation. The Italo-Canadians, in turn, found the greenhorns blatantly Italian, obtuse, and ungrateful.[42]

Although there are obvious changes in the *ambiente* and ecology of migration, the idea of a commerce of migration and of a *borghesia mediatrice* similar to that which existed at the beginning of the century, can be pursued in contemporary Toronto.[43] The most important changes are probably the aeroplane, the heightened consciousness of Italian nationality and higher literacy in the post-Fascist period, and the presence in the Canadian-Italian migration of more northern Italians and more urban people.

Despite higher literacy and the benign welfare state, immigrants still use a "middle class go-between" in the same manner that migrants once used *padroni*. Signing the wrong papers can bring anything from unwanted aluminum siding to deportation. It was estimated in 1961 that 25% of the Italians in Toronto spoke no English at all. Many others were surely functionally illiterate in English; most are more comfortable in dialect than in Italian itself.

There is in Italo-Toronto, dependence on middle-class "brokers" ranging from ethnic driver education schools and realtors to consulting only doctors from one's *paese*. The most typical broker in the community is probably the travel agent. The Italo-Canadian Commercial Directory for 1971 lists about 50 agents in Toronto, although the number would be far greater if it included formal and informal sub-agents.[44] Toronto agencies often have business or familial ties with sub-agents in Italy, and some also tend to serve a specific *paese*: e.g., the Trinacria agency for Sicilians, the Venezia agency for people from the northeast of Italy. The following, in order of frequency, are the services that first-generation Toronto Italians expected a travel agent to render: (1) Tickets, prepaid tickets for relatives in Italy and other travel arrangements, (2) Arrangement of passports, (3) "Going to Immigration," (4) Remittances, (5) Helping with unemployment insurance, (6) Making out Income Tax forms, (7) Dealing with the Workmen's Compensation Board, OHIP, Old Age Pensions, and, (8) Dissolving partnerships and other notarial work.[45] It is estimated that before the introduction of the current points system, 80% of the migrants to Toronto from Italy were "sponsored." Sponsorship constitutes the most obvious form of chain migration. Yet 60% of the people interviewed had consulted travel agents about sponsoring relatives, and some had depended on agents to find them sponsors. All had paid for the services rendered over and above the price of prepaid tickets.

All this is not intended to suggest the existence of a especially exploitative bourgeoisie or to justify the "waspish" response of those who always dismiss immigrant problems as the exploitation of "one dirty foreigner by another." It does maintain that a coherent class analysis can cross oceans in a way that the random and episodic study of separate kinds of enterprise cannot.

Along with problems of generational change and the persistence of regionalism among Toronto Italians, the differences between the old Italo-Canadians and the recent immigrants have not disappeared. The latter naturally tend to date the Italian presence in the city from their own arrival, and fail to realize that Toronto has seen all phases of Italian migration to North America. Properly understood, the continuity of the Italo-Canadian story reaches back across the war years and the arrival of new masses of Italians to the first migrant laborers of the late 19th century.

ENDNOTES

1. The term *ambiente* is used in this paper to designate a social and cultural atmosphere present in the ethnic neighborhood that was an evocation of the small towns of southern Italy and yet something that became a uniquely Italo-American setting.

2. *Royal Commission To Inquire into the Immigration of Italian Labourers (Montreal)*. Ottawa: Ministry of Labour, 1904, p. 44. Cited henceforth as *Royal Commission (Italian)*. Vol. IV, *The Cultural Contribution of the Other Ethnic Groups*, of the *Report of the Royal Commission on Bilingualism and Bicultural-*

ism (Ottawa, 1969) has convenient tables on yearly immigration. The statistics do not account for seasonal Italo-American work gangs or tally the rates of sojourning, return, and repatriation among young Italian laborers. The best general studies are R. F. Foerster, *The Italian Emigration of Our Times* (Harvard, 1919) and the articles in S. M. Tomasi and M. H. Engel, eds., *The Italian Experience in the United States.* (New York, 1970).

3. H. P. Fairchild, *Immigration* (New York, 1913), p. 148.

4. For the workings of the *padrone* system, see. L. Iorizzo, "The Padrone and Immigrant Distribution," in S. M. Tomasi and M. H. Engel, eds., *The Italian Experience in the United States*; and H. Nalli "The Italian Padrone System in the United States," in *Labor History* #2 Spring 1964. The chief employers were the CPR, the Grand Trunk, Dominion Coal Co. and a number of mining operations.

5. *Royal Commission (Italian)*, p. 168.

6. *Royal Commission (Italian)*, pp. 106-7.

7. Testimony of Mr. Burns, CPR hiring agent, to the *Royal Commission (Italian)*, p. 55.

8. M. Zaslow, *The Opening of the Canadian North, 1870-1914* (Toronto, 1971), p. 192. The author estimates that over 25% of the Ontario Italian population in the 1900s was in the North. That figure would be higher in summer. A spokesman for the Italian Immigrant Aid Society told the *Royal Commission (Italian)*, p. 12, that the Montreal Italian population went from 2 000 in summer to upwards of 10 000 in winter. The parallel seems to have held for Toronto's 1 000 permanent Italian residents.

9. First called A. Dini and Bros. and later known as the International Employment Association Ltd. Unless otherwise noted, detail about the Toronto community is drawn from the *Might's Toronto City Directory* and the Toronto Public Library Collection of Newspaper clippings on Immigration. The only scholarly narrative about Italians in Toronto can be found in the first chapters of Samuel Sidlofsky's *Post-War Immigrants in the Changing Metropolis with Special Reference to Toronto's Italian Population*, Ph.D. Thesis, University of Toronto, 1969. As the title indicates, the thesis is concerned with the later immigration.

10. A. Spada, *The Italians in Canada* (Ottawa, 1969), p. 265.

11. See J. Higham, *Strangers in the Land: Patterns of American Nativism, 1860-1925* (New York: Atheneum, 1963) and O. Handlin, "Old Immigrants and New," in his *Race and Nationality in American Life* (New York: Little, Brown & Co., 1957). The same views are expressed in J. S. Woodsworth, *Strangers Within Our Gates* (Toronto, 1909).

12. See the comments of the Secretary of the Charity Organization Society of Montreal in *Royal Commission (Italian)*, p. 27.

13. *Royal Commission on the Relation of Capital and Labor*, Vol. 5 *Evidence Ontario* (Ottawa, 1889), p. 628, cited henceforth as *Royal Commission (Capital and Labor)*. Italics are mine.

14. Goldwin Smith, *Canada and the Canadian Question*, ed. by C. C. Berger (Toronto, 1971), p. 34 (first published in 1891).

15. The intersections of Elm and Bay, Elm and Elizabeth, Elm and Centre had predominantly Italian storefronts. They represented the geographical center of the *ambiente*.
16. H. Nelli, *Italians in Chicago, 1880-1930. A Study in Ethnic Mobility* (New York: Oxford University Press, 1973), p. 25.
17. R. Glanz, *Jew and Italian: Historic Group Relations and the New Immigration* (New York: Ktav Publishing House, 1971), p. 9.
18. The decline of the Ward as a Little Italy, usually attributed to the expropriation of properties for hospitals, seems much more related to the arrival of new immigrants, the Chinese and then the Ukrainians pushing up from Dundas Street. Given the under-enumeration of transients and boarders in the City Directories, it is difficult to measure and record the impact of the newcomers.
19. The local enterprise was bought up by Catelli, the Montreal-based Italian food producer. Control of Toronto Italian foodstuffs showed the dualism between Montreal and New York influence. For example, the Tuscan style cigars that the immigrants enjoyed were either De Nobile, made in New York, or Marca Gallo, produced in Montreal.
20. Some of these tendencies can be found in C. Ware, *Greenwich Village, 1920-1930: A Comment on American Civilization in the Post-War Years* (New York: Octagon Books, 1965), p. 153. See also L. Tomasi, *The Italian American Family* (Staten Island, N.Y.: Center for Migration Studies, 1972). For this study, a number of Italian extended families in Toronto were followed over time, occupation, and residential change through city directories and interviews.
21. M. Puzo, "Chasing a Dream: Italians in Hell's Kitchen," in T. W. Wheeler, ed. *Immigrant Experience: The Anguish of Becoming American* (Baltimore: Penguin Books, 1972), pp. 47-48.
22. Attempts to see fruit vending as natural to former peasants or as indicative of entrepreneurial spirit lacking among the track laborers fail (1) to realize how many such peddlers were seasonal laborers looking for an extra hustle and (2) that pushing a fruit cart could be as heavy as track work.
23. Many of the families in the Ward had family members doing business in the Clinton-Mansfield Street area, just as other people of the Ward held jobs in the first settlement areas around Union Station and the Market. In turn, people from Clinton-Mansfield Street area commuted back to work in the City Dairy and the garment area. The correlation between work and residence is only loosely possible.
24. C. Ware, *op. cit.*
25. In the late 1920s and early 1930s, Brandon and Beaver both had higher Italian residential density than streets in the Ward, but there were few storefronts and little *ambiente*.
26. Regular emigration from Italy stopped, few political exiles arrived, but they moved on to more active centers of anti-Fascism.
27. Money made during Prohibition may have had connections with American organized crime; often it related to legitimate "chains" of extended family

that provided a natural avenue for such commerce.

28. G. G. Napolitano, "Il Treno degli Italiani" (Milan, 1933), quoted in G. Mingarelli, *Gli italiani di Montreal. Note e Profilo*, Montreal, 1957, pp. 64-66. The volunteers' cry, "Brittani accoci qua" demonstrates that there was no conflict between loyalty to Italy and to Canada.

29. *The Toronto Star*, 12 Dec. 1920.

30. I. Silono, *Bread and Wine*, (N.Y., 1962), p. 169.

31. A. Spada, *The Italians in Canada*, pp. 118-19.

32. The change came in May, 1927. For a statement about emigrants as overseas Italians, see B. Mussolini, *Onera Omnia*, Vol. XXIII, p. 187.

33. Now the home of C.O.S.T.I., the building was confiscated during the War years. Some of the Fascist organizations later outlawed by the Minister of Justice were the *Fasci italiani all 'estero, Depolavoro, Associazioni Combattenti Italiani, Organizzazioni Giovanili degli italiani all' estero*, and the Italian United Moral Front.

34. M. Duliani, *La Ville sans Femmes* (Montreal, 1945), p. 54.

35. Speeches of the Minister of Justice, 11 June and 13 June, 1940, *House of Commons Debates*, Vol. I (1940), p. 657 and pp. 744-45, respectively.

36. *Toronto Telegram*, 11 June 1940.

37. Speech of Mr. Church, Member for Broadview (12 June, 1948) *House of Commons Debates*, Vol. I (1940), p. 718.

38. *Manchester Guardian* article quoted by Mr. Church in *House of Commons Debates*, Vol. I (1940), p. 717.

39. Speech of A. R. Adamson, Member for York West (13 June 1940) *House of Commons Debates*, Vol I (1940), p. 757.

40. M. Duliani, *op. cit.*

41. Canadian Dept. of Citizenship and Immigration, *Annual Reports*, Ottawa, 1951-1959. See *Annuario Statistico Italiano* for the early 1950s. On the Friulians, see B. M. Pagani, *L'Emigrazione friulana dalla meta del secolo XIX al 1940*, Udine, 1968.

42. G. Mingarelli, *Gli Italiani di Montreal*, pp. 59-61, and O. Bressan, *Non Dateci Lenticchie. Esperienze, Commenti, Proseettive di Vita Italo-Canadese* (Toronto, 1958), pp. 106-10.

43. The impressions of Toronto's Italian community in this part of the paper are drawn mainly from two sources. For eight years, students in my Italian history course at the University of Toronto have written term papers on "anonymous immigrant history" subjects. Palmacchio Di Iulio, pre-Law student and Immigration Receiving Counselor at the Malton Airport, and Joseph Cornacchia, Law student, helped interview over a hundred first-generation Toronto Italians.

44. *Italo-Canadian Commercial Directory*, pp. 50-51.

45. Of a hundred people interviewed, 90% expected services 2 and 3 from a travel agent; about 70% expected service 4, and 40 to 60% expected the other services. To the migrant, the phrase "going to immigration" meant that the agent solved a problem or "arranged a difficult case". The agents seemed to protect their role as mediators by affecting an air of mystery about the nature of such transactions.

ALEXANDER MATEJKO   University of Alberta

Multiculturalism: The Polish-Canadian Case*

Poles in Canada today constitute a conglomerate of various local groups in limited touch with one another. A very substantial part of the more than 300 000 people of Polish origin have no contact with the Polish-Canadian ethnic institutions. Four fifths of them do not speak Polish at home (Radecki, 1976: 131).[1] Ethnic organizations are divided along ideological, educational and social class lines (Matejko and Matejko, 1974). Nevertheless, Polish-Canadians as a whole evidence a high degree of interest in their heritage and in the multicultural policy adopted by the federal government in 1971. This paper explores the bonds and diversity within the Polish-Canadian community.

Generations of Polish Canadians

The Poles who settled in Canada before World War II were predominantly peasants, and their whole ethnic lifestyle was very much influenced by values taken from the traditional peasantry (Matejko and Matejko, 1975). The scarce material resources and the limited good factor (Forster, 1965) favored the acceptance of an authoritarian rule imposed on peasants. The traditional peasant community[2] transplanted in North America reappeared in a multitude of self-help associations and ethnic parishes. Priests served as external brokers in dealing with the Anglo-Canadian environment (Matejko, J., 1974a).

The poverty of peasants in the northern and the western part of Poland led to a very clear differentiation of the "better-off" people. In Russia this differentiation was even much more evident (Shanin, 1972) and justified the statement that there are two different Russias: one poor and helpless, the other rich and powerful. The tensions which grew in Canada between the older peasant immigration and postwar intelligentsia immigration may be related to a large extent to the above-mentioned unhappy recollection of class distinctions. The social dualism which originated in the distant past may exist today but is less evident (Radecki and Heydenkorn, 1976).

* Reprinted from *The Polish Review*, vol. XXI, no. 3, 1976, pp. 177-94, with the permission of author and publisher.

In Canada where Anglo-Canadian urbanites predominate, there was no long-range possibility for the Polish peasant immigrants to continue the traditional patterns of behavior. They became urbanized, especially after the Second World War when the new tide of refugees from Poland consisted mostly of urbanites who had temporarily settled in Great Britain or in Germany. The closer integration into the Canadian urban-centered society has become simply unavoidable for the Poles. However, the general style of ethnic life originally established by peasant immigrants has remained, at least for a period of time, the same as in the beginning. The segmentation into local units which do not have very much in common with one another may be interpreted as the continuation of traditional villages. Human relations among Poles are still particularistic and diffuse; the organizational commitment is relatively weak; most common activities are of local importance; ethnic politics is highly personalized. The proliferation of local organizations may be partly explained by a demand for honorific social positions among people who are traditionally status-oriented and who are not able to find this status in the Anglo-Canadian world.[3]

Polish immigrants have gained a lot materially and politically.[4] It is true in general that conformity for European immigrants, including the Poles, is a way of guaranteeing respectability for those who are not sure they are respectable enough (Richmond, 1967b). "Ironically, then, in light of nativist fears that these immigrants would undermine middle-class patterns of life and threaten democratic political institutions, these (immigrant) ethnic and religious groups are among the principal defenders of the status quo" (Palmer, 1972: 247).

It is necessary to make a clear distinction among Polish Canadians between those who have improved their status and security by resettling in Canada, and those who have good reasons to feel less fortunate. For the peasants who entered Canada before World War II and went through the long crisis of the 1930s, what they have now is seen as a great achievement. "An experience of immigrants of downward occupational status mobility, followed by recovery or improvement of status, leads to higher levels of their satisfaction and adaptation to Canada" (Richmond, 1967b: 175). In general the lower-rank immigrants to Canada in the period 1945-65 were more satisfied with life in Canada than those who had high rank in their native country.

After the Second World War, the middle-class Polish people who refused to return to communist Poland and settled for good in Canada suffered the loss of their traditional status. In the late 1960s and in the 1970s many of them managed to improve their positions in the Canadian society. By the 1950s and early 1960s the Polish working class people also became well-established in their occupations.

With the progress of the Polish Canadians in education and income, and the entrance of the young generation into the scene, the traditional ethnic neighborhood integration ceases to exist or at least becomes much weaker. This is generally valid not only for Poles, but for all immigrants in North America, as could be ascertained, for example, in Toronto (Neumann, et al., 1973: 97). The young and educated Polish Canadian, who are ambitious enough to prove their worth, must move into the English-Canadian environment. "To young people fired by curiosity and equipped with a cosmopolitan education, the ethnic community can be intensely stultifying. It is likely to be suspicious, narrow-minded, riddled with prejudices" (Higham, 1974: 69).

For the Polish Canadians, an additional confusion derives from the conflict between the state socialism in Poland and the anti-communist orientation of the Poles in exile. This political orientation is particularly strong among the combatants from World War II who have their own association ties and who still maintain some political aspirations. When these people decided at the end of the war not to return to a Poland controlled by communists, this changed the social structure of the Polish community in Canada which before had been dominated by the lower classes.

In addition to peasants and manual workers, the ethnic middle class started to play an important role in the 1950s by establishing new associations, paying more devotion to common ideals and values, and strengthening a patriotic flavor. Many more Poles than before started to view themselves as an ethnic group that matters in Canada. The whole Polish ethnic group became more self-conscious and mature as a social entity.[5]

One of the obvious reasons for Poles to be proud was, among others, their direct participation in the growth of a "Third Power" in Canada. The ratio of non-British and non-French population in Canada had grown from one in ten in the last quarter of the 19th century to one in four in the 1960s. Catholics, which include most Poles, had grown from 39 to 46% of the total population in the period 1921-71 (only one fifth with an English background). These numerical gains made it possible to achieve some bargaining power, especially when the liberal Canadian government found in the policy of multiculturalism a vital support for its own political survival.

The Costs of Ethnicity

The stress experienced by Polish Canadians as members of a non-statutory ethnic group in Canada may lead to several possible outcomes. The prolonged maladaptation of an objective or subjective nature (personality difficulties) is the common cost in this respect. These are marginal people and there is no way to avoid it. However, "marginality may provide a perspective which enables one to gain keener insight into society and human behavior and can contribute to urbanity and sophistication. The challenge of marginality for the individual is to exploit the opportunity rather than to become a victim of it" (Martin and Franklin, 1973: 48).

Ethnicity should not be treated merely as a remnant of the past. "Even though modern development brings with it tradition-rending change, such as the rational division of labor and secularization, ethnicity per se may be equipped to adapt to the new conditions...The mobilization of ethnic groups may reflect the traumas of casting off tradition, but it may also portend innovative political forms for the future, beyond modernity" (Enloe, 1973: 274).

Ethnicity comes from the Greek word "ethnos" meaning people or peoples, and as such, is not necessarily in any basic disagreement with modernity. However, the ethnic group must have the will, ability and courage to become progressive, open-minded, up-to-date.

The parochialism that is often attributed to ethnic groups appears primarily to be the result of stereotyped thinking: in little concern for facts, in prejudgements and intolerance. Stereotypes "take less effort and give an appearance of order without the difficult work that understanding the true order of things demands. They are a way of classifying, which in itself is a necessary process for any kind of thinking...The traits assigned to a stereotype are selected for their ability to produce some desired effects or on the basis of an emotional predisposition" (Simpson and Yinger, 1972: 153-54).

Parochialism among majority and minority groups takes the form of keeping oneself at a distance from novelties. The first wave of Polish immigrants were mostly peasants who shared with other rural immigrant groups a lack of education and skills, maladaptation to the urban life, lack of mobility and an inadequate consumption pattern. These factors contributed to the prejudice of Anglo-Canadians[6] against the rural arrivals, Poles or Ukrainians (Krawchuk, 1966: 28-42). This prejudice was strengthened by the fear of at least some Anglo-Canadians that the Slavs could undermine the status quo (Matejko, A., 1974b). The intensity of personal attacks usually tended to be greater when the minority was seen as a political threat.

The lower class Poles who settled in North America came to consider their own status as a very touchy issue (Znaniecki-Lopata, 1976), especially when they started to enter the ranks of the middle class. Today any ridicule by others becomes a very vulnerable point (the Jews use their jokes as part of their survival kit, while jokes in North America are very often made *about* and not *by* Poles). With improvement in their economic status, more contact with other ethnic groups, and better acculturation, lower class Poles are now increasingly losing this feeling of isolationism or parochialism and the socio-psychological vulnerability related to it.

Better contact between the Poles and other ethnic groups is related, among other things, to the changing cultural content of ethnic life. The Polish immigrants who came after World War II brought some new elements and stimuli. They were more stable than other categories of arrivals; in the period 1946-61 Canada succeeded in retaining 70% of immigrants from Britain, 60% of those from the United States and 80% of those from other countries. In that period, the Poles and other immigrant groups contributed heavily to the growth of the country (the postwar immigration to Canada up to 1961 constituted a third of the population increase and half of the labor increase). While the postwar immigration substantially strengthened Polish ethnic identity, it also contributed to some confusion as to where exactly is the place of Poles in Canada. It is not the belonging to many groups that causes the difficulty, but an uncertainty of belongingness.

Polish Canadians share with Polish Americans[7] some mixed feelings about their ethnic identity. Michael Novak has spent a considerable effort in the U.S. to convince people that ethnic consciousness is not regressive; that it is not only for the old; that it must not be necessarily illiberal and divisive, and breed hostility; that it will not disappear; that intermarriage does not hopelessly confuse ethnicity; that intelligent sensitive ethnics, proud of their heritage, should not go around thumping their chests in ethnic chauvinism; that emphasis on the ethnic must not conflict with the American patriotism; and that ethnicity is all right not only for minorities, but also for the mainstream of society (Novak, 1971; 1972).

Ethnicity as the desire to uncover one's roots has become fashionable in North America, and the views held by Novak (1972) are quite popular. In the 1950s religion was popular not because of a deep interest in its doctrines, but because religion was a more respectable way of maintaining ethnic primary groups than ethnicity itself (Herberg, 1965). However, during the 1960s the status of being an ethnic became upgraded. The wave of ethnic feeling was evoked by domestic developments in the U.S., notably the formation of the Black Panther Party. Religion declined as a focus of ethnic identification (Glazer and Moynihan, 1970).

Ethnic voting becomes greatest when the ethnic group has produced a middle class. However, many people are restricted in their choice of a place to live by their race, religion or ethnic origin. Can one remain untrapped by the elements of an ethnic community which are limiting, yet be nourished by those elements which liberate?

Assimilation

Until the 1950s, the assimilation process of Poles in Canada was relatively slow. The percentage of those of Polish origin who spoke Polish
had decreased slightly in the period 1921-51 from 83% to 78% (Weinfeld,
1974: 21). However, among the Canadian-born of Polish descent, the
retention of the Polish mother tongue went down in that period from
82% to 39% and later in 1971 to 17%. The mother-tongue Poles have
decreased in the period 1951-71 from 7.8% to 4.8% of the total non-
English and non-French population (Ukrainians from 21.2 to 11.1%).
Only about half of mother-tongue Poles speak Polish at home. The
retention of the Ukrainian mother tongue among the Canadian-born of
Ukrainian descent declined in the period 1921-71 from 98% to 43%, and
the retention of the Italian mother tongue among the Canadian-born
people of Italian descent declined in the same period from 54% to 44%.
The appropriate percentages for the Canadian-born people of German
descent were 78% in 1921 and 27% in 1971. It seems that the Canadian-
born Polish Canadians are less inclined to retain the use of their native
language than other ethnic groups, with the exception of the Germans
and Scandinavians who lose their native languages particularly fast
(Weinfeld, 1974: 21, 23).

Intermarriages with other ethnic groups represented almost two thirds
of all the marriages in 1961 contracted by Polish males; for Ukrainians,
slightly more than half their marriages (57%) were formed with outsiders.
It is significant that the percentage of Polish males marrying Anglo-
Canadian females has risen from 3% in 1921 to 25% in 1961 (among
Ukrainians, from 0.5 to 25%, and among the Jewish, from 1.5 to 5%).
Among Canadian-born Poles in 1961, only a quarter had Polish wives in
comparison with 88% of Canadian-born Jews with Jewish wives and a
half of Canadian-born Ukrainians with Ukrainian wives (Weinfeld, 1974:
51, 52). Even among the Jews the ratio of intermarriages is growing
(from 2.5% in the late 1920s to 14% in 1970)[8], but the intermarriage rate
among the Polish people is particularly high. The assimilationist trend
undermines the existence of the Polish ethnic group.

Language ceases to be an important basis of social differentiation in
the second and subsequent generations, at least in large urban centers
like Toronto (Richmond, 1972: 61), and Poles in this respect are not
different from other ethnic groups. It is religion rather than ethnic
allegiance which remains (Richmond, 1972: 17; Herberg, 1955). With the
progressing acculturation there is less reason for Poles to stay in "Slavic"
areas or to limit their social contacts to their own compatriots. In a
sample of householders in Toronto in 1970 only 16% of Slavs expressed a

preference for living in an area where most people were of the same ethnic group in comparison with 27% among British and 29% among Jews and Italians (Richmond, 1972: 52). It is also significant that the most important reasons for such preference were language difficulties (33% of responses) and to a much lesser extent, the presence of friends, relatives and closer acquaintances (12% of responses) (Richmond, 1972: 53a). Most Slavs found living outside of their own ethnic group more interesting, although ironically, they rejected the idea of "total" Anglo-conformity.

Poles and other Slavs become more cosmopolitan in their general outlook following their socioeconomic advancement in the Canadian framework, fluency in English, higher security, and the broader societal contacts outside their own ethnic group. However, this does not necessarily mean that they rigidly conform to the Canadian lifestyle. The concept of "ethnic community" is no longer equal to an ethnic ghetto but is an extended social network "not necessarily confined to the immediate neighborhood" (Neumann, et al., 1973: 84). Such an ethnic community is highly differentiated internally, and fluency in English, educational level, income and class membership count a lot (Richmond, 1967a: 97). The institutional completeness of the Polish community cannot stop the progressive internal diversification.

The relative position of Poles in the class structure of Canada improves with the progress of their adaptation, but it still is less favorable than the position of some other ethnic groups. Among people of Polish origin in 1971, managerial, administrative and related occupations represented 2.8% in comparison with 3.6% among Germans, 5.2% among British, and 10.7% among Jews. The generally poorly paid services represented 13.1% among Poles in comparison with 10.6% among British and 4.9% among Jews (Perspective Canada, 1974: 279-80).

Upward social mobility is more open to the young generation of Poles than to the old and it is accompanied by their rapid assimilation to English Canada. Thus, there is not much hope for the preservation of ethnic languages on the North American continent. With people becoming too mobile, there are no longer strong supports in retaining distinctive ethnic cultures. Children of immigrants begin to lose their ethnic languages when they enter school. Everything which is relevant in life and work is conducted in English (or in French in Quebec). The immigrant cultures and languages are abandoned (Glazer, 1966). "These fragments of ethnicity that are retained in a disjointed and altered fashion are usually insufficient for the maintenance of functional bilingualism beyond the first generation" (Fishman, 1966: 395). Ethnic language retention is strongest among immigrants who have maintained greatest psychological, social, and cultural distance from the institutions, processes and values of the Anglo-Canadian core society (Fishman, 1966: 396).

Poles and Anglo-Canadians

If "the fundamental variable in majority-minority relations is a condition of unequal power between two more or less self-conscious groups" (Yetman and Steele, 1971: XIII) then in the relationships between Poles and Anglo-Canadians such a condition does not have any substantial explanatory value. Anglo-Canadians do not impose their will on Poles. Poles do not threaten the Anglo-Canadians, and vice versa. Nevertheless, differences exist that alienate the two. For example, the Poles put heavy emphasis on status-orientation (Matejko, A., 1970, 1973, 1974b), Roman Catholic background, nationalism, the gentry tradition, and collectivist background of peasantry. These factors have shaped the Poles in a manner different from the Anglo-Canadians.

Inequality of placement in the social hierarchy tends to entrench ethnic differences. Canada's elite of non-Anglo and non-French origin, including Poles, constituted in 1972-73 only 5% of the economic elite, 8% of the political elite and 4.5% of the bureaucratic elite. They constituted 27% of the total population while Anglo-Canadians constituted 45%; the latter represented 87% of the economic elite, 68% of the political elite and 72% of the bureaucratic elite (Clement and Olsen, 1974: 23).

The concept of public interest differs among various ethnic groups, including the Poles. Their experience in the last 200 years, based on the partitions of the Polish state and the long foreign rule, taught the members of the enlightened Polish strata to make a very clear distinction between national interest and state interest. Such a distinction is blurred in the Anglo democracies.

The social distance between people is also different among Poles in comparison with Anglo-Canadians. The social distance people are inclined to see and accept between themselves and their superiors, as well as how they value the informal group relationships, depends on the nature of the socio-cultural setting, which influences a person's participation in a given setting.[9] Historically, Poles had more exposure (in comparison with the British in North America) to social structures founded on nepotism and favoritism in which there was not much room for formalized participation. The informal Polish pressures effectively prevented people from acting in a way which was not socially prescribed for them. Social distance has been very much entrenched among Poles so that there is the distinction between "our people" ("our" family, "our" close friends, members of "our" stratum) and "strangers". The development of capitalist institutions which eliminated, or at least lowered, the impact of non-task considerations in the sphere of human relations, was slow and painful in the Polish ethnic territories. The contradictions of the capitalist growth led to several status incongruities. The traditional rural communities were undermined or even totally destroyed, but the new urban settlements were slow in providing people with an attractive material and cultural setting (Matejko, A., 1974b).

Poles in Europe today are exposed, on the one hand, to the influence of the gentry tradition on which the whole Polish culture is built, and, on the other hand, to the current bureaucratic patterns of state socialism brought from Russia. In this respect the problems of young generation Poles differ substantially from those of young Canadians. For the second or third generation of Polish Canadians it is relatively easy to conform to the patterns sponsored by the dominant Anglo-Canadian group. However, vivid interest in Poland is still cultivated at least by some Polish Canadian circles, primarily the Polish scouts, groups of university students, and until recently by the *Echo Magazine* in Toronto.

Current developments in Poland have only a minor impact on Polish Canadians, but they should not be underestimated. Young Polish Canadians visit Poland; some of them even study there, and the cultural influence of Poland is quite substantial. It is the ambition of at least some Polish Canadian intellectuals to play the role of middlemen between Poland and Canada. Under these circumstances, it is an open question how much the current Polish experience may be of some validity for the Canadian society. Multiculturalism makes sense when based on the assumption that something important and useful may be gained by Canadians from contact with other national cultures.

Conclusion

The issue of multiculturalism in the case of Poles in Canada is mainly limited to the preservation of at least a bicultural identity. The fact that the Canadian majority sets the cultural patterns and sustains them does not necessarily eliminate for Poles their own chance to survive as a socio-cultural entity. The critical issue in this respect is how Poles can cultivate their dual identity in a creative manner, namely by offering their own contribution to Canadian society. For the Canadians, it is a matter of becoming more perceptive of the creative potential in Slavic strangers. Poles must make a realistic evaluation of their own abilities as well as deficiencies. As long as they are not forced to accede to the demand of some ultra-conformists for full cultural assimilation, there is for them no reason to worry.

The transformation of the Polish ethnic group from a relic of the past to the "movement of self-knowledge" (the term of Novak, 1974: 18) is probably the most critical problem of this group. For the young generation of Polish Canadians it is a choice between becoming "like everyone else," namely petit bourgeois Canadian, or becoming truly bicultural and at the same time conscious of its own ethnic identity. The climate today in Canada for some kind of "Anglophilia" has, for several historical reasons, become less attractive than it used to be. There is now a place on the North American continent for new type of ethnic movements not of a purely defensive nature, but oriented to the highest self-awareness. They are not necessarily better than the old-fashioned ethnic identity.

The spiritual potential of various ethnic groups expresses itself in the ability to utilize a given ethnic background as a vehicle to effect external and internal change. It does not have anything in common with "the upper-class intellectual romanticism" which must serve, according to Myrdal, the conservative and reactionary interests (Myrdal, 1974: 30). It is rather, as in the case of Italian Americans, the result of the emergence of an ethnic intelligentsia which is bicultural, but at the same time rejects the melting pot concept (Vecoli, 1974: 39).

A new intellectual elite has emerged from the ranks of the Ukrainian Canadians which is committed to the resurgence of ethnic consciousness. For Polish Canadians it is still an open question whether, and to what extent, they will be able to go in the same direction. The old generation still occupies all important positions in the Polish ethnic movement and the problems specific to this generation dominate everything else. There are political divisions brought from Poland to Canada 30, 40 or even 50 years ago. The question is if, when and how the young generation will take over control of the Polish Canadian ethnic group. The Polish Canadian Congress which has existed for 40 years does not represent all Polish Canadians because the most important association, the Polish Alliance, withdrew from the Congress in 1972. Some Poles in Canada accept the Polish emigré government in exile, and some of them do not. Some maintain contacts with the authorities of the Polish People's Republic, and others do not. Some want to cooperate with the Ukrainians, while others are still preoccupied with whether the western Ukrainian territory now in Soviet hands should be returned to Poland in the event of a future major political upheaval in eastern Europe. The dividing lines are numerous (Matejko and Matejko, 1974); it is difficult for various generations of Poles to find a common language.

ENDNOTES

1. English is spoken mostly at home in Canada by almost all Scandinavians, 80-90% of Dutch, Germans and Jews, three quarters of Ukrainians and Poles, a half of Asians, but only 2/5 of Italians, and 1/7 of French. Among Canadians who speak Slavic languages at home only 1/10 are under 15. Among all Canadian Slavs only one fifth speak their native language most often at home (Statistics Canada).
2. "Community of descent and relatively low territorial mobility, primary personal contact and lack of anonymity, low division of labor and simple cooperation seem to underlie the high cultural cohesion of rural communities." (Shanin, 1972: 33).

3. For similar trends in other parts of the world, see Kuper, 1972: 140; Hunt & Walker, 1974. On Poles in the United States, see Znaniecki-Lopata, 1976; Sanders and Morawska, 1976.

4. Three quarters of immigrants to Canada in the period 1946-61 felt that they improved their standard of living. The British immigrants to Canada, compared with non-British immigrants, are less likely to be strongly positive in their attitudes to the Canadian way of life. English-speaking immigrants in Canada in the period 1945-65 tended to be recruited from skilled-manual and white-collar occupations. They tended to enter the middle and higher levels of the Canadian social structure (Richmond, 1967b).

5. I use the term "ethnic group" after Greeley (1972). The characteristics of an ethnic group are: (1) a consciousness of kind rooted in a sense of common origin; (2) interaction with each other most of the time; (3) sharing of ideals and values; (4) moralistic fervor and a sense of being persecuted; (5) distrust of those outside and a massive ignorance of them; and (6) tendency to view themselves as the whole of reality that matters. The arrival of Polish combatants to Canada has particularly contributed to points 3 and 6, while the previous ethnic experience of the lower class Polish people was focused in points 1, 2, and 5.

6. According to the Harris Survey conducted for the Urban League in the U.S. in 1970, prejudice exists more among Anglo-Americans than among European ethnic groups (Krickus, 1971).

7. In 1971 2.5% of Americans were of Polish origin (Statistical Abstract of the U.S., 1972: 33).

8. In the U.S. intermarriage is greater for every Jewish generation born in the U.S. and rises even more sharply among the college-educated. The intermarriage rate among the college-educated U.S. Jews is 2/5. Jewish men have a much higher intermarriage rate than Jewish women.

9. For example, in the field of industrial relations, "A man who does not expect to be consulted by his superior and is not inclined to trust either his superior or his peers will see little value in participating in decisions on a man-to-group basis." (Williams and Green, 1970: 258; see also Matejko A., 1976).

SELECTED REFERENCES

Bloch, Marc. *Feudal Society*. London: Routledge and Kegan Paul, 1965.

Clement, Wallace, and Dennis Olsen. "Official Ideology and Ethnic Power: Canadian Elites 1953-1973." Paper presented at the Annual Meeting of American Sociological Association, Montreal, 1974.

Enloe, Cynthia H. *Ethnic Conflict and Political Development*. Boston: Little, Brown, 1973.

Fishman, Joshua A. "Language Maintenance in a Supra-Ethnic Age: Summary and Conclusions," in J. A. Fishman et al. *Language Maintenance in the United States*. The Hague: Mouton, 1966.

Forster, G. M. "Peasant Society and the Image of a Limited Good." *American Anthropologist*, 67 (1965).

Glazer, Nathan. "The Process and Problems of Language-Maintenance: An Integrative Review." in J. A. Fishman, et al. *Language Maintenance in the*

United States. The Hague: Mouton, 1966.

Glazer, Nathan, and D. P. Moynihan. *Beyond the Melting Pot.* Cambridge: The MIT Press, 1970.

Gross, Feliks. *The Polish Worker. A Study of a Social Stratum.* New York: Roy Publ., 1945.

Herberg, William. *Protestant-Catholic-Jew.* New York: Doubleday, 1955.

Heydenkorn, Benedykt, ed. *Past and Present.* Toronto: Canadian-Polish Research Institute, 1974.

———, ed. *From Prairies to Cities.* Toronto: Canadian-Polish Research Institute, 1975.

———, ed. *Topics on Poles in Canada.* Toronto: Canadian-Polish Research Institute, 1976.

Higham, John. "Integration versus Pluralism: Another American Dilemma." *The Center Magazine,* VII: 4 (1974).

Hunt, Chester L., and Lewis Walker. *Ethnic Dynamics: Patterns of Intergroup Relations in Various Societies.* Homewood, Illinois: The Dorsey Press, 1974.

Krawchuk, P. "The Ukrainian Image in Canadian Literature," Tribute to Our Ukrainian Pioneers in Canada's First Century. Proceedings. Special Convention of the Association of United Ukrainian Canadians and the Workers' Benevolent Association of Canada, Winnipeg (May, 1966), pp. 28-42.

Krickus, J. "The White Ethnics." *City* (May-June 1971).

Kuper, Leo. "Religion and Urbanization in Africa," in Anthony H. Richmond, ed., *Readings in Race and Ethnic Relations.* London: Pergamon Press, 1972, pp. 129-48.

Manczak, K. "Spoleczny rachunek sumienia" (Examination of social consciousness), *Glos Polski-Gazeta Polska,* 40 (1974).

Martin, James G., and Clyde W. Franklin. *Minority Group Relations.* Columbus: Charles E. Merrill, 1973.

Matejko, Alexander. "Task versus Status." *International Review of Sociology,* VI, 1-3, 1970, pp. 329-54.

———. "Gestures or Deeds?" *International Review of History and Political Science,* X:4 (1973), pp. 18-33.

———. "The Slavic Influx." in B. Heydenkorn, ed., *Past and Present,* 1974a, pp. 73-80.

———. *Social Change and Stratification in Eastern Europe: An Interpretive Analysis of Poland and Her Neighbours.* New York: Praeger, 1974b.

———. "The Ethnic Middle Class." Paper presented to the Third Congress of the Polish Institute of Arts and Sciences in America, Montreal, May 1975. (forthcoming in *Migrant Echo,* 1978.)

———. *Overcoming Alienation in Work.* Meerut: Sadhna Prakashan, 1976.

Matejko, Joanna. "Rola Misjonarza wsrod polskich pionierow w Albercie" ("Role of missionaries among the Polish pioneers in Alberta"). *Migrant Echo* III:1 (1974), pp. 41-51.

———. "Polscy pionierzy w oczach Auglosasow" ("Polish pioneers in Canada as seen by the Anglo-Saxons"), *Zwiazkowiec* (Alliancer), 1974b, issues no. 70-74 (in Polish).

Matejko, Joanna, and Alexander Matejko. "Polish Canadians." in B. Heydenkorn, ed., *Past and Present.* Toronto: Canadian-Polish Research Institute,

1974, pp. 37-60.

———. "Polish Peasants in the Canadian Prairies." in B. Heydenkorn, ed., *From Prairies to Cities*. Toronto: Canadian-Polish Research Institute, 1975, pp. 9-34.

Myrdal, Gunnar. "The Case Against Romantic Ethnicity." *The Center Magazine*, VII: 4 (1974), pp. 26-30.

Neumann, Brigitte, et al. *Immigrant Integration and Urban Renewal in Toronto*. The Hague: Nijhoff, 1973.

Novak, Michael. "White Ethnic." *Harper's* (September 1971).

———. *The Rise of Unmeltable Ethnics*. New York: Macmillan, 1972.

———. "The New Ethnicity." *The Center Magazine*, VII:4 (1974), pp. 18-25.

Origins of the Canadian Population. 1961 Census of Canada 1966 Bulletin 7.1 – 6 Ottawa: Dominion Bureau of Statistics.

Palmer, Howard. *Land of the Second Choice. A History of Ethnic Groups in Southern Alberta*. Lethbridge: The Lethbridge Herald, 1972.

Perspective Canada. Ottawa: Information Canada, 1974.

Radecki, Henry. "Cultural Mosaic: A Micro View." in B. Heydenkorn, ed., *Topics on Poles in Canada*. Toronto: Canadian-Polish Research Institute, 1976.

Radecki, Henry, and B. Heydenkorn. *A Member of a Distinguished Family: The Polish Group in Canada*. Toronto: McClelland & Stewart, 1976.

Richmond, Anthony H. *"Immigrants and Ethnic Groups in Metropolitan Toronto."* York University (Institute for Behavioural Research mimeo)., 1967a.

———. *Post-War Immigrants to Canada*. Toronto: University of Toronto Press, 1967b.

———. *"Ethnic Residential Segregation in Metropolitan Toronto."* York University (Institute for Behavioural Research mimeo), 1972.

Sanders, Irwin T., and Ewa T. Morawska. *Polish-American Community Life: A Survey of Research*. New York: The Polish Institute of Arts and Sciences in America, 1976.

Shanin, Theodor. *The Awkward Class: Political Sociology of Peasantry in a Developing Country: Russia 1910-1925*. Oxford: Clarendon Press, 1972.

Simpson, E. S., and J. M. Yinger. *Racial and Cultural Minorities*. New York: Harper and Row, 1972.

Statistical Abstract of the U.S., 1972. Washington, D.C.: The U.S. Government Printing Office, 1972.

Thomas, W. I., and F. Znaniecki. *The Polish Peasant in Europe and America*. Boston: R. C. Badger, 1918-1920.

Vecoli, Rudolph. "The Italian Americans." *The Center Magazine* VII: 4 (1974), pp. 31-45.

Weinfeld, Mort. "Multiculturalism and Canadian Ethnic Groups." Manuscript, Ottawa: Department of Sociology. Carleton University, 1974.

Williams, Lawrence K., et al. "Do Cultural Differences Affect Workers' Attitudes?" in Henry A. Landsberger, ed., *Comparative Perspectives on Formal Organizations*. Boston: Little, Brown, 1970.

Yetman, Norman R., and C. Hay Steele, eds. *Majority and Minority*. Boston: Allyn and Bacon, 1971.

Znaniecki-Lopata, Helena. *Polish Americans*. Englewood Cliffs, N.J.: Prentice-Hall, 1976.

ALAN B. ANDERSON   University of Saskatchewan

Ukrainian Ethnicity: Generations and Change in Rural Saskatchewan*

Introduction

The inauguration in 1896 of the Sifton policy favoring the importation of farming settlers from eastern Europe brought in over 170 000 Ukrainians and Poles who settled in compact bloc settlements in the western Canadian prairies. Entire villages moved to Canada, ensuring ethnic self-awareness and a high degree of segregation of the new arrivals from the rest of Canadian society. Ukrainian consciousness in the prairie settlements was doubtless further augmented and inspired by the quest of Ukrainian nationalists in Europe for cultural and political autonomy, official recognition of the Ukrainian language, and permission to have their own schools using that language. Strongly pro-Ukrainian nationalistic sympathies were imported into Canada at the time of the Russian Revolution of 1917 and the ensuing brief period of an independent Ukraine. In Canada, Ukrainian nationalists, anxious to distinguish between Ukrainian and Russian identity, replaced some letters of the Russian alphabet with "Ukrainian" ones. It was also in Canada that the strongly nationalistic Ukrainian Orthodox Church was established after 1917. The Orthodox church regarded the Ukrainian Catholics as "mothered by Rome, fathered by the Polish state".[1] Ukrainian Catholics opposed "Latinization", anxiously preserving their own traditions, liturgy, vestments, and nationalistic accoutrements similar to their Orthodox coethnics. Both Orthodox and eastern-rite Catholic Ukrainians revealed a profound mistrust of western-rite Catholicism, no doubt enhanced by centuries of antipathy toward Polish and Austrian domination. Yet many western-rite Catholics identify themselves as Ukrainians rather than as Poles.[2]

Common identity as Ukrainians should not be overemphasized; there were many examples during the early years of settlement in Canada of

---

* Revised from Alan B. Anderson, "Ukrainian Identity Change in Rural Saskatchewan," in W. W. Isajiw, ed., *Ukrainians in American and Canadian Society: Contributions to the Sociology of Ethnic Groups* (Jersey City: M. P. Knots Publishing, 1976, in conjunction with the Ukrainian Center for Social Research, New York, and the Harvard Ukrainian Research Institute), with permission of the author and publisher.

rivalry, if not at times outright hostility, between these various ethno-religious subgroups within the larger Ukrainian-Polish group.[3] The regions from where most of the immigrants to Canada came – Galicia, Bukovina, Podcarpathian Ruthenia – were within the Austrian Empire; the rest of the Ukraine lay within the Russian Empire. Thus, the subjugated emigrants thought of themselves first as Galicians, Bukovinians, or Ruthenians; only secondarily as Austrians or Russians. Ukrainian identity was to emerge gradually *after* they had emigrated; *it was in Canada that they discovered their common identity*.[4]

Most of the first-generation respondents in our study were born in Europe between 1885 and 1915. Their parents were peasants forced to live in deplorable conditions unalleviated by the Austrian government's abolition of the traditional *panschyna* servitude. They owned little land, devoting much of their time to working the lands of the landlord. They were forbidden to speak their own traditional language, and they were heavily taxed. Very few peasant holdings were over thirteen acres.[5] After 1848, landlords (often Poles or Austrians) claimed the communal lands of whole peasant villages as a war indemnity.

How is Ukrainian identity expressed today? The experience of other ethnic groups reveals that ethnicity erodes with each subsequent generation born in the host society. This research focuses on the attitudes toward ethnic identity of three generations of Ukrainians in rural Saskatchewan.

Methodology

Four rural bloc settlements in north-central Saskatchewan with a combined Ukrainian-Polish population of 12 600 were studied over a four-year period (1968-72). In the sample (N = 252), 61.1% (154) of the respondents were Ukrainian Catholics, 32.9% (83) were Ukrainian Orthodox, and 6.0% (15) were "Polish" Catholics.[6] Table 1 presents the demographic characteristics of the sample.

The Settlements[7]

The four settlements studied were the Fish Creek settlement, with its center approximately 40 miles northeast of Saskatoon; Yellow Creek, some 40 miles southeast of Prince Albert; Redberry, with its nucleus about 50 miles northwest of Saskatoon; and Garden River, roughly 20 miles northeast of Prince Albert.

Fish Creek began to develop in 1897 with the arrival of immigrants from the Sokol, Cherniatyn, Horodenka, and Halychyna regions in Galicia. Although the first Independent Ukrainian congregation in Canada was established in this settlement at St. Julian in 1903 (thus laying the foundation for what would become the Ukrainian Orthodox Church in

TABLE 1 *Population characteristics of sample, per religious group*

	Orthodox (N=83)		Eastern-rite (Ukrainian) Catholic (N=154)		Western-rite (Polish) Catholic (N=15)	
Age						
13-19	8.5	(7)	13.0	(20)	0.0	
20-29	10.8	(9)	5.8	(9)	0.0	
30-49	20.5	(17)	38.3	(59)	26.7	(4)
50-69	50.6	(42)	27.9	(43)	40.0	(6)
70+	9.6	(8)	14.9	(23)	33.3	(5)
Total	100%	(83)	100%	(154)	100%	(15)
*Generation**						
First	26.5	(22)	24.7	(38)	40.0	(6)
Second	50.6	(42)	57.8	(89)	60.0	(9)
Third	22.9	(19)	17.5	(27)	0.0	
Total	100%	(83)	100%	(154)	100%	(15)
Sex						
Male	53.0	(44)	57.1	(88)	73.3	(11)
Female	47.0	(39)	42.9	(66)	26.7	(4)
Total	100%	(83)	100%	(154)	100%	(15)
*Occupation***						
Student	9.6	(8)	13.0	(20)	0.0	
Farmer (full-time)	36.1	(30)	55.2	(85)	86.7	(13)
Farmer (part-time)	2.4	(2)	1.3	(2)	0.0	
Clergy	3.6	(3)	1.9	(3)	6.7	(1)
Teacher	8.4	(7)	1.3	(2)	0.0	
Civil servant	7.2	(6)	1.9	(3)	0.0	
Indep. proprietor	16.9	(14)	14.9	(23)	0.0	
Employed (skilled)	2.4	(2)	5.8	(9)	6.7	(1)
Employed (unskilled)	2.4	(2)	1.9	(3)	0.0	
Other	10.8	(9)	2.6	(4)	0.0	
Total	100%	(83)	100%	(154)	100%	(15)
Education						
Grade school	41.0	(34)	32.5	(50)	66.7	(10)
Some high school	27.7	(23)	47.4	(73)	20.0	(3)
High school grad.	15.7	(13)	14.9	(23)	6.7	(1)
Some university	15.7	(13)	5.2	(8)	6.7	(1)
Total	100%	(83)	100%	(154)	100%	(15)

*"Generation" refers to generations resident in Canada; thus, the first generation consists of immigrants, the second and third are Canadian-born.
**"Occupation" refers to the primary source of income for each family interviewed; spouses are classified under their spouses' occupations though students are considered separately.

Canada), most communities and districts were largely Ukrainian Catholic by 1910, when the settlement expanded to approximately its present limits. Today there are 22 Ukrainian Catholic churches in the settlement (though many have small congregations and meet irregularly), compared to only seven Ukrainian Orthodox. Of the 10 Roman Catholic churches, only one is predominantly Polish. There is also one Stundist or "Russian" Baptist congregation. The total Ukrainian-Polish population of the settlement may be estimated at 3 900. The settlement has four towns, three incorporated villages, four hamlets which are not incorporated, and at least 53 rural localities of which 32 have distinctly Ukrainian names.

The *Yellow Creek* settlement developed between 1899 and 1912 with the immigration of Ukrainians and Poles from Galicia and Bukovina. The settlement soon expanded westward into districts originally settled by farmers of Hungarian, French, and German origin, so that it became virtually contiguous to the extended Fish Creek settlement. The Yellow Creek area remains a fairly small settlement, however, with only about 1 600 people of Ukrainian and Polish origin in a single incorporated village, five unincorporated hamlets, and 15 rural localities. The Orthodox are stronger here, with three active churches; the Ukrainian Catholics have three small congregations, the Polish Catholics two.

The *Redberry* settlement commenced with the migration of a number of Fish Creek Galicians into this area in 1904. Supplemented by immigrants from the western and eastern Ukraine as well as from Russia, by 1914 the new colony included a vast area. Today the 4 700 Ukrainians and Poles in this settlement live in a town, four villages, six hamlets, and no less than 60 rural districts, 20 with Ukrainian names. Ukrainian Catholics seem to outnumber Ukrainian Orthodox, though certain districts are largely Orthodox. There are 13 eastern-rite Catholic churches, compared to six Orthodox; and three out of the five western-rite Catholic churches have predominantly Polish membership. There are also two Stundist, Russelite, or "Russian" Baptist groups affiliated with the Mennonites.

The *Garden River* settlement began in 1906-7 when Ukrainians and Poles arrived near Prince Albert. They were joined in 1912-16 by farming families who had left the Stuartburn settlement in southeastern Manitoba because of the sandy soil and frequent flooding. In the new settlement the population was approximately evenly divided between Ukrainian Catholics and Poles from Galicia, on the one hand, and Ukrainian Orthodox from Bukovina, on the other hand; there were also a few Ukrainian and Polish immigrants from Russia. Today Garden River includes four Ukrainian Orthodox churches, five Ukrainian Catholic, and one of each of the following—Polish Catholic, Russian Orthodox, and Russian Baptist. A total of 2 400 Ukrainians and Poles live here.

Findings

Interviews covered such critical aspects of ethnicity as language usage, church attendance, adherence to various customs, and attitudes toward intermarriage.

TABLE 2 *Ukrainian ethnicity by generation and religious tradition*

Reported Behavior	Religion**	Generation* (%) First (N=60)	Second (N=131)	Third (N=46)	Total (N)
Identity preservation favored	Orth.	100	74	68	(83)
	ERC	100	82	55	(154)
English usage primary	Orth.	14	38	63	(83)
	ERC	10	36	44	(154)
Ethnic parish attendance regular	Orth.	96	57	7	(83)
	ERC	95	84	56	(154)
Ethnic intermarriage opposed	Orth.	68	33	26	(83)
	ERC	89	58	33	(154)
Religious intermarriage opposed	Orth.	68	33	36	(83)
	ERC	89	66	48	(154)

*Generation refers to generations resident in Canada; thus, the first generation consists of immigrants, the second and third are Canadian-born.
** Although other religious traditions were represented in the sample, the two most numerous reported here are Orthodox (Orth) and Ukrainian Eastern-Rite Catholic (ERC).

Generation

The common wisdom that the longer the period since immigration, the less emphasis will be placed on ethnicity finds support in the generational data presented in Table 2. Ethnic attitudes and behavior were found to weaken in a linear fashion between the first and third generation of Ukrainians, regardless of religious tradition. For example, while 89% of the first generation eastern-rite Catholics opposed ethnic intermarriage, 58% of the second generation registered disapproval, with opposition in the third generation dropping to a mild 33%.

It is difficult to ascertain whether the greatest step away from ethnic group consciousness occurs between first and second generation or between the second and third; the former may be the case for the Orthodox, the latter for the eastern-rite Catholics. While a fairly consistent rate of de-emphasis of ethnic identity was noted for all subgroups, it should also be noted that the majority of the third generation respondents still favored maintenance of their ethnic identity.

Age

Because of the strong inter-relationship between age and generation, one would expect the data when presented by age to show similar results to the data when presented by generation. Clearly, such is the case; the

TABLE 3 *Ukrainian ethnicity by age group and religious tradition*

Reported Behavior	Religion* Orth. (N=83) ERC (N=154)	Age Group (%)				
		13-19 (N=27)	20-29 (N=18)	30-49 (N=76)	50-69 (N=85)	70+ (N=31)
Identity preservation favored	Orth.	29	44	94	86	100
	ERC	45	44	83	95	100
English usage primary	Orth.	57	67	47	31	0
	ERC	50	56	42	19	0
Ethnic intermarriage opposed	Orth.	29	33	29	40	87
	ERC	20	44	58	72	96
Religious intermarriage opposed	Orth.	43	33	35	40	87
	ERC	45	44	61	81	96

*The Orthodox (Orth.) and Ukrainian Eastern-rite Catholic (ERC) are reported. There were Ukrainian Western-rite Catholics living in the area in small numbers, but none were third generation or under age 30; thus they were excluded from the generational analysis.

younger the Ukrainian, the less likely are strong ethnic attitudes and behaviors found. Concerning language, we see in Table 3 that the majority under 30 years of age use English exclusively or as a primary language. The situation is reversed for those over 30. Nevertheless, it should be pointed out that virtually all interviewed had some familiarity with their traditional mother tongue. Attitudes toward intermarriage reveal the younger generation to be more indifferent with greater tolerance for ethnic than religious intermarriage, the eastern-rite Catholics feeling more strongly about this issue than the Orthodox for most all ages.

Customs[8]

The visible features of Ukrainian culture are its customs. There are distinctly Ukrainian foods, crafts, ways of dressing, techniques for building homes and home decorating, types of farming, leisure-time activities, performing arts, and kinship networks. What concerns us is the extent to which certain customs have disappeared or have been retained.

Traditional foods remain of particular significance to rural people of Ukrainian and related Slavic origins in the Canadian prairies. All of the western-rite Catholic respondents, 92.2% of the Ukrainian Catholic ones, and 86.5% of the Orthodox replied that they frequently prepare or eat foods typically Ukrainian or Polish. Such foods include, for example, "borscht" (beet or cabbage soup), "perohi" (dumplings), "blintzi" (milk and egg pancakes), "kapusniak" (sauerkraut and buckwheat), poppy-seed bread, "holubtzi" (cabbage rolls), "kasha" (grain pudding), "Kulesha" or

"Mamalyga" (cornflour bread), "studenetz" (head cheese), "dushenya" (cooked meat with gravy), and "stynanka" (potato or dough soup). Special dishes are served on religious holidays, notably "paska" (Easter bread) and "kutia" (hulled wheat grains and honey at Christmastime).

A similar percentage of those interviewed make, wear or otherwise use distinctly Ukrainian or Polish crafts. Many of the other women still make "kilims" (handwoven tapestries) or "kylymy" (rugs); such work was particularly common among the Bukovinians in the Garden River settlement, but the art is seldom practised by their younger descendants today. Embroidered smocks, "obhortkas" (thick wool petticoats), embroidered white linen blouses, long billowing skirts, and leather boots, once common attire for Ukrainian women, were rapidly exchanged for typical Canadian clothing, though today it is not at all unusual to see the older women wearing "babushkas" (headscarves). Gone are the men's sheepskin coats, heavy boots, embroidered, bulky shirts, and coarse woolen trousers, though the older men typically wear loose-fitting clothing and floppy, broad-brimmed caps. Ukrainian homes used to be very distinctive, but today few examples of the original styles are left. In general, thatched roofs were replaced by shingled ones within only a few years after immigration (though many were still found in selected districts through the 1930s, and some still remain as barns and sheds), and sod or log walls were replaced by washed clay ones, then frame ones. Ukrainian homes today are less crowded; the typical homes several decades ago had one or two principal rooms occupied by as many as twelve extended family members and hired hands. Homemade furniture, religious icons, embroidery, and distinctive pottery remain quite common as decor in the homes, though less common now than was the case a generation back because of a decline in productivity.

The Ukrainian immigrants brought with them a culture rich in folk music, folk dances, art, and festivities. Ukrainian Canadians have long exhibited a keen interest in their folk arts. Many of their churches are lavishly decorated and built in the traditional Russo-Byzantine style. Folk music retains its popularity. Small bands, choirs, and folk dance troupes are still found in numerous Ukrainian communities. In the earlier years of non-mechanized agriculture, it was not unusual to hear Ukrainian peasants, including women and children, singing traditional work songs as they toiled in the fields of Saskatchewan and other prairie provinces. At small rural communities such as St. Julian there was the annual folk dancing of "Haiwka" (Easter Monday). Ukrainian-language plays, usually depicting Cossack days, were once common, held in conjunction with folk dancing in the schools; today the Cossack play-*cum*-dance routine remains popular with Ukrainian dance troupes in Canada. More often than not, Ukrainian weddings in rural areas are elaborate affairs lasting for several days and involving much drinking, dining, and dancing. Nevertheless, older respondents regretted that the younger generation Ukrainian Canadians reveal little real interest in Ukrainian history except for an amiable curiosity about the past. Ukrainian Christmas in Canada has become increasingly less traditional; largely gone during the past few years is the interest of young Ukrainian-Canadians in the traditional door-to-door carol singing, while the customary seasonal decorations and preparation of special foods are being replaced gradually by typical North American practices. Such occasions as Christmas and Easter have increasingly become simply nuclear family affairs when once they were very large gatherings for related extended kin networks.

Voluntary Associations[9]

Without doubt the Ukrainians remain one of the most highly organized, institutionally complete ethnic groups in the Canadian prairies. A wide variety of their organizations permeate the communities, large or small, within their bloc settlements. Participation in the "narodni domi" (community halls) was taken for granted for many decades. The Ukrainian Catholic and Orthodox "chulanyi proswitas" and "tovaristvos" (serving as halls of cultural activities, social centers, libraries, and folk dancing, music and drama theaters) were once far more common than they are today. Some voluntary associations were specifically nationalistic, such as the Ukrainian National Federation, the Ukrainian Hetmans Association, and the pro-monarchist, ardently anti-Communist Sich organization of the Ukrainian Catholic Church. However, participation in such "old guard" organizations has lost its appeal among the younger generation, necessitating a radical reinterpretation of the purpose of these organizations within Canadian society. Even when Ukrainian nationalistic sympathies were perhaps at their height during the 1920s in certain districts (e.g., the Bohdan district in the Redberry settlement) a vehement anti-Communist nationalism contrasted vividly with pro-Bolshevist sympathies.

Numerous organizations continue to function in Ukrainian communities across Canada, many of them connected with the churches. They have served in an extraordinary variety of capacities: as insurance agencies covering illness, death, and social welfare for orphans and the aged; as cooperatives for farmers and laborers; as federations of community centers; as university student hostels; as handicraft guilds; as folk culture centers; as nationalistic and political pressure groups; and as social centers.

Given the fact that the Ukrainians are still highly institutionalized in terms of ethnic-oriented voluntary associations, the question remains as to whether they actively participate in the associations. Our study of four bloc settlements seems to suggest that participation is very limited: 32.5%

of the Orthodox, 13.6% of the eastern-rite Catholics, and 26.7% of the western-rite Catholics. Who seemed most likely to be a participant? We discerned little correlation between participation and age, though second- and third-generation Orthodox and Polish Catholics were the most reluctant to participate. Moreover, in these two subgroups, the men were more likely to participate than the women; no significant correlations were noted for the third group, the Ukrainian Catholics. In general, participation in ethnic-oriented voluntary associations tended to increase with education, a weak correlation noted between participation and attitudes favoring identity preservation, ability to speak Ukrainian or Polish as a mother-tongue, frequent attendance at a Ukrainian or Polish parish church, and attitudes opposing physical mobility.

In order to arrive at a more precise portrait of the Ukrainian-Canadian resident in the bloc settlements, a larger sample, incorporating more control variables, would be necessary. To a limited extent, a higher proportion of Ukrainian Orthodox and Ukrainian Catholic females than males tended to favor identity preservation. Farmers, the clergy, and independent proprietors proved very conservative in all subgroups, as did skilled employees who were Orthodox and teachers who were eastern-rite Catholics; students were the least conservative. The more education the ethnic group member had, the less likely he or she was to stress ethnic identity up to the high school level; however, respondents with at least some university education tended to be largely conservative. Size of community, its accessibility, its location within the settlement, and even its degree of ethnic homogeneity apparently have little effect on the extent to which ethnic identity is emphasized. Wary of assimilation, about one half of the respondents were opposed to moving from the bloc settlements: 44.6% of the Orthodox, 62.9% of the eastern-rite Catholics, and 53.3% of the western-rite Catholics.

Conclusion

This research has concentrated on age and generation differences relating to the preservation of Ukrainian identity in selected bloc settlements in north-central Saskatchewan. While Ukrainian identity remains quite high in these settlements, there are many indications that this ethnic self-awareness is likely to continue to decrease, in all probability at an accelerating rate. We have observed that the older group member in the first generation tends to strongly favor the preservation of his ethnic identity, to speak his traditional mother-tongue, to attend an ethnic-oriented parish church as regularly as possible, to be familiar with numerous customs of his group, to participate, perhaps, in ethnic-oriented voluntary associations, and to be opposed to intermarriage. The typical Ukrainian- or Polish-Canadian teenager two generations removed from his immigrant forebears, on the other hand, is relatively indifferent toward preservation or emphasis of an ethnic identity, speaks English more often than Ukrainian or Polish, attends a Ukrainian or Polish parish church less often, is disinterested in or unfamiliar with many of the customs of his heritage, seldom participates in ethnic voluntary associations, and is rather indifferent toward intermarriage. While this is at best an over-generalization based on results from a limited number of interviews, it is at least suggestive for further research.

Considering that a strong sense of Ukrainian identity did develop among most of the first generation in Canada, why has so much of this feeling been lost among their third generation descendants? *Four basic reasons for assimilation may be set forth. First*, from the very beginning of their settlement in Canada, the immigrants had to come to terms with a conflict between their identity as Ukrainians and as Canadians. Despite the evidence that policies of Anglo-conformity were distasteful to them, there were indications also of an emergent pride in being Canadian. This pride could probably be accounted for if one recalls the dismal conditions of servitude as peasantry in the old country. Anglo-conformity in some instances has been replaced by multiculturalism so that toleration of ethnic group differences has become more characteristic of Canadian society, especially in the West. Ukrainian Canadians stressed their dual identity as Ukrainians and as Canadians; conflict was effectively translated into accommodation. While for the first generation the emphasis remained on *Ukrainian* Canadian, for the third, it is on Ukrainian *Canadian*.[10]

Second, increasing contact with Canadians of other ethnic origins meant inevitable acculturation. The first generation were segregated from contacts and largely illiterate in English.[11] With education in Canadian schools, considerable anglicization of Ukrainian dialects began to occur. Many new words derived from English were incorporated into the everyday language of Ukrainian Canadians; English combined with Ukrainian was heard increasingly; and the second generation typically imposed Ukrainian verb conjugation and sentence structure on the English they had learned.[12] The proportion of Ukrainians and Poles who abandoned their traditional religious affiliations slowly but steadily increased with intermarriage.[13] Ukrainian and Polish parish churches are increasingly adopting English in their services, though this practice is still limited.

Third, and most decisively, while the Ukrainians have maintained a high degree of institutional completeness through their voluntary associations, they were not able to maintain ethnic enclosure in the schools after 1919, when the provincial government legislated against foreign-language teaching in public schools. At the time there were perhaps as many as 50 small schools in the four Ukrainian-Polish bloc settlements in the north-central region still using, in whole or in part, instruction in the Ukrainian language.[14] During the 1920s many of these schools continued to teach the Ukrainian language after school hours, but during school hours English was the language of instruction. After 1927 the churches began to operate their own Ukrainian-language schools "to make better Canadians of their young members by helping them to become better Ukrainians". While the non-Ukrainian public school teachers had encouraged Ukrainian children to call themselves Canadians, they had to face considerable opposition from the parents, with the result that the Ukrainian-but-Canadian identity typical of the second generation emerged. While the public schools had once inculcated a strong sense of Ukrainian identity, they had become primary assimilation agencies. Their influence had to be offset, in part, by private church-run schools offering specifically Ukrainian education.

Fourth, technological change and rural depopulation have had a severely negative effect on ethnic identity maintenance. In north-central Saskatchewan, fairly intensive rural settlement has been gradually replaced by steady depopulation; physical and social isolation by increased mobility. Since 1929, repeated economic depressions and droughts have brought about virtually incessant population decline coupled with institutional consolidation. Largely gone are the intimate small communities upon which so many aspects of ethnic intra-group life were based. Older people have moved off their farms and into larger communities; the younger generation have been abandoning the rural life completely. The small country schoolhouses in the bloc settlements have been replaced since the 1950s by large consolidated schools, many of which are in ethnically heterogeneous centers, lessening the attention paid to considerations of ethnic origins. Country parishes have seen their membership fall by more than two thirds during the past ten years; many hold services very irregularly. The community halls which once dotted the countryside in the Ukrainian-Polish settlements are for the most part unused today except, perhaps, for the occasional wedding. If Ukrainian identity is to persist, it must do so in conditions vastly different from those existing at the time of immigration. The younger generation will have to forge an ethnic identity and build its social structural supports in an environment different from the one their elders lived in.

ENDNOTES

1. C. H. Young (1931), pp. 134-136, 143; and Rev. M. Schudlo (1951), pp. 5, 11, 21-24.
2. The distinction between Ukrainians and Poles seems to lie primarily in the former attending eastern rite churches and the latter attending western rite.

However, this distinction becomes blurred, at least in the settlements studied, for a variety of reasons: people identifying themselves as "Ukrainians" or "Poles" were commingled in virtually all of the eastern European regions from which they emigrated to the bloc settlements in the Canadian prairies, where not surprisingly they continued to settle together; their "Ukrainian" and "Polish" languages were actually similar if not identical regional dialects more than distinct languages; many of the "Poles" were culturally Ukrainian yet claimed Polish descent and citizenship upon emigrating; and in Saskatchewan informants suggested that a change in religious affiliation, usually due to intermarriage, is often accompanied by a change in ethnic identification, e.g., from Polish Catholic to Ukrainian Catholic or Ukrainian Orthodox. For these reasons respondents identifying as "Poles" were treated essentially as a sub-group, along with Ukrainian Catholics and Ukrainian Orthodox, of a larger Ukrainian-Polish group. See, for example, C. H. Young (1931).

3. Conflict between ethno-religious factions within the Ukrainian-Polish group has been documented by J. Hawkes (1924), C. H. Young (1931), M. Schudlo (1951), O. S. Trosky (1968), and others. Conflict between these closely related factions dated back for centuries in Europe prior to emigration. O. S. Trosky (1968) and D. Millett (1971) have described the history of the Ukrainian Orthodox Church in Canada, and B. Kazymyra (1975) and E. Tremblay (1960), the Ukrainian Catholic Church.

4. On the lack of a Ukrainian national identity in Europe prior to emigration, see, for example, C. A. McCartney, "Nationalism and the Minorities," O. Jaszi, "Reversals of Dominance in Central Europe," and S. and B. Webb, "National Minorities in the Soviet Union," in Alain Locke and Bernhard J. Stern (eds.), *When Peoples Meet: A Study in Race and Culture Contacts* (New York: Hinds, Hayden, & Eldridge, 1946); see also Erich Goldhagen, (ed.), *Ethnic Minorities in the Soviet Union* (New York: Praeger, 1968).

5. T. Skwarok (1959).

6. A 2% controlled quota sample yielded 252 cases, or one interview for every fifty persons of the relevant ethnic origin in each settlement. The extent of each settlement was determined by the limit beyond which the Ukrainian-Polish proportion constitutes less than 25% of the general population in a certain rural area. To avoid bias, not more than one member of a single nuclear or extended family could be interviewed, and no respondent was less than thirteen years of age. But to arrive at findings approximately representative of the larger ethnic group population in each settlement, interviews were conducted throughout the settlements and the sample was stratified to some extent by age, generation, and sex. Data analysis was by computer univariate, bi-variate, and tri-variate cross-tabulations; only significant results are reported in this paper.

7. Among the many sources describing the development of Ukrainian and Polish bloc settlements in the prairies are R. England (1929), C. H. Young (1931), C. A. Dawson (1936, 1940), V. Lysenko (1947), V. J. Kaye (1964), A. B. Anderson (1972), and H. Radecki and B. Heydenkorn (1976).

8. This description of Ukrainian customs is based largely on J. Hawkes (1924), R. England (1929), C. A. Dawson (1940), V. Lysenko (1947), and data from the Archives of Saskatchewan: Martin papers, file 168.

9. For further details on Ukrainian voluntary associations, see C. H. Young (1931), C. A. Dawson (1940), V. Lysenko (1947), O. S. Trosky (1968), and the Report of the Royal Commission on Bilingualism and Biculturalism, Book IV, part II, chap. 4 (1970).

10. Sources on changing Ukrainian-Canadian identity include: C. H. Young (1931), V. Lysenko (1947), E. Wangenheim (1971), and W. W. Isajiw (1976).

11. For details on illiteracy among Ukrainian settlers in the early years of settlement, see R. England (1929); C. H. Young (1931); and the Archives of Saskatchewan: Martin 168. Examples of Anglicization of Ukrainian may be found in J. T. M. Anderson (1918), and V. Lysenko (1947).

12. On language use among Ukrainian and Polish Canadians, see: Archives of Saskatchewan: Martin 168, R. England (1929), C. H. Young (1931), A Milnor (1968), A. Royick (1968), Royick and Pohorecky (1968), Y. Grabowski (1975), and A. B. Anderson (1976).

13. Recent sources referring to intermarriage among Ukrainians in Canada include M. Stefanow (1962), W. Darcovich (1967), the Report of the Royal Commission on Bilingualism, op. cit. (1970), A. B. Anderson (1974), D. M. Heer and C. A. Hubay Jr. (1975), S. P. Wakil (1976).

14. For further details on the use of Ukrainian as a language of instruction in Saskatchewan public schools, see J. T. M. Anderson (1918), R. England (1929), C. H. Young (1931), T. Skwarok (1959), O. S. Trosky (1968), Keith A. McLeod (1968), and Archives of Saskatchewan: Martin 53, 56, 60, Education file 12A, Scott 18c, Latta 7.

APPENDIX: FRENCH ETHNICITY IN NORTH CENTRAL SASKATCHEWAN*

The Ukrainian data reported in the body of the paper are drawn from a larger study comparing identity change among seven ethno-religious groups in north-central Saskatchewan. In order that the Ukrainian data may be placed in a comparative ethnic perspective, corresponding data on French ethnicity are presented here.

In all but one of the French settlements studied, most of the original settlers came directly from France rather than Quebec although today the various French origins—Métis, Bretons from France, Belgians, Québécois, Acadians, Franco-Americans—have been mixed into a common Saskatchewan French Canadian identity.[1] Table 1 provides the demographic

---

* The data in this Appendix and in the body of the paper are drawn from the larger study by Alan B. Anderson, "Assimilation in the Bloc Settlements of North-Central Saskatchewan," Unpublished Ph.D. thesis in sociology, University of Saskatchewan, 1972. The French ethnicity data have appeared in Alan B. Anderson, "Ethnic Identity Retention in French Canadian Communities in Saskatchewan," A paper presented to the Canadian Sociology and Anthropology Association, Toronto, Ontario, 1974.

TABLE 1 *Population characteristics of the French sample and proportions of respondents favoring identity retention*

	Proportion of total sample in category		Proportion of respondents within each category favoring identity retention	
	%	N	%	N
Age				
13-19	14.9	(30)	36.7	(11)
20-29	9.9	(19)	52.6	(10)
30-49	35.6	(72)	73.6	(53)
50-69	26.7	(54)	79.7	(43)
70+	13.4	(27)	92.6	(25)
*Generation**				
First	19.8	(40)	87.5	(35)
Second	45.5	(92)	80.4	(74)
Third/more	34.7	(70)	47.2	(33)
Sex				
Male	50.5	(102)	70.3	(71)
Female	49.5	(100)	70.3	(70)
*Occupation***				
Student	14.9	(30)	30.0	(9)
Farmer (full-time)	49.5	(100)	80.0	(80)
Farmer (part-time)	1.0	(2)	100.0	(2)
Clergy	3.5	(7)	85.7	(6)
Teacher	1.5	(3)	100.0	(3)
Civil servant	3.5	(7)	71.4	(5)
Indep. proprietor	13.9	(28)	64.3	(18)
Employed (skilled)	6.9	(14)	57.1	(8)
Employed (unskilled)	4.0	(8)	100.0	(8)
Other	1.5	(3)	100.0	(3)
Education				
Grade school	22.3	(45)	86.6	(39)
Some high school	59.9	(121)	67.7	(82)
High school grad.	11.4	(23)	52.2	(12)
Some university	6.4	(13)	69.2	(9)

*"Generation" refers to the number of generations resident in western Canada; thus the first generation consists of immigrants from France, Belgium, or the U.S.A., or settlers born in Quebec.
** "Occupation" refers to the primary source of income for each family interviewed; spouses were classified under their spouses' occupations though students were considered separately. Teaching nuns were included as teachers, not clergy.

characteristics of the French sample and the proportion of respondents in each category favoring identity retention. The data in Table 2 present ethnicity as distributed by age group. Table 3 is a description of the settlements where the sample interviews were conducted. The overall distribution of French Canadians throughout Saskatchewan by rural or urban dwelling is presented in Table 4.

TABLE 2 *French ethnicity by age group*

Reported Behavior	Age Group (%)				
	13-19 (N=30)	20-29 (N=19)	30-49 (N=72)	50-69 (N=54)	70+ (N=27)
Identity Preservation favored	37	53	74	80	93
French Usage primary*	53	68	78	89	93
Ethnic Inter-marriage opposed	13	21	46	54	81
Religious Intermarriage opposed	37	68	89	91	100
Ethnic Parish Attendance regular	83	84	89	96	100

*89% of the sample is bilingual; 10% is unilingual French; 1% is unilingual English. Primary usage refers to the language commonly used as a first preference.

In the 1880s through the 1930s the bloc settlement became the typical pattern of settlement for all the major ethnic groups in the Prairies. Although more than 30 bloc settlements were developed by the French in Saskatchewan, they were not as vast as the settlements populated by the Ukrainians, German Catholics, and Mennonites nor as extensive as the rural French settlements in Manitoba and Alberta.[2] The small French pockets in Saskatchewan made them prey to the encroachment of other ethnic groups.[3]

In the north-central region of Saskatchewan, the proportion speaking French has always been higher than the proportion in the province as a whole: 97.0% in 1941, 79.7% in 1951, 71.5% in 1961, and 66.9% in 1971.[4] If we exclude the cities of Prince Albert and North Battleford, where in 1971 only 55.7% of the French-origin population spoke French, the proportion of French Canadians in the region speaking French came to 75.1% in the last census. In other words, it is reasonable to conclude that

TABLE 2A *French ethnicity by generation*

Reported Behavior	Generation (%)		
	First (N=40)	Second (N=92)	Third (N=70)
Identity preservation favored	88	80	47
English usage primary	10	16	36
Ethnic parish attendance regular	100	95	81
Ethnic intermarriage opposed	70	49	27
Religious intermarriage opposed	95	90	62

TABLE 3 *French-origin population and derived sample per settlement*

Settlement	Estimated French-origin population		Sample (Total N = 202)
	(1961)	(1971)	
Batoche & area	3 900	3 000	78 families
Léonville-Debden	2 700	2 000	54 families
Prud'homme – St-Dénis	1 100	900	22 families
Marcelin & Coteau	900	800	18 families
St-Brieux area	900	700	18 families
Albertville area	600	600	12 families

today more than three quarters of the French Canadians in the bloc settlements of this region still speak French. While it is virtually impossible to determine the exact proportions speaking French within each settlement, due to the settlement limits not coinciding with census delimitation areas (incorporated communities plus rural municipalities), approximate proportions may be calculated. We estimate that over 90% of the French-origin population in the Duck Lake and St-Louis settlement speak French, about 85% in the Prud'homme and St-Dénis settlement, 80% in the Léoville and Debden settlement, 80% in the Albertville settlement, 75% in the St-Brieux settlement, and 65% in the Marcelin and Coteau settlement.

An exceptionally high proportion (90-100%) of French Canadians in several incorporated communities still speak French, notably at St-Brieux, Debden, Duck Lake, and St-Louis. Moreover, if unincorporated communities were also taken into consideration, several would stand out as having exceptionally high proportions of French-speakers; we would estimate that well over 90% of the French Canadians in such hamlets as St-Isidore-de-Bellevue, St-Dénis, and Victoire speak French fluently and often.

From the brief account of French settlements in north-central Saskatchewan, we are able to conclude that French language usage is higher in these rural settlements than in urban areas in the province and that it falls off considerably among the young. Of more interest, when French are compared with Ukrainians, the following observations emerge:

TABLE 4 *Proportion of French Canadians able to speak French in urban and rural areas of Saskatchewan, 1951-71*

	Urban	Rural Non-Farm	Rural Farm	Total	French Cdn. Population
1951	53.9%	72.0%	78.9%	70.9%	51 930
1961	41.6%	58.2%	65.8%	54.5%	59 824
1971	46.3%	66.0%	65.7%	56.2%	56 200

Source: *Census of Canada*, 1951, 1961, 1971.

(1) A higher proportion of the group under 30 years old uses French as compared with Ukrainian as a primary language.[5]

(2) Ethnic data by age tend to be linear for French and Ukrainians, with older people in both groups more strongly supportive of traditional ties. What is not known is whether the young will acquire a stronger ethnicity as they age. It is commonly assumed, however, that ethnicity is dying out with the older generations and will not be replaced in a similar form or content by the younger members.

(3) Both French and Ukrainian samples tend to oppose religious exogamy more strongly than ethnic exogamy.[6] One would no doubt find other similarities among these ethnic groups if one were to pursue the analysis further. Given the overwhelming assimilative forces in the larger society, perhaps ethnic groups more closely resemble each other on certain core attitudes than the larger society. The hypothesized similarity of "ethnics", is not to deny their uniqueness, but to point to the fact that they all have the same basic problems to solve if they are to successfully maintain their ethnic identity. To the extent that they solve these problems (e.g., language retention and in-group marriage), their attitudes concerning their identity may be similar.[7]

ENDNOTES

1. While a synthesized French Canadian identity may have emerged gradually in Saskatchewan, a couple of qualifications merit mention. First, there was little mixing of French origins in particular settlements when the settling process originally took place. Most settlements in the northern series were established by immigrants directly from France, whereas most in the sourthern series were settled by Québécois. Second, certain settlements—better yet, specific rural communities—still retain the identity of a francophone subgroup to an appreciable degree. For example, St-Laurent-Grandin is still Métis, St-Brieux and Kermaria are largely Breton, Gravelbourg remains essentially Québécois, and Acadian families and Franco-Americans from Minnesota settled around St-Isidore-de-Bellevue; but far more communities have francophone residents of more diverse origins.

2. The two most extensive areas of French settlement in Saskatchewan are: first, in southern Saskatchewan, the Gravelbourg settlement (with approximately 2 000 French, plus another 5 200 in the contiguous settlements around Coderre and Courval, Willow Bunch, Ferland, Val Marie, Ponteix, and Lac Pelletier); second, in north-central Saskatchewan, the settlement around Duck Lake, Batoche, St-Louis, Domrémy, Bonne-Madone, St-Isidore-de-Bellevue, and Carlton (with almost 4 000 French). On the other hand, there are over 11 000 people of French descent in the Peace River country and over 12 000 in the St-Paul, Bonnyville, and Lac-La-Biche region in northern Alberta, or over 12 000 in the adjoining Rivière Rouge and Rivière Seine settlements in Manitoba.

3. A good illustration is the Ukrainian "invasion" of the Batoche Métis settle-

ment, which has been so complete that today Métis landowners hold title to only 15 of the original 76 river lots between Batoche and Fish Creek. In southern Saskatchewan, the French element in the once largely French communities of Sedley, Lebret, and Forget has all but vanished.

4. In the Province of Saskatchewan as a whole, the proportion of French Canadians speaking French was approximately 75% in 1941, 65% in 1951, 55% in 1961, but then this trend of decline was arrested, so that in 1971, 56% were francophone. It could also be noted that a consistently higher proportion of people of Ukrainian origin, but a lower proportion of people of German or Scandinavian descent, could speak their traditional mother tongues. For further details see A. B. Anderson, "Linguistic Trends Among Saskatchewan Ethnic Groups," research paper presented at the National Conference on Ethnic Studies and Research, University of Regina, Oct. 1976.

5. The survey data indicated that a lower proportion of Ukrainian, Doukhobor, German Catholic, and Scandinavian respondents under 30 years of age were familiar with their traditional group language than the French respondents. A higher proportion of teenage Mennonite respondents, but a lower proportion in their 20s, retained their German dialect. These survey data tend to support census data for the province as a whole. In 1971, 32.8% of people of French origin in Saskatchewan in the 0-9 age cohort could speak French, compared to 44.6% in the 10-19 cohort, and 53.6% in the 20-34 cohort. A lower proportion of people of Ukrainian, Polish, German, or Scandinavian origin for these cohorts were able to speak their traditional mother tongue. See A. B. Anderson, *op. cit.*, 1976.

6. This finding also applied to German Catholics, Mennonites, Poles, and Scandinavians, but not Doukhobors, interviewed. The survey data further indicated that the Hutterites, Mennonites, Ukrainian Catholics, and Scandinavians interviewed were more opposed than the French respondents, to *ethnic* intermarriage, while German Catholics, Ukrainian Orthodox, Poles, and perhaps Doukhobors interviewed were less opposed. Respondents representing all of these ethnic or ethno-religious groups (except Hutterites) were less opposed to *religious* intermarriage than were the French respondents. For details see A. B. Anderson, "Intermarriage in Ethnic Bloc Settlements in Saskatchewan: A Cross-Cultural Survey of Trends and Attitudes," research paper presented at the annual meetings of the Western Assoc. of Sociology and Anthropology, Banff, Dec. 1974; and A. B. Anderson, "Ethnic Identity in Saskatchewan Bloc Settlements: A Sociological Appraisal," in H. Palmer, ed., *The Settlement of the West* (Calgary: Comprint Publishing, Univ. of Calgary, 1977), ch. 10.

7. Certain key identificational factors will be de-emphasized more readily than others, depending on group differences (for example, adherence to a traditional language may decline more rapidly than adherence to a traditional religious affiliation for some groups but not for others). Most important, while it must be stressed that apparently every group studied (except the Hutterites) is changing with each new generation, the actual rate and extent of assimilation differs markedly from one group to another. In many ways French and Ukrainian Canadians in general in Saskatchewan have proven to be far more conservative of their ethnic identity than people of Scandinavian or German descent (excluding Hutterites and many Mennonites).

SELECTED REFERENCES

Anderson, Alan B. "Assimilation in the Bloc Settlements of North-Central Saskatchewan: A Comparative Study of Identity Change Among Seven Ethno-Religious Groups in a Canadian Prairie Region." Ph.D. thesis in sociology, University of Saskatchewan, 1972.

———. "Intermarriage in Ethnic Bloc Settlements in Saskatchewan: A Cross-Cultural Survey of Trends and Attitudes." Research paper presented at the annual meetings of the Western Association of Sociology and Anthropology, Banff, Dec. 1974.

———. "Linguistic Trends Among Saskatchewan Ethnic Groups." Research paper presented at the National Conference on Ethnic Studies and Research, University of Regina, Oct. 1976.

———. "Ethnic Identity in Saskatchewan Bloc Settlements: A Sociological Appraisal," in Howard Palmer, ed., *The Settlement of the West*. Calgary: Comprint Publishing, Univ. of Calgary, 1977, ch. 10, pp. 187-225.

Anderson, J. T. M. *The Education of the New Canadian*. Toronto: J. M. Dent, 1918.

Archives of Saskatchewan: Martin Papers, files 53, 56, 60, 168; Scott Papers, file 18c; Latta Papers, file 7; Education file 12a.

Darcovich, William. *Ukrainians in Canada: The Struggle to Retain Their Identity*. Ottawa: Ukrainian Self-Reliance Assoc., 1967 (booklet).

Dawson, C. A., et al. "Group Settlement: Ethnic Communities in Western Canada, and Pioneering in the Prairie Provinces: The Social Side of the Settlement Process," respectively volumes vii (1936) and viii (1940) in the *Canadian Frontiers of Settlement* series. Toronto: Macmillan, 1936 & 1940.

England, Robert. *The Central European Immigrant in Canada*. Toronto: Macmillan, 1929.

Grabowski, Y. "Languages in Contact: Polish and English," in Paul Migus, ed., *Sounds Canadian: Languages and Cultures in Multi-Ethnic Society*. Toronto: Peter Martin Associates, 1975, pp. 59-68.

Hawkes, John. *The Story of Saskatchewan and Its People*. Regina: S. T. Clarke, 1924.

Heer, David M., and Charles A. Hubay, Jr., "The Trend of Interfaith Marriages in Canada: 1922 to 1972," in S. Parvez Wakil, ed., *Marriage, Family and Society: Canadian Perspectives*. Toronto: Butterworth, 1975, ch. 6, pp. 85-96.

Isajiw, Wsevolod W. "Ethnic Status, the Process of Assimilation, and Ethnic Identification of Ukrainians in North America," (in Ukrainian), in W. W. Isajiw, ed., *Ukrainians in American and Canadian Society*. Jersey City: M. P. Knots, 1976, pp. 212-27.

Kaye, Vladimir J. *Early Ukrainian Settlements in Canada, 1895-1900*. Toronto: Univ. of Toronto Press, 1964.

Kazymyra, Bohdan Z. "The Ukrainian Catholic Church as a National Institution," in Paul Migus, ed., *Sounds Canadian: Languages and Cultures in Multi-Ethnic Society*. Toronto: Peter Martin Associates, 1975, pp. 110-13.

Lysenko, Vera. *Men in Sheepskin Coats: A Study in Assimilation.* Toronto: Ryerson, 1947.

McLeod, Keith A. "Politics, Schools, and the French Language, 1881-1931," in Norman Ward and Duff Spafford, eds., *Politics in Saskatchewan.* Lindsay, Ont.: Longmans, 1968, ch. 8, pp. 124-50.

Millett, David. "The Orthodox Church: Ukrainian, Greek and Syrian," in Jean L. Elliott, ed., *Minority Canadians*, vol. 2: *Immigrant Groups.* Scarborough, Ont.: Prentice-Hall of Canada, 1971, ch. 4, pp. 47-65.

Milnor, Andrew. "The New Politics and Ethnic Revolt," in Norman Ward and Duff Spafford, eds., *Politics in Saskatchewan.* Lindsay, Ont.: Longmans, 1968, ch. 9, pp. 151-77.

Radecki, Henry, with Benedykt Heydenkorn. *A Member of a Distinguished Family: The Polish Group in Canada.* Toronto: McClelland & Stewart, 1976.

Report of the Royal Commission on Bilingualism and Biculturalism, Book IV, part II, ch. 4 (1970).

Royick, A. "Ukrainian Settlements in Alberta." *Canadian Slavonic Papers*, vol. 10, no. 3, 1968.

Royick, A., and Zenon S. Pohorecky, "Ethno-Linguistic Overview of Ukrainian-speaking Communities in the Province of Alberta, Canada," in *Napao: A Saskatchewan Anthropology Journal*, 1:2 (Nov. 1968).

Schudlo, Rev. Michael, C.Ss. R. *"Ukrainian Catholics."* Yorkton, Sask.: *Redeemer's Voice*, 1951 (booklet).

Skwarok, T. *The Ukrainian Settlers in Canada and Their Schools, 1891-1921.* Toronto: Basilian Press, 1959.

Stefanow, Marlene. "A Study of Intermarriage of Ukrainians in Saskatchewan." M.A. thesis in Sociology, University of Saskatchewan, 1962.

Tremblay, Rev. Emilien, C. Ss. R. *Le Père Delaere et l'Eglise Ukrainienne du Canada.* Berthierville, P. Q.: l'Imprimerie Bernard Ltée., 1960.

Trosky, Odarka S. *The Ukrainian Greek Orthodox Church in Canada.* Winnipeg: Bulman Bros., 1968.

Wakil, S. Parvez. "Marriage and Family in Canada." *Journal of Comparative Family Studies* (1976).

Wangenheim, Elizabeth. "The Ukrainians: A Case Study of the 'Third Force'," in W. E. Mann, ed., *Canada: A Sociological Profile*, 2nd ed. Toronto: Copp-Clark, 1971, pp. 165-77.

Young, Charles H. *The Ukrainian Canadians: A Study in Assimilation.* Toronto: Thomas Nelson & Sons, 1931.

JARMILA L. A. HORNA   University of Calgary

The Entrance Status
of Czech and Slovak Immigrant Women*

Introduction

Immigrants tend to have a "depressed entrance status" in the process of building a new life in the host country. This is primarily manifested in the labor market, more specifically in the sphere of occupational status. For example, A. Richmond (1967: 118) found that "the large majority of immigrants experienced some degree of occupational status dislocation as a consequence of migration"; he defined such dislocation as "any change of social position consequent upon geographic movement and either necessitated or facilitated by it." Similarly, J. Porter, in his *Vertical Mosaic* (1969: 63), characterized this phenomenon: "entrance status implies lower level occupational roles and subjection to processes of assimilation laid down and judged by the charter group. Over time the position of entrance status may be improved or it may be a permanent caste-like status."

Although job mobility may be the usual scenario if the immigrant is male, what is the experience if the immigrant is female? As a group as well as individuals, female immigrants generally experience differential entrance treatment. Discrepancies in labor force participation by immigrant women as compared with men and irregularities in women's access to occupations have been documented statistically over many years (Davis and Gupta, 1968, Department of Manpower and Immigration, yearly, and 1974; Kalbach, 1970, 1974; Parai, 1965, 1974; Richmond 1967, 1974).

Other studies have approached this problem of inequality on a macro-societal level (Boyd, 1975; Royal Commission on the Status of Women, 1970). For example, M. Boyd (1975: 415) concluded her study on the status of immigrant women by stating that "immigrant women bear a double burden with respect to their status in Canadian society: they are frequently classified as dependents at the border when *de facto* they may make substantial labor force contributions; and when they work, they are

* Written expressly for *Two Nations, Many Cultures: Ethnic Groups in Canada*. The research was supported by Canada Council Grant No. S71-1245. The support is gratefully acknowledged.

likely to find themselves in the predominantly female and less-rewarded occupations compared to those of their male and native born counterparts, respectively." M. Boyd's findings are further supported by the statement made by the Royal Commission on the Status of Women (1970: 360): "we have been informed that when a husband and wife both seek admission as independent applicants, it is fairly common practice to consider only the husband's application, presumably on the assumption that his wife will enter the country as a member of his immediate family." Even without further documentation it appears to be beyond any doubt that women's entrance status in the majority of cases is lower than the status of men.

Invaluable as the above-mentioned studies are, they require additional illumination from empirical, microsocietal data drawn from in-depth case studies. The primary aim of this paper is to add to the statistical data and the macrosocietal, immigrant studies information about a specific group of immigrant women. The somewhat unique admittance circumstances of the Czech and Slovak women in this study do not detract from the fact that their experiences on arrival in Canada may be similar to those of many other immigrant women. A second purpose of this paper is to show the impact of such a differentially depressed entrance status on women's self-esteem and adaptation to Canadian life.

The Research Design

This study is derived from a larger project dealing with the process of initial adjustment and adaptation of immigrants who left Czechoslovakia after the upheaval of August 1968, and settled in Edmonton, Alberta, between September 1968 and the first months of 1969. Data reported in this paper represent only a small fraction of an extensive body of information obtained in the course of the original investigation. The original data were largely acquired from a survey utilizing a mailed questionnaire supplemented by a series of informal interviews (Horna, 1973)[1].

In comparison with other immigrant groups such as the Ukrainians or Germans, the Czechs and Slovaks are a relatively small group in Canada as well as in Edmonton. The 1971 statistical data prepared by Statistics Canada on immigrants residing in Edmonton who were of the Czechoslovak origin by birthplace show that there were 390 Czechoslovaks 20 years of age and over (245 males, 145 females) who arrived during the 1967-68 period, and 95 Czechoslovaks aged 20 and over (50 males, 45 females) who arrived in 1969. Since there were only 10 arrivals in 1966, it can be assumed realistically that the majority of Czechs in those enumerations were members of the group under study. The total number of Czechs and Slovaks in Edmonton at the time of the 1971 Census was 2 860; this includes both the foreign born and native born (Alberta Culture, Youth and Recreation).

The sample consisted of 103 men and women 20 years of age and older who were contacted approximately three years after their arrival; they were approximately one fifth of the 1968-69 total emigration. Their composition is shown in Table 1. In some respects this sample of Czechs and Slovaks may be representative of immigrants in general. Findings based on the longitudinal survey of the economic and social adaptation of immigrants (Department of Manpower and Immigration, 1974c: 109) state that "persons in the same group [of Czechoslovaks admitted under the emergency operation from September 1968 until January 1969] have progressed as rapidly as other immigrants admitted during the same period and have been readily accepted into the Canadian communities where they live and work."

The respondents were instructed to complete questionnaires on their own behalf, not as a couple; the basic unit of investigation was an individual. Given the very rigid observance of confidentiality and ano-

TABLE 1 *Distribution of respondents*

Sex	No.	%
Males	63	61.2
Females	40	38.8
Total	103	100.0

Age at respondent's last birthday

Age	No.	%	Age	No.	%
under 19	0	0.0	45-49	7	6.8
20-24	7	6.8	50-54	1	1.0
25-29	36	35.0	55-59	4	3.9
30-34	23	22.3	60-64	1	1.0
35-39	16	15.5	65 and over	0	0.0
40-44	8	7.8	Total	103	100.0

Marital status of respondents before emigration and at the time of survey

Marital status	before emigration		at survey	
	No.	%	No.	%
Single	30	29.1	13	12.6
Married	68	66.0	85	82.5
Divorced, separated	4	3.9	4	3.9
No response	1	1.0	1	1.0
Total	103	100.0	103	100.0

TABLE 2 *Respondents' economic activity*

Type of Activity	Present Activity (1972-73)						Original Intent (1968-69)	
	Males		Females		Total		Total	
	No.	%	No.	%	No.	%	No.	%
Employed, salary/wages	43	68.8	20	50	63	61.2	79	76.8
Self-employed or farmer	2	3.2	1	2.5	3	2.9	2	1.9
Student	17	27	7	17.5	24	23.3	16	15.5
Housewife	–	–	11	27.5	11	10.7	2	1.9
Other	1	1.6	1	2.5	2	1.9	4	3.9
Total	63	100.0	40	100.0	103	100.0	103	100.0

nymity of respondents, it has been impossible to match pairs of individual questionnaries. All comparisons of the husband's and wife's experience have been obtained in the course of informal interviews.

The educational level of the sample was not representative of the total Czech and Slovak population in Edmonton. Those with post-secondary education were over-represented. At the time of their arrival, 79.4% of the males and 82.5% of the females had secondary or post-secondary education. With the exception of one woman, all respondents were either employed or full-time students before their emigration from Czechoslovakia. To their great disadvantage, the abrupt, unplanned decision to flee the home country resulted (among other problems) in a very poor command of English. Upon arrival, about three quarters of respondents could not speak English satisfactorily. Fifty-seven percent of the women reported no knowledge at all; 38% of the men were in a similar situation. By the time of the survey, however, an equal proportion of men and women (54%) reported good-to-fluent command of English.

Research Findings on Women's Status

Even if not recorded on the papers of the immigration office, virtually all female respondents intended at the time of their entry to continue to work outside the home or pursue their former studies (Table 2). In spite of their original intentions, 27.5% of women were at home as housewives at the time of the survey, and a considerably lower proportion of women than men were full-time students. Among those who were housewives in 1972-73 there were two women who came to Canada intending to remain at home. Another eight (i.e., 72% of all housewives) reported that they

TABLE 3 *Type of the respondents' first job*

Type of job	Males		Females	
	No.	%	No.	%
Same as former occupation	8	15.4	3	8.8
Former field but different position	15	28.8	10	29.4
Nothing in common with the former one	29	55.8	21	61.8
Total	52	100.0	34	100.0

Note: Only those who were employed reported the type of occupation. Also important is to note that 10 among those employed reported that they did not wish to pursue their former occupation since they were forced into it by a quota system back home.

did not wish to stay at home. Although numerically small, this group of respondents consisted of many well-educated and professional women. Thus, it did not come as a surprise that these women were quite disappointed over their under-utilization and dependent position (Table 3).

The women who managed to find employment reported all sorts of problems. These problems cannot be explained totally by the poor command of English since most women have mastered English at least "fairly" well. On the other hand, it should be recognized that for most of the skilled and professional occupations, a good knowledge of the language is beyond dispute; it is not expected that the very first job would be of the same level as the former one in the home country. Table 4 shows that the downward shift in fact took place for the majority of respondents, again for more women than men.

The female respondents recollected many instances of differential treatment overtly related to their sex. A female doctor, with the same credentials and years of experience as her husband, could work only as a laboratory technician at a hospital while her husband was accepted as a resident doctor and given the opportunity to write examinations. Said she:

They just wouldn't talk to me at all—like I couldn't possibly know any medicine. They showed me that I should be quite grateful for their generosity in letting me wash the glass in their lab. I would not say a word when they did something awfully wrong about the sanitation standards or lab procedures. But when a patient was involved...I just couldn't stop myself, I felt responsible for him—even without those Canadian papers. I *am* a doctor, am I not? I signed my Hippocrates' oath, I had to tell them. So I got transferred, and the next time again: and no doctor would "lower" himself and go for coffee with me, and the girls thought of me as a snob. If not for the money we needed so desperately, I would quit right away.[2]

TABLE 4 *Respondents' relative social status in Canada as compared with the former status in Czechoslovakia, at the time of survey*

Canadian status as compared with Czechoslovakia	Males		Females	
	No.	%	No.	%
Higher	20	33.3	6	17.1
Same	16	26.7	12	34.3
Lower	24	40.0	17	48.6
Total	60	100.0	35	100.0

Note: Three men and five women did not answer this question without further explanation.

Unmarried female professionals did not fare much better at the beginning, especially if they possessed diplomas in the "masculine" fields. A female engineer surveyor with a technical university diploma and two years of work experience expressed it this way:

When I first applied for that job (with the government) they did not even look at my engineering credentials. But they gave me this job as a draftsman because it would be nice to have such a pretty chick in our office . . . Our men on a surveying crew would never work seriously for you. Besides, we don't have a camper just for you. Anyway, I did drafting during my office hours and studied toward my recognition exams in the evenings. Not long ago I passed all, and now I have my certificate.[2]

Some of the female respondents mentioned during the interviews that they realistically accepted the deep plunge in their career development as inevitable at the beginning. However, they felt bitter when they realized that their marginality label was firmly attached to them and could be removed only if they were to "remove themselves" from their places of employment. These women were startled when told that they had aspired for promotions in vain. A woman with a Ph.D., ten years of university teaching and several publications to her credit described her experience thus:

At first, I did all little jobs, even went to buy cigarettes from a vending machine and brought coffee for my supervisor. And studied—English as well as literature in my field. Boy! I studied really hard; I felt that my whole life depended on it. And soon I also carried out research and presented a few papers, and gave several guest lectures. Do you think that somebody would recognize it; admit that I really could do it? That I have progressed . . . I couldn't understand why—until I was frankly told that, 'well, you know we sort of got used to your low position and it would be hard for us to have you in our midst as our equal'. So, I was flatly turned down when I applied for a faculty appointment. But my male colleagues are doing just fine—all are professors by now.[2]

Several women were unsuccessful when they applied for admittance to the basic English course sponsored by the Canada Manpower Center. Those who were married and had children could not easily gain access to an intensive learning course from the Manpower.

> The officer (at the Canada Manpower) told me that he must place his men and couldn't waste (his allotment of places) on women. Why do I need a course? I've got a husband and can learn at home from my kids and their friends.[2]

Those who were students before immigration and could speak some English applied for admittance to the university, usually as special students. The same pattern of differential, unequal status applied in these cases. While practically all men were accepted at the time of their first application, women were not as fortunate; they often succeeded only after repeated applications. If the woman was single and needed some means of livelihood, she was given referrals by her Manpower officer—all of them for menial jobs. One of the former students recalled:

> When the lunch-hour rush started (in the student cafeteria), I would hide in the farthest corner of the kitchen. Nobody could send me to the front counter. I just couldn't bear it—to see all those boys who were not any better than I, speaking English as poorly as I, and all of them students. I was not ashamed of my job, I was not living off anyone, but I was really furious because of that inequality. . . . [2]

It cannot be said that no women have been successful. Also, some men were similarly as unfortunate as the above women. However, as a group, women have suffered an entrance status more depressed than their male counterparts, and it has taken them longer to recuperate from the plunge. Table 3 illustrates this point quite clearly, although it is based on subjective evaluations by the respondents.

Several of our respondents commented that they had three considerations when accepting a low-status employment or home-making: (1) financial, (2) family needs and priorities, and (3) long-range plans. They soon learned to calculate whether the woman's income was "worth all that frustration at the job".

> If I could make only some two or three hundred dollars a month—and then pay the transportation costs, babysitting expenses, buy decent clothing and cosmetics, there would be very little left for our needs. Besides, I am qualified to be their supervisor, but they wouldn't understand that if I couldn't express myself in English it didn't mean there was nothing to express. Don't take me wrong. I didn't ask for a supervisory position. I knew I couldn't do it yet because of my English (it involved report writing), but why should they treat me as if I were dumb?[2]

This complaint came from a former head nurse, but similar complaints were expressed by many others as well. Couples, on realizing the hardships they would encounter if they both worked, decided to "take turns". That involved one of the spouses staying at home and freeing the other from the family and household obligations in order to facilitate his/her rapid advancement. Given the aforementioned financial formula and the tradition, it was almost exclusively the wife who stayed at home. Curiously enough, when several of the housewives eventually entered the labor market, they progressed at a very rapid pace. Perhaps because of the benefit of the shared experience, they avoided many mistakes typical of newcomers.

Among the female university graduates, the majority has accepted the inevitable low status and employment considerably below their qualifications and long-range plans.

> I just *had* to be there, every day—to breathe that air (I never noticed before that a university has actually a smell of its own), to see the students changing classes, milling around. Oh, no! That's too emotional although that was a part of it too. I believed that I could eventually meet some colleagues, gain familiarity with my specialization in this continent, learn as much as I could absorb, and gradually flow into the mainstream of the university life. I wouldn't say that I didn't mind my second "apprenticeship", but I tried to benefit from it as much as I could. I am confident that it will eventually work for me but, I am telling you, it's tough.[2]

Discussion

The Czech and Slovak immigrant women in this study were concentrated in less prestigious or sex-typed occupations, or had withdrawn into their homes, only *after* their immigration to Canada. This phenomenon of a permanent or continuing depressed entrance status has taken place in spite of the high credentials these women possessed at the time of their arrival. In contrast, the same degree of downward mobility seems not to have occurred for the comparable group of male immigrants.

One of the standard explanations for the discrepancies between the men's and women's entrance statuses, i.e., that they do not possess equal qualifications, does not hold true in the case of the Czech and Slovak women. Women did not fall behind men in their mastery of English after their arrival. Moreover, they were willing to learn. In fact, it seemed that more women than men requested an English course but were discouraged by their immigration officers. As a result these women find it increasingly difficult to keep pace with their male counterparts and move out of their lower or homemaking positions.

Another explanation usually mentioned in connection with differential statuses is the time span between arrivals of various immigrant groups. Such an explanation is also not applicable since the Czech and Slovak men and women arrived within the same period and general economic conditions; moreover, the married couples landed together.

It is very difficult to avoid the conclusion that the severely depressed entrance status of those Czech and Slovak immigrant women is related to the Canadian occupational structure, with its unequal opportunities for men and women and its differential allocation mechanisms. Immigrant women may suffer more than their native-born Canadian sisters although this hypothesis is not within the scope of our research.

Finally, at the time of the survey, substantially more men than women indicated that they already experienced a "feeling of being more Canadian than Czechoslovak". Fifty-one percent of the women seldom or never felt this way as opposed to 27% of the men. Unfortunately the nature of our data does not allow us to conclude that there is a direct causal relationship between the lower status of women and their lesser identification with Canada. Even if this correlation were spurious, the difficulties faced by the immigrant women *qua* women may not have enhanced their identification with their new country.

ENDNOTES

1. The methodology of this survey as well as complete results pertinent to the entire sample are available by contacting the author.
2. Translated verbatim quote from respondent.

SELECTED REFERENCES

Alberta Culture, Youth and Recreation. *Ethnic Group Distribution in Alberta, 1971.* Edmonton: Cultural Heritage Branch, n.d.

Boyd, Monica. "The status of immigrant women in Canada," *Canadian Review of Sociology and Anthropology* 12 (4) Part I (1975), pp. 406-16.

Davis, N.H.W., and M. L. Gupta. "Labour Force Characteristics of Post-War Immigrants and Native Born Canadians, 1956-1967," *Dominion Bureau of Statistics Special Labour Force Studies No. 6.* Ottawa: Queen's Printer, 1968.

Department of Manpower and Immigration. *Immigration Statistics* (yearly). Ottawa: Queen's Printer.

——. *Immigration and Population Statistics.* Canadian Immigration and Population Study. Ottawa: Information Canada, 1974a.

——. *Three Years in Canada: First report on the longitudinal survey on the economic and social adaptation of immigrants.* Ottawa: Information Canada, 1974b.

———— . *The Immigration Program*. Canadian Immigration and Population Study. Ottawa: Information Canada, 1974c.

Horna, Jarmila. *Adjustment of Refugees: A Case Study*. Population Research Laboratory Discussion Paper No. 3. Edmonton: University of Alberta, Department of Sociology, 1973.

Kalbach, Warren E. *The Impact of Immigration on Canada's Population*. 1961 Census Monograph. Ottawa: Queen's Printer, 1970.

———— . *The Effect of Immigration on Population.*. Canadian Immigration and Population Study. Ottawa: Information Canada, 1974.

Parai, Louis. *Immigration and Emigration of Professional and Skilled Manpower During the Post-War Period*. Economic Council of Canada. Ottawa: Queen's Printer, 1965.

———— . *The Economic Impact of Immigration*. Canadian Immigration and Population Study. Ottawa: Information Canada, 1974.

Porter, John. *The Vertical Mosaic: An Analysis of Social Class and Power in Canada*. Toronto: University of Toronto Press (first ed. 1965).

Report of the Royal Commission on the Status of Women. Ottawa: Information Canada, 1970.

Richmond, Anthony H. *Post-war Immigrants in Canada*. Toronto: University of Toronto Press, 1967.

———— . *Aspects of the Absorption and Adaptation of Immigrants.*. Canadian Immigration and Population Study. Ottawa: Information Canada.

Statistics Canada. *Census of Canada 1961*.

———— . *Census of Canada 1971*.

WILLIAM SHAFFIR   McMaster University

Jewish Immigration to Canada*

Introduction

Although Canadian society is often conceived of as a mosaic of ethnic groups, there is a relationship between the structure and organization of the ethnic community and the history of its immigration. A community's ability to maintain a set of cultural boundaries, and to provide those within the group with a distinctive identity, is linked to the circumstances under which members of the groups chose to come to Canada, when they arrived, and how, both collectively and individually, they attempted to retain their separate culture.

The following discussion of the patterns of Jewish immigration to Canada outlines the stages through which Jews settled in this country and then suggests how the successive waves of immigration helped to shape and reshape the organization of the Jewish community. Finally, a brief analysis is made of the Candian Jewish community today, focusing on its cultural and religious formation.

Phase of Immigration[1]

Immigration patterns can be understood in terms of underlying motivations, which themselves must be considered within the social, economic and political contexts in both the country of origin and arrival. The "push/pull" concept has been used to partially explain the emigration of groups or individuals. Movement of people from one country to another may be the result of forced or impelled migration (Fairchild, 1926; Peterson, 1958), and immigrants may also be attracted to a country by the promise of security and stability. Movements of people may also be directly affected by specific trends in immigration policy. The chronological analysis of Jewish immigration to Canada is chiefly organized around these phenomena.

Montreal Origins

The presence of Jewish settlers in Canada has been traced to about 1760; the beginning of a stable Jewish settlement coincides with the time when the country came under British rule and previously existing bars against

---

* Written expressly for *Two Nations, Many Cultures: Ethnic Groups in Canada*. Appreciation is expressed to Berkeley Fleming for comments on an earlier draft of this paper.

non-Catholic settlers were removed. The first official census of the number of Jews in Canada, taken in 1831, showed 107 residents in Upper Canada. By 1841, almost 80 years after the beginning of settlement, 154 Jewish residents were listed. Most of the first Jewish settlers, relatively wealthy and coming from the 13 colonies, encountered few obstacles in their adjustment. Of Sephardic origin from Spain, Portugal and North Africa, they maintained a distinctive religious identity while adapting to the larger community. Most lived in Montreal, and in 1768 a congregation—"Shearith Israel" ("Remnants of Israel")—was founded there. Commenting on the founding period of Jewish settlement in Canada, Kage observes:

> Firstly, there was established a Jewish communal structure with which the newly arrived immigrant could identify himself; and secondly, this community could extend a guiding hand to the immigrant in his adjustment to the socio-economic conditions of the country (1962: 11).

A new phase in Jewish immigration, beginning in 1840 and extending to about 1900, occurred with the arrival of immigrants first from Germany and Poland and later from the Russian Empire. During this period, Canadian policy encouraged immigration and assisted in colonization. German migration to Canada in the 19th century was primarily caused by economic and population pressures, for Jews as well as for others. The 154 Jews in 1841 had increased by the first census after Confederation to 1 333 and had almost doubled to 2 393 ten years after (Kage, 1962: 18).

The pioneering efforts of German Jews laid the community foundation for the subsequent Jewish mass migration from eastern Europe. Thus, the influx of German Jews, along with those of Polish and English descent, influenced the religious life of the Montreal community. Although the older Sephardic element continued to exercise its influence on every facet of communal life, the new arrivals helped increase the sphere of Jewish activity, and provided a sharp contrast to the Sephardic Jews:

> While the latter (Sephardic Jews) were largely merchants and men of means, the new arrivals came unencumbered with possessions. No great opulence could they bring with them. Poverty, defeat and suffering were their heritage. ... Yet if they brought no material riches, they brought something else—a deeper consciousness derived from generations of closely-welded unity with the living sections of their people. This consciousness soon began visibly to affect the physiognomy of Jewish life in the new country (Sack, 1945: 145).

Unfamiliar with the Sephardic mode of prayer and service, some of the Ashkenazic (German and Eastern European) arrivals broke off from the Spanish and Portuguese synagogue in Montreal and organized in 1846 a German-Polish congregation—the Shaar Hashomayim Congregation—establishing for themselves an independent place of worship after the manners and customs of English, German and Polish Jews.

Western Settlement

The eastern European phase of Jewish immigration started in the 1870s, intensified toward the end of the century, and continued to grow until 1914. The "push" forces for immigration during this period included quests for economic betterment, increased social status and greater religious freedom, all thought to be realizable in the countries of immigration. For many Jews in Russia, the home of the largest group of Jews in any one land, emigration was the solution to the persecutions and pogroms there in the 1880s. The outbreak of the pogroms led to a colonization drive in Canada's West. Till this time, most Jews lived in Quebec and Ontario. Until the 1880s, except in Victoria and Vancouver, a few Jewish settlers were to be found in Western Canada. In Manitoba, in 1881, there were only 33 families, numbering perhaps 100 Jewish souls. With the large scale Russian immigration, their numbers increased dramatically. The burden of receiving the victims of Czarist oppression fell heavily on the Jewish colony in Winnipeg. Although many who arrived in Canada in 1881 and 1883 remained in Montreal, most were dispersed throughout the country, particularly in the West.

Most of the early Jewish colonists in Western Canada were Russian refugees who had been persuaded to settle on the land. Often they were employed on the construction of the Canadian Pacific Railway, though many later availed themselves of "homestead" grants. While institutional life was most developed in Montreal and Toronto, by the early decades of the 20th century fledgling Jewish communities were sprinkled across the Prairie provinces. In Winnipeg, the first informal congregation, organized in 1897, held a service on Yom Kippur (Day of Atonement); at the end of the 19th century Winnipeg Jewry had established two congregations. When only two dozen Jews lived in the city, the Edmonton Talmud Torah was established in 1907; by 1922 more than twelve hundred Jews inhabited Calgary. Only two decades earlier, the city boasted only one Jew. A congregation had already been established in Regina by 1913, while the Saskatoon Hebrew Congregation was built one year earlier.

Between 1840 and 1900 roughly 15 000 Jewish immigrants came to Canada. Unlike the Montreal Jewish population, which included a relatively high proportion of Rumanian Jews, the Jews in Toronto and Winnipeg were predominantly Polish and Russian-Ukrainian. It was during the first two decades of the current century, however, that the largest influx of Jews to Canada occurred (see Table 1). These Jews were only a small fraction of the more than 30 million immigrants, both Jews and non-Jews, from central, eastern, and Balkan Europe who flocked to the United States and Canada between 1880 and 1924. It is thought that this migration might be the largest in the history of the world; it was responsible for many of those who are referred to today as the "white

TABLE 1 *European Jewish immigration to Canada 1900-52*

Period	Jewish Immigration	Jewish Immigration as % of Total Immigration
1900-20	138 467	4.3%
1920-30	48 434	3.9%
1930-40	11 005	5.4%
1940-47	1 852	3.6%
1947-52	11 064*	11.3%

* Displaced persons (refugees)

ethnics". The mass out-migration from Europe coincided with an active Canadian immigration policy receptive to newcomers from Europe as well as the British Isles, including the Jewish. The out-migration was interrupted by the advent of World War I.

The National Jewish Community: Cohesion during the War Years

The inflow of immigrants and their distribution throughout the country changed the shape of the Jewish community. Several features of communal life during this period are noteworthy. While the synagogue served as the religious center, the secular mode of communal effort expanded. The Jewish labor movement was organized to protect the interests of Jewish workers in predominantly Jewish industries. Yiddish, the language of the Jewish masses in eastern Europe, became a central means of communication and cultural expression. In 1907 the "Kanader Odler", the first Yiddish daily in Canada, was established in Montreal. Another was established in Toronto, and a weekly in Winnipeg. Jewish newspapers and magazines also began to appear in English. Although the Jewish community displayed a keen interest in Canadianization, there was also an active concern to retain aspects of Jewish life.

Community cohesion was fostered not only through the internal dynamics of growth and development, but also by way of external tragedies which struck Jewish populations in Europe, serving to unify the community on a national level. The dislocations, caused by the outbreak of World War I, of the Jewish populations in Russia, Poland, Rumania and Austria created within the Canadian Jewish community the recognition of their responsibility to help kin and friends overseas.

The serious dislocation of Jews in eastern Europe because of the war spurred emigration. The Jews often served as convenient targets against whom could be channelled the hostilities of certain segments of the population. Another factor that strengthened the desire for emigration following the First World War was the internal political, social and economic conditions in Poland, Rumania, Latvia and Lithuania. In addition, the Peace Treaties coordinated by the League of Nations which guaranteed to the minorities in various eastern European countries basic civil, economic and political rights never materialized in practice. Thus, the problems resulting from the war, fueled by practices of discrimination, led many Jews to seek resettlement through emigration.

The postwar years, however, witnessed a curtailment of emigration opportunities. Traditional countries of immigration such as the United States and Canada inaugurated restrictive admission policies in 1918 in response to their inundation in the pre-War era that resulted from a permissive "open door" policy. The Revised Immigration Act of 1927 introduced a series of immigration restrictions and prohibited the admission of all persons with the exception of those who fit the admissible categories. These restrictions, affecting mainly the immigrants from eastern Europe, had a significant effect on Jewish immigration. In response to the new immigration policy, the Canadian Jewish Congress was organized in 1919 to coordinate a Jewish effort on a national basis. In that same year a specialized immigrant aid agency, the JIAS (Jewish Immigrant Aid Services) was established to provide direction to the community's formation of an immigration policy.

Canada's immigration policy became even more restrictive during the depression, barring all but a few categories of immigrants. The possibility of admitting into Canada refugees from the Nazi regime became an acute question. For a long time the major source of Jewish immigration to Canada had been eastern Europe; now it shifted back to western Europe.

In January 1934 the Canadian Jewish Congress focused its efforts on behalf of German Jewish refugees. The Congress at times was opposed by anti-refugee forces who were against the relaxation of immigration regulations in favor of German Jews. Nevertheless, between April 1, 1930 and March 31, 1940, 11 005 Jewish immigrants were admitted to Canada and on a percentage basis, Jewish immigration reached its peak (see Table 1).

The Second World War drastically reduced immigration in general and Jewish immigration in particular. Efforts during the war years concentrated on assisting various groups of Jewish refugees, including those from Poland, Spain, Portugal and Tangiers. In 1940, after the fall of Dunkirk, British authorities interned all former German citizens, including Jewish refugees from Germany who resided in England; in the summer of 1940, about 2 500 males of this group were transferred to internment camps in Canada. Through the efforts of The Canadian Central Committee in Interned Refugees, a special body organized to plead their cause, certain categories of internees were released to become Canadian residents (Kage, 1962: 107).

At the end of the war, Jewish immigration efforts were concentrated on adjusting the status of certain Jewish refugees who were threatened with deportation and pleading for the admission of special cases.

Between 1947 and 1952, immigration to this country was expanded, and 11 064 of the 98 057 displaced Jews from Europe were admitted to Canada.

In 1952, Canada's immigration policy entered a new phase, resulting in a general curtailment of Jewish admissions. The major sources of Jewish immigration in this decade included uprooted displaced persons, Hungarian escapees and Egyptian expellees (1956). In the late 1950s, the appearance of Jews from North Africa and Israel represented a departure from the traditional source of Jewish immigration, eastern Europe. Between 1953 and 1960, 24 381 Jews, forming about 2% of the total immigration, entered Canada. This 2% figure held in the next decade as well.

Trends first noticed in the late 1950s strengthened in the 1960s with 30 773 Jews emigrating between 1960 and 1969 primarily from Morocco, Israel, and Russia. In the 1970s an estimated 3 500 Jews annually choose Canada as their adopted homeland.

Jewish immigration in Canada is best understood against the background of conditions which prompted Jews to leave their respective countries. For many, intolerable political, economic and social conditions made emigration inevitable; for others, Canada offered the possibility of better economic opportunities, a more tolerant environment, and lessened possibilities for discrimination. The settlement of Jews in this country was also directly influenced by the prevailing policies toward immigration. While the Jews attempted to become integrated into the larger society, they also sought to retain their ethnic and religious identity. The internal organization of the Jewish community shifted with the arrival of immigrants from different countries. In the next section, the Jewish community's contemporary social and religious organization will be examined.

The Contemporary Jewish Community

By the time of the 1971 census, the Jewish community had reached 296 940, comprising 1.3% of the total population. Excluding the British and French, 5.2% of the ethnic population are Jews, up from 3.7% in 1961. The provinces of Ontario, Quebec and Manitoba show the highest concentration of Jews and the cities of Montreal, Toronto, Winnipeg, Vancouver and Ottawa have the largest number of Jewish residents. Most Jews—approximately 99%—live in urban areas and are concentrated in the secondary and tertiary areas of the economy. They are largely represented in the following occupations: managerial, administrative and related—10.7%; clerical and related—18.8%; sales—24.2% and production, fabrication, assembly and repair—6.4%. The Jews' relatively high representation in higher occupational levels must not be confused with power, for Jews are hardly represented at the higher levels of Canada's corporate institutions (Porter, 1965; Clement, 1975).

Although Jews have become integrated into the larger society, their community retains a proliferation of institutions and associations which cater exclusively to social and economic needs of Jews of all ages.[2] The origins of these organizations can be traced directly to the flow of immigrants into this country. The numerical growth of the Jewish community and the distribution of immigrants throughout the country resulted in the establishment of houses of worship, charitable and welfare institutions, cultural activities and other forms of communal efforts. With the wave of immigrants which began during the middle of the 19th century, the Jews in Canada recognized the need to respond to their brethren's misfortunes and organized the first charitable agency, the Hebrew Philanthropic Society, in Montreal in 1847.

The arrival of immigrants also saw the organization of *lands-mann-schaften*, consisting of groups of individuals who came from the same town or region in Europe. Such organizations, which provided social and economic assistance and psychological support, were extremely helpful to the newly arrived immigrant and provided him with a sense of group belonging. Some of these *lands-mannschaften* still exist today, but many have been replaced by local, national and international organizations which provide members with a sense of belonging and support. The distinctive communal organization of Canadian Jewry, with its high degree of institutional completeness (Breton, 1964), has been directly responsible for initiating and maintaining a distinctive ethnic identity among this country's Jewish population.

While an analysis of Jews in Canada may be organized around the institutional and associational framework that has come to surround the Canadian Jewish community, Jews' religious affiliation and identification crosscut their organizational and communal involvement. From the outset, the synagogue has been the most significant form of communal organization, serving not only as a house of worship but also as a means of bringing the members of a community together. As soon as a "minyan" could be gathered in any community, shortly a synagogue would almost certainly be built.

Religious identification among the Jews is related to their affiliation to one of three movements that have developed in modern Judaism— Orthodox, Conservative and Reform. These groups are best seen as three intersecting circles, each with different dimensions and distinctive philosophies but all sharing some common beliefs.[3] Adherents to Orthodox Judaism believe that every question and problem facing the individual can be answered according to the divine teachings in the Code of Jewish Law—the *Shulchan Orech*. Attempts to adjust Judaism to the spirit of the time are rejected by Orthodox Jews who claim that it is not the values of any given age but rather the revealed will of God that provides the ultimate standards. In contrast, Conservative Judaism "places high priority on the need to examine the Code of Jewish Law, and to change it wherever necessary, in accordance with its spirit, but based upon a desire to direct its growth" (Rosenberg, 1966: 60). Reform Judaism, which began in the middle of the 19th century as an answer to new discoveries in science and history, has broken with tradition in its attitude toward Jewish law, and has denied the binding authority of the Bible and Talmud on questions of ritual law (Rosenberg, 1966). In Canada today, communities with sizable Jewish populations are likely to support congregations of each kind, but smaller Jewish communities are more likely to maintain only Orthodox and Conservative congregations.

Although modern Judaism can be subdivided into three major components, each is, in turn, comprised of a number of subgroups. What mark the various bodies in the Jewish community are different practices with ritual variations shading from one group to the next. The most striking example on the Orthodox landscape is the Chassidim, considered ultra-Orthodox even as judged by other Orthodox Jews. Their zealous and meticulous observance of the Code of Jewish Law isolates them from other Orthodox segments. They are recognizable by their attire as this is one way they attempt to protect themselves from assimilative forces (Shaffir, 1974).

Although a small number of Chassidic Jews reside in Toronto, most have established their communities in Montreal.[4] The Lubavitcher Chassidim were the first to settle in Montreal in 1941, with adherents arriving mainly from Russia throughout the 1940s and early 1950s. The Chassidic Jews established their religious institutions in the existing Jewish neighborhoods. As the larger Montreal Jewish community shifted its location to the more westerly areas of the city, the Lubavitcher followed while other groups of Chassidic Jews elected to remain in their initial location even though, in time, it became almost entirely non-Jewish in ethnic composition.

The contribution of the Chassidic to the larger Jewish community and the ambivalence with which they are viewed were the objects of comment by the Royal Commission on Bilingualism and Biculturalism:

... the Jewish cultural group has been augmented by small numbers of Hassidic Jews. ... These later arrivals have attempted to transfer their traditional way of life, including their mode of dress, to their new home. They pose a threat to some members of the Jewish cultural group for they hinder the process of integration into Canadian society. At the same time other Jews, who have themselves given in to the forces of assimilation, welcome the Orthodox arrivals because they guarantee the survival of traditional Jewry in Canada, without demanding any sacrifices on the part of those with less strict devotion to the traditions of their religion (Volume IV, 1969: 98).

Taken as a whole, the question of the integration of the Jewish community into Canadian society can be answered in terms of acculturation without assimilation (Rosenthal, 1960). On the one hand, it has attempted to become actively involved in contributing to social, economic and political events. On the other hand, as an ethnic group, it has sought to maintain its distinctive forms of communal organization to ensure its persistence. Encounters with prejudice, discrimination and anti-Semitism have had the effect of fortifying the boundaries of the community, fostering its institutional completeness, and both hindering and accelerating efforts on the individual and community levels towards integration with the larger Canadian society.

ENDNOTES

1. Much of the analysis in this section is derived from Kage's (1962) excellent account of Jewish immigration to Canada. The statistical information is based on the figures provided by Kage (1962), Rosenberg (1939) and the Canadian census.
2. In line with Gordon's (1964) analysis of assimilation, it may be argued that the Jews have experienced a high degree of behavioral assimilation whereas the extent of their structural assimilation has not been considerable.
3. It would be fallacious to believe that all Jews could be neatly classified as being either Orthodox, Conservative, or Reform. There are many Jews who may be referred to as secular Jews, who follow many of the traditions handed down through generations, but who do not adhere to the laws.
4. What commonly is referred to as the Chassidic community is, in fact, a number of Chassidic groups, each with its loyalty and devotion to its own *Rebbe* (leader). While it is true that these groups share the desire to maintain the integrity of Orthodox Judaism, they are sometimes sharply divided on points of practice and philosophy and personalities; leadership styles may conflict.

SELECTED REFERENCES

Breton, Raymond. "Institutional Completeness of Ethnic Communities and the Personal Relations of Immigrants." *American Journal of Sociology* 70 (September 1964), pp. 193-205.

Clement, Wallace. *The Canadian Corporate Elite: An Analysis of Economic Power.* Toronto: McClelland and Stewart Limited, 1975.

Fairchild, H. P. *Immigration: A World Movement and Its American Significance.* New York: Macmillan Company, 1926.

Gordon, Milton M. *Assimilation in American Life: The Role of Race, Religion, and National Origins*. New York: Oxford University Press, 1964.

Peterson, William. "A General Typology of Migration." *American Sociological Review* 23 (April 1958), pp. 256-66.

Porter, John. *The Vertical Mosaic: An Analysis of Social Class and Power in Canada*. Toronto: University of Toronto Press, 1965.

Rosenberg, Louis. *Canada's Jews*. Montreal: Bureau of Social and Economic Research, Canadian Jewish Congress, 1939.

Rosenberg, Stuart E. *The Jewish Community in Canada*. Toronto: McClelland and Stewart Limited, 1970.

Rosenthal, Eric. "Acculturation Without Assimilation? The Jewish Community of Chicago, Illinois." *American Journal of Sociology* 66 (November 1960), pp. 275-88.

Sack, B. G. *History of the Jews in Canada*. Montreal: Harvest House, 1965.

Shaffir, William. *Life in a Religious Community: The Lubavitcher Chassidim in Montreal*. Toronto: Holt, Rinehart and Winston of Canada, Limited, 1974.

The Cultural Contribution of the Other Ethnic Groups. Royal Commission on Bilingualism and Biculturalism. Volume 4. Ottawa: Queen's Printer, 1969.

Third World Immigration
a. Racial Prejudice and Discrimination

ANTHONY H. RICHMOND   York University

Immigration and Racial Prejudice in Britain and Canada*

Background Factors: Britain and Canada Compared

Britain and Canada differ from each other very substantially as far as major demographic characteristics are concerned. Canada has a population of 22.5 million distributed at a low density across a country that is the largest in the Western Hemisphere. In contrast, Great Britain (England, Wales, and Scotland) has a population of approximately 55 million living mainly in urban areas and at high densities, in a small island. Traditionally, Britain has been a country of emigration, providing a constant flow of migrants to those countries now sometimes described as the "old Commonwealth". In addition, Britain has a long history of colonialism, the economic consequences of which have persisted even with the achievement of political independence by almost all the countries that formerly made up the "British Empire". In contrast, Canada's population has grown as a consequence of natural increase and substantial net migration in the 19th and 20th centuries. Whereas the foreign-born (including the Irish) constituted only 6.5% of the population of England and Wales in 1971, 15% of the population of Canada were immigrants at that date. Furthermore, an additional 19% of those born in Canada were of immigrant parentage. Notwithstanding Welsh, Gaelic, and some regional and local dialects, the population of Great Britain is

---

* Revised version of a paper originally titled "Urban Ethnic Conflict in Britain and Canada: A Comparative Perspective" first published in S. E. Clarke and J. L. Obler, eds., *Urban Ethnic Conflict: A Comparative Perspective*, Chapel Hill: Institute for Research in Social Science, University of North Carolina, 1977.

relatively homogeneous from a linguistic and cultural point of view. In contrast, 27% of the Canadian population is French-speaking. Although the majority of francophone Canadians live in the Province of Quebec, there are French-speaking minorities in all provinces. Another demographic difference of some significance concerns the age distribution of the respective populations. Whereas Canada has only 8% of its population 65 years and over, the proportion for Great Britain is 14%, reflecting fluctuations in natural increase since the turn of the century, together with the contribution of young adults to the Canadian population through net immigration.

Economically, the two countries exhibit major differences. Although the gross national product of Great Britain considerably exceeds that of Canada, the average annual *per capita* income is almost 50% higher in Canada than in Britain. Canada's wealth is still based heavily on the exploitation of its natural resources. Agriculture, forestry, fisheries, trapping, mining and the production of electric power together account for a quarter of the value added in Canadian goods-producing industries. (Canada Year Book, 1973: 860.) In contrast, Britain depends more heavily on manufacturing, industry and services. Both countries have a substantial export trade, but in the case of Canada, this tends to be predominantly primary products in an unprocessed or semi-processed form. Only about one third of Canada's exports are in the form of manufactured end products.

Both countries experienced significant labor shortages, particularly in the 1950s and early 1960s. As a consequence, immigrants played an important role in the labor force, facilitating the growth of both economies. However, Canada actively promoted immigration from Britain and other countries, whereas Britain moved more quickly to control the inflow of immigrants who tended to serve as a replacement population in geographic and occupational terms.[1] (Peach, 1968). Tables 1A-2B show the trends in immigration and emigration in the two countries. Both experienced high immigration in 1967, but there has been considerable fluctuation in levels since then. Britain consistently lost more people than it gained, but Canada has continued to experience positive growth from net migration.[2]

Attitudes toward Black and Asian Immigration

The different attitudes toward immigration in the two countries may be related not only to their respective demographic and economic circumstances, but also to the different historical role which each country played in the international relations. This, in turn, may be related to the major ideological differences between the two countries. Britain imposed con-

TABLE 1A *Immigration to the U.K. by citizenship and total emigration: 1967-72 fiscal years (thousands)*

Citizenship	1967-68	1968-69	1969-70	1970-71	1971-72
Aliens	62	61	66	61	53
Canada, Australia, New Zealand	15	15	16	18	19
Other Commonwealth*	87	76	64	61	54
British (U.K.) (returnees)	78	76	77	87	74
All in-migrants (excluding Irish)	242	228	224	227	201
All out-migrants	286	296	306	266	240
Net migration	−44	−68	−82	−39	−39

*Includes India, Pakistan, Ceylon, West Indies and others.
Source: U. K. Government Statistical Service (International Passenger Survey)

trols on alien immigration at the turn of the century but permitted the free movement of people from Commonwealth and colonial territories until 1961. Even prior to the first Commonwealth Immigration Act, 1962, Britain had relied on constraints imposed by Commonwealth countries such as India, which restricted the number of passports issued for travel to the United Kingdom, to ensure that the increasing speed and ease of air transportation did not break down the traditional insularity of the country completely. When these "gentlemen's agreements" ceased to function effectively, Britain introduced a series of acts designed to control the flow of immigration from the so-called "new Commonwealth". The most recent legislation is the Immigration Act, 1971, which determines admissibility to Great Britain for permanent residence on the basis of a "patrial" clause concerning the birthplace of the parents of a potential immigrant. Although leaving the door open to persons of mixed racial descent (e.g., some Anglo-Indians), the legislation, in effect, removed the right of many Blacks and Asians living in Commonwealth countries to move to Britain even if, as in the case of some Kenya and Uganda Asians, they were in possession of British passports.

Britain's imperialist history gave rise to conflicting ideologies concerning the admission of "colored" immigrants and ambivalent attitudes toward them when they did immigrate to the "mother country". Political and economic relations between Britain and her former colonial dependencies tended to induce a movement of labor from the newly independent countries to the former imperial country which, in turn, benefited

TABLE 1B *Immigration to the U. K. by citizenship and total emigration: 1972-75 calendar years (thousands)*

Citizenship	1972	1973	1974	1975
Aliens*	57	68	62	59
Overseas Commonwealth*	53	45	43	53
United Kingdom	111	83	79	85
All in-migrants	222	196	184	197
All out-migrants	233	246	269	238
Net migration	−11	−50	−85	−41

*Pakistani citizens are included in Overseas Commonwealth in years to 1972 and in Aliens from 1973.
Note: Figures for 1975 and onwards are not directly comparable with earlier years due to a re-weighting of the sample.
Source: Adapted from Office of Population Census and Surveys in *Population Trends* (7), Spring 1977, p. 53.

from a supply of professional, skilled and unskilled labor at the times of shortage. However, when this movement began to threaten traditional ways of life and cultural values and appeared to aggravate the competition for housing and other services, attitudes toward colored immigrants tended to be hostile. Less attention was paid to immigration from other countries including the United States, old Commonwealth countries such as Australia and Canada, and the immigration from Europe. In practice, the "new Commonwealth" immigration during the 1960s was only about one third of the total inward movement of population. (Central Statistical Office, 1973.)

Canada's attitude toward Black and Asian immigration was almost the reverse of that in Britain. Even before the Canadian Confederation in 1867, there had been some Asian immigration, particularly to the West Coast, but opposition to it grew in the latter part of the 19th and early 20th centuries. As a consequence, prior to 1962, Black and Asian immigration to Canada was negligible and immigration regulations were explicitly discriminatory in terms of social and ethnic background (Richmond, 1967). However, the official position was reversed in 1962 when all bases of discrimination were removed from the criteria for admission to Canada. The adoption of a "points system" of selection, based on education and occupational qualifications, increased substantially the proportion of Black and Asian immigrants entering Canada. Prior to 1967, they constituted less than 4% of all immigrants compared with approximately one third in 1973 and 1974. (C.I.P.S. 3, 1974.)[3]

There are important differences between the two countries in the expectations with regard to cultural assimilation and structural integra-

TABLE 2A *Immigration to Canada by citizenship and total emigration 1967-71 (thousands)*

Citizenship	1967	1968	1969	1970	1971
U.K. (Britain and Colonies)	65	41	37	30	20
U.S.A.	18	19	21	23	23
Australia & New Zealand	6	4	4	4	2
Other Commonwealth*	15	12	19	19	17
All other foreign	125	108	81	72	60
Canada (returnees estimated)	34	32	33	31	29
All in-migrants	263	216	195	179	151
All out-migrants (estimated)	108	105	101	100	97
Net migration	+ 155	+ 111	+ 94	+ 79	+ 54

* Includes India, Pakistan, Ceylon and West Indies only.
Source: Department of Manpower and Immigration (adapted)

tion. Canada's dualistic origins in which special constitutional rights were accorded to the French Canadian population, together with the multicultural nature of immigrants in the 100 years since Confederation, resulted in greater acceptance of structural and cultural pluralism among immigrant minorities. In contrast, despite some lip service paid to the desirability of immigrants' retaining some of their cultural characteristics after arrival and not being forced into too rapid an "Anglo-conformity", immigrants in Britain were expected to conform more rapidly to what were regarded as appropriate British norms of behavior. Whereas the federal and provincial governments of Canada have financially supported and encouraged language and cultural maintenance among first and second generation immigrants, Britain has been more actively concerned with community relations problems and eventual anglicization (Patterson, 1969).

In contrast with single party totalitarian states, politically pluralistic democratic societies are characterized by competing ideologies reflecting the needs and interests of various classes and groups within the society. In Britain, the dominant ideologies concerning the situation of racial and ethnic minorities range from the explicitly racist and jingoist views of the extreme right, which would be happy to ban all non-white immigration and repatriate the existing Black and Asian populations, to the somewhat

TABLE 2B *Immigration to Canada by citizenship and total emigration, 1972-76* (thousands)*

Citizenship	1972	1973	1974	1975	1976
U.K. (Britain and Colonies)	24	38	48	40	28
U.S.A.	21	24	25	19	16
Australia & New Zealand	2	2	2	2	2
Other Commonwealth**	15	32	35	28	21
All other foreign	59	88	108	98	82
Canada (returnees estimated)	27	25	23	21	19
All in-migrants	148	209	241	208	168
All out-migrants*** (estimated)	90	80	75	70	65
Net migration	+58	+129	+166	+138	+103

*These differ from figures published by Department of Manpower and Immigration because of the inclusion of an estimated number of returning Canadian residents.
**India, Pakistan, Ceylon and West Indies only.
***Estimates of emigration differ from those published by Statistics Canada. See endnote 2.
Source: Department of Manpower and Immigration (adapted).

condescending and patronizing attitude of the liberal establishment. The latter accepts the necessity for continued immigration from the new Commonwealth and is concerned with effecting integration with a minimum of overt conflict. Countervailing ideologies and utopias are articulated on behalf of minority groups ranging from those who espouse a "Black Power" philosophy and confrontation tactics to those who would prefer to see colored immigrant minorities working through official channels and voluntary organizations toward fuller social integration.

In Canada, Black and Asian immigration has been more recent and on a smaller scale. Blacks and Asians constitute less than 2% of the total population. Despite the racist character of some extreme right-wing organizations, there has been little or no support in recent years for exclusionist policies and no question of repatriation. However, the recent economic situation has led to some opposition to immigration in general, although few people have openly favored a return to racially discriminatory immigration policies. The linguistic and cultural heterogeneity of immigration to Canada has made it difficult for any organization to represent effectively the interests of immigrants as a whole. A large number of ethnic organizations have arisen and these serve the cultural needs, and to a lesser extent, the economic and political interests, of the many nationalities represented. Partly influenced by the geographic proximity of the United States, there has been some manifestation of "Black Power" ideologies, but the organizations concerned do not appear to command much support (Ramcharan, 1974).

It should be emphasized that the urban ethnic conflicts associated with Black and Asian immigration are not necessarily the only ethnic conflicts or even the most serious ones in the two countries. However, the systematic testing of hypotheses, using the comparative method, necessarily involves focussing on those conflicts which are not unique and which do not have a high degree of historical specificity. To provide a more systematic basis for comparative analysis, using available quantitative data, the situation of Black and Asian immigrant minorities in the two countries will be examined in the area of housing. To some extent these recent immigrant minorities, with their high visibility in the receiving societies, have become the scapegoats for more deep-seated conflicts arising from demographic conditions and economic problems existing in Britain and Canada.

Blacks and Asians as Neighbors

When considering the attitudinal dimension of ethnic conflict, two separate questions must be considered. First, under what conditions does ethnic prejudice become widespread in a particular sub-culture so that racist ideologies are a part of the cognitive repertories of the population concerned? Second, what are the factors associated with a differential propensity to select or reject these ethnocentric or racist attitudes? The first question involves an examination of the historical context and the particular structural and situational determinants. The second question generally involves an exploration of the individual socioeconomic and socio-psychological determinants of attitudes and personality characteristics. The two approaches are complementary rather than mutually exclusive ways of explaining ethnic prejudice.[4]

There is no doubt that, in both countries, racist ideologies have been a persistent element in the prevailing culture and that, among the stereotypes and antipathetic beliefs are many that represent Black and Asian families as unsuitable neighbors. In both countries, myths concerning the effects on property values of colored families moving into a neighborhood can be found. Among the derogatory allegations made are that such people are dirty, rowdy, given to crime and delinquency and sexual promiscuity. These attitudes co-exist with more favorable ones which, in Britain and Canada, emphasize that all human beings are equal irrespective of race and which emphasize the more positive qualities of colored immigrants (Rose, 1969; Hughes and Kallen, 1974).

TABLE 3 *Attitudes of a national sample toward colored people as neighbors, Canada: 1963, 1969, and 1975*

1963	Region				
Would you move if colored people came next door?	*Maritimes* %	*Quebec* %	*Ontario* %	*Western* %	*Total* %
Definitely, Yes	7	5	3	1	3
Might do so	7	6	6	4	5
No	86	89	91	95	92
	100	100	100	100	100
					N = 718
1969					
Definitely, Yes	6	4	5	2	4
Might do so	10	5	6	5	6
No	84	91	89	93	90
	100	100	100	100	100
					N = 722
1975					
Definitely, Yes	5	2	5	3	3
Might do so	6	4	11	5	7
No	89	94	84	92	90
	100	100	100	100	100
					N = 1 067

Source: Canadian Institute of Public Opinion

In August 1963, May 1969, and June 1975, the Canadian Gallup Poll made national sample surveys on the reaction that people might have to colored families moving into the neighborhood. One of the questions was the respondent's likely reaction if a colored family moved next door. This was followed by a question concerning the likely reaction if many colored families moved into the area. Predictably, the latter situation was more likely to make people say they would move. There was only a small difference between the responses in 1963, 1969 and 1975, on a national basis. The results are tabulated by the region of residence of the respondent in Tables 3 and 4. Over the 12-year period there is some evidence of a slight increase in the proportion living in Ontario and the western provinces who answered "yes" or "might do so" to the first question, but no comparable change in attitudes on the second question. Overall, attitudes have remained the same or improved.[5]

TABLE 4 *Attitude of national sample to many coloreds moving into area, Canada: 1963, 1969, and 1975*

1963			Region		
Would you move if many coloreds moved into your area?	Maritimes %	Quebec %	Ontario %	Western %	Total %
Definitely, Yes	22	11	14	8	12
Might do so	34	18	29	26	26
No	44	71	57	66	62
	100	100	100	100	100
					N = 718
1969					
Definitely, Yes	21	11	16	12	14
Might do so	28	14	31	28	25
No	51	75	53	60	61
	100	100	100	100	100
					N = 722
1975					
Definitely, Yes	9	11	16	8	12
Might do so	11	10	25	24	19
No	80	79	59	68	69
	100	100	100	100	100
					N = 1 067

Source: Canadian Institute of Public Opinion.

The British Institute of Public Opinion asked the question "if colored people come to live next door to you, would you want to move away or wouldn't you mind?" on three separate surveys in 1958, 1961, and 1968. It is interesting to compare the trend over time and also to compare the results with the Canadian survey. Table 5 shows that the proportion of respondents indicating that they would be inclined to move almost doubled in a decade from 9% in 1958 to 19% in 1968. The proportion of those who thought they might move also increased, and there was a very substantial decline in the proportion who indicated they would not move, from 70% in 1958 to only 31% in 1968. It is reasonable to suppose that this increase was directly related to the growth in the size of the so-called colored immigrant population in Britain and the very significant change

TABLE 5 *Attitude of national sample toward colored family as neighbors, Britain: 1958, 1961, and 1968*

Would you move if colored people came next door?	1958 %	1961 %	1968 %
Yes	9	11	19
Might	21	33	43
No	70	50	31
Don't know, etc.	–	6	7
	100	100	100

Source: British Institute of Public Opinion.

in the climate of opinion as a result of the widespread publicity given to the alleged problems created by Black and Asian immigration. Despite the increased Third World immigration to Canada after 1967, there does not appear to have been any similar hardening of attitudes. This suggests that these new immigrants were not perceived by Canadians as threats, at least in the context of housing and neighborhood.

Social Distance

It is also possible to compare the responses of selected samples in the two countries to a Bogardus social distance scale. Table 6 compares the acceptability of the French, the East Indians and the Blacks as relatives or neighbors. The Canadian sample is representative of household heads in Metropolitan Toronto. The British sample is from an urban area in southern England. (Bagley, 1970.) It is evident that the general level of antipathy toward Blacks and Asians as potential neighbors is very much higher in the British sample. Almost four times as many of the British respondents reject Blacks and six times as many reject East Indians. However, the general level of prejudice-proneness does not seem to differ to the same extent. Using a six-item scale of racial prejudice on a sample in five English cities, approximately one third were found to be "tolerant; a little over half fell in the middle range and 14% were intense-outspoken i.e., prejudiced on five or six of the items." Using a five-point scale, with somewhat different items, but measuring underlying prejudice, a sample of householders in Metropolitan Toronto showed a very similar distribution. Approximately 36% fell into the two lowest categories, 52% in the middle categories and 12% obtained the highest prejudice score.[6] This suggests that the specific responses concerning colored immigrants as relatives and neighbors are a result of situational determinants rather than a difference in the two populations with regard to the underlying psychological dimensions of ethnic prejudice. It would lead to the

TABLE 6 *Comparison between Canada and Britain in degree of acceptability of selected ethnic groups as relatives by marriage or as neighbors*

	Canada* %	Britain** %
Accept French person as relative by marriage or neighbor	80	75
Accept French person as neighbor only	15	10
Not accept French person as relative or neighbor	5	15
Total	100	100
Accept East Indian person as relative by marriage or neighbor	40	20
Accept East Indian person as neighbor only	50	27
Not accept East Indian person as relative or neighbor	10	53
Total	100	100
Accept Black person (Negro) as relative by marriage	33	34
Accept Black person (Negro) as neighbor only	54	17
Not accept Black person (Negro) as relative or neighbor	13	49
Total	100	100

* Metropolitan Toronto survey of householders, 1970; based on 3 218 respondents.
** Survey conducted by Dr. Christopher Bagley in an urban area of southern England, 1971; based on 206 respondents.

hypothesis that antipathetic attitudes toward Black and Asian immigrants in Toronto might increase if conditions were more like those in Britain. In particular, an increase in the size of the "colored" population and a shortage of housing leading to an intensification of competition might be expected to aggravate the situation in Toronto. By the same token, an improvement in attitudes in Britain might come about as a consequence of a perceived reduction in the competition for housing or a redefinition of the situation in less competitive terms.

In this connection, it is interesting to note the conclusion of one study in Britain which found that *relative deprivation* in housing was related to extreme manifestations of racial prejudice. It was found that individuals whose housing quality was below that enjoyed by the majority of members of their occupational class, were more likely to score very high on the prejudice scale. It was shown that this was not a consequence of those in poor housing being more likely to come into contact with colored immigrants. On the contrary, the study showed that when other things were equal in terms of occupational class, the effect of proximity to colored neighbors was to reduce the level of prejudice. (Bagley, 1970: 53-67.) However, in practice "other things are not equal" and housing deprivation tends to coincide with living in or near those areas with high concentrations of colored immigrants. Although in Canada colored immigrants are more residentially dispersed than they are in Britain, there is also some tendency for recently arrived Black and Asian immigrants to locate in the older areas where housing is of poorer quality. (Richmond, 1972.) This is particularly true of single male immigrants congregating in the "rooming house" areas in both countries.

There is no doubt that the quality of housing available in Canada is better than in Britain, where there is more serious overcrowding and homelessness. Nevertheless, in large metropolitan areas such as Toronto, the rate of population increase and family formation has exceeded the rate of new housing starts after allowing for loss through other forms of urban development. (Wheeler, 1969.) Furthermore, the cost of purchase and rental housing has escalated with inflation and high mortgage interest rates. In this situation, recently arrived immigrants, irrespective of nationality, tend to be at a competitive disadvantage. It seems likely that in both Britain and Canada, non-white immigrants will feel a sense of "fraternal" deprivation in a number of social contexts including that of housing. It would seem to follow that individual relative deprivation may generate attitudes of hostility on the part of members of the dominant white group while a more generalized group deprivation, in absolute and relative terms, may create the conditions for collective action by the minority groups concerned.

Although situational determinants may be important in gauging the general level of attitudes between one country and another, or between different cities and localities within the same country, further factors must be taken into account in order to explain variations in attitude *within the same neighborhood.* A study of Sparkbook, England, emphasized the importance of situational determinants, minimizing the importance of psychological and other influences. It was argued that hostility towards immigrants was rational in the light of the "class struggle over the use of houses". The authors considered that the attitude of the native white residents of an area into which immigrants were moving was determined by their objective housing situation and position in a competitive housing market (Rex and Moore, 1967). In a study of Bristol, England, an attempt was made to test this hypothesis. Three indices were used to represent the housing situation: whether the respondent owned or rented his present accommodation; whether he had placed his name on the waiting list for public housing; and whether he was satisfied with his present conditions. No significant correlation between these items and the measures of racial prejudice was found among the white residents of a neighborhood having a large number of non-white immigrants. There was a slight, but not statistically significant correlation between prejudice and whether the respondent had placed his name on the waiting list for public housing, but this did not appear to be as strongly linked with expressions of prejudice as other variables, such as ethnocentrism, localism, having low socioeconomic status and being elderly and female (Richmond, 1970; 1973.)

Housing Conditions and Discrimination

The availability of housing for immigrants has been a major problem in Britain, but has only recently become contentious in Canada. Britain has suffered a severe housing shortage since the First World War. Despite a major building program, the rate of housing starts has never kept pace with the growth of population and the loss of usable housing space due to age, dilapidation, and war damage in Britain. In contrast, despite an even more rapid growth of population through natural increase and immigration, Canada experienced a construction boom in the 1950s and the 1960s partly assisted by the immigration of large numbers of skilled tradesmen in the building industry. (Richmond, 1974b.) However, that situation is now changing and housing in Canada is becoming relatively scarcer and more expensive. Although the objective housing conditions of the foreign-born improved between 1961 and 1971, there may have been some deterioration since.

Separate data for the housing conditions of Black and Asian immigrants in Canada are not available. However, the situation of postwar immigrants in general, and that of certain nationalities having low socioeconomic status, such as the Italian, was inferior to that of the Canadian-born. Although multiple occupation and overcrowding were not nearly as serious as in Britain, they were more frequent characteristics of immigrant households than others. Households consisting of two or more families were characteristic of only 4% of Canadian-born households in 1961, compared with 13% of all immigrant households. However, the latter figure had fallen to 6% by 1971. Overcrowding was particularly characteristic of the most recently arrived immigrants. Among those who had arrived in Canada in the five years preceding the 1961 census, 21% were living more than one person per room, compared with only 9% of the Canadian-born. In Metropolitan Toronto, which experienced the largest influx of immigrants and the greatest pressure on housing resources, 90% of Canadian-born families had exclusive use of bath and toilet facilities whereas a quarter of the postwar immigrant families living in the central city did not have exclusive use of these facilities at that date. By 1971, the actual housing conditions of postwar immigrants had improved, but there was increasing competition for available housing which had not kept pace with the rate of population growth.

An important difference between the housing situation in Britain and Canada is the role of municipal governments and the public housing sector. In Britain, public or "council housing" accounts for 31% of the total housing stock. In Canada, public housing is only a very small proportion of the available housing. Nevertheless, in a city such as Toronto, there has been a growing demand for public housing which cannot be met with the available resources. For example, in Metropolitan Toronto in the first quarter of 1968, more than 3 000 additional names were added to the list of applicants for family housing, but, during the same period, only 734 families actually lived in public housing. The size of the waiting list has been growing ever since. Allocations are made according to a "points system" related to the housing conditions of the applicant, income, family size, health and other factors. Very recently, the housing authorities imposed residence restrictions on eligibility for recent migrants to the city, whether from other parts of Canada or abroad, similar to those which have been used by most municipal authorities in Britain for many years. Clearly, such policies are related to the increasing competition and pressure on limited housing resources.

Various studies in Britain have shown that non-white immigrants were living in older houses with fewer amenities and experiencing a much more severe overcrowding than the Canadian white population (Burney, 1967). Even when careful controls for the education, income, family size and other characteristics of the immigrant group were taken into account, there was overwhelming evidence that their housing conditions were inferior. For example, the Bristol study used a matched control group and concluded that differences in housing conditions between white and non-white households, where both were in-migrants to the central city area, could not be explained by factors such as age, sex, family type, socioeconomic group or length of residence. (Richmond, 1973: 114-26.)

More recently, a general household survey carried out by the government social survey in Britain has indicated that in the housing field, the biggest disadvantage is to be colored. The survey showed that colored immigrants were younger, lived in a larger household, and had more insecure housing tenure, less bedrooms, and more persons per room than the white population. The survey, which was carried out in 1973, indicated that there had been a considerable increase in the number of non-

TABLE 7 *Housing discrimination in Britain as indicated by field tests in 1967 and 1973*

	1967 % discrimination against West Indian tester	1973 % discrimination against West Indian and Asian testers	
Rental accommodation (telephone)	62	27	
Rented accommodation (personal)	75	NA	
House purchase (personal)	64	17	(different treatment)
		12	(inferior treatment)

Source: McIntosh and Smith: *The Extent of Racial Discrimination*, p. 19.

white immigrants living in local authority dwellings (i.e., public housing), but they were still under-represented in this type of accommodation and in privately rented unfurnished houses and apartments. They were significantly over-represented in furnished rented accommodation. (C.R.C., 1974.)

Other studies have shown that the poorer housing conditions, higher rents, mortgage payments, and other problems experienced by colored immigrants in Britain were definitely due to racial discrimination. Definitive investigations of this question have been undertaken by Political and Economic Planning, an independent research organization, on two occasions. Carefully controlled field tests were carried out by a team of actors carefully matched in respect of their social backgrounds. In 1967 the comparisons were made between a West Indian, a Hungarian and a white tester. (Daniel, 1968.) In 1973, similar tests were repeated with West Indian and Asian testers compared with an Italian and a white English person. Racial discrimination was indicated when the West Indian or Asian tester was refused accommodation or received differential treatment while the European or white applicants were not. (McIntosh and Smith, 1974.) The results of the 1967 and 1973 tests are compared in Table 7.

The table shows that there was a significant decline in the incidence of discrimination between 1967 and 1973. This was most marked in the case of house purchase through estate agents and in connection with obtaining a mortgage. In this connection, it should be noted that the earlier study was carried out before the 1968 Race Relations Act which imposed

TABLE 8 *Self-reported experience of discrimination in housing by Black and Asian immigrants, Britain and Canada*

Britain 1967	All %	At Risk %
Black	39	65
Asian	16	60
All colored	26	55
Britain 1973		
Black	19	70
Asian	6	55
All colored	18	61
Canada (Toronto) 1970		
Black	38	47
Asian	13	21
All colored	26	38

Sources: Studies by Political and Economic Planning, 1967 and 1973 in Britain, and Metropolitan Toronto Survey, 1970 (York University).

penalties for racial discrimination in the sale or rental of accommodation. Following this, the building societies offering loans for house purchase removed the discriminatory practices which they had previously followed. The authors of the study note that although discrimination in the field of accommodation has decreased since 1967, discrimination against applicants for rented accommodation is still substantial.

It is possible also to compare the extent of self-reported discrimination by Black and Asian informants in 1967, compared with 1973 in Britain. Unpublished data from the PEP survey in 1973 can be compared with that reported in the earlier survey.[7] (Daniel, 1968: 165.) Very similar questions concerning discrimination in housing were also asked in a survey carried out in Metropolitan Toronto in 1970. This enables a direct comparison to be made between Britain and Canada (see Table 8).

In 1967, more than a quarter of all non-white immigrants interviewed in Britain indicated that they had personal experience of discrimination when endeavoring to rent private accommodation. Respondents were further asked if they had either applied for a house, flat or room from a white landlord who was a complete stranger. This enabled the number of persons actually "at risk" to be ascertained. When the results of the 1973 study are compared with the earlier investigation, it is evident that the absolute level of reported discrimination had fallen very considerably. However, when only the population "at risk" is considered, the level of discrimination appears to have risen. In other words, Black and Asian immigrants in Britain have adapted to the experience of discrimination by withdrawing from those situations where they are most likely to experience it. Instead, they have rented accommodation from Black or Asian landlords or become home owners. The increased availability of public housing through a relaxation of discrimination and increased eligibility through longer residence in Britain have probably also resulted in fewer non-white immigrants seeking private rented accommodation from white landlords. In this connection, it is notable that the PEP study finds no comparable diminution in the degree or extent of discrimination against colored immigrants in the employment sector.

The Canadian data in Table 8 are not precisely comparable with those from Britain. The question asked in Toronto concerned all forms of housing and was not limited to private rentals. The actual figures for self-reported discrimination are very similar to those found in the 1967 survey in Britain, but some differences appear when the population "at risk" is considered. The definition of "at risk" in this case was the total reported discrimination as a proportion of all those in rented accommodation. Given the Toronto housing situation in 1970, it was reasonable to assume that mortgages would be available and that Black and Asian respondents would not have any difficulty in obtaining a home to purchase if they could afford it. In fact, a high proportion of Asian respondents (who included some who were Canadian-born) were home owners. (Richmond, 1972: 87-90.) In both countries, it seemed that Black respondents were likely to experience more discrimination than Asians.

Comparatively few of the actual cases of discrimination that occur in any community result in a formal complaint being lodged with the appropriate authorities. Both Britain and Canada have civil rights legislation which outlaws discrimination, on grounds of race or ethnicity, in such areas as employment, housing and provision of services, although details of the legislation, the procedures adopted and the penalties available differ considerably. In the case of Canada, there is considerable variation by province in the nature and extent of the legislation and the machinery for its enforcement. Ontario has the most developed system; the Ontario Human Rights Code was first introduced in 1962 and was a consolidation of human rights legislation going back to 1944. It has since been amended and extended on a number of occasions; in 1972, provisions governing discrimination in regard to sex, marital status and age were introduced.

The Race Relations Act in Britain was not passed until 1968 and has more limited powers. However, it is interesting to compare the trends in complaints received by the two agencies as shown in Table 9. Given the much smaller population of Ontario (only 6.5 million compared with Britain's 55 million), it is significant to note the larger number of complaints made. This can hardly be explained by the different form of legislation or the incidence of discrimination itself. Instead, it suggests that the Ontario Human Rights Commission, through its longer history and the effective publicity given to its work, succeeds in providing a channel for the redress of grievances in a larger proportion of the actual cases of discrimination that occur, than does the Race Relations Board in Britain. In both countries, cases concerning discrimination in *housing* constitute 12% of all those reported. (OHRC, Annual Report, 1974; RRB, Annual Report, 1974.)

Conclusion

In the last 20 years, both Canada and Britain have experienced a substantial immigration of Black and Asian workers and their families so that the proportion of non-white immigrants in major metropolitan areas is quite similar although the earlier immigration into Britain means that the number of younger people born or mainly educated in that country, who are of Black or Asian immigrant parentage, is probably larger. The impact of these highly visible immigrant minorities has been rather different in the two countries. Measures of underlying socio-psychological predisposition to prejudice do not suggest any large difference between the populations concerned, but hostility toward the so-called colored people is much more outspoken in Britain. In particular, there has been growing opposition to colored immigrant families as neighbors in Britain while, over the same period and despite increased competition for housing in large cities, Canadian respondents remain tolerant in their expressed attitudes toward non-white neighbors and are also less opposed to intermarriage.

Despite these more tolerant attitudes, self-reported discrimination in housing by Blacks and Asians, both foreign and Canadian-born, is almost as high as in Britain, although the latter exhibits higher rates when only those 'at risk' in the private rental housing market are considered. However, housing discrimination in Britain has declined since 1968. This points to important structural differences between the two countries. In Britain a much larger proportion of the population depends on rental housing, particularly in the public or "council" house sector, whereas home ownership is more common in Canada.

Probably the most serious problems, in both Britain and Canada in the future, will surround the generation born, or mainly educated, in the receiving country whose relative socioeconomic deprivations will be combined with an identity crisis, likely to be even greater than that of other second generation immigrants because of the added effect of the ascriptive racial and visibility factor.

ENDNOTES

1. It is often assumed that adverse economic conditions in Britain led to the imposition of immigration controls. This is not the case. On the contrary, it was economic growth and a low rate of expansion of the indigenous labor force, due to demographic factors, that created a strong pull factor attracting immigrants to Britain. Political rather than economic considerations led to the first Commonwealth Immigration Act, 1962; subsequent amendments were a response to situations arising externally, such as the expulsion from Kenya and Uganda of Asians having United Kingdom citizenship. For a discussion of economic aspects of immigration to Britain, see Peach (1968) and Jones and Smith (1970).

2. Official statistics of immigration to Canada, published by the Department of Manpower and Immigration, are misleading on two counts. First, they refer to date of obtaining "landed immigrant" status (i.e., permission for permanent residence) and not date of entry to the country, which would be demographically more useful. No attempt is made in Tables 2A or 2B to correct for this. Secondly, Canadian immigration statistics do not include the return migration of Canadian citizens or landed immigrants who have been absent from the country for twelve months or more, which is the conventional definition of an immigrant or an emigrant for international comparative purposes. Therefore, a crude estimate of return migration has been included in Table 2, based on trends evident at the time of the 1971 census. Official statistics of emigration from Canada published by Statistics Canada are also misleading. Based on an annual estimate the official figures for 1966-71 are 317 200 for the quinquennium and 217 100 for the period 1971-76. However, the method used by Statistics Canada seriously underestimates the actual outward movement. Therefore, the estimates in Tables 2A and 2B are adjusted on the basis of trends evident in the 1971 census. (See J. J. Kelly, "Alternative estimates of the volume of emigration from Canada, 1961-71," *Canadian Review of Sociology and Anthropology*, Vol. 14. No. 1., February, 1977, pp. 57-67.)

3. The absolute number of Black and Asian immigrants that came to Canada between 1962 and 1974 is estimated at approximately 400 000. This compares with 600 000 for Great Britain in the same period although the labor force component of the colored immigration to Britain in the last decade has been smaller than in Canada. Allowing for earlier immigration and the effects of re-migration and return, the total *foreign born* populations of Black and Asian origin in 1974 are estimated as 930 000 in Britain and 404 000 in Canada. As a percentage of the total population, this represents a little under 2% in both cases. Britain has a larger proportion of children born in that country to recent immigrants. Therefore, the total non-white population of Britain may be estimated at 2.6% in 1974 and that of Canada about 2.4%, including Native Peoples. For a fuller discussion, see Richmond (1975).

4. Attitudinal data alone are notoriously inadequate to explain behavior, in the absence of relevant information concerning structural and situational determinants. In particular, a knowledge of subjective aspects of prejudice will not necessarily predict discrimination or avoidance behavior. The evidence from a

study in Bristol, England suggested that underlying ethnocentric and racist tendencies are good predictors of verbal hostility, but are only weakly associated with behavior, such as degree of personal contact with members of a racial minority. Demographic factors and socioeconomic status were more strongly associated with the behavioral indicators, with elderly females and those of low socioeconomic status exhibiting the greatest tendency to discriminate against and avoid contact with colored immigrants (Richmond, 1973: 211-38).

5. An analysis of the Canadian data based on the question of whether people would move if many colored people moved into the neighborhood suggests that age is a most important determinant. In all three surveys those under 30 years are much less likely to move than others. Furthermore, a cohort analysis shows that between 1963 and 1975 hostility declined in the middle-aged category as those born and educated after 1933 moved into the older group. In other words, the aging process itself did not make people more inclined to move away. At the same time, it should be noted that the Ontario and British Columbia respondents were consistently more likely to say they would move. Since these are the areas with the largest numbers of Black and Asian immigrants, and with the most serious housing problems for a rapidly growing population, it seems likely that these situational determinants are important. Unfortunately, the size of the Gallup Poll samples do not permit a reliable analysis of the figures, by Province or Metropolitan area, with controls for age and socioeconomic status.

6. A problem of construct validity arises when scales using very different items are compared, but both the British and Canadian scales appeared to be measuring an underlying factor that might be called "racial prejudice proneness." The alpha reliability score of the British scale was .67 and that of the Canadian, .66. For a methodological discussion, see Bagley (1970) and Goldlust and Richmond (1974).

7. I am indebted to Mr. David Smith of Political and Economic Planning for providing access to unpublished data included in Table 8.

SELECTED REFERENCES

Bagley, Christopher. *Social Structure and Prejudice in Five English Boroughs.* London: Institute of Race Relations, 1970.

_____ . *The Dutch Plural Society: A Comparative Study in Race Relations.* London: Oxford University Press, 1973.

Burney, Elizabeth. *Housing on Trial: A Study of Immigrants and Local Government.* London: Oxford University Press, 1967.

Canada Year Book 1973. Ottawa: Statistics Canada and Information Canada, 1973.

Central Statistical Office. *Social Trends.* No. 4. (ed. M. Nissel.) London: Her Majesty's Stationery Office, 1973.

C.I.P.S. *Immigration and Population Statistics.* Canadian Immigration and Population Study, Vol. 3. Ottawa: Manpower and Immigration and Information Canada, 1974.

C.R.C. *Facts and Figures about Commonwealth Immigrants.* London: Community Relations Commission, 1974.

Daniel, W. W. *Racial Discrimination in England: Based on the PEP Report.* Harmondsworth: Penguin Books, 1968.

Hughes, D. R., and E. Kallen. *The Anatomy of Racism: Canadian Dimensions.* Montreal: Harvest House, 1974.

McIntosh, N., and D. J. Smith. *The Extent of Racial Discrimination.* (Broadsheet 547). London: PEP: The Social Science Institute, 1974.

Ontario Human Rights Commission Annual Report, 1973-1974. Ontario: Department of Labour, 1974.

Patterson, Sheila. *Immigration and Race Relations in Britain, 1960-1967.* London: Oxford University Press, 1969.

Peach, Ceri. *West Indian Migration to Britain.* London: Oxford University Press, 1968.

Ramcharan, S. "Adaptation of West Indians in Canada." Unpublished Ph.D. dissertation, York University, 1974.

Race Relations Board. *Annual Report 1974.* London: Her Majesty's Stationery Office.

Rex, J. and R. Moore. *Race, Community and Conflict: A Study of Sparkbrook.* London: Oxford University Press, 1967.

Richmond, A. H. *Post-war Immigrants in Canada.* Toronto: University of Toronto Press, 1967.

———. "Housing and Racial Attitudes in Bristol." *Race* 12:1 (1970), pp. 49-58.

———. *Ethnic Residential Segregation in Metropolitan Toronto.* Toronto: Institute for Behavioural Research, York University, 1970.

———. *Migration and Race Relations in an English City: A Study in Bristol.* London: Oxford University Press, 1973.

———. "Migration, Housing and Urban Planning in Toronto." *Current Research in Sociology* (ed. M. Archer). The Hague: Mouton, 1974b.

———. *Black and Asian Immigrants in Britain and Canada: Experiences of Prejudice and Discrimination.* New Community, 1975.

Rose, E. J. B., et al. *Colour and Citizenship: A Report on British Race Relations.* London: Oxford University Press, 1969.

Runciman, W. G. "Race and Social Stratification." *Race* 4 (April 1972), pp. 497-510.

Saywell, John. *Quebec 70: A Documentary Narrative.* Toronto: University of Toronto Press, 1971.

Smith, D. J. *Racial Disadvantage in Employment.* Vol. XL Broadsheet 544. London: Political and Economic Planning, The Social Science Institute, 1974.

Wheeler, M. *The Right to Housing.* Montreal: Harvest House, 1969.

Jane Sawyer Turrittin

"We Don't Look for Prejudice": Migrant Mobility Culture among Lower Status West Indian Women from Montserrat*

Introduction

Explanations of the mobility process among immigrants have primarily focused on migrants' educational and occupational characteristics, giving little attention to their social skills. Recent studies (Anderson, 1974; Turrittin, 1976), however, describe how migrants create and use their social networks and what roles cultural brokers play in promoting geographic and occupational mobility. The ways migrants activate their social networks may be patterned by cultural norms which, in turn, may vary by ethnic and class sub-culture. Cultural attributes thought to promote the upward mobility of lower status West Indian women from Montserrat[1] in Canada are the focus of this research.

West Indian Migration

Since the passage of the 1967 Immigration Act, Canada has experienced a major migration from the West Indies—a migration that has perceptibly changed the color composition of our urban populations. Current estimates of the West Indian population in Metro Toronto, for example, are in the order of 100 000. Unlike migration from other parts of the world, West Indian immigrants have been and continue to be made up primarily of females. This has been attributed to the availability in Canada of domestic work as an occupation open to West Indian women. With the passage of the 1967 Immigration Act, the Canadian-West Indian Female Domestic Scheme, in effect between 1955 and 1967, became anachronistic, but the availability of domestic work continues to motivate large numbers of women from the Caribbean to come to Canada. The ratio of female to male West Indians entering annually has, however, declined from 61.2% in 1964 to 53.1% in 1974.

* Written expressly for *Two Nations, Many Cultures: Ethnic Groups in Canada.*

311

Canadians do not consider themselves racists and have in recent years taken pride in their non-discriminatory immigration policy. Studies show that the Canadian social structure is somewhat open and mobility is possible for minority ethnic groups, but the evidence also indicates full structural assimilation has not been achieved (Porter, 1965; Richmond, 1967, 1972; Kalbach, 1970; Hawkins, 1972). Comparative data collected on the occupational mobility of immigrants from ethnic groups in Toronto whose first jobs were in the "unskilled laborer" category indicate that "respondents with English mother-tongue experience greater upward occupational mobility than either those with a non-English mother tongue or West Indians" (Ramcharan, 1974: 80). Although "the majority of (West Indian) respondents" were found to be "successful in obtaining employment in their intended occupations" (Ramcharan, 1974: 77), a correlation between lower-class status and discrimination against West Indians was also reported.

The Research Problem

If Montserratian women were successful in moving from domestic labor to blue- or white-collar jobs in Canada, one might be tempted to con-clude that neither racial nor sexual discrimination was significantly encountered. Nevertheless, to say these women have not been prevented by their skin color, sex, or cultural background from experiencing mobil-ity is to misrepresent their history. They have been discriminated against. It is argued that certain features of their cultural background, however, have equipped them, both psychologically and socially, to "make it", despite the fact that they are not only black and lower-status, some speaking a dialect unintelligible to most Canadians, but also women (Boyd, 1975). It is further argued that the West Indian women from Montserrat reported on here have certain expectations concerning the goals of their migration. These expectations color the interpretations of their experiences in Canada. The women are thought to possess specific culturally developed interpersonal skills which contribute to their ability to overcome "barriers". Finally, it is suggested that where the potential for discrimination against a category of immigrants is high, cultural attributes possessed by these immigrants may be potentially critical in enabling mobility to occur.

The Sample of Women from Montserrat

In 1974, I interviewed 15 women from Montserrat who had migrated to Canada between 1967 and 1972. Ten of the women first worked in Canada as "domestics", a job ascribed to them on the basis of a racist, sexist stereotype. At the time of the interviews, nine were doing white-collar work and eleven had upgraded their educational qualifications. The representativeness of these women to the total population of Mont-serratian women or other West Indian women in Canada cannot be assessed. Our interest in the case histories of these women lies in the ways in which they were able to achieve their migration goals.

Montserrat: Culture of Origin

A century and more of out-migration from Montserrat has resulted in the development of a whole body of customs and behaviors which facilitate the ability of individuals to go out and make their way in urban, industrial settings. As a "migration-oriented" society, Montserratian culture has bequeathed these women a "migrant ideology" or "cognitive model . . . concerning the nature and goals of their migration" (Philpott, 1973: 69). In Montserrat, youths have little opportunity to earn a living, even by agricultural pursuits, and children are reared with the expectation that they will migrate and work abroad so that they can contribute to the economic support of their families. Families are large (8 to 12 children is common) and the social environment is full of reminders of the importance of migrants who have gone out. Photographs of one or more brothers and sisters, or parents, who have migrated are displayed on the walls of homes, and these individuals are frequent topics of conversation. Letters with news and remittance money are awaited eagerly. Social recognition of the departure and return of migrants is marked on the community level with a "fête", in much the same way as a christening or wedding is celebrated.

Anticipatory socialization with respect to migration and occupational goals within the family is reinforced by the presence in the community of migrants who have returned. Many of these migrants have obviously improved their material standard of living while abroad, and all, by virtue of having been out, enjoy enhanced prestige. Teacher Alice, head of the primary school in a village in the eastern district of the island, had studied in England on three different occasions. She lived in a modern concrete-block house, drove a car and was undoubtedly a salient role-model for her six- and seven-year-old pupils. Whether migration confers adulthood on women, as Philpott found it did on men, I do not know, but there is a definite glamor in going abroad. The economic necessity underlying migration, then, has made it not only an altruistic but a self-interested act.

Because of contacts with Canadians living in a retirement colony on the island, Montserratian women know about the availability of domestic work in Canada and view the "opportunity of doing domestic" as a means of contributing to the support of their families, perhaps enabling those with ambition to pursue a career. Five of the women interviewed migrated so that they could contribute to the support of their own children. Other women without children, however, were also important sources of financial aid to their families.

The necessity for migrants to make their way in urban, industrial settings has resulted in a high priority being put on education by islanders. Many youths desire not only to migrate, but to "achieve something". Expectations about the proper occupations for women outside the household reflect traditional sex-role stereotypes. In answer to a questionnaire given to students in Standards 5 and 6, Philpott found nursing, teaching, dressmaking, and clerical work the most frequent occupational choices of girls (1973: 100).

Until recently out-migration from Montserrat was primarily male. One consequence of the absence of males is that women remaining on the island assumed greater responsibility in economic and social life than is customary in North America. Surveys in two of the rural districts on the island indicate the effects this male migration has had on lower-class domestic organization. In "the East" and Cudgoe Head 56% and 42% of the households, respectively, were headed by women (Philpott, 1973: 150).

The absence of men has also resulted in children making a contribution to the functioning of the household at a younger age than is customary in North America. Children's help in the production and harvesting of crops and running errands is essential to domestic organization in Montserrat. One informant, for example, spoke of how she knew how to iron at the age of nine. Philpott reports: "At 13 or 14 years of age girls are usually almost fully socialized to their adult domestic roles and take a major part in caring for younger children, laundering, and preparing meals" (1973: 139). The assumption by Montserratian women of economic and social responsibilities toward their families and their familiarity with work at what North Americans consider an early age equip women who migrate with the qualities necessary to earn a living without necessarily relying on a man.

Migration to Canada

The Patron-Client Relationship

Perhaps the most important social skill possessed by these women which enables them to make their desire to migrate a reality is their ability to cultivate "friendships" with higher-status, often white, individuals. The propensity among lower status women to enter into the lopsided friendships characteristic of patron-client relationships (Pitt-Rivers, 1954) is perhaps one of the legacies of the colonial and post-emancipation eras. As reported previously (Turritin, 1976) the ability to secure white patrons on the island itself enabled six of these women to migrate and obtain domestic work in Canada, while the ability to manipulate her relationship with her employer in Canada enabled at least one woman, who came as a visitor, to solicit his patronage to secure landed immigrant status.[2]

The relationship established between Evelyn[3] and her employer well illustrates the nature of the lopsided friendships characteristic of patron-client relationships:

> There were 16 of them, not all of them Jean X's and I had to do the work for them too. Mr. X did construction. He built highrises all around. That job was near Eglinton and Bathurst. I lived in and got $150 per month. They never raised my wages but Mrs. X used to buy me things. I would tell her I saw some nice sheets when I had been out shopping and she would get them for my room. Or I would buy a dress and she would pay for it. We got along real good. We used to talk together a lot. She would let me go out with her husband. She would say "Hurry and get through these things and you can go out with Mr. X. I saw a lot of Toronto that way.... They used to tell me to bring my boy-friend over. Even now, we see them and she calls me up. "If you want to leave your husband, you can come here." She told me, "Stay and I'll leave you something in my will." But I had a disagreement with one boy and I left.

Because "a minimal charge of affect invests the relation of patron and client" (Wolf, 1966: 16), if a domestic no longer needs her employer's patronage to reach her goals, no matter how satisfactory the rapport established between them, she will leave domestic work.

Response to Whites

The skill with which women solicit patrons is related to their attitude toward whites, and Montserratians are perhaps less ready to evaluate individuals on the basis of color than are "big islanders", i.e., migrants from Trinidad and Jamaica. As one informant put it, "I don't look for prejudice." Even though some whites act in discriminatory ways, these women hold the attitude that whites can be useful in helping them attain their goals, and they do not generalize experiences of discrimination from some whites to all whites.[4] They are confident that "genuine" whites can be found, and that they can enter into the lopsided friendships characteristic of patron-client relationships, as well as primary group relationships with them.[5]

Women find a different attitude between the races in Canada than they are familiar with at home. "From the start," said one informant, "I found a complete difference to home in racial attitudes. It is worse to work for a colored family on Montserrat than for a white family in Canada. Here they let me sleep in the children's bed." Canadians may be superficially more liberal about color, but this does not prevent communication problems from arising between domestics and their employers. The women exhibit a certain tenacity in sticking to jobs, and appear to be willing to tolerate some degree of discrimination provided they are able to meet economic goals, but if the work situation is so bad that it does not merit compromising, a woman will quit. The initial working conditions of three women who first worked as domestics were so bad they quit and found different positions as domestics as soon as they could, two within two months of entering the country. Quitting takes courage and entails risk, especially for a woman who has been in the country only a few months and who will have "no reference" and few friends to fall back on.

Response to Other West Indians

Another aspect of the migrant culture which promotes mobility and aids Montserratian women in overcoming barriers is their attitude toward interaction with non-Montserratian migrants. Montserratians place "little moral value on interaction with other Montserratians" (Philpott, 1973: 180) and find it easy to enter into primary group relationships with West Indians from other islands. As reported previously (Turrittin, 1976), the ability of women to make friends out of chance acquaintances met at points central to the networks of West Indian migrants enabled several women to get basic information concerning job and educational opportunities and to leave domestic work and enter blue-collar jobs. Without this friendly attitude Montserratian women would be severely limited with respect to the size of the pool of individuals from which they could choose friends (and husbands), since the number of Montserratians in Toronto is extremely small, in the order of 250 to 300 people.

Positive Work Attitudes

Montserratian women look for blue-collar jobs, which have work-styles similar to those on the island, such as nurses' aide, salesclerk, or sewing in the garment industry. (Most women have probably never been in a factory until they secure their first factory job in Canada.) Unlike many Canadians, Montserratian women believe there are plenty of jobs available; the problem is not to find work, but to find long-term satisfactory work. Employers effectively discriminate against immigrants by making jobs available only to those with "Canadian experience". The barrier women fear most is discrimination on the basis of their lack of Canadian experience, but they are aware that this may co-occur with discrimination on the basis of color. The self-assurance the women now convey may be in part a result of having obtained "Canadian experience", but they are also possessed of good manners and a maturity generally lacking in Canadian women of similar age. This manner undoubtedly aids their ability to secure jobs, and their ability to secure patrons. Once gained, "Canadian experience" is the object of disparaging humor among islanders. One informant's brother claimed he was going to write a song about it.

A good work record is an asset, and women do not like to change jobs. Changes are necessitated as often by the fortunes of the companies they work for as by their own needs. Women try to line up new jobs quickly when it is necessary to transfer from one blue-collar job to another, and they take pride in their ability to do so. At the time the women were interviewed, none had experienced more than six months' unemployment since arriving in Canada. Ironically, those who had first worked in non-domestic jobs experienced longer periods of unemployment than former domestic workers. The latter were longest unemployed when looking for their first non-domestic jobs. While unemployed, with the exception of one woman who had briefly received unemployment insurance, the women had lived on their savings or had been supported by a husband or relatives.

The evaluations Montserratian women make of their blue-collar experiences underscore the value they put on independence and the ability to live socially satisfying lives. Job histories reflect the search, within the relatively narrow range available to them, for jobs in which there is opportunity to develop social relationships. Most women who had done blue-collar work evaluated service jobs more highly than factory work, and their work histories indicate the move from factory into service jobs; that is, alienation with factory work motivated these women to look for jobs as service workers, where they would have opportunity for social interaction and where they could exercise some discretion in how to go about doing their work. Evelyn, for example, could not remember the brand names of items she packed in a factory job she had in Canada: "We packed food—Tang, coffee—I can't remember," but made the following comment about her job as a waitress in a coffee shop: "It is small. There are just four of us there, and it doesn't pay very well, ... but I prefer it to working sewing." Celia, who left her factory job after only two weeks because she "didn't like that work; it was too tiring," liked her job as a salesclerk. "I have responsibility for keeping boys' wear and men's socks."

The blue-collar career of only one woman shows the move from service to factory work. In addition to an economic incentive for making this move, there is some indication of a social incentive. She quit her job as a nurses' aide because "I could not get along with my supervisor," and took a job in a factory where she worked for over three years.

> Fourteen girls worked in our unit, opposite the men, who did the heavy work. I worked with two other women at a machine which works the hose clamps once they have been cut. . . . Once my boss's sister, who is 67 years old, told me to "shut-up", and I told her to "shut-up." I don't take anything from anybody here in Canada. Down home you can make a joke. I work with my hands and talk with my mouth. You would be a savage to work all day and not talk.

In addition to ranking the narrow range of jobs available in blue-collar work on the basis of wages and work hours, women rank jobs on the basis of relatively minor benefits: whether there is opportunity for over-time, opportunity for social interaction, and so on. Some of these were well-articulated by Betty in her anticipation of a new factory job where the pay and "little benefits" were better.

> I am looking forward to many things about this new job. I will be able to make my bed in the morning and pack a proper lunch. I'll leave about 6:40 a.m. but not have to rush the way I had to for my old job. If I get hospitalized, I'll have a semi-private room.

Some women, like Agnes, look for jobs which enable them to exercise initiative. After working in the garment industry, in a factory, and as a waitress, Agnes eventually found a job which enabled her to exercise her managerial abilities. Agnes had been engaged in multiple occupational pursuits on Montserrat as a trafficker[6] and as a seamstress.

> Through the paper I got a waitress job at the Bathurst subway—Garfield News. I was the head of the evening shift and worked from 2:30 to 10. I had the keys to lock up, and earned $62/week, $55 take-home. I was in charge of two other girls and I took the cash. It was not too hard and people were quite friendly. Of course I used to help the girls take out the garbage etc. but I was in charge. This was an excellent job and I worked there for one year. I did not get tips but did get my meals, and eventually they made me manageress.

Most women prefer blue-collar work to domestic work. Some inform-ants were able to find satisfactory blue-collar jobs, although many did not find blue-collar work advantageous in the long run. It may be that many bosses in small factories and businesses in Toronto treat women badly. Fortunately, the women interviewed who did not find blue-collar work satisfactory had the social resources to get out.

Female Friendship Networks

Friendship with another woman from home is probably the most durable social relationship a Montserratian woman in Canada has until she marries, and perhaps the most important social resource Montserratian women have in Toronto is the presence of at least one close friend whom they can count on (Bled, 1965; Henry, 1968). To ensure that individuals will not be totally isolated when they migrate, it is customary, among women at least, to come with a friend. Two or three women may come up on the same plane together, or within a few weeks of one another. With few exceptions, even migrants who come alone do not enter a social vacuum, knowing at least one person, if only a distant relative, already in Canada. As Eldecka said, "You've got to have some resource."

On Montserrat people are able to ask and secure favors from friends with the understanding that these favors will be repaid at some unspecified time in some unspecified way, and the customs of reciprocity characteristic of the island, although modified, are carried over into city life (Philpott, 1973: 174). Women do personal favors for each other such as sewing, or fixing hair or they work together to organize social events such as parties or weddings. Women put up siblings when they first arrive in Toronto, or friends who are visiting from other cities.

The ability to call on friends for help without having to repay immediately is an invaluable resource for Montserratians who migrate, and the presence of a small network of people from home, including at least one close friend, is of crucial importance to these women. This small, close-knit network of friends functions to socialize women into the migrant situation, enabling them to benefit from the experiences of others. It is important to emphasize that the embeddedness of women in a supportive network of friends and relatives promotes rather than retards the mobility process (Bled, 1965), and does not serve as a liability, as has been suggested by some researchers (Ramcharan, 1974). As these women's success in securing the aid of patrons and making friends with non-Montserratian West Indians attests, being able to count on close friends does not prevent women from activating extended network ties when necessary.

Consider the function of a woman's social network in promoting her educational aspirations. Like North Americans, Montserratians put a high priority on education. Access to secondary education for these women, however, was severely limited on Montserrat and most had Standard 7, the equivalent of Grade 8 in Canada, at the time they migrated. The importance of the encouragement of friends in motivating women to pursue educational and occupational goals is revealed clearly in the following statements:

Agnes: When you say domestic, people think different. . . . It's only a start. A bright looking girl like you, people said, should go to school.
Doreen: Folks say, "Don't stay and do housework. Go to school." I saw ads and would send for them and read them over. But I couldn't afford it. A girl

from Montserrat encouraged me. She was in England. I was glad to have opportunities.

It is of interest to note that these women are the beneficiaries not only of support from friends in Toronto, but also from friends who are literally thousands of miles away. Agnes had not completed Standard 7 on Montserrat but eventually became a keypunch operator while Doreen, who had attended but not completed secondary school on Montserrat, became a bookkeeper.

In order to enter the white-collar jobs to which they aspire, the women have to upgrade their educational credentials considerably. The usual pattern is for women to begin going to school part-time, taking evening courses, while working as domestics or in blue-collar jobs, but for most women the ability to obtain proper credentials necessitates going to school full-time. Although the women interviewed paid for their part-time courses, they could not afford to finance their own full-time education, and thus had to solicit the aid of Manpower.

It is through her social network that a woman learns about the availability of Manpower-financed training courses, and how to deal with Manpower counsellors. Specifically, she learns that she must prove to the Manpower counsellor she has worked in Canada for at least one year and has a good work record, that she knows what occupation she wants to enter and has made some effort on her own to begin to get the necessary qualifications for that occupation. She learns that her own experience of rejection the first time she applied for a Manpower training course is relatively common, that she might have better luck with a particular counsellor at another Manpower office who has been sympathetic to another West Indian woman. Manpower counsellors have considerable discretionary power over the entry of applicants into training programs. Without exception the women who succeeded in getting into Manpower-financed training programs also completed their courses, securing white-collar jobs on this completion. Although sceptical about Manpower's desire to take them seriously, the women know Manpower can help them and are grateful to Manpower once they are successful in getting into a training program.

By the time they attempt to go back to school to secure the qualifications which enable them to get into white-collar work, most women interviewed had established relatively secure social lives. Having been out of school several years, going back necessitates a change in their lives for which they plan carefully. They may lack self-confidence about their ability to do school work and be embarrassed that as adults they must take Grade 9 or 10 subjects. They want to devote themselves full-time to their studies, but it is only after women have established their own households that they can confidently pursue their studies full-time.

Delayed Marriage

The necessity to migrate and contribute to the support of one's family is related to late marriage for Montserratian women in Canada. Late marriage is also customary on Montserrat, but there it is related to the desire not to marry until one is financially secure. At the time of writing, nine of the fourteen women who were single at the time they migrated had married. Of these, two married before they were 25 years old, five married between the ages of 25 and 30, while two married after the age of 30. This differs considerably from marriage patterns among Canadian women.

Because of the demographic imbalance in the West Indian population in Toronto, it may be difficult for West Indian women to meet men, and especially among domestic workers limited interaction with men may last as long as a year. Once met, a man may be willing to enter into a sexual relationship with a woman, but be reluctant to marry, especially if she has a child or children. Thus, West Indian women face potential exploitation not only from white employers, but in their relationships with West Indian men, and a boyfriend may be an economic burden.

> Eldecka and her brother Matthew shared an apartment, dividing the costs of rent and food equally, but Eldecka's boyfriend Michael often ate with them. Michael occasionally paid for a bag or two of groceries, or bought a bottle of liquor, but Eldecka paid more often, and this situation caused tension between Eldecka and Matthew, who had to pay part of the costs of entertaining Michael. Once, when the telephone company threatened to cut off his phone, Michael phoned Eldecka at 6:30 a.m., awakening her to ask if she would pay his phone bill.

Another Montserratian woman told the following story:

> I used to see Lawrence from time to time. One day he asked me if he could borrow my credit card to buy a camera. I have good credit and I let him have it. Then he changed his phone number and I didn't see him again. Believe me, every penny of that $288 hurt a lot.

The basis of social life among Montserratian immigrants in Toronto is the sibling household—a household composed of a single woman and one or more siblings, either brothers or sisters. Most women interviewed were able to establish their own household within one or two years of their arrival in Canada, once they found relatively steady non-domestic work. The establishment of a household symbolizes for these women the attainment not only of economic, but of psychological and social independence, and often coincided not only with the move out of domestic work into relatively stable non-domestic work, but with the arrival in Canada of a sibling whom they had sponsored.

Residential patterns among Montserratian migrants reflect the importance of island-based friendships among women, and women who knew each other on Montserrat may choose to live near one another in Toronto. For example:

Several migrants from Kinsale live in the Bathurst-Eglinton area near where Ona, one of the first women to migrate to Canada from the island on the Canadian-West Indian Female Domestic Scheme, is still employed as a domestic. When one of Ona's sisters married, she and her husband lived with another of her sisters within walking distance of Ona's employer. When their second child was born they got an apartment on the same block as the sister with whom they had previously lived. Another sister and her husband later bought a house about a fifteen minute walk, but only a three to five minute drive by car, from this apartment.

The Bathurst-Eglinton area was also attractive to another group of women from the same area of the island.

When she married, Evelyn got an apartment not far from her original employer in the Bathurst-Eglinton area. Similarly, when she married in 1971 Edna found an apartment in the area, although she had been living in Scarborough with a married cousin, so that she could be near Evelyn, as well as another friend, Doreen. Doreen was working days at a clerical job, but continued to live-in with her original domestic employer, in part because of the convenience of being near Ona, whom she saw frequently.

Once women are able to establish their own households, they can recreate, although on a restricted scale, the kinds of social relationships similar to home.

An account of the cultural traits promoting mobility among these Montserratian women would be incomplete without giving some indication of the personal costs of this mobility for them. Migration results in a dramatic change in a woman's life, necessitating both separation from family and separation from friends. Perhaps the greatest liability women struggle to overcome is loneliness which they associate with domestic work because the hours and conditions of employment give little scope for the development of social relationships. Even though a woman may have at least one friend in Toronto, the excessive dependence of women on each other, or on close relatives, may lead to a "clash." Unless a woman has developed alternative social ties, such a clash can be disastrous for the women involved. The establishment of their own households, however, widens their social networks and enables them to live more satisfying lives.

Montserratian women deal with loneliness by taking on a part-time job in addition to a full-time job. At the time they were interviewed four of the seven women who were then single had part-time jobs, while none of the married women did. For some women, working or going to school part-time may take the place of social life at home. There is, however, a reluctance to take on part-time jobs permanently. Once a woman has a fuller social life, meets certain special expenses, or gets a salary raise at her full-time job, she will quit part-time work.

Conclusion

The relative success of these particular migrant women rests fundamentally on cultural factors as well as on the opportunity structure in Canada. In our view, a migrant mobility culture enables individuals to take advantage of opportunities which exist. Occupational or social mobility — the alteration of an individual's position in the social structure—is related to a number of factors, including the degree to which various ethnic groups are welcomed or discriminated against in Canada, the educational and occupational assets individuals have, and the ways in which these assets are channeled into the economic system through various types of brokers. Finally, the cultural background of the migrant interacts with the above, determining, in part, the ultimate outcome.

An explanation of the mobility of these Montserratian women, therefore, necessitates making reference to their "migrant ideology" as seen by their ability to manipulate the patron-client relationship, to make friendships with other West Indians, to maintain at least one reliable friend from home, and to work hard, sometimes holding multiple jobs despite prejudice and personal costs such as loneliness. In fact, when the potential for discrimination against a category of worker is high, a cultural background supportive of the mobility process may be an essential factor in the migrant's success.

ENDNOTES

1. Montserrat is one of the Leeward Islands in the Eastern Caribbean and has almost no industry, its economy being based on small-scale agricultural production, with cotton as the cash crop, and dependent on remittance money (Philpott, 1973). To make a living most adults engage in a number of occupational pursuits. For men this involves producing cash and subsistence crops, raising goats and perhaps some dairy cattle, being employed by the government on road construction, or by private builders, engaging in carpentry or another trade, etc. The term "lower status" is therefore preferable to "lower class" in describing the social origins of these women.

2. The patron-client relationship always implies exploitation. Manipulation of a patron does not mean a reversal of the basic relationship of super-ordination and sub-ordination.

3. Although the names used in this paper are common Christian names on Montserrat, the names of individuals quoted here have been changed to ensure anonymity.

4. Lloyd Fallers' description of Bantu informant's attitudes to relationships of super-ordination and sub-ordination may also be applicable to these Montserratian women. He writes: Their social world was pervaded by great "objective" differences in wealth and power, but my informant stoutly refused to conceptualize these in terms translatable as "classes" or "strata", and they behaved, for the most part, in accord with their own conceptualization of inequality in dyadic, patron-client, master-servant terms. (1973: 4).
5. Of 26 marriages that took place in Toronto involving at least one Montserratian which came to my attention, five were with white Canadians, seven were island endogamous, and 14 were with other islanders.
6. 'Trafficking' is a common female occupation in the Caribbean. Traffickers act as middle persons between small-scale agricultural producers and consumers, travelling distances to get produce which they then bring to local markets to sell for a small profit.

SELECTED REFERENCES

Anderson, G. *Networks of Contact: The Portuguese and Toronto.* Waterloo: Wilfrid Laurier University, 1974.

Bled, Y. "La Condition des Domestiques Antillaises à Montréal." MA Thesis, University of Montreal, 1965.

Boyd, M. "The status of immigrant women in Canada." *Canadian Review of Sociology and Anthropology* 12:4 (1975), pp. 520-26.

Fallers, L. *Inequality: Social Stratification Reconsidered.* Chicago: University of Chicago Press, 1973.

Hawkins, F. *Canada and Immigration, Public Policy and Public Concern.* Montreal: McGill-Queen's University Press, 1972.

Henry, F. "The West Indian Domestic Scheme in Canada." *Social and Economic Studies* 17:1 (1968), pp. 83-91.

Kalbach, W. *The Impact of Immigration on Canada's Population.* Ottawa: Dominion Bureau of Statistics, 1970.

Philpott, S. B. "West Indian Migration: The Montserrat Case." *London School of Economics Monographs on Social Anthropology 47.* London: Athlone Press, 1973.

Pitt-Rivers, Julian. *The People of the Sierra.* N.Y.: Criterion Books, 1954.

Porter, J. *The Vertical Mosaic.* Toronto: The University of Toronto Press, 1965.

Ramcharan, S. "The Adaptation of West Indians to Toronto." Ph.D. Thesis, University of Windsor, 1974.

Richmond, A. *Post-War Immigrants in Canada.* Toronto: University of Toronto Press, 1967.

————. *Ethnic Residential Segregation in Metropolitan Toronto.* Toronto: Institute for Behavioural Research, York University, 1972.

Turrittin, J. "Networks and mobility: the case of West Indian domestics from Montserrat." *Canadian Review of Sociology and Anthropology* 13:3 (1976), pp. 305-20.

Wolf, E. "Kinship, friendship and patron-client relations in complex societies," in M. Banton, ed., *The Social Anthropology of Complex Societies*, A.S.A. Monograph No. 4. London: Tavistock, 1966.

b. Asian Immigration

NORMAN BUCHIGNANI   Lethbridge University

Recent East Indian
Immigration to British Columbia:
Identity Formation among Fijians*

Introduction

Immigration has brought together people of different class, nationality, culture, and race. Immigrants and native-born Canadians interacting in ways different from their prior experiences have made behavioral and ideological adjustments to each other necessary. Immigrants have had to quickly "make sense" out of Canadians and Canadian society in the same way that Canadians have had to go through a process of developing explanations for what various immigrant groups were about, where they fitted into Canadian society, and how one would behave towards them.

This process of mutual definition and adjustment between Canadians and immigrants is related to the long history of Canadian immigration which has brought in peoples of diverse backgrounds. Changes in the Canadian immigration regulations in 1964 and 1967 have meant that today's immigrants come from a far wider range of ethnic and national backgrounds than ever before. As late as 1965, European and American immigration to Canada accounted for about 85% of all immigrants, and Asian countries contributed less than 7% of the total.[1]

Today, about one half of all immigrants come from places other than the United States and Europe; about one half of these come from Asia.[2] This increase in the range of cultural and national backgrounds has had two predictable effects. First, Canadians have had to develop new patterns of belief and social interaction to encompass these immigrants.

* An extensive revision of a paper presented at the Canadian Society for Asian Studies in Fredericton, New Brunswick, May, 1977. The financial support of the Secretary of State, Ottawa, which made the earlier draft possible, is gratefully acknowledged.

Second, the expansion in the number of source countries has generated many new immigrant groups. These new Canadians are presently formulating their ideas of Canada, Canadians, and their relationship to both.

This paper attempts to understand an ethnic interaction pattern that has developed between an East Indian sub-community and other Canadians in Vancouver.[3] While I do not provide a total explanation of this situation, I hope to show that the everyday events to which we often crudely apply terms like *racism* and *prejudice* are underlain by very complex, human processes of understanding on both sides of the ethnic boundary (Barth, 1969). In particular, I would like to describe how the transmission and reception of ideas of the social worth of ethnic individuals takes place and is channelled by social interaction and prior belief.

East Indian Immigration

People of East Indian origin have become one of the largest sources of Canadian immigrants. While East Indians first established a community in British Columbia shortly after the turn of the century, Indian immigration to Canada was legally barred from 1908 to 1947, and the small, predominantly Punjabi Sikh population of that era remained numerically stable until after the Second World War.[4] As the last of British Columbia's three early Asian immigrant groups to arrive in Canada, the East Indians suffered all of the economic and social liabilities of the Chinese and Japanese who came before them. They could not vote, become citizens, or be elected to public office (Angus, 1937). Neither could they work for the government, nor be employed on Crown lands or in public works. They were informally barred from the professions and from white society, and were channelled into unskilled, blue-collar labor, chiefly in the lumber mills. In short, they became a subordinate racial caste in early British Columbia.

Formal restrictions against the East Indians in Canada were removed after the Second World War. They were allowed to vote in 1947, when the immigration ban was lifted. Through a series of postwar changes in the immigration regulations, East Indian immigration has dramatically increased. There are now more than 150 000 East Indians in Canada from such diverse countries as Pakistan, Uganda, and Guyana.[6]

Fijian East Indians

Fijians are one of the many ethnic and national groups called "East Indian" which has participated in this increase. There are now over 10 000 Fijian Indians in Canada, and chain migration has resulted in about 8 000 of them taking up residence in the metropolitan area of

TABLE 1 *East Indian immigration to Canada, 1956-76**

Years	No. of Estimated Immigrants
1956-61	3 301 (actual)
1962-67	18 000
1968-73	57 000
1974	20 000
1975	17 000
1967	12 000
Estimated total	127 301

*The estimated data in the table are the sum of immigration from India, Pakistan, Sri Lanka, Uganda, Tanzania and Fiji for those years and are therefore likely to be an underestimate (Department of Manpower and Immigration, *Annual reports 1967-76*).

Vancouver. This newly-formed community has recently experienced an enormous population increase. As can be seen from Table 2, over 60% of these immigrants have come in the past four years (1973-76). This rapid influx has made for a considerable degree of uncertainty and lack of understanding of their new home. This is particularly so of their perceptions of how others value their presence in Canada. For these reasons, Fijian East Indians will provide the focus of this paper.

When they come to Canada, Fijians bring with them Fijian Indian values and expectations, and it is through those values that they must make some sense out of their new context; this is a self-evident point, but one which is often overlooked in studies of how one type of person develops notions about other social groups. Because the basic values which allow one to make sense out of the world often differ markedly

TABLE 2 *Fijian immigration to Canada**

Year	No. of Immigrants	Year	No. of Immigrants
pre-1962	50 (estimate)		
		1970	776
		1971	721
1962-1964	209	1972	636
1965	304	1973	987
1966	271	1974	1 530
1967	172	1975	2 323
1968	253	1976	1 081
1969	590	Estimated total	9 903

*Virtually all Fijians who come to Canada are East Indians; therefore one can use the source country immigration figures with some certainty.
Source: Census of Canada.

across an ethnic boundary, even such fundamental determinants of human behavior as one's idea of what "that other fellow" thinks about oneself may not be identical with what that other actually thinks. This is the case between Fijians and others in Vancouver.

Social Identity

An individual's *social identity* is that set of collectively-held ideas which others hold about that individual by virtue of his or her membership in a social group. These are the beliefs which allow one to explain the situation of others and to predict their likely behavior in a given situation. An excellent illustration of a social identity is seen in Braroe's account of native Indians in rural Saskatchewan (Braroe, 1975).

Perceived Social Identity

Framed in this manner, Fijian Indians' *perceptions* of their social identity and that identity itself are very different indeed. In short, Fijians have created a view of their own social situation which is decidedly off-base as judged from the viewpoint of the larger society. Nevertheless, the way in which they have assembled this view of their world is neither incoherent nor arbitarily constructed. The principal determinants of this perceived social identity are information on their self-worth received in interaction across the ethnic boundary, ideas communicated by other Fijians, and by the media.

Social Identity Formation

Sources of Information

As a geographically and occupationally dispersed minority in an urban industrial context, Fijians must of necessity interact a great deal with other Canadians, resulting in a contradictory set of expressions of their social worth. Because of the short time during which they have resided in Canada, and the prior social distance between Indians and Europeans in Fiji, Fijian adults have developed few personal relationships with Euro-Canadians. For example, many Fijians have never been in a Euro-Canadian house, nor have they informally socialized with Euro-Canadians outside of the context of work.

While Canadian-Fijian social contacts are increasing at present, the general level of personal interaction is still low, with several exceptions. Younger Fijian adults have been moderately successful in attracting European friends. The world of Fijian Indian children in Vancouver is dominated by non-Fijian compatriots. For adolescents, the interactional customs of the particular school are important determinants. Some high schools have developed sharp network cleavages along ethnic lines; others have not.

While these Canadian-Fijian relationships are relatively few, those which do exist have contributed to the idea that, basically, Canadians are a friendly, fair, socially and ethically acceptable people, who are willing to accept Fijians into their society, given that Fijians acquiesce to most Canadian customs. This basic assessment of Canadians as "good" people stands at the center of Fijians' beliefs about their place in Canadian society, for they have not yet chosen to change this assessment as they attempt to reconcile the fact that some Canadians are overtly hostile to them.

Most social relationships between Fijians and Canadians are rather highly institutionalized, routinized, and role-dependent. Most involve contact at work or in the acquisition of goods and services; the former is particularly important in reinforcing an essentially positive view of Canadians. In contrast to earlier Asian immigration (Japanese and Chinese) to British Columbia, Fijians have not concentrated in any one occupation that would be perceived as an economic or social threat by Canadians. They are mainly skilled or semi-skilled workers in a very wide range of occupations, notably automotive repair, factory work, furniture manufacturing, food processing, janitorial service, and office work. Their spread of employers is equally wide, and by far, most of them work in situations where Fijians are a minority in the workforce. But it is within other institutionalized relationships that Fijians receive most of their perceptions about their ethnic social identity, and the formidable constraints which prohibit its perfect transmission must be outlined in detail.

Social identities are normally complex; yet often, the social constraints of ethnic interaction are such that only a very small measure of this total picture can be effectively packaged and transmitted across the ethnic boundary. The East Indians in Vancouver are no exception to this rule; most of the ideas Fijians receive from Canadians about their social identity come through the "shorthand" of routinized statements like "Punjab, go home", or through forms of anti-East Indian behavior which are similarly limited in their semantic depth.

Many aspects of this East Indian social identity do not have such readily dispensable packaging and can only be conveyed by that very sort of detailed discussion which so rarely occurs across an ethnic boundary. For instance, the presence of East Indians in Vancouver was at one time being used to explain the sudden rise in house prices which occurred in 1973 and 1974. This notion did not evolve an appropriate form for its easy transmission, and Fijians were largely oblivious to the charge.

Social constraints limit the transmission of Canadian ideas about East Indians even further. Those situations where it is still socially acceptable to air racist statements in British Columbia are severely limited, particularly if a member of the group in question is present. Moreover, the routine, everyday nature of many East Indian-white relations also prevents the flow of such statements.

In spite of the constraints, Fijians do receive fragmentary information about their social identity, and this reception finds its ideal type in those extraordinary incidents where the anti-East Indian critique is overt and is central to the event. Incidents of this sort range from a harangue delivered to a Fijian in a bank "sending all his money to India", to a Fijian woman out shopping being taunted as a "dirty raghead", to vandalism of one's home, and to inter-ethnic violence.

These incidents are in fact quite rare, and most Fijians may claim not to have directly participated in one. Such incidents, nevertheless, have great impact; news is rapidly telegraphed across dense Fijian social networks to a great number of individuals, making events of this sort appear to be far more common than they actually are. When, for instance, a Fijian woman was mysteriously murdered in Vancouver in 1976, information about the event flashed across the community in about two days and made the national news in Fiji, and returning visitors to Fiji were asked about the level of racism in Canada for the first time.

Information received from other Vancouver Fijians constitutes another important source of ideas about their social identity. The person-to-person exchange of these ideas abstracts culturally-relevant material out of individualized stories and such information is unconsciously molded into patterns which are psychologically and semantically acceptable to Fijians. Intra-ethnic communication is, therefore, the integrating mechanism of this perceived social identity.

The media also play their part in conveying an image of East Indians to Fijians. In particular, Fijians watch a great deal of television; it is a new experience for them. The presentation of East Indians on television suffers from many of the same weaknesses as does the portrayal of many other aspects of society; this medium focuses on the unique and different, and neglects everyday life. "Ram Singh", the nice guy with a happy family life and a steady job, is not news, while "Mohammed Khan", the wife-beater, is. Coverage of East Indians in Vancouver is predictably dominated by immigration stories, and by the presentation of East Indians as criminals or as the victims of crime (Indra, 1977).

Reception and Integration

Like its transmission, the reception by East Indians of their social identity is severely constrained, chiefly by the fact that Fijians are culturally different from Canadians. Often Fijians do not realize that an evaluation of their social worth is being conveyed because they lack familiarity with the nuances of Canadian linguistic usage or customary behavior. In general, Fijians may be far more often the small-scale victims of their ethnicity than they ever notice. Different cultural values may occasionally result in Fijians incorrectly seeing racism in situations in which there was no intent on the part of Canadians to slight them.

Because Fijians and Canadians do not entirely participate in the same universe of meaning, the *same* transmitted signal does not usually convey the same meaning on both sides of the ethnic boundary. To see how this occurs, it is necessary to introduce some elements of the East Indian social identity.

Let us begin with the general category itself—"East Indian"—or alternatively, "Punjab" or "Hindu". In present day British Columbia, any of these terms refer to all those people who are recognizably "East Indian-looking". Most British Columbians do not recognize that any significant differences exist between people of the several ethnic groups which they would include under the rubric of East Indian. Most do not in fact realize that in no real sense does there exist an East Indian community in Vancouver; rather, there are a number of small social sub-communities like the Fijian one which are the "real" bases for the social life of East Indian individuals.

The relatively meager interaction which other British Columbians have with East Indian people has also determined a large part of the semantic configuration which goes with these labels. Social identity has been assembled around folk ideas about Punjabi Sikhs—ideas which have persisted for over seventy years (Dodd, 1907; Lockley, 1907). Fijian East Indians are quite invisible in this homogeneous social identity, and not many British Columbians know that they are here at all.

On their part, Fijians do not accept the validity of either the label "East Indian" or the social identity which goes with it. Fijians have therefore begun to reassemble their social identity by displacing the stigma elsewhere: "We're not East Indians, we're *Fijians*." This process is easily accomplished because of their own strong sense of Fijian self-identity; moreover, in Fiji an *East Indian* was a person who came from India itself. About 10 000 out of the total 260 000 Indian population of Fiji were born in India. There are sharp social cleavages between these two populations.

Many of the criticisms which underlie these general terms concern differences in material culture, as suggested by the phrases "dirty Hindu" and "raghead". It is beyond the bounds of this work to argue whether these charges are actually used with their semantic implications of uncleanliness and dress differences, respectively, but as with other such statements, these are the literal interpretations to which Fijians will affix meaning. Those which have had particular impact concern dress (turbans, saris, "pointy shoes", beards, odd color combinations), personal hygiene (cleanliness, smell), and household practices (condition of houses, use of curried food). Others concern presumed East Indian social customs and "modal personality". East Indians as an ethnic group are claimed to be clannish (they keep together, live together, and have their own social rules), violent (both with each other and with other Canadians), unfriendly, argumentative (they bargain on prices, are loud about their "rights"), and generally do not meet Canadians on their own terms (with respect to language use, social customs, and the like).

Social Identity Interpretation

Ideological Defense

How do Fijians react to these charges? The first reaction is one of total rejection. Fijians possess a well-developed sense of self-worth and of high personal morality, and they consider their behavior in Canada as being faultless. They believe themselves to be acting in ways which are accept-able both to their own ethical code *and* to Canadian ones.

If they are firmly convinced that the charges are not true and that Canadians are basically fair, knowledgeable, and good, how are these convictions to be reconciled with the overt criticism East Indians often face from Canadians? The means are twofold, yet interconnected. First, the criticism itself is displaced onto the Sikhs. This ideological accom-plishment is non-problematical and straightforward. The social identity of East Indians has been constructed around vague notions of Sikhs, down to the categorical terms "Punjab" and "raghead". In this regard, Fijians have either taken the taunts quite literally, or have chosen to note and over-stress some, while patently ignoring those others for which there is no ideological escape. A few examples are in order. They have taken messages like "Punjab, go home" to mean just that—*Punjabs* (i.e., not Fijians) go home. "Raghead", which for Canadians would read "East Indian", for Fijians reads "Sikh".

In their selective acknowledgement of messages, Fijians have made use of *a priori* Fijian and continental Indian stereotypic ideas about Sikhs to confirm their belief that Sikhs are acting similarly here. Many Fijians firmly believe that Canadian Sikhs *are* dirty and unkempt, don't keep up their houses, and tend to be socially distant unless they "really trust you"; they are perceived to be mechanically inclined, but are a bit oxen-like and unimaginative with "nothing much under the turban". Those Canadian charges which "fit" this Sikh social identity are duly noted by Fijians as being basically *valid* observations of Sikh practice. For example, all those aspects of the East Indian social identity which concern personal or familial cleanliness have become central to Fijians, as in "dirty Hindu" and "East Indians don't keep up their houses", which Fijians translate as "'*dirty* (i.e., Sikh) Hindu' and '*Sikhs*' don't keep up their houses". Fijians believe that Sikhs *are* a violent, argumentative, and militaristic people, and so the made-in-Canada labels of East Indians are also transferred over to the Sikhs. That Canadians are good people can still be maintained because the reason for their anti-East Indian hostility is perceived to be improper Sikh behavior. This ideological transfer of stigma is also aided by the very high social distance between Fijians and Punjabi Sikhs in Canada today. This distance allows Fijians less of an insight into everyday Sikh life than they have into the Canadian. Neither group seem to see much in common with the other, and both possess essentially negative evaluations of the other's social worth.

As important as those elements which support the charge that it is the Sikhs who are at fault, other elements which do not become activated are also crucial. In the main, they are those where Fijians must acknowledge that they, too, do something which resembles the charge. As such, these elements cannot so easily be transferred, for the polarization between Fijian self-identity and East Indian social identity does not exist.

Fijians are clean and industrious house owners, perhaps to the extreme, and this acknowledged practice can therefore easily do battle with the accusation that they are not. But what of the charges that they "live 83 in a house", have "forced" arranged marriages, or eat different foods? While they do none of these things in anything like the way the social identity charges, within their understandable, everyday world Fijians do things which do correspond to them. They also act in ways which parallel "bringing all their relatives over" and "sending all their money to India", although to say parallel is not to imply equivalence.

These situations are directly confronted by feelings of the essential correctness of the activities which stand behind them, whenever to compromise would result in high social or economic costs. Thus, extended households, the use of Indian food, the nomination of relatives to come to Canada, the remittance of money to dependants in Fiji, the use of Hindi in homes, the private practice of non-Christian religion, and the arrangement of marriage are considered as appropriate and continue to be major themes in first-generation Fijian life in Canada.

The Presentation of Self: Announcing Fijian Identity

The transference of some of these stigmatic inputs to Sikhs and the avoidance of others certainly constitute a remarkable accomplishment; Fijians have been able to maintain feelings of positive self-identity and equally positive evaluations of Canadians in the face of anti-East Indian hostility. But in itself, this is hardly sufficient; Fijians must daily interact with people who only see them as East Indians. They are socially stigmatized until their identity is proven otherwise by that closer interaction which rarely comes. At the same time, it would be inaccurate to infer that Fijian convictions about the propriety of their behavior are so strong as to make them incapable of any accommodation to the behavioral demands which Canadians put upon them. However, it should not be unexpected that Fijians have responded with a large-scale presentation of self as Fijians and with an even more massive acceptance of Canadian customs in the public sphere.

Although it is difficult to assess the degree to which they are consciously motivated to do so, several Fijian strategies may be attempts to provide Canadians with positive diacritica of their Fijian, rather than their East Indian, identity. In conversation, they actively over-communicate their Fijianness and give a positive, idyllic assessment of life in Fiji. Fijian males often dress in a particularly Fijian style with south-sea island and Hawaiian prints, while adolescents of both sexes are more direct, and often wear shirts emblazoned with the word "Fiji". With increasing frequency, Fijians' cars are similarly labelled with decals and bumper stickers. At home, the public areas of Fijian homes are inevitably filled with explicitly marked mementos of Fiji, ranging from wall posters and chairs to Fijian mats. In these ways, Fijians are using physical markers to differentiate themselves from what Canadians label as a biologically and culturally homogeneous population of East Indians. Unfortunately, most of this effort has been in vain; the Canadian perceptual grid is not fine enough to have yet sorted out Fijians on *any* basis, let alone on the basis of their own presentations of self.

Another significant response comes at the level of the place Fijians see for themselves in Canadian society. If as a group they had been historically united by adversity and minority status, one might expect that they would express "separate but equal" tendencies in the face of this social stigmatization, but they have not. Rather, while firmly holding on to a definitive self-ascribed Fijian identity, they perhaps have opted for a far more extensive acceptance of Canadian values and practices than I believe has occurred among any of Canada's other Asian ethnic groups.

In virtually all respects, Fijians conform to their ideas of proper Canadian behavior in public. Save for their own volunteered ethnic diacritica, they are largely indistinguishable in dress from other Canadians, and saris are rarely worn in public, except by older women or by visiting Fijians. Women's hair and makeup styles are also rapidly adjusting to Canadian practice. Equipped with some considerable prior experience with English, their inter-ethnic linguistic etiquette has been sharpened to the point where they rarely use the Indian languages in public. At home, Fijian family structure largely remains intact, but a massive potential for its radical change is building in the almost totally Canadian-ized second generation. In terms of decor, personal privacy, and the like, Canadian patterns have largely won out.

On the whole, it is difficult to assess to what degree this process of assimilation has been internally motivated or structurally necessary, or whether this results from an accommodation to what are perceived to be demands for "Canadian" behavior on their part. Some aspects clearly derive from each.

Conclusion: Social Identities and Sociological Realities

Fijian East Indians in Vancouver have developed a sense of how others view them; this illustrates many characteristics which seem to be inherent in the interaction between social groups. Because the boundaries of social groups are normally barriers to communication, both information and values are only selectively transmitted. Because group membership implies normally a degree of common culture, individuals will assemble information from the outside in accordance with what they collectively hold to be true.

Fijian versions of their social identity constitute explanatory attempts to understand the nature of their new social setting in such a way as to maintain their own sense of self-worth and their convictions as to the nature of the world. While their analysis of this social setting is not in accordance with how "outsiders" would assess the same situation, the conclusions which they draw are nevertheless logical, rational, and con-sistent with their past and present experiences.

The same process of reality construction takes place when Canadians attempt to categorize their East Indian neighbors. Most of their ideas are "inaccurately" drawn conclusions about "East Indians" based on tenuous and selective evidence. Despite their factual weaknesses, these ideas also reflect an attempt by a social group to explain another group's behavior in terms of one's own cultural values. Both Fijians and Canadians believe that they possess *the* true version of reality, and both are convinced of the rightfulness of acting upon that knowledge. The results are prejudice, discrimination, ethnocentrism, and ideological uncertainty on both sides of the ethnic boundary. But at the same time, these beliefs are the products of very human attempts by people to explain and understand the nature of their social world.

ENDNOTES

1. By European and American, I have included immigrants who are from Europe or from the United States, as well as from Australia, New Zealand, South Africa, or Rhodesia. This 85% figure is an average over the years 1964, 1965,

and 1966 (Source: Department of Citizenship and Immigration Annual Reports 1964-1966).
2. These figures are approximate, as the Department of Manpower and Immigration no longer collects data on the ethnic backgrounds of immigrants. These percentages are derived from averages for the years 1973-75 (Department of Manpower and Immigration Annual Reports 1973-75).
3. The data in this study are derived from my thesis research (Buchignani, 1977a), carried out between 1974 and 1977. The reliability and validity of my data is discussed therein.
4. There are a number of historical sources of information on East Indians in Canada (Buchignani, 1977b). Several easily accessible works are included in the selected references of this paper.
5. This figure adds 1971 Census totals to immigration since that date.

SELECTED REFERENCES

Angus, H. F. "The Legal Status in British Columbia of Residents of Oriental Races and their Descendants," in N. A. M. Mackenzie, ed., *The Legal Status of Aliens in Pacific Countries*. London: Oxford University Press, 1937, pp. 77-87.

Barth, F., ed. *Ethnic Groups and Boundaries*. Boston: Little, Brown and Co., 1969.

Bhatti, F. M. "East Indian Immigration into Canada, 1905-1973." Ph.D. Dissertation, University of Surrey, 1974.

Braroe, Neils. *Indian and White: Self Image and Interaction in a Canadian Plains Community*. Palo Alto, California: Stanford University Press, 1975.

Buchignani, Norman L. "Immigration, Adaptation, and the Management of Ethnic Identity: An Examination of Fijian East Indians in British Columbia." Ph.D. Dissertation, Simon Fraser University, 1977a.

——— "A Review of the Historical and Sociological Literature on East Indians in Canada." *Canadian Ethnic Studies*, 9:1 (1977b).

Cheng, Tien Fang. *Oriental Immigration in Canada*. Shanghai: Commercial Press, 1931.

Das, Rajani Kent. *Hindustanee Workers on the Pacific Coast*. Berlin: Walter de Gruyter, 1923.

Department of Citizenship and Immigration. *Annual Report 1964-66*.

Department of Manpower and Immigration. *Annual Report 1967-76*.

Dodd, W. D. "The Hindu in the Northwest." *World To-Day* 13 (1907), pp. 1157-60.

Ferguson, Ted. *A White Man's Country: An Exercise in Canadian Prejudice*. Toronto: Doubleday, 1975.

Indra, Doreen. "The Portrayal of Ethnicity in the Vancouver Press, 1906-1976." Ph.D. Dissertation, Simon Fraser University, 1977.

King, William L. Mackenzie. *Report of the Royal Commission appointed to inquire into the Method by which Oriental Labourers have been induced to come to Canada*. Ottawa: King's Printer, 1908.

Lal, Brij. "East Indians in British Columbia, 1904-1914: A Historical Study in Growth and Integration." M.A. Thesis, University of British Columbia, 1976.

Lockley, Fred. "The Hindu Invasion." *Pacific Monthly* (1907), pp. 584-95.

Mayer, Adrian C. *A Report on the East Indian Community in Vancouver*. University of British Columbia. Mimeo. 1959.

Morse, Eric W. "Immigration and Status of British East Indians in Canada: A Problem of Imperial Relations." M.A. Thesis, Queens University, 1935.

Srivastava, Ram P. "Family Organization and Change among Overseas Indians with Special Reference to Indian Immigrant Families of British Columbia, Canada," in G. Kurian, ed., *Family in India: A Regional Review*. The Hague: Mouton, 1975.

K. VICTOR UJIMOTO   University of Guelph

Postwar Japanese Immigrants in British Columbia: Japanese Culture and Job Transferability*

Introduction

Historically, any society developed by successive waves of migrations tends to have certain high status positions reserved for the native born, while conferring a lower "entrance status" upon newcomers. According to Porter (1965: 63), "entrance status implies lower level occupational roles and subjection to processes of assimilation laid down and judged by the charter group." An entrance status is further defined by ethnic and social class dynamics.

Although the interplay between ethnicity, social class, and entrance status affects in large measure how immigrants fare in Canada, research in this area is limited, especially on the non-white immigrant. Prior to the adoption in 1967 of the "point system", an immigration policy that bases entry on "merit", research on immigration from Asia and elsewhere in the Third World was negligible. Ramcharan's work (1976) on West Indian economic adaptation in Toronto, for example, reflects the "new" immigration of the late 1960s.

While the new Japanese immigrant (*gijutsu imin*), with high technical and educational qualifications, is a result in part of the point system, the Japanese have been resident in Canada for over a century extending back in time to 1877. Before falling victim to racial prejudice and the War Measures Act during World War II, the Japanese were industrious workers in the West coast's primary occupations—fishing, agriculture, mining and lumbering.

Although there has been a history of discrimination against the Japanese in Canada (Adachi, 1976), the reaction of the host society to the Japanese is beyond the scope of this research. Our study of Japanese immigrants focuses upon ethnicity and entrance status, specifically that

* Revised version of a paper presented at the *Conference on the Adaptation and Attitude Change of Asian Emigrants*, East-West Center, University of Hawaii, Honolulu, May, 1977. Canada Council support for this research is gratefully acknowledged.

aspect of entrance status concerned with the matter of securing employment in the same occupation as that held previous to emigration; or, in other words, job transferability.

It is hypothesized that there is a relationship between the ethnicity of immigrants and their employment history. This research attempts to examine the cultural baggage immigrants carry to Canada which may influence their search for jobs and their subsequent work performance. Possible cultural differences in the work setting in Japan and Canada will be suggested. Secondly, the entrance status and career lines of a sample of postwar Japanese immigrants in British Columbia will be analyzed by occupational group.

Japanese Work Culture

To the casual observer, the organizational structure of a Japanese firm would appear similar to that of Canadian firms of comparable size. In both Japanese and Canadian companies, offices are arranged in hierarchical order, but a closer examination will reveal less flexibility in the Japanese case. Nakane describes the bureaucratic structure of business enterprises in Japan as

> ... a proliferation of sections accompanied by finer gradings in official rank ... there appeared uniforms for workers, badges (lapel buttons) worn as company insignia and stripes on the uniform cap to indicate section and rank. Workers thus came under a more rigid institutional hierarchy.[1]

One might expect that the emphasis on finer rank differentiation in Japanese firms would result in different occupational administrative procedures employed by firms in Japan when compared to those in Canada.

Some of the problems facing the Japanese immigrant seeking employment in Canada may have their source in these organizational and procedural differences. In Japan, an individual's social and educational background is considered quite important when it comes to employment, but a letter of recommendation submitted with the job application is equally important. Employment in a medium-to-large Japanese firm is usually a lifetime commitment, and it is difficult to differentiate between the normal social relations of one's home and those of the company. A Japanese company provides housing, medical and hospital benefits, recreational facilities, group outings, and numerous other services. Given this paternalistic nature of a Japanese firm, the letter of recommendation serves a similar purpose as the *nakodo* (marriage broker) and often the procedure followed in the employment process can be as time-consuming as that of an arranged marriage.

The Japanese term for the "go-between" in the employment process is *kone*, which means "connection."[2] It refers to a person, or a friend of a person, who is already employed in a company in which the individual is seeking employment. Thus, a letter of introduction by a *kone* is always in great demand. In actual fact, most people have to be satisfied with letters written by a friend or a friend of a *kone*. In other words, the resources of a social network are frequently employed in securing employment in Japan.[3] In contrast, the newly arrived Japanese immigrant in Canada is unable to utilize the social network well-established in Japan. Furthermore, in Canada, the curriculum vitae and letters of recommendation are not of importance to the same extent as in Japan, and the immigrant is forced to seek out his own source of employment.

Even with the absence of a *kone* in Canada, Japanese immigrants soon establish social contacts to whom the traditional role performed by the *kone* in Japan is directly transferred. If the social contact happens to be a Japanese immigrant who had arrived in Canada a few years earlier, then he or she acts as the *sempai* or senior immigrant and subsequently assumes the role assigned to the *kone* in securing employment. In Canada, this results not in writing letters of recommendation, but in making personal visits to possible employment sources together with his *kōhai* or junior immigrant friend. Even in the event that immediate employment is not obtained, the *kōhai* immigrant can more or less rest assured that his *sempai* will eventually succeed in finding him suitable employment. In this manner, a system of mutual obligations is established between the *sempai* and *kōhai*.

If the new social contact in Canada happens to be a Canadian or a Japanese Canadian, the role of a *kone* cannot be readily transferred as this is an alien concept altogether in Canada. Numerous Japanese immigrants have assumed that once a friendly contact was made with a Canadian or a Japanese Canadian, employment opportunities would soon materialize, but such contacts alone have not been very fruitful.

When seeking employment in Canada, the Japanese immigrant often does not make a second call back to a prospective employer, because a person brought up in Japan tends to attach greater significance to indirect answers. In Japan, it is often common not to give a negative response to a question too directly. A series of indirect and abstract excuses will often suffice to convey to the respondent the negative feelings of the speaker. Thus, in the Canadian situation, if an employer should reply that possible job vacancies will not occur until the following month, the Japanese immigrant interprets this to mean an outright job refusal and consequently fails to return for a follow-up job application.

The Japanese practice of inducing lifetime commitments through numerous incentives at regular intervals contrasts sharply with the experience of abrupt termination of employment without any explanation in Canada. The possibility that termination of employment in Canada is less related to the technical or professional competence of the Japanese immigrant and more to Canadian economic circumstances is seldom understood by the immigrant. Such unexpected job terminations are often understood at first as manifestations of racial discrimination. However, similar experiences by immigrants of other ethnic groups, as well as by migratory Canadians, tend to dispel notions of discrimination. The critical difference in employment patterns can be best illustrated by Abegglen's observation:

> When comparing the social organization of the large factory in Japan and the United States one difference is immediately noted and continues to dominate and represent much of the total difference between the two systems. At whatever level of the organization in the Japanese factory, the worker commits himself on entrance to the company for the remainder of his working career. The company will not discharge him even temporarily except in the most extreme circumstances. He will not quit the company for industrial employment elsewhere. He is a member of the company in a sense resembling that in which persons are members of families. . . . [4]

Abegglen's comparison of a Japanese company to that of a family or fraternal organization is quite appropriate. The parent-child role of family relationship is also manifested in the *oyabun-kobun* relationship of a Japanese business firm regardless of its size. Various descriptions of the *oyabun-kobun* relationship have been given. Iwao Ishino notes that:

> The *oyabun-kobun* institution is one in which persons usually related by close kin ties enter into a compact to assume obligations of a diffuse nature similar to those ascribed to members of one's immediate family. The relationship is formally established by means of a ceremony involving many of the expressive symbolisms of birth and marriage. Both the terms of address and the assignment of roles within the group are patterned on the Japanese family system: the leader becomes a ritual parent and his followers, symbolic children. These "children," in turn, are ritual brothers to each other and seniority among them is formally recognized by terms which imply elder brother-younger brother distinctions. [5]

Nakane's description of *oyabun-kobun* relationship is similar to that given by Ishino. Nakane comments that "the essential elements in the relationship are that the *kobun* receives benefits or help from his *oyabun*, such as assistance in securing employment or promotion, and advice on the occasion of important decision-making. The *kobun*, in turn, is ready to offer his services whenever the *oyabun* requires them." [6] The extent to which the *oyabun-kobun* relationship is practised in Japan is subject to considerable debate, and it may not be as extensive throughout Japanese society as Nakane asserts. Whitehill and Takezawa state that its current usage is limited to certain social groups only. Cole suggests that the *oyabun-kobun* pattern of relations is found "most often in certain industrial sectors peripheral to the key industries associated with modern industrial development. They are found in construction, longshoring, and forestry where the labor contractor continues to play a key role."[7] Nakane aptly describes the effects of the *sempai* and *kohai* relationship in daily conversations:

> The consciousness of rank which leads the Japanese to ignore logical procedure is also manifested in the patterns and practices of daily conversation, in which a senior or an elderly man monopolizes the talk while those junior to them have the role of listener. Generally there is no development of dialectic style in a Japanese conversation, which is guided from beginning to end by the interpersonal relations which exist between speakers. In most cases a conversation is either a one-sided sermon, the "I agree completely" style of communication, which does not allow for the statement of opposite views; or parties to a conversation follow parallel lines, winding in circles and ending exactly where they started. . . .
>
> Hence most conversations are intellectually dull, emotionally enjoyable to the speaker, with a higher status, rather than the listener, with a lower status.[8]

If the immigrant had observed in Japan the rules of propriety associated with either the *sempai-kōhai* or *oyabun-kobun* relatonships, then one possible consequence in Canada might be the restrained nature of conversations during the employment interview. This hesitancy to speak openly is conditioned by rank consciousness which evolved out of the *sempai* and *kōhai* system in Japan. These differences in social relations as well as differences in the degree of commitment and in the duration of employment in Japanese and Canadian firms account for the variations in the patterns of employment shown by the postwar Japanese immigrants in Canada.

Japanese Immigration History from World War II to Present

The outbreak of the Second World War resulted in the mass evacuation of all persons of Japanese ancestry from the coastal areas of British Columbia. One of the consequences of the Canadian government's War Measures Act was that Japanese families, both citizens and aliens, were relocated to various centers in the interior of British Columbia, and in Alberta, Manitoba, and Ontario. After the relocation, those who elected to return to Japan renounced their Canadian citizenship and were repatriated.

After the end of World War II, a number of Japanese-Canadians returned to Canada. They were known as the *kika nisei* or the "returned second generation" and were usually sponsored by relatives who resided in Canada. It is extremely difficult to determine whether the *kika nisei* were officially included in the Canadian government immigration statistics for the period 1946 to 1952 since it was only after the legislation of the 1952 Immigration Act that a Canadian citizen resident in Canada was able to sponsor a wife, husband, or an unmarried dependent under 21 years of age.

The number of Japanese immigrants to Canada gradually increased as a result of the 1952 Immigration Act. This increase was further facilitated by the 1957 Order in Council PC 1957 – 1975 which "enabled residents (non-citizens) to sponsor the admission from Asia and other countries of their spouses, unmarried minor children and aged parents."[9] Sponsored Japanese immigration to Canada, or the *yobiyose*, was the highest between 1952 and 1965.

Until 1965, postwar Japanese immigrants to Canada were mostly relative-sponsored which enabled immigrants who lacked both educational experience and occupational skills to enter Canada. This usually resulted in the employment of the Japanese immigrant in his or her sponsor's family occupation or in some other makeshift work arrangement within the ethnic community. The only Japanese community in British Columbia is Steveston. It had its origin in the mass transplantation of a fishing village from Mio-mura, Wakayama Prefecture, Japan. Emigration from Mio-mura reached its peak in 1926.[10] Consequently, after World War II, a number of sponsored immigrants came to reside in the Steveston and Richmond areas and were employed in the fishing industry.

Sponsored Japanese immigrants were also destined to the various agricultural areas of southern Alberta, Manitoba, and Ontario. Perhaps, next to those immigrants who were employed in the fishing industry, the immigrants in the various agricultural occupations constituted the second largest group of sponsored immigrants to Canada.[11] The remainder of the sponsored immigrants did not immediately enter the labor force and included children, housewives, and "picture-brides".

With the establishment of the Canadian visa office in Tokyo in 1966, a vigorous advertising campaign was launched in Japan to attract highly qualified technical and professional people. There were significant differences between those Japanese immigrants who entered Canada after 1966 and those who had arrived previously. Japanese immigrants to Canada after 1966 were known as *gijutsu imin* or literally translated "technical

TABLE 1 *Postwar Japanese immigrants: respondents' characteristics (N = 100)*

Respondents' Characteristics	At time of 1972 Interview (N = 100)
Marital Status	
Non-married women	14
Married women	8
Non-married men	18
Married men	60
Age Distribution	
21 - 25	5
26 - 30	37
31 - 35	27
36 - 40	19
41 - 45	7
45 and over	5
Duration of Residence in Canada	
1 year	11
2 years	19
3 years	15
4 years	26
5 years	15
6 years	3
7 years or more	11
Family Composition	
Self only	26
Self and spouse	17
One child	24
Two children	20
Three children	9
Four children	4

immigrants." Unlike their predecessors, the *gijutsu imin* consisted of both professional and technical people, were highly educated, had several years of experience in their own occupations, and were able to converse in English.

Unlike the Chinese, Italian, and East Indian immigrants,[12] the Japanese social networks tend not to be kin-oriented. Extremely few postwar Japanese immigrants were sponsored by relatives in Canada. The relative absence of kin-oriented social networks has had implications for the job hunt as immigrants have had to find jobs largely through other than familial channels.

Postwar Japanese Immigrants in British Columbia

Research Design

The universe of all postwar Japanese immigrants consisted of the *kika nisei* (returned second generation), the *yobiyose* (sponsored immigrant), and the *gijutsu imin* (technical immigrant). Because of the atypical career line of the *kika nisei*, our survey was limited to *yobiyose* and *gijutsu imin* who entered Canada since the 1952 Immigration Act. The demographic characteristics of our random sample of postwar Japanese immigrants surveyed in 1972 are provided in Table 1.

Occupations are defined as "readily transferable" if the immigrant's skill can be utilized in Canada without retraining of more than a few weeks. It is assumed that those selected to come to Canada will try to secure employment in the same or related occupation to that held previously in Japan. It is the policy of the government to grant immigration visas to those people whose occupational skills are in demand.

It is not a simple task to select out the various factors that contribute to job transferability as some factors may be crucial only to certain

FIGURE 1 *Work history of a single professional worker*

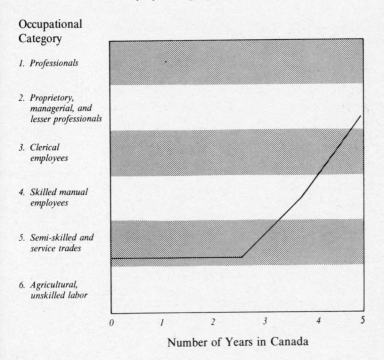

Occupational
Category

1. *Professionals*

2. *Proprietory, managerial, and lesser professionals*

3. *Clerical employees*

4. *Skilled manual employees*

5. *Semi-skilled and service trades*

6. *Agricultural, unskilled labor*

0   1   2   3   4   5

Number of Years in Canada

FIGURE 2 *Work histories of professional workers*

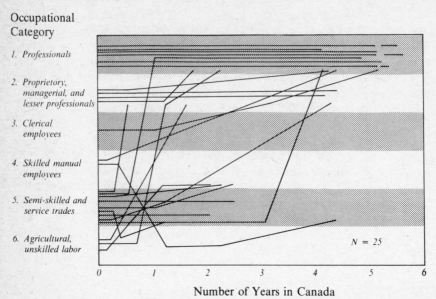

Occupational
Category

1. *Professionals*

2. *Proprietory,*
   managerial, and
   lesser professionals

3. *Clerical*
   employees

4. *Skilled manual*
   employees

5. *Semi-skilled and*
   service trades

6. *Agricultural,*
   unskilled labor

N = 25

0   1   2   3   4   5   6

Number of Years in Canada

occupations. For example, a farmer may be able to secure employment in Canada without having any English speaking ability or without having to satisfy professional requirements, unlike the immigrant who is a nurse or a pharmacist. In order to provide a graphic representation of the various jobs held by the immigrants and the changes in the work positions between various occupational classifications, the job histories for each of our respondents were plotted. These are shown in Figures 1 to 7.

An example of how we have charted the various job changes of our respondents is given in Figure 1. Here, the charting refers to one respondent who was a professional worker at the time of emigration. The horizontal axis represents the number of years resident in Canada and the vertical axis represents the six major occupational classifications arranged according to Blishen Scores. (See Appendix A.) The respondent charted in Figure 1 was a mechanical engineer in Japan, but upon arrival in Canada, he obtained a job as a welder and remained in this trade for two years. He then changed jobs and became a tool and die maker. After a year in this trade, he managed to establish his own machine shop and thus became a proprietor. The graphical representation follows the technique employed by Miller and Form[13] and the last job, which is represented by a circular dot, is used as the criterion to place our respondent in one of the occupational groups shown along the vertical axis. A heavy dot denotes the occupational group the worker was in at the time of our interview.

FIGURE 3 *Work histories of proprietory, managerial, and lesser professional workers*

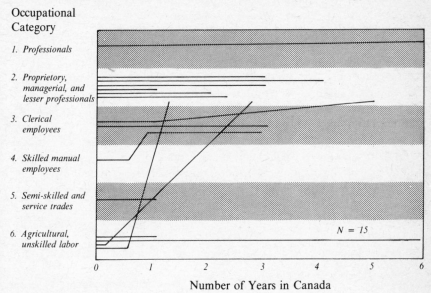

Occupational Category

1. *Professionals*

2. *Proprietory, managerial, and lesser professionals*

3. *Clerical employees*

4. *Skilled manual employees*

5. *Semi-skilled and service trades*

6. *Agricultural, unskilled labor*

N = 15

0   1   2   3   4   5   6

Number of Years in Canada

Findings

Figure 2 shows the job histories for the 25 immigrants who were in the *professional* occupational category at the time of emigration. In this group, six subjects or 24% of the respondents were able to maintain employment in the same occupational category after arrival in Canada. At the end of one year, only one respondent was able to return to the professional level. Two respondents took two years, two more took three years, and two required four years to return to professional status. In other words, at the end of four years of residence in Canada, 13 respondents or 52% of the immigrants in the professional occupational group were able to achieve the same professional status as that held prior to emigration. For others, our chart illustrates the many different occupational levels in which the professional immigrants remained.

Several explanations can be provided to account for the variations in the job histories presented in Figure 2. Immigrants who secured immediate employment in Canada in the same professional occupations were fluent in English, had minimal professional requirements to satisfy, and all had established some form of contact with Canadian employers prior to leaving Japan. They also possessed six or more years of experience in their professions while in Japan. Those who were unable to satisfy the professional requirements entered the labor force at a lower occupational status level and later, some were able to return to their original professional occupation. Immigrants who were unable to speak English took whatever job that was available and usually, remained at the same occupational level for a few years.

The job histories in Canada for immigrants who were in the *proprietory, managerial,* and *lesser professional* occupations in Japan are shown in Figure 3. Six respondents (40%) were able to secure employment in the same occupations after arrival in Canada. After a duration of residence of one year, two respondents (13%) were able to reach the proprietory, managerial, and lesser professional level. For the second, third, and fourth year of residence in Canada, one immigrant per year achieved the proprietory, managerial, and lesser professional status. The remainder of the respondents were at various occupational levels. Apart from those immigrants who secured employment in Canada in the same occupation as that held in Japan, only two immigrants exhibited any stability. This occurred in the clerical and agricultural occupational category. Again, immigrants who secured immediate employment in the same occupations were characterized by fluency in English, had established contact with someone in Canada prior to emigration, had six or more years of experience in Japan, and all had experienced minimal occupational certification requirements.

Figure 4 represents the job histories for those who were in the *clerical* occupations at the time of emigration. All respondents were female. Five

FIGURE 4 *Work histories of clerical employees*

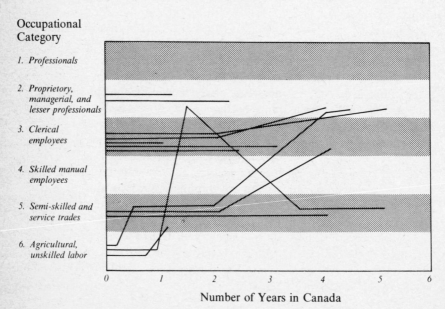

Occupational
Category

1. *Professionals*

2. *Proprietory, managerial, and lesser professionals*

3. *Clerical employees*

4. *Skilled manual employees*

5. *Semi-skilled and service trades*

6. *Agricultural, unskilled labor*

0   1   2   3   4   5   6

Number of Years in Canada

subjects (41%) were able to secure jobs in the clerical occupations in Canada. Two immigrants (17%) obtained jobs in a higher occupational status group and the remainder (42%) secured jobs at the semi-skilled, service trades, and agricultural occupational level. From this group, only one respondent managed to return to the clerical employee occupational level and this was achieved after four years of residence in Canada. For the clerical occupations, complete fluency in English was essential and although the test given to secretarial job applicants cannot be classified in the same category as professional certification requirements, nevertheless, Japanese clerical employees were seriously handicapped by their lack of knowledge and experience in Canadian office practices. The network of social contact became important only when employment was sought in a branch office of a Japanese firm in Canada. This was because "clerical duties" in Japanese firms included everything from making tea, arranging flowers, to seeing your boss off at the railway station. Thus, it was not so much the clerical competence of the job applicant, but his or her general personality, loyalty, and resourcefulness that mattered the most. Hence the heavy reliance on proper introductions and the network of personal affiliations.

Immigrants who were in the *skilled* occupational category were the most successful of all immigrants to secure immediate employment in Canada in the same occupation as that held prior to emigration. As shown in Figure 5, eight out of the nine respondents in this occupational

FIGURE 5 *Work histories of skilled employees*

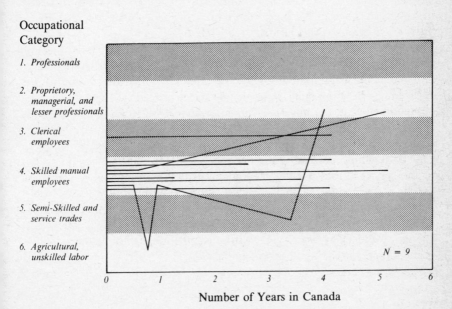

Occupational Category

1. Professionals
2. Proprietory, managerial, and lesser professionals
3. Clerical employees
4. Skilled manual employees
5. Semi-Skilled and service trades
6. Agricultural, unskilled labor

N = 9

0   1   2   3   4   5   6

Number of Years in Canada

FIGURE 6 *Work histories of semi-skilled and those in service trades*

Occupational
Category

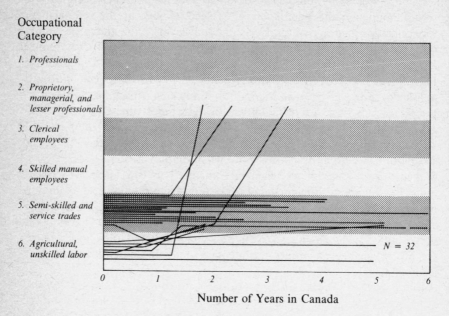

1. *Professionals*

2. *Proprietory,
   managerial, and
   lesser professionals*

3. *Clerical
   employees*

4. *Skilled manual
   employees*

5. *Semi-skilled and
   service trades*

6. *Agricultural,
   unskilled labor*

N = 32

0   1   2   3   4   5   6

Number of Years in Canada

category (89%) obtained employment in Canada at the same occupational status level. This group was also characterized by the stability manifested in their job histories. Only one immigrant exhibited a downward and then extreme upward mobility. Immigrants in the *semi-skilled* and *service trades* occupations also exhibited great stability. This is shown in Figure 6. Here again, 24 of the 32 respondents (75%) were able to secure immediate employment in Canada in the same occupations as that held in Japan. Of the remaining eight respondents who secured employment at a lower occupational status level, six managed to achieve higher occupational status within two years after arrival.

Immediate employment in both the skilled employee, semi-skilled and service trades occupational levels occurred because of the demand in Canada for those possessing the necessary skills. In particular, immigrants in the service trades usually secured immediate employment because of the heavy demand for their service skills. English ability and contact network were not crucial but some service occupations such as hairdresser and barber required professional certification. Although frequent job changes were manifested, very little occupational mobility from one occupational level to another was indicated.

The last chart, Figure 7, represents the job histories of those immigrants who were in the *agricultural, fishing,* and *general laborer* occupa-

FIGURE 7 *Work histories of farmers, fishermen, and unskilled laborers*

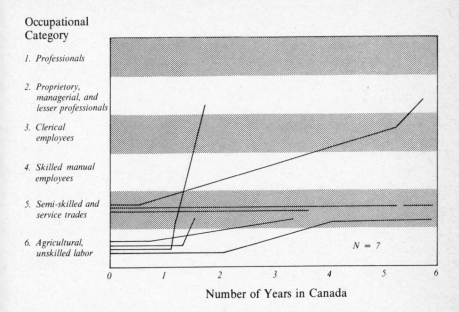

Occupational
Category

1. *Professionals*

2. *Proprietory,
   managerial, and
   lesser professionals*

3. *Clerical
   employees*

4. *Skilled manual
   employees*

5. *Semi-skilled and
   service trades*

6. *Agricultural,
   unskilled labor*

N = 7

Number of Years in Canada

tional groups. Although there were only seven immigrants in this group, three were able to obtain employment in occupations of a higher occupational status. The others secured employment in the same occupation as that held in Japan but by the end of the second year of residence in Canada, all had moved up into other occupations. Employment in the agricultural sector occurred mainly through sponsored immigration and hence the importance of social contact prior to emigration is self-evident. Sponsored immigration also meant that the job vacancies available in Canada were not being filled by Canadians. Our sample included only a few immigrants who came to Canada as farmers or farm laborers. This was because most of the sponsored farm immigrants settled in southern Alberta and only those who migrated to British Columbia were included in our population of postwar immigrants.

Summary and Conclusion

It has been suggested that both entrance status and ethnicity are important factors to consider when studying aspects of adaptation of immigrants in Canada. One of the important implications of entrance status was that the less preferred ethnic groups will be relegated to lower level occupational roles by the charter group. The extent to which entrance

TABLE 2 *Immediate employment in Canada in the same occupation as that held in Japan*

Occupational Category at time of Emigration (1966-72)	No. in Survey	% who secured immediate employment in the same occupation as that held in Japan
1. Professional	25	24
2. Proprietory, Managerial, and Lesser Professionals	15	40
3. Clerical Employees	12	41
4. Skilled Manual Employees	9	89
5. Semi-Skilled and Service Trades	32	75
6. Agricultural, Unskilled Labor	7	57
	N = 100	

status may be operational with reference to the Japanese immigrants may be determined from the patterns of job history. Table 2 provides a summary of the distribution of immigrants in the various occupational categories who managed to secure immediate employment in the same occupation as that held prior to emigration. It will be noted that only 24% of the immigrants in the professional occupations secured immediate employment in Canada in the same occupation as that held in Japan. Thus, it would appear from our data that the most pronounced indication of entrance status requirements is in the professional occupational category. In contrast to the immigrants in the other occupational categories, this low percentage stemmed from the fact that a number of factors such as the immigrant's English ability, occupational certification requirements, the number of years of experience in Japan, and the immigrant's contact or lack of contact with Canadian employers all acted in concert to determine the immigrant's immediate employability in Canada.

For those in the proprietory, managerial, and lesser professional categories, one's ability to speak English, work experience in Japan, and contact established prior to emigration were also important. However, occupational certification requirements were not so crucial as in the professional occupations. Similarly, immigrants in the clerical occupations required a working knowledge of English but were less constrained by certification requirements.

Immigrants in the technically skilled, semi-skilled, and service trades secured immediate employment mainly because of the demand in Canada for their services and consequently, English ability was not as critical as in the professional occupations. With the exception of barbers and hairdressers, occupational certification requirements were also minimal.

Those immigrants in the agricultural and unskilled labor category who secured immediate employment in Canada were able to do so through contacts established prior to emigration. Most immigrants in this latter category were sponsored and thus job availability in Canada and social contacts were the two important factors for both emigration and employment.

Lacking comparative data, we are unable to measure the effect of ethnicity on entrance status. Our data suggests that for the Japanese, entrance status requirements are heavily determined by the immigrant's occupational characteristics. The immigrant's ability to read, write, and speak English was most crucial for those in the professional occupations and in the service trades in which occupational certification was mandatory but in contrast, English ability was not as important for sponsored agricultural immigrants. Immigrants who were fluent in English took less time to pass the required occupational certification examinations.

Although immigrants in the clerical and secretarial occupations were not required to meet the rigid occupational certification requirements such as those required in the professional occupations, the immigrant's ability to read, write, and converse in English was nevertheless an important factor for securing immediate employment in Canadian companies. A few immigrants who experienced difficulty in oral English managed to obtain employment in Japanese speaking companies; however, because of the limited number of Japanese firms in Vancouver, it was not always possible to obtain work if one's ability to speak English was limited. Regardless of occupation, if the immigrant was unable to find employment because of language difficulties, the Department of Manpower and Immigration sponsored the immigrant to attend an English language school.

Another important determinant of job transferability was the availability of jobs in Canada. Occupational demand accounted for fifteen points and area demand for five points toward the required fifty points necessary to secure an immigration visa. Information on both occupational and area demand is available at the head office of the Department of Manpower and Immigration in Ottawa. In addition, Manpower projections for various labor force requirements in Canada are also available and all immigration offices abroad have access to this information. Thus, the granting of an immigration visa to Japanese applicants was closely related to the employment opportunities available in Canada. The question of whether job vacancies still existed or not when the Japanese immigrant arrived in Canada was another matter.

In our conclusion, we have appeared to place more stress on the immigrant's English ability and less on ethnicity or cultural factors. This is not to suggest that once the Japanese immigrants become fluent in the English language, they will be on an equal footing with other European immigrants. It is suggested that cultural factors will undoubtedly have some influence which will affect the immigrant's later occupational mobility. As the Japanese immigrants become assimilated, they will learn that lifetime commitment to the firm is not the most rapid means for occupational mobility; in fact, the opposite appears to be true in North America. The constraints in daily social interaction because of specific task roles assigned to the *kone*, the *sempai-kōhai*, and *oyabun-kobun* will also tend to become less important as assimilation into the host society continues. The decreasing importance of ethnic behavior patterns will be further reinforced by the smaller number of family-sponsored immigrants from Japan and more generally by the decreasing trend in the number of immigrants from Japan since reaching its all time peak in 1973 (see Table 3).

TABLE 3 *Number of Japanese immigrants entering Canada, 1946 – 76*

Year	Number	Year	Number
1946 *	3	1961 **	114
1947	2	1962	141
1948	6	1963	171
1949	13	1964	140
1950	13	1965	188
1951	3	1966	500
1952	7	1967	858
1953	49	1968	628
1954	73	1969	698
1955	102	1970	785
1956	124	1971	815
1957	185	1972 ***	684
1958	193	1973	1 020
1959	197	1974	810
1960	169	1975	587
		1976	474

*Source: Warren E. Kalbach, *The Impact of Immigration on Canada's Population*. Ottawa: Dominion Bureau of Statistics, 1970. pp. 426-27. (By ethnic origin).
**Source: *Immigration Statistics*, Department of Manpower and Immigration. (By country of citizenship).
***Source: *Quarterly Immigration Statistics*, Department of Manpower and Immigration. (By country of citizenship).

APPENDIX A *Postwar Japanese immigrant sample: occupation at time of emigration*

1. *Professionals (Blishen Score 70.14 to 76.69)*[*]

Professor
Geological Engineer
Mineral Engineer
Communication Engineer
Mechanical Engineer
Civil Engineer

Computer Engineer
Medical Doctor
Architect
Pharmacist
School Teacher

2. *Proprietory, Managerial, and Lesser Professionals (Blishen Score 51.11 to 68.80)*

Sales Manager
Manager and Owner of Business
Office Administrator
Accountant
Librarian
Draftsman

Arts Designer
Computer Programmer
Nurse
Dietician
Interpreter

3. *Clerical Employees (Blishen Score 40.05 to 50.98)*

Bookkeeper
Cashier
Office Appliance Operator

Secretary
Clerical Occupation

4. *Skilled Manual Employees (Blishen Score 40.05 to 50.93)*

Mechanic and Repairman, Radio and TV
Mechanic and Repairman, Aircraft
Electrician, Electronic Technician
Dental Technician

Medical Technician
Toolmaker
Diemaker
Photographic Processor

5. *Semi-Skilled and Service Trades (Blishen Score 29.43 to 39.86)*

Tailor
Dressmaker
Bartender
Steward
Sales Clerk
Barber, Hairdresser
Leather Cutter
Cabinet and Furniture Maker
Taxi Driver
Painter
Motor Vehicle Mechanic

Cook
Waiter
Welder
Piano Tuner
Plasterer
Delivery Boy
Dry Cleaner
Launderer
Cosmetologist

6. *Agricultural, Unskilled Labor (Blishen Score 25.36 to 29.41)*

Farm Laborer
Orchard Farmer
Fisherman
Artificial Inseminator

[*]Bernard R. Blishen, "A Socio-Economic Index for Occupations in Canada," *Canadian Review of Sociology and Anthropology*, 4 (February, 1967), pp. 41-53.
Note: Socioeconomic position for occupations not listed in Blishen scale obtained from *Occupational Classification Manual Census of Canada* 1971, Ottawa: Information Canada, 1971.

ENDNOTES

1. Chie Nakane, *Japanese Society* (Berkeley: University of California Press, 1970), p. 17.
2. For a brief description on how to establish a *kone*, see Ezra F. Vogel, *Japan's New Middle Class* (Berkeley: University of California Press, 1965), p. 61.
3. For the North American case, see Fred E. Katz, "Occupational Contact Networks," *Social Forces*, 37 (October, 1958), pp. 52-55.
4. James Abegglen, "Social Structure in a Japanese Factory," in Charles R. Walker (ed.), *Modern Technology and Civilization* (Toronto: McGraw-Hill Book Company Inc., 1962), p. 349.
5. Iwao Ishino, "The Oyabun-Kobun: A Japanese Ritual Kinship Institution," *American Anthropologist*, 55 (1953), p. 696.
6. Nakane, *op. cit.*, pp. 42-43.
7. Robert E. Cole, *Japanese Blue Collar* (Berkeley: University of California Press, 1971), pp. 196-97.
8. Nakane, *op. cit.*, pp. 34-35.
9. Kalbach, *op. cit.*, p. 23.
10. Fukutake, *op. cit.*, p. 152.
11. An attempt was made to obtain statistical information from the Department of Manpower and Immigration on sponsored Japanese immigrants to Canada, such as their intended occupation and destination in Canada. Unfortunately, this information was not available due to the confidential nature of other information also on the microfilm of the immigrant's application form.
12. See Stanford M. Lyman, "Contrasts in the Community Organization of Chinese and Japanese in North America," *Canadian Review of Sociology and Anthropology*, 5 (1968), pp. 51-67. Clifford J. Jansen, "The Italian Community in Toronto," in J. L. Elliott, (ed.), *Immigrant Groups* (Scarborough: Prentice-Hall, 1971), pp. 207-15. Joy Inglis and Michael N. Ames, "Indian Immigrants in Canada," *The Indo-Canadian*, Vol. 4,-Vol. 5, No. 1, 1968, pp. 2-6.
13. Delbert C. Miller and William H. Form, *Industrial Sociology* (New York: Harper and Row, 1963), p. 576.

SELECTED REFERENCES

Adachi, Ken. *The Enemy that Never Was: A History of the Japanese Canadians.* Toronto: McClelland and Stewart, 1976.

Abegglen, James C. *The Japanese Factory.* Glencoe, Ill.: Free Press, 1958.

Blishen, Bernard R. "A Socio-Economic Index for Occupations in Canada," *Canadian Review of Sociology and Anthropology*, 4 (February 1967), pp. 41-53.

———. "Social Class and Opportunity in Canada," *Canadian Review of Sociology and Anthropology*, 7 (May 1970), pp. 110-27.

Department of Manpower and Immigration. *Canadian Immigration Policy.* Ottawa: Queen's Printer, 1966.

———. *Immigration Statistics.* Annual Issues 1965-1971. Ottawa: Queen's Printer, 1971.

Office Consolidation of the Immigration Act. Ottawa: Queen's Printer, 1968.

Cole, Robert E. *Japanese Blue Collar.* Berkeley: University of California Press, 1971.

Cornell, John B., and Robert J. Smith. "Japanese Immigrants Abroad," *Rice University Studies,* 56 (Fall 1970), pp. 267-82.

Elliott, Jean Leonard, ed. *Minority Canadians,* vol. 2, *Immigrant Groups.* Scarborough: Prentice-Hall of Canada Ltd., 1971.

Fukutake, Tadashi. *Man and Society in Japan.* Tokyo: University of Tokyo Press, 1962.

Inglis, Joy, and Michael N. Ames. "Indian Immigrants in Canada." *The Indo-Canadian,* 3rd and 4th quarter (1968).

Ishino, Iwao. "The Oyabun-Kobun: A Japanese Ritual Kinship Institution." *American Anthropologist,* 55:5 (1953), pp. 695-707.

Jansen, Clifford J. "Leadership in the Toronto Italian Ethnic Group." *International Migration Review* 4 (1969), pp. 25-43.

Kalbach, Warren E. *The Impact of Immigration on Canada's Population.* Ottawa: Dominion Bureau of Statistics, 1971.

Katz, Fred E. "Occupational Contact Networks." *Social Forces* 37 (1958), pp. 52-55.

Laviolette, Forest E. *The Canadian Japanese and World War II.* Toronto: University of Toronto Press, 1948.

Lyman, Stanford M. "Contrasts in the Community Organization of Chinese and Japanese in North America." *Canadian Review of Sociology and Anthropology,* 5 (May 1968), pp. 55-67.

Marsh, Robert M., and Hiroshi Mannari. "Lifetime Commitment in Japan: Roles, Norms, and Values." *American Journal of Sociology,* 76 (March 1971), pp. 795-812.

Miller, Delbert C., and William H. Form. *Industrial Sociology: The Sociology of Work Organizations.* New York: Harper and Row, 1964.

Nakane, Chie. *Japanese Society.* Berkeley: University of California Press, 1970.

Porter, John. *The Vertical Mosaic.* Toronto: University of Toronto Press, 1968.

Ramcharan, Subhas. "The Economic Adaptation of West Indians in Canada." *Canadian Review of Sociology and Anthropology* 13:3 (1976).

Ujimoto, K. Victor. "Post-War Japanese Immigrants in Canada: Job Transferability, Work, and Social Participation." Unpublished PhD Dissertation, University of British Columbia, 1973.

———. "Contrasts in the Prewar and Postwar Japanese Community in British Columbia: Conflict and Change." *Canadian Review of Sociology and Anthropology* 13:1 (1976), pp. 80-89.

Vallee, Frank G. "Multi-Ethnic Societies: The Issues of Identity and Inequality," in Dennis Forcese and Stephen Richer, eds., *Issues in Canadian Society: An Introduction to Sociology.* Scarborough: Prentice-Hall of Canada Ltd., 1975.

Vogel, Ezra F. *Japan's New Middle Class.* Berkeley: University of California Press, 1965.

Walker, Charles R., ed. *Modern Technology and Civilization.* Toronto: McGraw-Hill, 1962.

Whitehill, Arthur M. Jr., and Shinichi Takezawa. *The Other Worker.* Honolulu: East-West Center Press, 1968.

GRAHAM E. JOHNSON   University of British Columbia

Chinese Family and Community in Canada: Tradition and Change*

Introduction

Chinese-Canadians, although constituting a relatively small ethnic group, are long established in Canada. Chinese migrants first came to western Canada in the late 1850s, and the first community of Chinese was established at Barkerville, B.C., the center of activities during the Fraser River gold rush. The first Chinese migrants were young peasants from South China. They were followed in the late 1870s and 1880s by similar young peasants who labored, under appalling conditions, to build the CPR and thus contributed handsomely to the realization of building a Canada "from sea to sea". Chinese communities were established throughout B.C. and were extended to other parts of Canada upon completion of the CPR and the founding of Vancouver.

The center of Chinese migration and the most significant Chinese community in the late 19th century was Victoria. As Vancouver grew it assumed a dominant position for the Chinese population of Canada and by the first decade of the 20th century was the largest community (Sedgewick, 1973). Chinese communities in Canada, especially the larger ones, followed a pattern in their development which has been replicated in virtually every part of the world to which Chinese have migrated (Crissman, 1967; Watson, 1975; Johnson, 1977).

The development of a Chinese ethnic identity in Canada occurred in the context of massive prejudice and discrimination. The Chinese population, from the earliest period, was subject to a most astonishing series of efforts at harassment, legal and otherwise, which had a profound effect upon the nature of community and the possibility for family formation. Such prejudicial attitudes and discrimination against a Chinese population were not peculiar to Canada. The behavior of western Canadians followed that of the white population of California and other Pacific states of the U.S. (Saxton, 1971). White populations in other parts of the

* Written expressly for *Two Nations, Many Cultures: Ethnic Groups in Canada*. Research support from the Canada Council and the Citizenship Branch, Secretary of State, Ottawa, is gratefully acknowledged.

Pacific region behaved similarly (Price, 1974). Thus, the emergence of a particular kind of community in scattered and culturally distinct parts of the world—although reflective of certain *Chinese* cultural patterns—was also a consequence of a common effort on the part of dominant political authorities, often colonial and often British, to exclude the Chinese segment of the population from full participation in social life.

The Chinese migrant before 1923 was said to be possessed of a "sojourner" mentality in that his commitment remained to his homeland rather than to a new country, such as Canada. A casual glance at the literature on migration suggests that many, if not most, of the peasant migrants were sojourners (Lopreato, 1967; Mangin, 1970). For Chinese migrants in the late 19th and early 20th centuries, distinctive cultural characteristics became marks not merely of disability but of inability to assimilate to new cultural frameworks. The assumption in the early years was that the Chinese themselves were largely responsible for the lack of commitment. But from the beginnings, legal disability made it impossible for Chinese migrants to even contemplate commitment to a society that so categorically rejected them from full membership. When we look to Chinese-Canadian family structure it is determined partly by the cultural characteristics of China but largely by Canadian law—especially immigration law—which severely constrained the kinds of family structures that could emerge. For much of Chinese-Canadian history it was simply impossible for most Chinese-Canadians to form families in Canada.

The Cultural Background

Community Organization

China was, and is, a society composed overwhelmingly of peasants. Chinese migrants in the period before 1923 were typically rural in origin, most coming from an area of several adjacent counties to the southwest of Kwangchow (Canton). Overseas Chinese communities in Canada, like those in other parts of the world, were essentially urban. China itself had a substantial degree of urbanization in the past. The adaptation of Chinese rural migrants to Chinese cities is a clue to how Chinese were to behave when they moved abroad and formed communities overseas (Willmott, 1970).

The Chinese abroad have a well-established genius for associational formation. This is reflective of the Chinese urban past (Morse, 1909; Burgess, 1928), but it also seems a common sociological pattern when extensive economic change is involved (Johnson, 1975). Voluntary associations for the Chinese population of Canada, from very early times,

FIGURE 1 *Hypothetical stages in the development of Chinatown*

Involuntary Choice (Discrimination & Prejudice towards the Chinese)	Defensive Insulation (Need for mutual help)	Voluntary Segregation	Gradual Assimilation
(1)	(2)	(3)	(4)

became an important mechanism employed to deal with both the strangeness of a new culture, separation from familiar cultural assumptions, and the racial prejudice and discrimination which were a constant feature of life in Canada.

In the wake of Chinese coolie labor on the CPR, Chinese migrants to Canada established communities in Canada's larger cities. The "Chinatowns" which grew up in the late 19th and early 20th centuries were "ghettos" of the classical kind (Wirth, 1956: 4). But the ghettos that fascinated North American sociologists tended to crumble or change their character as migrants enjoyed upward social mobility. Residents of Chinatowns, however, did not have the prospects of either social or geographical mobility that other immigrant groups enjoyed. In western Canada, for example, certain occupations, such as law and medicine, were closed to Chinese; in Vancouver, restrictive covenants prevented Chinese from purchasing property outside of the Chinatown area until the late 1930s. It has been argued that Chinese communities (Chinatowns) in the United States have followed a predictable set of stages in their development (Yuen, 1965: 277-84). Such a pattern can also be seen in the development of Canadian-Chinese communities.

The first stage in community formation is a consequence of prejudice and discrimination and leads to the second, where solidarity is a necessary defence against a hostile environment. Voluntary segregation is a strategy for cultural survival in an environment that denied the legitimacy of certain aspects of the culture. It arose in the Canadian context after the Exclusion Act of 1923. Only after repeal of the Act in 1947 did the possibility of an end to voluntary associations as key mechanisms of defence and mutual aid occur (Johnson and Wickberg, 1977).

Chinese Family Life

A definition of traditional peasant life draws attention to land ownership and the working of that land through family labor. A great deal of peasant life is defined with respect to kinsmen. Other elements, such as the nature of production, political power, and class relationships are clearly of great importance in the development of peasant society. But when a Chinese migrant left his native place for the uncertainties of life in Canada, separation from his kinship structures was especially traumatic.

In the past in China, the cardinal social values were those which had a direct relationship to the family. The individual derived his status from his kinship group and the individual was controlled to some important degree through the kin group. The system of kinship in traditional China had one dominant characteristic—it was based on male predominance. Descent and inheritance were strictly patrilineal, residence was patrilocal and the pattern of authority in the family ideally patriarchal. Patrilocal residence was in part a consequence of the fact that marriages were arranged, for marriage was a question for the family, not the individual. And this was in turn a consequence of the belief that the Chinese family was a corporate group that transcended the life of any individual at a point in time. A man was but a link in a chain which consisted of his ancestors and his descendants. From classical times it was seen as a moral transgression to let the family die out. One of the most famous quotations from the classical period of Chinese history is by Mencius who said "Of the three unfilial acts, the greatest is to have no progeny."

The Chinese family in traditional times was a cooperating economic unit. Its economic basis was the property that it held in common. For a peasant family this property was the land it tilled and the house in which it lived. A key relationship in the Chinese family was that between father and son. This was in part a consequence of the demand that sons should continue the line and as a matter of course inherit the family property and continue the economic unit. But sons also had important ritual obligations to worship their ancestors and their parents after death. This is, again, an aspect of the definition of the kin group as an endless chain. In addition, therefore, to the economic solidarity which resulted from working jointly-held property, there was a significant religious aspect to the structure of the traditional Chinese family.

There is another aspect to the traditional Chinese kinship system. Beyond the household there is a wider kinship grouping—the lineage. A group of families living together in the same locality who regard themselves as relatives since they are descended from a common ancestor through the male line is said to constitute a lineage. The lineage, like the household, was a corporate group with common property although there was no cooperative working of the property. It was a ritual unit and its members collectively worshipped their common ancestors. The income derived from lineage properties was used to support ancestor worship and could also be divided among the households which constituted the lineage. There was thus an admixture of the economic and the religious which gave the group of related families an important degree of solidarity.

There are many issues in the study of Chinese kinship in the traditional period. For the present discussion two aspects are important. The area from which most Chinese migrants to Canada originated was notable for the presence of large localized lineages (Freedman, 1958; Woon, 1975). It was only among the wealthy that the ideal form of Chinese family, of several generations living harmoniously together under one roof, prevailed. Few peasant families possessed family estates big enough for more than one son. If there were younger sons they were often obliged to leave. Young and poor peasants left in increasing numbers from South China for Canada in the late 19th and 20th centuries. They remained part of their family corporations and their localized lineages and they felt their obligations to those kinship units keenly.

The Canadian Experience

Chinese organizational skills facilitated the adaptation of Chinese migrants to Canadian society. Solitary communities developed but they were demographically imbalanced. Many immigrant communities are initially dominated by males. It is characteristic of the migration process for men to form the first links in a chain that sees women, children and aged parents following. This did not occur in the migration of Chinese to Canada. The initial phase of single men laboring at unskilled jobs was extended partly as a consequence of efforts to stem Chinese in-migration through a series of legal regulations, the most prominent being the "head-tax" which Chinese migrants were obliged to pay from 1844 until they were denied admission to Canada in 1923.[1] Under such circumstances Chinese males tended to come to Canada alone; the cost of bringing over a wife or aged parents was prohibitive, especially after 1905.

"Involuntary choice" or "defensive insulation" had the collorary that, despite the distance and discomfort of a long sea voyage, close links with the homeland were maintained. The "sojourner" mentality had as part of its pattern remitting sums of money both for the support of the kinship units (household and lineage) and for the acquisition of valued resources (land and house space) to be enjoyed after the migrant could return to live permanently in China, in old age if not before. The impact of overseas migration was often to revive and make more splendid aspects of traditional social life, particularly that relating to kinship and its attendant ritual, but also the local economy (Chen, 1936; Watson, 1975; Woon, 1975).

The traditional system of kinship was not carried abroad but flourished in the homeland through the system of remittances and frequent visits. Canadian immigration legislation had the effect, initially, of discouraging

FIGURE 2 *Stages in the development of Chinese-Canadian families*

		Period
The Bachelor community (a) Coolie Phase (b) Exclusion Phase Family focus in China	(1)	1880s – mid-1940s
Attempts at normalization Reuniting of husbands and wives in Canada	(2)	1947 – 1967
Beginnings of the "second generation" Canadian families of Chinese descent – complete families in Canada	(3)	1967 – present

the in-migration of Chinese women and then, in 1923, of preventing it. It was only after 1947 that there existed the possibility of substantial in-migration of women and children. Social disorder in the mid-1940s and the formation of the People's Republic of China in 1949, changed the relationship between the Chinese-Canadian communities and the Chinese homeland. Land Reform in China in the early 1950s and the gradual socialization of the economy not merely effectively destroyed the Chinese lineage but blocked a most important avenue of investment for Canadian-Chinese. Social changes under the new government began to compromise aspects of traditional kinship structures. Revolution in China effectively brought to an end the sojourning mentality. There followed demands from the Canadian-Chinese community to remove completely the restrictive nature of immigration legislation. Gradually those demands were met. In the post-1967 period this has led to a revitalization of the Chinese communities in Canada and the development of a new form of community that stands in great contrast to the "bachelor society" (Nee and Nee, 1972) of an earlier period.

The families of Chinese-Canadians are thus a reflection of the historical development of Chinese communities in Canada. The development of the Chinese-Canadian family thus parallels the stages of development which Yuen (1965) has suggested characterize Chinatowns in North America (Fig. 2).

Chinese communities in Canada were characterized by a preponderance of men until 1947. In 1931, for example, there were but 3 468 women in a total Chinese population of 46 519 (Table 1). Hoe reports that in the late 1920s there were only five married Chinese women in Calgary and six in Edmonton as late as 1935 (1977: 268). Among British Columbia's Chinese population in 1931, less than a thousand women

TABLE 1 *Chinese population, Canada and British Columbia: 1931*

	Canada	British Columbia
Male	43 051	24 900
Female	3 468	2 239
Total	46 519	27 139

Source: Census of Canada, 1931.

were aged 15 to 44 and there were only 1 101 females below age 14 (Table 2). The preponderance of males was such that Lyman reports fist fights over the favors of women (1961: 346) but substantial numbers of men were nonetheless married, their families presumably being established in China (Table 3). What does not seem to have happened during this period was any degree of intermarriage. This is most likely an effect of prejudicial attitudes; it may also reflect the commitment of Chinese migrants to their homeland kinship structures.

The focus of Chinese communities during the "bachelor" phase was the voluntary associations. This was in part a very traditional response to urban or overseas migration where it was inappropriate or impossible to establish conjugal units. The associations themselves, however, often constituted *fictive* kinship groupings. Certain particularistic principles—territory, dialect or surname were the normal ones—were used as criteria of membership and recruitment. The members, as in a pre-industrial Chinese city, constituted a "brotherhood" replete with worship of tutelary gods or putative ancestors. The association provided facilities for dealing with the alien and prejudicial environment of Canada. It also facilitated the transmission of remittances to the homeland, kept its members in touch with the affairs of the homeland and, if necessary, transported bones of the deceased for suitable burial. The associations were also important sources of welfare for indigent members. It is a feature of the Chinese community which has remained to the present. For those older members of the community who have never married, were too poor to

TABLE 2 *Chinese population, British Columbia: sex by age, 1931*

Age	Male	Female
0 – 14	1 158	1 101
15 – 44 }	23 580	938
45 + over }		200
Not stated	162	
Total	24 900	2 239

Source: Census of Canada, 1931.

TABLE 3 *Chinese population, British Columbia: conjugal status, 1931*

	Rural	Urban	Total
Single	1 280	4 479	5 759
Married	4 572	12 442	17 014
Widowed	50	118	168
Divorced	11	1	12
Not given	463	3 733	4 196
	6 366	20 774	27 139

Source: Carrothers, 1938: 211.

return to their native places or unable to maintain contacts over the years, they live in retirement in the associational halls as remnants of the old bachelor society. For such men collective households have been part of their lives since coming to Canada. During the days of the bachelor society most residents of the Chinese community lived in *fang-k'ou*—formally organized collective households for Chinese "bachelors". A few still exist and can be found in the backstreets of Vancouver, Victoria, Toronto and Montreal.

During the bachelor phase there was a small segment of the community which consisted of conjugal units. In British Columbia in 1931 there were, perhaps, a thousand Chinese families. It was not until after the repeal of the Chinese Exclusion Act in 1947 that it became even possible for most Chinese migrants to abandon their "bachelor" status and establish their own conjugal units in Canada. In the period after 1947, husbands were reunited with their wives and sometimes children whom they barely knew, or men in their late forties married in China and brought their brides to Canada and began the second generation—late! There is the not uncommon feature in the community today of elderly men with children a half-century their juniors who are separated not merely by a generation gap but by a version of the ethnic community which is totally different.

Restrictions on Chinese immigration were not entirely removed until 1967, although the 1962 law considerably eased the disabilities and went a long way to putting Chinese on an equal footing with other potential migrants to Canada. Changes in the law allowed the Chinese population of Canada to grow in size after long years of decline. In the decades 1951-60, 1961-70, the Chinese population of Canada doubled (Table 4). As immigration law grew more liberal, the climate of prejudice and discrimination also seemed to diminish. Canadian citizens of Chinese origin were enfranchised and could practise professions such as law and medicine in British Columbia. They were able to buy property in Van-

TABLE 4 *Chinese population of Canada: 1881-1971*

1881	4 383
1891	9 192
1901	17 312
1911	27 774
1921	39 587
1931	46 519
1941	34 627
1951	32 528
1961	58 197
1971	118 815

couver and its surrounding communities without restriction. The dominant society was thus less hostile to its Chinese minority and the Chinese community began to change. Not least in impelling change was the increasing numbers of new migrants, especially in the period after 1967.

The kind of Chinese migrant has changed. Peasants from a relatively impoverished area of the Canton delta coming to work as laborers or shop assistants are a memory of the past. Direct migration between China and Canada ceased in 1949; it was not to be reestablished until 1967. The funnel for Chinese migration to Canada became the booming, sophisticated and wealthy British colony of Hong Kong. The migrant population since 1962 has a degree of wealth, sophistication and education which contrasts sharply with previous Chinese migrants to Canada. Above all they are no longer sojourners but have a commitment to Canada. They see themselves and their children, especially their children, as Canadians. In 1971, almost 70% of the Chinese Canadian population held Canadian citizenship. Canada has become a land of opportunity where it is possible to avoid the rigidities of the class structure and the uncertainty of the future that characterizes Hong Kong.

TABLE 5 *Chinese population by province: 1971*

	%
New Brunswick*	0.4
Nova Scotia	1.0
Quebec	10.2
Ontario	32.3
Manitoba	2.6
Saskatchewan	4.0
Alberta	11.9
British Columbia	37.6

Source: Census of Canada, 1971.
*The numbers of Chinese in P.E.I. and Newfoundland are too small to enter in calculations.

The focus in the bachelor community were the old associations and Chinese politics. Today the old associations have given way to new organizational forms (Johnson and Wickberg, 1977), and the politics of pre-Liberation China (i.e., the conflict between the Nationalists and the Communists for the control of China) has become irrelevant. China is the People's Republic of China and China's increasing international stature has led to pride in the Chinese heritage. The kinds of politics that now dominate are the politics of multiculturalism and a struggle to ensure that Chinese-Canadian culture can be represented in the Canadian mosaic. Migration from Hong Kong has revived the Chinese community in Canada and has made possible a family structure which, while recognizing a particular cultural heritage, sees adaptation to Canadian society as the dominant mode. The Canadian-Chinese family by the mid-1970s seems little different from other Canadian families.

The Chinese Community Today

In the 1970s the Chinese community is less confined geographically than it was in earlier periods of history. British Columbia still has the largest concentration of Chinese-Canadians but that preeminence is challenged by Ontario (Table 5). This is a reflection of the economic attraction of Metropolitan Toronto for an immigrant population that seems upwardly mobile with now the possibility of achieving career and other success. Educational achievement does not guarantee success, but among the Chinese population it has been seen traditionally as an important attribute. It is one tradition that has persisted (Tables 6 and 7).

The influx of new migrants has done much to change the character of Chinese communities in Canada. "Chinatowns" have become an important cultural focus and the focus for the assertion of a Canadian-Chinese cultural identity. The older associations persist, some have flourished, but a new structure has been grafted onto the old. In the absence of a

TABLE 6 *Chinese population, Montreal and Toronto: educational achievement, 1971*

	%
University	21.4
Grade 12 – 13	15.4
Grade 11	6.5
Grade 8 – 10	25.2
Less than Grade 8	23.8
None	6.5

Source: Census of Canada, 1974.

TABLE 7 *Chinese population, Vancouver: educational achievement, 1974*

	%
University	23.9
High School Graduate	16.8
Some High School	27.1
Elementary	19.8
None but literate	3.8
Illiterate	5.3
N = 338	

"family community" the bachelors of an earlier period attempted to create fictive kinship structures. Such a response by new Chinese migrants is no longer necessary.

And yet the past is not totally without relevance. For all the sophistication and urbanity of many new migrants, family and kinship remain important. The majority of Chinese migrants in Vancouver, although largely coming via the funnel of Hong Kong (others come from Southeast Asia, South Africa, the West Indies and Peru), trace their ancestry to the eight adjacent counties that gave Canada its first Chinese migrants. That association is indicative of the kinship links that tie the new Canadian-Chinese to the old. Chinese communities in the 1970s have a complexity that is derived from the differing periods of migration and the differing class position that is held by its members. It is possible, for example, to isolate the "old overseas Chinese", the "native born" and several varieties of "new migrants". But beneath the complexities there is a common thread—the web of kinship. In a Vancouver sample of Chinese residents in 1974, 75% were sponsored or nominated immigrants, the great majority by their immediate families. The possibilities for independent migration were opened by the 1967 immigration legislation. Only one in four of the Vancouver sample chose to come without the apparent support of relatives. It is also significant that almost 70% of the Vancouver sample came as whole families, in great contrast to the experience of their granduncles.

Kinsmen were in Canada to establish the beachhead for the Chinese migrants, to assist in setting up a household and in finding a job. In the days of the bachelor community such tasks were the preserve of the associations. By the 1970s fictive kinship was no longer crucial to the process of migrant adaptation. Associations within the Chinese communities in the 1970s are largely to establish a cultural identity or to assist the migrant to make accommodations to the demands of Canadian society. The Chinese Canadian in the 1970s is not obliged, as was his kinsman 50 years ago, to rely on the resources of the ethnic community for his livelihood, his welfare and his emotional support. A vibrant and outgoing "family society" has replaced the bachelor society of the past. The kin network is perhaps less extensive than in the Chinese society of Hong Kong or the homeland but it is, nonetheless, substantial. Chinese families in Vancouver are not isolated but enjoy frequent interaction with kinsmen. "Chinatown" has become an important meeting ground for shopping, eating and movie-going and the celebration of festivals, weddings, and anniversaries. Such activities are frequently enjoyed in the company of large numbers of kinsmen and their offspring.

In some respects there is the continuity in traditional familial values. One such is the respect that is accorded parents and the expectation that as one mark of respect resources are committed to the support of parents. Seventy percent of the Vancouver sample that had living parents contributed to their support. This raises another point. Almost a quarter of the Vancouver sample had one or both parents living in the same house. In terms of child-rearing it would seem that grandmothers are crucial to the Chinese population of Vancouver. The presence of a grandparent allows both parents to work, which is an enormous asset in the adaptation process. The presence of a member of the senior generation also has an important influence on the cultural knowledge, and especially language skills, which young Chinese-Canadians possess.

In other respects, however, there are breaks with tradition. Traditional kinship gatherings, such as grave worship, which are very significant in Hong Kong, seem of little importance. But other aspects of traditional ritual have also declined. Only ten percent of the households in the Vancouver sample possessed ancestral tablets in the home, which suggests that the domestic ancestor worship of traditional Chinese households has not survived the passage from the Chinese homeland. On the other hand, a quarter of the sample households did perform traditional worship of some kind, mostly on major lunar festivals. In the stores of Vancouver's Chinatown traditional ritual paraphernalia can be bought in substantial quantities. Testimony from shopkeepers suggests that traditional rituals are far from moribund.

Canadian-Chinese family structure is the result of a particular configuration of historical forces. In the past, prejudice and discrimination and especially immigration legislation gave rise to a singular community structure. In it fictive kinship had an important role to play in the absence of the possibility to develop a family society. Liberalism of the immigration law has allowed, in the late 1960s, a new and vibrant form of ethnic community to emerge. With it there has developed a family structure that, while recognizing its cultural heritage, sees adaptation to the Canadian milieu as its prime task.

ENDNOTES

1. The head-tax was increased as follows: 1884 – $10; 1885 – $50; 1900 – $100; 1905 – $500.
2. Since 1967 Ontario (Toronto) has consistently attracted more Chinese migrants than British Columbia (Census of Canada, 1971).

SELECTED REFERENCES

Burgess, J. S. *The Guilds of Peking.* New York: Columbia University Press, 1928.

Carrothers, W. A. "Oriental Standards of Living," in H. A. Innis, ed., *The Japanese Canadians.* Toronto: University of Toronto Press, 1938.

Chen Han-seng. *Agrarian Problems in Southernmost China.* Shanghai: Kelly & Walsh, 1936.

Crissman, L. "The Segmentary Structure of Urban Overseas Chinese Communities." *Man* 2:2 (June 1967), pp. 185-204.

Freedman, M. *Lineage Organization in Southeast China.* London: Athlone Press, 1958.

Hoe, B. S. *Structural Changes in Two Chinese Communities in Canada.* Ottawa: National Museum of Man, 1976.

Johnson, G. E. "Voluntary Association and Social Change: Some Theoretical Issues." *International Journal of Comparative Sociology* xvi: 1-2 (1975), pp. 51-63.

———. "Leaders and Leadership in An Expanding New Territories Town." *China Quarterly*, 69 (Jan-March 1977), pp. 109-25.

Johnson, G. E., and E. Wickberg. "Immigration and Organizational Change in Canadian Chinese Communities Since 1947," Unpublished paper, 1977.

Lopreato, J. "Emigration and Social Change in Southern Italy," in C. Bell and H. Newby, ed., *The Sociology of Community.* London: Cass, 1967, pp. 84-96.

Mangin, H. B. *Peasants in Cities: Readings in the Anthropology of Urbanization.* Boston: Houghton Mifflin, 1971.

Morse,.H. B. *The Guilds of China.* London: Longman, Green & Co., 1909.

Nee, V., and B. De Bary Nee. *Long Time Californ': A Documentary Study of an American Chinatown.* New York: Pantheon, 1973.

Price, C. *The Great White Walls Are Built: Restrictive Immigration to North America and Australia 1836-1888.* Canberra: Australian National University Press, 1974.

Sedgewick, C. "The Context of Economic Change and Continuity in an Urban Overseas China Community." Unpublished M.A. thesis, University of Victoria, 1973.

Saxton, A. *The Indispensable Enemy.* Berkeley & Los Angeles: University of California Press, 1971

Watson, J. L. *Emigration and the Chinese Lineage.* Berkeley: University of California Press, 1975.

Wickberg, E. B. *The Chinese in Philippine Life: 1850-1898.* New Haven, Conn.: Yale University Press, 1965.

Willmott, W. E. *The Political Structure of the Chinese in Cambodia.* London: Athlone Press, 1970.

Wirth, L. *The Ghetto.* Chicago: University of Chicago Press, 1956.

Woon, Y. F. "Social Organization in South China 1911-1949. The Kwaan Lineage of Hoi-ping." Unpublished Ph.D. dissertation, University of British Columbia, 1975.

Yuen, D. Y. "New York Chinatown," in A. M. Rose & C. B. Rose, eds., *Minority Problems.* New York: Harper & Row, 1965, pp. 277-84.

c. Arab Immigration

BAHA ABU-LABAN   University of Alberta

Arab Immigration to Canada*

Introduction

In the summer of 1883, a Syrian youth, Joseph Jebawy, was strolling along the main streets of Montreal. Nothing looked familiar. The layout of the city, the buildings, the people, the languages spoken, the culture, all these and more were radically different from Syria, the country from which he had emigrated with his father. In the vicinity of the Notre Dame Cathedral, across from the famous Place d'Armes Square, he glimpsed a face which did not look so strange. The young man with the familiar appearance was selling artifacts on the street. Peter Tady, the peddler, was a Syrian, like myself, who had emigrated to the New World. The news of Jebawy's discovery soon reached his father, and Abraham Bounadere, yet another youthful Syrian, who had arrived in Montreal a year earlier. The four Syrian men had a joyous social gathering in Bounadere's residence, a simple room located at the corner of Laguache-tiere and St Andre Streets. These men were the first four Arabic-speaking immigrants to set foot on Canadian soil.[1]

The Syrian Arabs

The early immigrants from the Arab world were not in any way representative of the Arab population. They were largely males, young, and mostly unmarried. More importantly, they were overwhelmingly Christians from Syria. Although they were classified officially in Canada as Syrians, and later as Syrian-Lebanese, they were Arabs. They carried with them to Canada the Arab cultural heritage and they spoke the

---

* Excerpted from Baha Abu-Laban, *An Olive Branch on the Family Tree: A Study of Arabs in Canada*, with permission of author and publisher, the Multicultural Programme, Department of the Secretary of State, Ottawa (forthcoming).

Arabic language. Some of these early immigrants and their descendants prefer(red) to be called *Arabic-speaking* Syrian or Lebanese rather than Arabs. There are several reasons underlying this preference, chief among which is the desire not to be mistaken for Moslems. But the fact remains that they are Arabs, both in language and culture.

The beginning of Syrian immigration coincided with a period during which increasing numbers of immigrants from other parts of the world were gravitating toward this country. For example, in 1882, Canada admitted a total of 112 458 immigrants, compared to only 47 991 admitted in the year preceding. Also, between 1881 and 1890, Canada admitted a total of 886 177 immigrants, compared to only 342 675 admissions during the ten-year period immediately preceding. More importantly, in the final two decades of the 19th century, an increasing number of immigrants to Canada came from countries other than the United States and those of western Europe. During this period, the proportions of immigrants from eastern, central and southern Europe were increasing.[2] Thus, Canada's ethnic mosaic began to take on a more variegated form. The admission of Syrian immigrants to this country added a new dimension to the Canadian ethnic mosaic.

The Growth of the Early Arab-Canadian Community

According to the best available evidence, the number of Syrian residents in Canada increased from 4 in 1883, to 10 in 1885, and to 50 in 1890.[3] The formative period for the Arab-Canadian community was toward the end of the 19th century when increasing numbers of Syrians joined their kindred in Montreal and elsewhere in Canada. On the average, about 80 Syrian immigrants arrived in Canada annually during that decade. By the end of the 19th century, the Syrian-born immigrants in Canada totaled 826.[4]

Immigration statistics show that a substantial number of Syrians crossed the Atlantic in the first decade of the 20th century. Syrian immigration to Canada in the first twelve years of this century has been recorded as follows:[5]

1900 – 1901	464
1901 – 1902	1 066
1902 – 1903	847
1903 – 1904	369
1904 – 1905	630
1905 – 1906	336
9 months ended March 31, 1907	277
1907 – 1908	738
1908 – 1909	189
1909 – 1910	195
1910 – 1911	184
1911-1912	144

TABLE 1 *Syrian-born Arabs in Canada by sex, 1911-41.*

Year	Total	Male	Female
1911	2 907	1 885	1 022
1921	3 879	2 395	1 484
1931	3 953	2 305	1 648
1941	3 577	2 057	1 520

Sources: *Census of Canada*, 1931, Vol. I, Table 24; and *1941*, Vol. IV, Table 18.

Thus, between 1900 and 1912, a total of 5 373 Syrian immigrants arrived in this country.

From 1911 to 1951, the rate of growth of the Arab-Canadian community was very slow and was based largely on natural increase. Arab immigration to Canada during this period was reduced to a trickle. Table 1 shows the number of Syrian-born Arabs in Canada for the period 1911-41. Part of the decline in the number of Syrian-born immigrants may be due to return migration, but we do not have information on this process.

The decline in the immigration of Syrian- or Arab-origin people to Canada in the 40-year period following 1911 is due to two sets of conditions. The first may be summarized in terms of the limitations on the free movement of people resulting from World War I, the depression of the 1930s, and World War II. During these disastrous events, Canada followed a very restrictive immigration policy. The policy was applied more or less uniformly to all national-ethnic groups except those from Britain and the United States.

The second, and perhaps more critical, set of conditions curbing the entry of Syrian- or Arab-origin people to Canada during that period were the 1908 Order-in-Council, P.C. 926, which placed severe restrictions on

TABLE 2 *The Arab population of Canada, by sex, 1921-71*

Year	Total	Male	Female
1921	8 282	4 595	3 687
1931*	10 753	5 796	4 957
1941	11 857	6 288	5 569
1951	12 301	6 469	5 832
1961	19 374	10 112	9 262
1971**	28 550	16 135	12 415

Sources: *Census of Canada, 1921*, Vol. 1, Tables 22 and 25; *1941*, Vol. IV, Table 1; *1951*, Vol. I, Table 32; *1961*, Vol. 1.2, Table 35; *1971*, Bulletin 1.3-4, Table 18; and W. Burton Hurd, *Ethnic Origin and Nativity of the Canadian People*, (Ottawa: Dominion Bureau of Statistics, 1941), p. 193, Table 2.
*The total for 1931 is obtained from Hurd. The corresponding sex distribution is determined on the basis of 116.9 males per 100 females, which is four points higher than the comparable 1941 sex ratio. See Hurd, p. 75, Table XXXIV.
**The 1971 figures are based on "mother tongue" rather than "ethnic origin". As such, they are an underestimate of the Arab origin population of Canada.

the admission of all Asiatic immigrants[6]; the negative public attitudes toward Syrian immigrants; and the mistaking of these immigrants for Turks—Canada's enemy during World War I.

The above discussion has been confined to first-generation (i.e., Syrian-born) Arab-Canadians, which is a portion of the ethnic community. Table 2 shows the growth of this community by sex, for the period 1921-71. The effects of restrictive immigration on the size of the Arab-Canadian population are clearly reflected in this table. The figures in Table 2 show that between 1921 and 1951 the growth rate of the Arab ethnocultural group was relatively small. Specifically, it increased from a total of 8 282 in 1921 to 12 301 in 1951. In relative terms, the size of this ethnic community increased by 22% between 1921 and 1931; 18% between 1931 and 1941; and only 4% between 1941 and 1951. The main contributor to growth was natural increase (i.e., surplus of births over deaths).

The Postwar Arab-Canadian Community

Since 1951, the change in the size of the Arab-Canadian community has been influenced more by immigration than natural increase. Again, Table 2 shows the effects of a more open immigration policy on the size of this ethnic community. Between 1951 and 1961, the Arab population of Canada increased by about 57%, from a total of 12 301 in the former year to a total of 19 374 in the latter. For reasons which are discussed below, the 1971 figure of 28 550 (Table 2) is a substantial underestimate of the actual size of the Arab ethnic group. Nevertheless, between 1961 and 1971, the resident Arab population in Canada increased by over 47%. A more realistic growth rate for this period, involving an upward adjustment of the 1971 census figure, would be 300%.

The 28 550 figure for 1971 is based on the number of Arab-Canadians claiming Arabic as their mother tongue. This figure does not include those Arab-Canadians whose mother tongue is not Arabic (and there are many of those) or is not reported as Arabic. Technically, the 1971 figure is not comparable to the figures given for the preceding decennial years. Since the 1971 Canadian census does not record a total for the Arab-Canadian community, as distinct from mother-tongue affiliation, we are forced to rely on estimates. Judging from the inflow of Arab immigrants to Canada, and allowing for natural increase, there were an estimated 50 000 to 60 000 people of Arab origin in Canada in 1971; and 70 000 to 80 000 at the end of 1975.

The two significant periods of growth in the history of the Arab-Canadian community are the formative period 1891-1911, and the postwar period, starting in 1951. Both migration and natural increase have played a significant role in the demographic evolution of the Arab ethnocultural group, but net migration has been the more important of the two.

TABLE 3 *Arab immigrants to Canada, 1946-75*

Year of Arrival	Number	Year of Arrival	Number
1946 – 1955*	1 491	1966	3 114
1956**	571	1967	3 608
1957**	563	1968	5 437
1958**	353	1969	3 256
1959**	404	1970	2 641
1960**	337	1971	1 967
1961**	301	1972	2 123
1962	1 912	1973	3 595
1963	2 281	1974	4 533
1964	3 379	1975	3 839
1965	2 914		
TOTAL (1946 – 1975)			48 619

Sources: Department of Manpower and Immigration, *Immigration Statistics, 1956; 1957; 1958; 1959; 1960; 1961; 1962; 1963; 1964; 1965; 1966*, Table 2; *1967; 1968; 1969; 1970; 1971; 1972; 1973; 1974*, Table 3; and *1975, Fourth Quarterly Report*, Table 1.
*The figure for the period 1946-55 is taken from *Immigration Statistics*, 1970, Table 13.
**For the period 1956-61, the figures are based on "ethnic origin". For the preceding and following years, the figures are based on "country of former or last permanent residence".

Postwar Arab Immigration to Canada

Between 1946 and 1975, Canada received nearly 4 million immigrants. About one out of every 100 of these immigrants was of Arab origin. Table 3 shows the numbers of Arab-origin immigrants admitted annually during this period. The total number of immigrants from the Arab world is 48 619, giving an average of over 1 600 admissions annually for 30 years. The table also shows that the heaviest influx of immigrants from Arab countries came in the second half of this period (during which the average number of persons admitted annually reached about 3 000).

The statistics reported are based on "ethnic origin" for the period 1956-61, and on "country of last permanent (or former) residence" for the preceding and following years. This means that for all years, except 1956-61, some non-Arabs, whose country of last permanent residence is recorded as Arab, are included in the statistics. By the same token, some Arab immigrants, whose country of last permanent residence is recorded as non-Arab, are excluded.

The period following World War II, particularly the decade of the 1960s, has witnessed not only a substantial growth in Arab immigration to Canada, but also significant changes in the characteristics and national origins of Arab immigrants. For example, prior to 1945, virtually all of the Arab immigrants in Canada came from Syria and Lebanon. Between 1946 and 1975, the largest number of immigrants from the Arab world came from Egypt (18 115), followed by immigrants from Lebanon

(16 333), Morocco (7 234), Syria (3 713), Jordan (737), and Tunisia (583). In addition, a total of 1 904 immigrants originated from other Arab countries. Of these, 441 immigrants were officially classified as "Arabian", but their countries of origin were not specified. The balance, or 1 463, originated from Algeria (391), Saudia Arabia (301), Kuwait (285), Iraq (187), Libya (87), Sudan (55), Bahrain (45), Qatar (45), United Arab Emirates (U.A.E.) (23), Somalia (13), Mauretania (12), Yemen (12), and Oman (7).

Patterns of Change in Sex Composition

In the first few years of Syrian immigration to Canada, women were almost totally absent. However, in the late 1880s, couples, some with children, as well as unattached women began to arrive in Canada.[7] Also, as men became more established socially and economically, wives reunited with their husbands and, as well, there were marriages between Arab-Canadian men and women from the old country.

The unattached women immigrants in general did not come to Canada as fully independent persons, but rather as relatives, e.g., as a sister or daughter, or as persons sponsored by a Syrian resident or a family already in this country. This is consistent with the Arab cultural tradition of female dependency and emphasis on the nurturant role. The presence of Syrian women provided not only a secure and stable home environment in a strange land, but also a complementary economic role to that of the husband or guardian.

The sex composition of a given group of people is often depicted in the form of a "sex ratio", expressed as the number of males per 100 females. Two sets of sex ratios are available. The first set of sex ratios is for foreign-born Arab-Canadians, i.e., immigrants, and the second set of sex ratios is for Canadians of Arab origin regardless of whether they were born overseas or in Canada (Table 4).

Several important facts may be derived from Table 4. First, for any given year, the sex ratio is higher among immigrants than Arab-origin Canadians. Second, between 1911 and 1961 there was a steady decline in the percentage of men to women for both immigrants and the Arab-Canadian ethnic group. The trend toward a steady decline in the percentage of males to females may be explained in large measure by marital status. Marriage and parenthood have a decisive balancing effect on the sex distribution of a given group of people, immigrant or otherwise. The evidence points to the presence of an increasing number of married couples with children among Arab immigrants in recent years, and to the eventual marriage of those who landed in Canada as unattached immigrants.

TABLE 4 *Percentage of males to females for Arab immigrants and Arab-origin Canadians, 1911-71*

| Year | Males as % of Females | |
	Arab Immigrants	Arab-origin Canadians
1911	184	—
1921	161	125
1931	140	117
1941	135	113
1951	—	111
1961	127*	109
1971	115	112**

Sources: See Tables 1 and 2 which give the numbers of males and females for the 1911-1941 immigrant groups and for the Arab-Canadian community (1921-1961); and Department of Manpower and Immigration, *Immigration Statistics, 1956; 1957*, Table 7; *1958; 1959; 1960; 1961; 1962; 1963; 1964; 1965*, Table 8; *1966; 1967; 1968; 1969; 1970; 1971*, Table 9.
*This percentage is based on the sex distribution of the 1956-61 immigrant groups.
**This percentage is an estimate, representing the mid-point of the figures given for the Arab-Canadian community for 1961 (109) and Arab immigrants for 1971(115).

Factors in Migration

The Early Syrian Immigrants

As discussed earlier, the Arabs who migrated to Canada in the latter part of the 19th and the first few decades of the 20th centuries had two striking characteristics: they were mostly Syrians and Christians. Estimates of the proportion of Christians among early Syrian immigrants to North America have ranged, but they have been variously set, at between 90 and 97%. The 1931 Census of Canada records only 645 Moslems in the country, out of a total of 10 070 Arab-origin Canadians. Why did emigration occur mostly from Syria? Why were Christians more inclined than other religious groups to migrate?

The larger portion of the Arab world was under Turkish control until the end of World War I. As a colonized people, Moslem and Christian Syrians were highly oppressed under the Turkish rule—more so, for example, than the geographically more distant inhabitants of Arabia. The oppression of the Syrian Moslems was mitigated by their religious affinity with the colonial administration. No such mitigating circumstance existed for Syrian Christians. Compared to their Moslem compatriots, the Syrian Christians in general felt greater pressure from the Turkish rulers.

The aversion of Canada's early Syrian immigrants toward the Turkish rule was well expressed by the Very Reverend Michael Zarbatany, parish priest of St. Nicholas Cathedral of the Syrian Eastern Othodox Church, Montreal, who migrated to Canada in 1902.

Syrian Christians were, therefore, living under the shadow of oppression, with the massacre of the 60's [1860] still fresh in their memories, never knowing what fatal surprises the morrow held for them, and constantly discriminated against in their contacts with constituted authority. In view of all this and of their natural bent towards trade, and fondness for travel, is it to be wondered at that they should finally have found in emigration to America "the Land of Freedom", relief from all their fears and worries?[8]

In a similar vein, a Syrian-Canadian writer attributed the migration of Christian Syrians "to the pressure of the Turkish rule and the well known discrimination of that vindictive power against the Christian elements of its empire . . . "[9]

One important aspect of the Turkish government's misrule concerns the *millet* system of administration whereby non-Moslem sects were given a high degree of autonomy in matters affecting the personal status of their members. Although religious separateness was not new to the region and the goals of the *millet* system were worthwhile, the way it was applied intensified the social separation of sects and religious groups. One of the fiercest conflicts, for example, occurred in 1860, mainly between the Druse and the Maronites. The dislocations resulting from that conflict were felt for many decades and were an important factor in the migration of Syrian nationals.[10]

Another important element in the structure of Syrian society, relevant to the migration of Syrian Christians to the New World, was the presence of a large number of European (and, later, American) nationals in the region. Largely because of their presence, westernization progressed more rapidly in that region than anywhere else in the Arab world. Lebanon, in particular, is frequently identified as the most modern and most westernized among the Arab states. The role of missionaries was particularly important, for in addition to their religious function they opened western-type schools and established strong social relations with the local residents. French missionaries worked closely with the Maronite communities while the British missionaries established strong relations with the Druse and the Greek Orthodox sects. Typically, it was the Syrian Christians, not the Moslems, who acquired a western orientation.

During this period, the economy of The Lebanon (the mountainous region of modern Lebanon) was hard hit by the decline of the silk industry, low agricultural productivity and increasing population pressure. The mountain peasants, many of whom were Christians, were searching for the slightest hint of possible relief. Canada-bound Syrian immigrants came with little education and hardly any capital, but with a strong commitment to hard work and success. The goal frequently expressed by these immigrants was to live in Canada for a short period and then return to Syria with enough money to guarantee their economic security there.

Canada was seen as a land of freedom and economic opportunities. This "pull" factor was revitalized constantly in Syrian villages when remittances were received from relatives abroad or success stories were told of Syrians in the New World. Immigrants who returned to Syria, either permanently or for a short visit, provided concrete evidence of the promise which Canada held for immigrants.

The Recent Arab Immigrants

Canada's postwar immigrants from the Arab world were more heterogeneous than their earlier counterparts. For example, more recent migrants included a larger proportion of non-Christians; they came from more diverse Arab countries; they represented a wider range of educational and occupational backgrounds; and they carried varying political ideologies and orientations.

The results of our survey of Arab-origin Canadians provide insights into the reasons underlying their immigration. The following question was asked of all foreign-born respondents: "For what reason(s) did you come to Canada?" Forty-five percent of the responses centered around inducements in Canadian society. Included in these inducements are job and economic opportunities (23%), educational opportunities (12%), better future (6%), and better standard of living (4%).[11]

Postwar Arab immigrants included a large number of professionals and highly skilled individuals for whom emigration was not an economic necessity, but rather an avenue for the fulfillment of higher career and professional aspirations. Moreover, many of the occupationally well-placed among recent immigrants referred to the goal of higher education as a primary reason for coming to Canada. Some of these respondents entered the country as students and later decided to seek permanent residence. The goal of higher education was almost totally absent among the pioneer Arab immigrants.

Kin-related considerations constitute the second most important factor in postwar Arab immigration to Canada. Twenty-one percent of the responses given referred to family reunions, maintaining an intact family unit, and aspirations for children. In a few cases, friendship considerations played a role in the motivational structure of immigrants. It is interesting to note that female respondents, as well as respondents with lower educational qualifications, tended to refer to family reasons more frequently than their opposite counterparts.

The third most important contribution to postwar emigration from the Arab world is the factor of political estrangement, which accounts for about 12% of the responses. Such terms as political instability, insecurity, loss (or fear of loss) of freedom, political repression, discriminatory treatment, and government policy (e.g., socialism) illustrate the nature of "push" factors involved. Respondents from Palestine added expulsion from and inability to return to the homeland.

Since 1961, increasing numbers of alienated Egyptian nationals have been emigrating to different parts of the world, and a significant number of them have been non-Moslems. Immigrants from Egypt tended to verbalize political disaffection and hopes for a higher standard of living and better future more frequently, and family reasons less frequently, than immigrants from other Arab states. In some cases, respondents attributed their migration, and that of their compatriots, partly to what they considered to be discriminatory treatment of non-Moslems in Egypt, and partly to lack of opportunities for advancement. The infrequent reference to family as an underlying reason for immigration is due to the short history of this stream of immigration to Canada, and to the Egyptian immigrants' tendency to move in family units.

And lastly, 22% of the responses to the question on reasons for immigration to Canada refer to such miscellaneous factors as search for adventure, change, and tourist travel followed by a decision to stay permanently. This composite factor is certainly not unique to Arab immigrants, but its presence as a motivating element in this group should be acknowledged.

Summary

The history of the Arab-Canadian community is relatively short. Arab immigrants began to come to Canada in the 1880s as a part of a larger stream of Syrian immigration to the New World. By 1901, Canada had an estimated total of 2 000 people of Arab origin. By 1911, the size of this ethnocultural group rose to 6 000 – 7 000 people. For the 40-year period ending in 1951, relatively few Arab immigrants were admitted to this country because of severe restrictions on the admission of immigrants from Asia.

The second phase of Arab immigration to Canada began in the 1950s and reached its peak in the decade following. Between 1946 and 1975, 48 619 of Canada's immigrants originated from the Near East and Arab North Africa. The majority of these immigrants, or 44 599, arrived after 1961. Unlike the earlier wave which consisted almost entirely of Syrians, the recent wave consisted of immigrants from many different Arab states, notably Egypt. Today, it is estimated that there are in Canada 70 000 to 80 000 people of Arab origin. The vast majority of these people, or more than nine out of ten, live in Ontario, Quebec and, to a lesser degree, Alberta and Nova Scotia.

While the sex ratio among the Arab immigrants was about 184 males per 100 females in 1911, by 1971 it had dropped to about 115 males per

100 females. In the postwar period, there were significant differences in the age-sex composition of immigrants from different Arab states. Considering the whole of the Arab-Canadian ethnic group, the percentage of males to females declined from 125 in 1921 to about 112 in 1971. The steady decline in sex ratio is due not only to the increasingly more balanced sex ratios among Arab immigrants, but also to family formation among the resident Arab population and the possible return of some immigrants, usually male, to their ancestral homeland. The important point is that the decline in sex ratio is symptomatic of the increasing stability and permanence of the Arab ethnic group in Canada.

Since the 1880s the reasons for Arab immigration to Canada have been associated with the unfavorable social, political and economic conditions in the ancestral homeland. The details of these conditions varied from one immigrant to another and from one country to another, but they have always been an important component of the motivational structure of Arab immigrants. For the disaffected as well as the achievement-oriented Arab migrants, Canada has offered freedom and ample economic opportunities. The nucleus of Canada's Arab community was established as early as 1901. Over the years, this community attracted increasing numbers of newcomers from the Near East, partly because of its capacity to accommodate new immigrants and partly because of the strength of filial ties among its members.

ENDNOTES

1. Elias Karam, "Syrian Immigration to Canada," in Elias Karam, ed., *The Syrian Canadian National Review* (Ottawa, 1935), p. 19.
2. For a relevant discussion of immigration during this period, see Norman MacDonald, *Canada: Immigration and Colonization, 1841-1903* (Toronto: Macmillan, 1966).
3. Karam, "Syrian Immigration to Canada," pp. 19, 21 & 23.
4. Baha Abu-Laban, "The Arab-Canadian Community," in *The Arab Americans: Studies in Assimilation*, Elain C. Hagopian and Ann Paden, eds. (Wilmette, Ill., 1969), p. 21.
5. Recorded by the Superintendant of Immigration, Ottawa, in a January 16, 1913, letter to Hon. Dr. Roche. See Records of the Immigration Branch, RG76, Vol. 431, File No. 622436: "Immigration from Syria and Lebanon, 1905-1910, 1913."
6. P. C. 926 required immigrants of Asian origin to have in their possession $200 upon arrival. In view of the destitution which characterized the overwhelming majority of these immigrants, the $200 requirement was severe. In practical terms, it meant debarment from entry to Canada.
7. Cf. Karam, *op. cit.*, p. 21.

8. Michael Zarbatany, "A Short History of Syria," in *The Syrian Canadian National Review*, Elias Karam, ed. (Ottawa, 1935), p. 17.

9. Karam, *ibid.*, p. 25.

10. Some non-Christians adversely affected by the civil war also were prompted to migrate. In his biography, an early Druse immigrant to Canada, for example, relates his father's experience. See Sheikh Muhammad Said Massoud, *I Fought As I Believed* (Montreal, 1976), p. 5ff.

11. The survey carried out in 1974 was based on structured interviews with 349 Arab-Canadians living in the Toronto and Montreal areas. The interview schedule was designed to yield information on background characteristics, reasons for emigration to Canada, social and economic adjustment, survival of ethnic patterns, and attitudes toward Canada and the ancestral homeland. On the average, each interview lasted for about one hour.

Statistical Appendix

TABLE 1 *Population counts of Native People*

	Registered Indian population*		Census of Canada** Indians	Inuit
1929	108 012	1881	108 547	
1939	118 378	1901	127 941	
1949	136 407	1921	110 814	2 910
1961	191 709	1941	118 316	7 205
1966	224 164	1951	155 874	9 733
1971	257 619	1961	208 286	11 835
1974	276 436	1971	295 215	17 550

Source: *Perspective Canada* II, Statistics Canada, Ottawa, 1977.
*The Department of Indian and Northern Affairs annually counts the number of Registered Indians under its jurisdiction. Prior to 1960 this count was made every five years.
**The Census of Canada counts as Indian anyone who calls himself Indian, whether registered or not, and who can trace Indian ancestry through the father's line. Prior to 1951 people of mixed Indian and non-Indian parentage were included in the native population. In the 1951, 1961 and 1971 Censuses, people of mixed parentage were counted in the same way as other ethnic groups i.e., through the line of the father.

TABLE 2 *Provincial distribution of registered Indians and Inuit*

	Registered Indians 1974	Inuit 1971
	%	%
Newfoundland	—	6.0
Prince Edward Island	0.2	—
Nova Scotia	1.9	0.1
New Brunswick	1.8	—
Quebec	10.9	21.4
Ontario	21.8	4.3
Manitoba	14.6	0.7
Saskatchewan	14.8	0.4
Alberta	11.8	0.8
British Columbia	18.7	1.2
Yukon	1.0	0.1
Northwest Territories	2.5	65.0
Canada	100.0	100.0
Total population	276 436	17 550

Source: *Perspective Canada* II, Statistics Canada, Ottawa, 1977.

TABLE 3 *Registered Indians by location of residence*

	On reserves	On crown lands	Other*	Total	
	%	%	%	%	number
1959	73.2	9.9	16.9	100.0	179 126
1966	70.3	10.2	19.5	100.0	224 164
1968	68.1	9.1	22.8	100.0	237 490
1970	65.2	9.3	25.5	100.0	250 781
1972	63.7	8.6	27.7	100.0	264 680
1974	63.8	9.2	27.0	100.0	276 436

Source: *Perspective Canada* II, Statistics Canada, Ottawa, 1977.
*Includes Registered Indians whose type of residence was not known.

TABLE 4 *Indian and Inuit population by place of residence*

	Urban and Rural Distribution	
	1961	1971*
	%	%
Rural	87.1	69.3
Farm	6.8	3.9
Non-farm	80.3	65.4
Urban	12.9	30.7
Cities of:		
100 000 +	6.6	15.9
30 000 – 99 999	1.3	2.9
10 000 – 29 999	1.1	4.5
5 000 – 9 999	0.8	2.0
2 500 – 4 999	0.9	1.6
1 000 – 2 499	2.2	3.8
TOTALS	100.0	100.0
Number	220 121	295 215

Source: *Perspective Canada*, Statistics Canada, Ottawa, 1974.
*Does not include Inuit.
Note: The cities chosen were those which in 1971 had the largest number of Indian residents. The numbers are probably underestimated since many new arrivals in a city are itinerant and are, therefore, very difficult to count in a census.

TABLE 5 *Indians and Inuit in urban centers*

	1951	1961	1971*
Calgary	62	335	2 265
Edmonton	616	995	4 260
Hamilton	493	841	1 470
London	133	340	1 015
Montreal	296	507	3 215
Prince Albert	211	225	1 045
Prince Rupert	—	880	1 780
Regina	160	539	2 860
Saskatoon	48	207	1 070
Toronto	805	1 196	2 990
Vancouver	239	530	3 000
Winnipeg	210	1 082	4 940

Source: *Perspective Canada*, Statistics Canada, Ottawa, 1974.
*Does not include Inuit.
Note: The cities chosen were those which in 1971 had the largest number of Indian residents. The numbers are probably underestimated since many new arrivals in a city are itinerant and are, therefore, very difficult to count in a census.

TABLE 6 *Enfranchisements* of registered Indians*

	Enfranchisements upon application		Enfranchisements following marriage to a non-Indian		Total enfran-chisements
	Adults	Children**	Women	Children**	
1955-56 to 1959-60	912	724	2 078	484	4 198
1960-61 to 1964-65	401	239	2 198	694	3 532
1965-66 to 1969-70	207	107	2 440	655	3 409
1970-71 to 1974-75	54	20	1 823	117	2 014

Source: *Perspective Canada* II, Statistics Canada, Ottawa, 1977.
*On enfranchisement an Indian permanently gives up his rights under the Indian Act. Enfranchisement in this sense has nothing to do with the possession of voting rights which were guaranteed to all Indians in 1960.
**Prior to 1972-1973 minor, unmarried children were automatically enfranchised with their parent(s). Since 1972-1973 minor, unmarried children have been enfranchised only when it is requested by the parent(s) and when the application is approved by the Department of Indian and Northern Affairs.

Table 7 *Age distribution of the registered Indian population*

	Age group					Dependency ratios*		
	0-14 years	15-64 years	65 years and over	No age given	Total	Population	Young	Aged
				percent				
1924	32.2	51.2	5.9	10.7	100.0	104 894	62.9	11.5
1934	34.7	55.4	6.2	3.7	100.0	112 510	62.7	11.1
1944	37.5	55.9	6.6	—	100.0	125 686	67.0	11.8
1954	41.7	53.2	5.1	—	100.0	151 558	78.5	9.6
1964	46.7	49.1	4.2	—	100.0	211 389	95.0	8.6
1974	43.2	52.4	4.2	0.2	100.0	276 436	82.4	8.1

* The dependency ratios reflect the relationship between the groups least likely to be involved in the work force, (i.e. the young and the elderly,) and the working age population. The ratios are calculated as follows:

Young- Persons aged 0-14 ÷ Persons aged 15-64 × 100

Aged- Persons aged 65 and over ÷ Persons aged 15-64 × 100

A high dependency ratio suggests that the working age population must support a larger non-productive population than a similar working age population with a low dependency ratio.
Source: *Perspective Canada* II, Statistics Canada, Ottawa, 1977.

TABLE 8 *Causes of death by international classification, 1974*

	Indians and Inuit	All Canada
	%	%
Diseases of the circulatory system	20.0	49.3
Diseases of the respiratory system	10.5	1.2
Diseases of the digestive system	5.1	3.7
Diseases of the nervous system	2.3	1.1
Neoplasms	7.6	20.4
Infective and parasitic diseases	3.1	0.7
Congenital anomalies ··	1.6	1.0
Perinatal morbidity	4.6	1.5
Accidents, poisoning and violence	34.8(1)	10.1
Other causes	10.4	11.0
Total	100.0	100.0
Total deaths	1 973	166 794

(*) "Accidents, poisoning and violence" includes motor vehicle accidents (8.8%), drowning (5.6%), exposure (1.7%), burns (3.8%), falls (1.2%), firearm mishaps (2.7%), drug overdoses (1.1%), and others (9.9%).
Source: *Perspective Canada* II, Statistics Canada, Ottawa, 1977.

TABLE 9 *Population by ethnic group*

	1871	*1911*	*1921*	*1931*	*1951*	*1961*	*1971*
				percent			
Austrian	—	3.8	7.3	2.4	1.1	2.3	0.7
Belgian	—	0.8	1.4	1.3	1.2	1.3	0.9
Czech and Slovak	—	—	0.6	1.5	2.1	1.6	1.4
Dutch	10.1	4.9	8.0	7.2	8.9	9.1	7.4
Finnish	—	1.4	1.5	2.1	1.5	1.3	1.0
German	69.4	35.2	20.1	22.9	20.8	22.3	22.9
Greek	—	0.3	0.4	0.5	0.6	1.2	2.2
Hungarian	—	1.0	0.9	2.0	2.0	2.7	2.3
Italian	0.4	4.0	4.6	4.7	5.1	9.6	12.7
Jewish	—	6.7	8.6	7.6	6.1	3.7	5.2
Lithuanian	—	—	0.1	0.3	0.5	0.6	0.4
Polish	—	2.9	3.6	7.0	7.4	6.9	5.5
Roumanian	—	0.5	0.9	1.4	0.8	0.9	0.5
Russian	0.2	3.9	6.8	4.3	3.1	2.5	1.1
Scandinavian*	0.6	9.8	11.4	11.0	9.5	8.2	6.7
Portuguese**	—	—	—	—	—	—	1.7
Ukrainian	—	6.6	7.3	10.9	13.2	10.1	10.1
Yugoslav	—	—	0.3	0.8	0.7	1.4	1.8
Other European	1.3	0.6	1.2	0.4	1.2	1.9	1.7
Chinese	—	2.4	2.7	2.3	1.1	1.2	2.1
Japanese	—	0.8	1.1	1.1	0.7	0.6	0.6
Other Asiatic	—	0.6	0.7	0.7	0.6	0.7	2.2
Native Indian and Inuit	7.9	9.2	7.8	6.2	5.6	4.7	5.4
Other and not stated	10.1	4.6	2.7	1.4	6.3	5.2	3.5
TOTALS (other than French and British)	100.0	100.0	100.0	100.0	100.0	100.0	100.0
Number in thousands	293	1 147	1 465	2 068	2 980	4 699	5 764
French	31.1	28.6	27.9	28.2	30.8	30.4	28.7
British	60.5	55.5	55.4	51.9	47.9	43.8	44.6
Other	8.4	15.9	16.7	19.9	21.3	25.8	26.7
TOTALS	100.0	100.0	100.0	100.0	100.0	100.0	100.0
Number in thousands	3 689	7 207	8 788	10 377	14 009	18 238	21 568

Source: *Perspective Canada*, Statistics Canada, Ottawa, 1974.
*Includes Danish, Icelandic, Norwegian and Swedish.
**Included with "Other European" prior to 1971.

TABLE 10 *Age by ethnic group, 1971*

	0-4	5-9	10-14	Years 15-24	25-44	45+	Total	Total persons
				percent				*no.*
British	8	10	10	19	23	30	100	9 624 120
French	8	11	12	20	26	23	100	6 180 120
German	8	10	10	17	29	26	100	1 317 200
Italian	11	12	10	16	31	20	100	730 820
Ukrainian	7	9	9	17	25	33	100	580 655
Netherlands	9	12	13	18	26	22	100	425 945
Indians and Inuit	16	16	13	20	21	14	100	312 765
Scandinavian	7	9	10	18	26	30	100	384 795
All other	9	9	9	17	29	27	100	2 011 890
Canadian average	8	10	11	19	25	27	100	21 568 310

Source: *Perspective Canada*, Statistics Canada, Ottawa, 1974.

TABLE 11 Ethnic group by occupational group, 1971

	British Isles	French	German	Hungarian	Italian	Jewish	Netherlands
				per cent			
Managerial, administrative and related	5.2	3.7	3.6	2.8	1.8	10.7	3.5
Natural sciences, engineering and mathematics	3.1	1.8	2.7	4.7	1.3	2.6	3.3
Social sciences and related	1.0	0.9	0.6	0.6	0.3	3.3	0.7
Religion	0.3	0.4	0.3	0.2	0.1	0.2	0.4
Teaching and related	4.3	4.5	3.6	3.1	1.6	5.2	3.2
Medicine and related	4.1	3.6	3.5	3.4	1.1	4.9	3.6
Art, literature, performing arts and related	1.0	0.9	0.7	1.3	0.6	2.1	0.8
Clerical and related	18.5	14.7	13.4	11.5	9.7	18.8	11.9
Sales	10.4	8.7	8.7	6.7	6.7	24.2	8.8
Service	10.6	11.2	10.6	11.9	13.0	4.9	10.6
Farming, horticulture and animal-husbandry	5.4	4.4	12.5	9.4	1.8	0.4	14.2
Fishing, hunting, trapping and related	0.4	0.2	0.1	—	—	—	0.2
Forestry and logging	0.6	1.3	0.5	0.4	0.2	—	0.4
Mining, quarrying including oil and gas field	0.6	0.9	0.7	0.7	0.4	—	0.4
Processing	3.1	4.9	3.7	4.2	6.2	1.4	3.8
Machining	2.4	2.8	3.4	5.8	5.2	0.6	3.1
Production, fabrication, assembly and repair	5.9	8.2	7.6	9.7	15.6	6.4	6.9
Construction trades	5.6	6.9	7.9	7.2	15.3	1.7	8.1
Transport equipment operation	4.2	4.5	3.5	2.5	2.6	1.7	3.5
Material handling and related	2.4	2.2	2.3	2.4	3.4	0.8	2.3
Other crafts and equipment operation	1.4	1.3	1.1	1.0	0.7	0.6	1.1
Not stated and not elsewhere classified	9.5	12.0	9.0	10.5	12.4	9.5	9.2
TOTALS	100.0	100.0	100.0	100.0	100.0	100.0	100.0

Source: *Perspective Canada.* Statistics Canada. Ottawa. 1974.

TABLE 12 *Mother tongue and language spoken in the home, 1971*

	Mother tongue (1)	Language of the home (2)	Percentage change from (1) to (2)
English	12 973 810	14 446 235	+ 11.3
French	5 793 650	5 546 025	− 4.3
German	561 085	213 350	− 62.0
Italian	538 360	425 235	− 21.0
Ukrainian	309 855	144 760	− 53.3
Native Indian	164 525	122 205	− 25.7
Netherlands	144 925	36 170	− 75.0
Polish	134 780	70 960	− 47.4
Greek	104 455	86 830	− 16.9
Chinese	94 855	77 890	− 17.9
Portuguese	86 925	74 765	− 14.0
Magyar (Hungarian)	86 835	50 670	− 41.6
Serbo-Croatian	74 190	29 310	− 60.5
Yiddish	49 890	26 330	− 47.2
Other	41 835	31 900	− 23.8
Finnish	36 725	18 280	− 50.2
Indo-Pakistani	32 555	23 110	− 29.0
Russian	31 745	12 590	− 60.3
Arabic	28 550	15 260	− 46.5
Czech	27 780	15 090	− 45.7
Norwegian	27 405	2 160	− 92.1
Danish	27 395	4 690	− 82.9
Spanish	23 815	17 710	− 25.6
Swedish	21 680	2 210	− 89.8
Gaelic	21 200	1 175	− 94.5
Slovak	17 370	9 465	− 45.5
Japanese	16 890	10 500	− 37.8
Inuit	15 295	15 080	− 1.4
Lithuanian	14 725	9 985	− 32.2
Estonian	14 520	10 110	− 30.4
Flemish	14 240	3 190	− 77.6
Lettish	14 140	9 250	− 34.6
Romanian	11 300	4 455	− 60.6
Icelandic	7 860	995	− 87.3
Welsh	3 160	370	− 88.3
TOTALS	21 568 310	21 568 310	

Source: *Perspective Canada*, Statistics Canada, Ottawa, 1974.

TABLE 13 *Language most often spoken at home, 1971*

	English	French	Other	Total
		per cent		
CANADA	67.1	25.7	7.2	100.0
Newfoundland	99.1	0.4	0.5	100.0
Prince Edward Island	95.7	3.9	0.4	100.0
Nova Scotia	95.5	3.5	1.0	100.0
New Brunswick	67.9	31.4	0.7	100.0
Quebec	14.7	80.8	4.5	100.0
Ontario	85.1	4.6	10.3	100.0
Manitoba	82.6	4.0	13.4	100.0
Saskatchewan	89.9	1.7	8.4	100.0
Alberta	90.8	1.4	7.8	100.0
British Columbia	92.8	0.5	6.7	100.0
Yukon	95.0	0.7	4.3	100.0
Northwest Territories	58.1	1.7	40.2	100.0

Source: *Perspective Canada*, Statistics Canada, Ottawa, 1974.

TABLE 14 *Population by mother tongue, 1971*

	Linguistic Group		Provincial Population			
	English	French	English	French	Other	Total
			percent			
CANADA	100.0	100.0	60.2	26.9	12.9	100.0
Newfoundland	4.0	0.1	98.5	0.7	0.8	100.0
Prince Edward Island	0.8	0.1	92.4	6.6	1.0	100.0
Nova Scotia	5.7	0.7	93.0	5.0	2.0	100.0
New Brunswick	3.2	3.7	64.7	34.0	1.3	100.0
Quebec	6.1	84.1	13.1	80.7	6.2	100.0
Ontario	46.0	8.3	77.5	6.3	16.2	100.0
Manitoba	5.1	1.0	67.1	6.1	26.8	100.0
Saskatchewan	5.3	0.5	74.1	3.4	22.5	100.0
Alberta	9.7	0.8	77.6	2.9	19.5	100.0
British Columbia	13.9	0.7	82.7	1.7	15.6	100.0
Yukon	0.1	—	83.4	2.4	14.2	100.0
Northwest Territories	0.1	—	46.9	3.3	49.8	100.0

Source: *Perspective Canada*, Statistics Canada, Ottawa, 1974.

TABLE 15 *Official language of specified ethnic groups*

	Converse in neither English nor French 1961	1971	Converse in English Only 1961	1971	Converse in French Only 1961	1971	Converse in both English and French 1961	1971	Total
					percent				
British	0.1	–	95.5	94.1	0.4	0.6	4.0	5.3	100.0
French	0.2	–	8.6	8.2	61.2	60.1	30.1	31.7	100.0
German	1.3	11.2	95.7	94.0	0.5	0.8	2.6	4.0	100.0
Italian	17.4	16.6	65.2	63.3	6.8	6.0	10.6	14.1	100.0
Jewish	1.3	0.9	79.9	74.3	0.5	1.4	18.4	23.4	100.0
Netherlands	1.6	0.7	95.3	94.6	0.2	0.3	2.9	4.4	100.0
Polish	2.5	2.6	91.3	89.6	0.7	0.7	5.5	7.1	100.0
Russian	2.7	3.8	90.3	89.3	0.5	0.6	6.5	6.3	100.0
Scandinavian	0.2	0.2	97.4	96.6	0.3	0.3	2.1	2.9	100.0
Ukrainian	2.5	2.0	94.6	93.6	0.2	0.2	2.6	4.2	100.0
Other European	4.9	9.2	85.4	79.8	2.0	2.2	7.7	8.8	100.0
Asiatic	11.2	12.0	80.9	78.3	1.3	1.6	6.6	8.1	100.0
TOTALS	1.3	1.5	67.4	67.1	19.1	18.0	12.2	13.4	100.0

Source: *Perspective Canada*, Statistics Canada, Ottawa, 1974.

TABLE 16 *Educational attainment by mother tongue, 1971**

	Elementary	Secondary	Post-secondary	University
		percent		
English	26.2	42.5	17.5	13.8
French	49.5	29.0	12.8	8.7
German	47.0	25.7	18.7	8.6
Indians and Inuit	79.5	15.0	3.8	1.7
Italian	74.0	16.0	5.7	4.3
Dutch	37.6	30.7	21.6	10.1
Scandinavian	45.7	29.8	16.2	8.3
Ukrainian	54.8	27.3	9.9	8.0
All other	48.0	25.7	11.4	14.9
TOTALS	36.8	36.0	15.4	11.8

*Persons 20 years of age and over.
Source: *Perspective Canada*, Statistics Canada, Ottawa, 1974.

TABLE 17 *Population by religion*

	1871	1901	1911	1921	1931	1951	1961	1971
			percent					
Anglican	14.1	12.8	14.5	16.1	15.8	14.5	13.2	11.8
Baptist	6.8	6.0	5.3	4.8	4.3	3.7	3.3	3.1
Greek Orthodox[1]	–	0.3	1.2	1.9	1.0	1.2	1.3	1.5
Jehovah's Witnesses	–	–	–	0.1	0.1	0.2	0.4	0.8
Jewish	–	0.3	1.0	1.4	1.5	1.4	1.4	1.3
Lutheran	1.1	1.8	3.2	3.3	3.8	3.1	3.6	3.3
Mennonite[2]	–	0.6	0.6	0.7	0.9	0.9	0.8	0.8
Pentecostal	–	–	–	0.1	0.3	0.7	0.8	1.0
Presbyterian	16.2	15.8	15.6	16.0	8.4	5.5	4.5	4.0
Roman Catholic	42.9	41.7	39.5	38.6	39.5	42.7	45.8	46.3
Salvation Army	–	0.2	0.3	0.3	0.5	0.5	0.6	
Ukrainian Catholic	–	–	–	–	1.8	2.8	1.0	1.1
United Church	3 689	5 371	7 207	8 788	10 377	14 009	18 238	21 568

1) Includes those churches which observe the Greek Orthodox Rite such as Russian Orthodox, Ukrainian and Syrian Orthodox
2) Includes Hutterite.
3) Includes Evangelican United Brethren.
4) Included with "Other".
Source: *Perspective Canada*, Statistics Canada, Ottawa, 1974.

TABLE 18 *Birth rates, Canada and Provinces, 1951-74*

	1951	1956	1961	1966	1971	1972	1973	1974
			Rate per 1 000 population					
Canada	27.2	28.0	26.1	19.4	16.8	15.9	15.5	15.4
Newfld.	32.5	35.0	34.1	28.5	24.5	24.2	22.0	18.9
P.E.I.	27.1	26.8	27.1	20.3	18.8	17.8	16.4	16.6
N.S.	26.6	27.5	26.3	20.1	18.1	17.0	16.5	15.9
N.B.	31.2	29.9	27.7	20.6	19.2	18.4	17.5	17.3
Quebec	29.8	29.4	26.1	19.0	14.8	13.8	13.8	14.0
Ont.	25.0	26.6	25.3	19.0	16.9	16.0	15.6	15.3
Man.	25.7	25.8	25.3	18.7	18.2	17.6	17.0	17.1
Sask	26.1	27.3	25.9	19.9	17.3	16.9	16.3	16.7
Alta.	28.8	31.1	29.2	20.9	18.8	17.7	17.4	17.4
B.C.	24.1	25.9	23.7	17.3	16.0	15.4	14.8	14.8
Yukon	38.0	40.1	38.1	25.7	27.5	23.9	21.3	25.5
N.W.T.	40.6	41.3	48.6	40.3	37.0	34.4	31.9	27.8

Source: *Vital Statistics*, Vol. 1, Births, Statistics Canada, Ottawa, 1974.

CHART 1 *Infant mortality in the registered Indian, Inuit and Canadian populations*
Rate per 1 000 live births

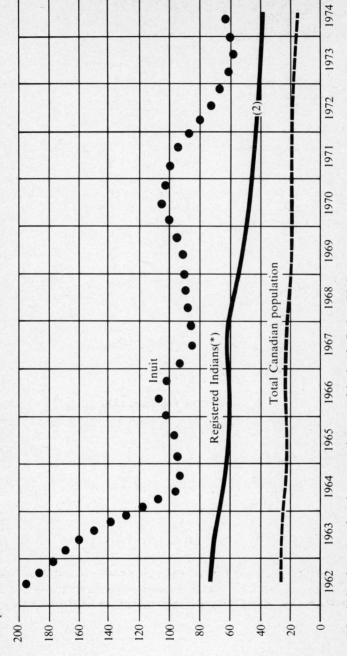

(*) See the introductory text for a short note re the source of the data for Registered Indians.
(**) No national figure was available for Registered Indians in 1972.
Source: *Perspective Canada* II. Statistics Canada. Ottawa. 1977.